Daily Truths from the Gospel
of Luke for Followers of Jesus

disciple

365
DEVOTIONAL READINGS FOR
EVERY DAY OF THE YEAR

PAUL CHAPPELL

Striving Together Publications
4020 E. Lancaster Blvd.
Lancaster, CA 93535
800.201.7748

Cover design by Andrew Jones
Layout by Craig Parker and Jocelyn Allen
Edited by Monica Bass and Robert Byers

The contents of this book are the result of decades of spiritual growth in life and ministry. It is not our intent to claim originality with any quote or thought that could not readily be tied to an original source.

ISBN 978-1-59894-338-2

Printed in the United States of America

Table of Contents

A Word from the Author

Dear Friend,

The longer I walk with the Lord, the more convinced I am that knowing and loving Jesus Christ is really what the Christian life is all about.

As the pastor of a local church, more than I want my church family to experience any outward change in their lives, I want them to fall in love with Jesus and walk with Him in fully-committed, heart-deep discipleship. Over and over I've seen that those who love Jesus purely do experience radical change—both heart change and life change.

This is the heart of the Bible word *disciple*. The original twelve disciples were personal followers of Christ, and today, God still calls us to follow Him as disciples.

Each of the daily readings in *Disciple* will take you on a journey through the Gospel of Luke and the chronological account of the life of Christ. (Because we celebrate Christmas in December, I've included the early part of Luke, which tells of Christ's birth, in the December devotions.) It is my hope that this study will help deepen your love for Jesus.

The end of each devotion includes "Today's Discipleship Principle." This summary of the devotion provides a solid takeaway principle which you can apply to your life immediately.

In addition to the daily devotions, you'll find some tools for effective Christian growth—including Bible reading schedules—in the front. Many devotions refer to passages of Scripture from throughout the Bible, so in the back we have included a Scripture reference index.

It is my prayer that each devotion in *Disciple* will help you in your spiritual growth and encourage you to purposefully follow the Lord every day. As you study the life of your Saviour, may your daily walk with Him be strengthened.

Sincerely in Christ,
Paul Chappell

practices
of effective
christians

The Effective Christian Memorizes Scripture

The following principles for effective Scripture memory are taken from *Homiletics from the Heart*, written by Dr. John Goetsch.

1. **Choose a specific time and a quiet place.**
    What gets scheduled gets accomplished. When memorizing the Word of God, you want to free yourself from all distractions.

2. **Organize by topic.**
    Many people attempt to learn the "Golden Chapters" or whole books of the Bible. While this is a noble attempt, it is not the way the Word of God will be used while teaching or preaching. Choose a topic you would like to study and then memorize every verse that deals with it. The next time you are speaking on that particular subject, your mind will be able to tie these verses together to truly allow you to "preach the Word…"

3. **Work out loud.**
    Even though it may sound odd, your mind memorizes better and faster that which it audibly hears. This is why you should choose a specific time and a quiet place!

4. **Walk while you memorize.**
    Your body has a natural sense of rhythm. This is why we memorize the words of songs so quickly. We will memorize much more quickly (and retain it longer) if we are walking around.

5. **Review, review, review.**
    Repetition is the key to learning. The one who is serious about memorizing Scripture cannot simply keep learning new passages weekly. Rather, he must also make the time to review the previous passages already committed to memory. It becomes readily apparent that memorization will take work, but the rewards are worth it!

6. **Set goals of time.**
    If you are not careful, you may ask for disappointment by setting goals of verses per week. The reason why is that some verses are more difficult to learn than others. If you set goals of time spent in memorization, God will honor that.

On the following pages you will find many major Bible doctrines and key verses to memorize. It is time to put into practice these six principles.

The Bible

Psalm 119:160—*Thy word is true from the beginning: and every one of thy righteous judgments endureth for ever.*

Isaiah 40:8—*The grass withereth, the flower fadeth: but the word of our God shall stand for ever.*

2 Timothy 3:16–17—*All scripture is given by inspiration of God, and is profitable for doctrine, for reproof, for correction, for instruction in righteousness: That the man of God may be perfect, throughly furnished unto all good works.*

Hebrews 4:12—*For the word of God is quick, and powerful, and sharper than any twoedged sword, piercing even to the dividing asunder of soul and spirit, and of the joints and marrow, and is a discerner of the thoughts and intents of the heart.*

John 17:17—*Sanctify them through thy truth: thy word is truth.*

Matthew 24:35—*Heaven and earth shall pass away, but my words shall not pass away.*

1 Thessalonians 2:13—*For this cause also thank we God without ceasing, because, when ye received the word of God which ye heard of us, ye received it not as the word of men, but as it is in truth, the word of God, which effectually worketh also in you that believe.*

God

Psalm 111:9—*He sent redemption unto his people: he hath commanded his covenant for ever: holy and reverend is his name.*

Isaiah 57:15—*For thus saith the high and lofty One that inhabiteth eternity, whose name is Holy; I dwell in the high and holy place, with him also that is of a contrite and humble spirit, to revive the spirit of the humble, and to revive the heart of the contrite ones.*

Lamentations 3:22–23—*It is of the LORD's mercies that we are not consumed, because his compassions fail not. They are new every morning: great is thy faithfulness.*

Deuteronomy 32:4—*He is the Rock, his work is perfect: for all his ways are judgment: a God of truth and without iniquity, just and right is he.*

Psalm 138:2—*I will worship toward thy holy temple, and praise thy name for thy lovingkindness and for thy truth: for thou hast magnified thy word above all thy name.*

John 4:24—*God is a Spirit: and they that worship him must worship him in spirit and in truth.*

Psalm 90:2—*Before the mountains were brought forth, or ever thou hadst formed the earth and the world, even from everlasting to everlasting, thou art God.*

Jesus Christ

John 1:1, 14—*In the beginning was the Word, and the Word was with God, and the Word was God. And the Word was made flesh, and dwelt among us, (and we beheld his glory, the glory as of the only begotten of the Father,) full of grace and truth.*

Philippians 2:6–8—*Who, being in the form of God, thought it not robbery to be equal with God: But made himself of no reputation, and took upon him the form of a servant, and was made in the likeness of men: And being found in fashion as a man, he humbled himself, and became obedient unto death, even the death of the cross.*

Colossians 1:16–17—*For by him were all things created, that are in heaven, and that are in earth, visible and invisible, whether they be thrones, or dominions, or principalities, or powers: all things were created by him, and for him: And he is before all things, and by him all things consist.*

1 Timothy 2:5–6—*For there is one God, and one mediator between God and men, the man Christ Jesus; Who gave himself a ransom for all, to be testified in due time.*

Hebrews 1:8—*But unto the Son he saith, Thy throne, O God, is for ever and ever: a sceptre of righteousness is the sceptre of thy kingdom.*

Luke 19:10—*For the Son of man is come to seek and to save that which was lost.*

Holy Spirit

John 14:16—*And I will pray the Father, and he shall give you another Comforter, that he may abide with you for ever;*

John 14:26—*But the Comforter, which is the Holy Ghost, whom the Father will send in my name, he shall teach you all things, and bring all things to your remembrance, whatsoever I have said unto you.*

John 15:26—*But when the Comforter is come, whom I will send unto you from the Father, even the Spirit of truth, which proceedeth from the Father, he shall testify of me:*

John 16:13–14—*Howbeit when he, the Spirit of truth, is come, he will guide you into all truth: for he shall not speak of himself; but whatsoever he shall hear, that shall he speak: and he will shew you things to come. He shall glorify me: for he shall receive of mine, and shall shew it unto you.*

1 Corinthians 3:16—*Know ye not that ye are the temple of God, and that the Spirit of God dwelleth in you?*

Ephesians 4:30—*And grieve not the holy Spirit of God, whereby ye are sealed unto the day of redemption.*

Ephesians 5:18—*And be not drunk with wine, wherein is excess; but be filled with the Spirit;*

Mankind

Genesis 1:26–27—*And God said, Let us make man in our image, after our likeness: and let them have dominion over the fish of the sea, and over the fowl of the air, and over the cattle, and over all the earth, and over every creeping thing that creepeth upon the earth. So God created man in his own image, in the image of God created he him; male and female created he them.*

Job 14:1, 14—*Man that is born of a woman is of few days, and full of trouble. If a man die, shall he live again? all the days of my appointed time will I wait, till my change come.*

Psalm 8:4–5—*What is man, that thou art mindful of him? and the son of man, that thou visitest him? For thou hast made him a little lower than the angels, and hast crowned him with glory and honour.*

Isaiah 64:6—*But we are all as an unclean thing, and all our righteousnesses are as filthy rags; and we all do fade as a leaf; and our iniquities, like the wind, have taken us away.*

Romans 3:10–11—*As it is written, There is none righteous, no, not one: There is none that understandeth, there is none that seeketh after God.*

Romans 3:23—*For all have sinned, and come short of the glory of God.*

Sin

Numbers 32:23—*But if ye will not do so, behold, ye have sinned against the LORD: and be sure your sin will find you out.*

Ezekiel 18:20—*The soul that sinneth, it shall die. The son shall not bear the iniquity of the father, neither shall the father bear the iniquity of the son: the righteousness of the righteous shall be upon him, and the wickedness of the wicked shall be upon him.*

Romans 6:23—*For the wages of sin is death; but the gift of God is eternal life through Jesus Christ our Lord.*

James 1:15—*Then when lust hath conceived, it bringeth forth sin: and sin, when it is finished, bringeth forth death.*

1 John 1:8–10—*If we say that we have no sin, we deceive ourselves, and the truth is not in us. If we confess our sins, he is faithful and just to forgive us our sins, and to cleanse us from all unrighteousness. If we say that we have not sinned, we make him a liar, and his word is not in us.*

1 John 3:4—*Whosoever committeth sin transgresseth also the law: for sin is the transgression of the law.*

Jeremiah 17:9—*The heart is deceitful above all things, and desperately wicked: who can know it?*

Salvation

Isaiah 45:22—*Look unto me, and be ye saved, all the ends of the earth: for I am God, and there is none else.*

Isaiah 43:11–12—*I, even I, am the LORD; and beside me there is no saviour. I have declared, and have saved, and I have shewed, when there was no strange god among you: therefore ye are my witnesses, saith the LORD, that I am God.*

John 14:6—*Jesus saith unto him, I am the way, the truth, and the life: no man cometh unto the Father, but by me.*

Acts 4:12—*Neither is there salvation in any other: for there is none other name under heaven given among men, whereby we must be saved.*

Romans 10:9–10—*That if thou shalt confess with thy mouth the Lord Jesus, and shalt believe in thine heart that God hath raised him from the dead, thou shalt be saved. For with the heart man believeth unto righteousness; and with the mouth confession is made unto salvation.*

Ephesians 2:8–9—*For by grace are ye saved through faith; and that not of yourselves: it is the gift of God: Not of works, lest any man should boast.*

Titus 3:5—*Not by works of righteousness which we have done, but according to his mercy he saved us, by the washing of regeneration, and renewing of the Holy Ghost;*

Church

Matthew 16:18—*And I say also unto thee, That thou art Peter, and upon this rock I will build my church; and the gates of hell shall not prevail against it.*

Colossians 1:18—*And he is the head of the body, the church: who is the beginning, the firstborn from the dead; that in all things he might have the preeminence.*

Ephesians 5:25–27—*Husbands, love your wives, even as Christ also loved the church, and gave himself for it; That he might sanctify and cleanse it with the washing of water by the word, That he might present it to himself a glorious church, not having spot, or wrinkle, or any such thing; but that it should be holy and without blemish.*

Acts 2:46–47—*And they, continuing daily with one accord in the temple, and breaking bread from house to house, did eat their meat with gladness and singleness of heart, Praising God, and having favour with all the people. And the Lord added to the church daily such as should be saved.*

1 Corinthians 12:13—*For by one Spirit are we all baptized into one body, whether we be Jews or Gentiles, whether we be bond or free; and have been all made to drink into one Spirit.*

1 Timothy 3:15—*But if I tarry long, that thou mayest know how thou oughtest to behave thyself in the house of God, which is the church of the living God, the pillar and ground of the truth.*

Angels

Genesis 3:24—*So he drove out the man; and he placed at the east of the garden of Eden Cherubims, and a flaming sword which turned every way, to keep the way of the tree of life.*

Psalm 148:2, 5—*Praise ye him, all his angels: praise ye him, all his hosts. Let them praise the name of the Lord: for he commanded, and they were created.*

Isaiah 6:1–3—*In the year that king Uzziah died I saw also the Lord sitting upon a throne, high and lifted up, and his train filled the temple. Above it stood the seraphims: each one had six wings; with twain he covered his face, and with twain he covered his feet, and with twain he did fly. And one cried unto another, and said, Holy, holy, holy, is the Lord of hosts: the whole earth is full of his glory.*

Mark 13:32---*But of that day and that hour knoweth no man, no, not the angels which are in heaven, neither the Son, but the Father.*

Hebrews 1:5–6—*For unto which of the angels said he at any time, Thou art my Son, this day have I begotten thee? And again, I will be to him a Father, and he shall be to me a Son? And again, when he bringeth in the firstbegotten into the world, he saith, And let all the angels of God worship him.*

1 Thessalonians 4:16—*For the Lord himself shall descend from heaven with a shout, with the voice of the archangel, and with the trump of God: and the dead in Christ shall rise first:*

End Times

1 Thessalonians 4:13–18—*But I would not have you to be ignorant, brethren, concerning them which are asleep, that ye sorrow not, even as others which have no hope. For if we believe that Jesus died and rose again, even so them also which sleep in Jesus will God bring with him. For this we say unto you by the word of the Lord, that we which are alive and remain unto the coming of the Lord shall not prevent them which are asleep. For the Lord himself shall descend from heaven with a shout, with the voice of the archangel, and with the trump of God: and the dead in Christ shall rise first: Then we which are alive and remain shall be caught up together with them in the clouds, to meet the Lord in the air: and so shall we ever be with the Lord. Wherefore comfort one another with these words.*

John 14:1–3—*Let not your heart be troubled: ye believe in God, believe also in me. In my Father's house are many mansions: if it were not so, I would have told you. I go to prepare a place for you. And if I go and prepare a place for you, I will come again, and receive you unto myself; that where I am, there ye may be also.*

Acts 1:10–11—*And while they looked stedfastly toward heaven as he went up, behold, two men stood by them in white apparel; Which also said, Ye men of Galilee, why stand ye gazing up into heaven? this same Jesus, which is taken up from you into heaven, shall so come in like manner as ye have seen him go into heaven.*

Revelation 22:20—*He which testifieth these things saith, Surely I come quickly. Amen. Even so, come, Lord Jesus.*

How to Lead a Person to Christ

Someone once said: "The fruit of a Christian is another Christian." There is a lot of truth in that statement. The Christian leader will influence people to be more soul-conscious. Yet, sometimes a person will be very active in sharing the Gospel, but will not see much fruit. It is the responsibility of the Christian leader to "Train Every Available Member" to not only be available, but effective. Here are some truths that every soulwinner must remember as he prepares to help another soul spend an eternity with Christ.

1. **A soulwinner should start with the truth of God's love for every individual.**
   John 3:16 is perhaps the most familiar verse in all the New Testament. *"For God so loved the world...."* There are sinners living today who actually believe that God hates them and wants them to go to Hell because of their sin. A sinner will never accept a Saviour who he believes will never love him.

2. **A soulwinner must emphasize the fact that we are all sinners— there are no exceptions.**
   There have been some who understand the "love" of God and feel that He would never send anyone to Hell. These sinners must also understand that the God of "love" is also first, and foremost, holy. All men fall short of the holy standard He has set. As a result of this "falling short," we are condemned to an eternity in Hell. Romans 3:23 includes all men everywhere.

3. **A soulwinner must teach the sinner that his sin carries with it an expensive price tag.**
   According to Romans 6:23, *"the wages of sin is death...."* In Ezekiel 18:20, the Israelites learned that the soul that sinned would die. As a soulwinner, the person you are dealing with has the wrath of God already abiding on him (John 3:36).

4. **A soulwinner should demonstrate the good news that Jesus has already paid this price.**
Not only does Romans 6:23 deal with the penalty of sin, it also deals with the promise of salvation. Romans 5:8 continues with this theme by showing the sinner that Christ died for us while we were yet sinners.

5. **A soulwinner must remember that a sinner must personally accept Christ as Saviour.**
This promise is given in Romans 10:13—*"For whosoever shall call upon the name of the Lord shall be saved."* A sinner may believe that God loves him, may understand the fact that he is a sinner, and may further understand that Jesus died to pay his sin debt and still be lost. The soulwinner is not after a simple mental assent to a list of subscribed facts. He is looking for a sinner to repent, to confess, and to know the joy of being a Christian.

6. **Ask the sinner, "Is there anything that would hinder you from trusting Christ right now, today, as your Saviour?"**
This question will show the soulwinner if there are still any "obstacles" that must be removed before a sinner trusts Christ. It will also serve as a good transition into drawing the Gospel net. After a sinner is saved, the Great Commission is still unfulfilled. We are commanded to go, to win, to baptize, and to teach (disciple). An effective soulwinner will determine to see each aspect of the Great Commission come to fruition with those he leads to Christ.

Verses Remembered by Effective Christians

When you lose sight of His greatness:
Jeremiah 32:17; Jeremiah 33:3; Psalm 147:5; Romans 11:33–36; and 1 Chronicles 29:11–14

When you have needs:
Matthew 6:33; Philippians 4:19; Psalm 37:3; Psalm 37:25; and Deuteronomy 2:7

When you are overwhelmed:
Psalm 55:5; Psalm 55:18; Psalm 107:6–8; and 2 Corinthians 4:16

When problems seem insurmountable:
2 Corinthians 4:15–18; Romans 8:18; Psalm 32:7; Psalm 60:12; Psalm 61:2; and Psalm 62:6–8

When you need purpose:
1 Corinthians 10:31; Ephesians 3:16–21; John 10:10; and Psalm 139:14

When you have stress:
Philippians 4:4–7; Deuteronomy 20:1–4; and Jeremiah 32:27

When you are under pressure:
Psalm 27:1–2; Psalm 27:13–14; Psalm 46:1–2; and 2 Corinthians 12:9–10

When you worry:
Philippians 4:6–7; 1 Peter 5:7; Psalm 55:22; and Psalm 46:10

When you are afraid:
Psalm 56:3; Genesis 15:1; Psalm 27:1; 2 Timothy 1:7; and John 14:27

When you have a big decision to make:
Psalm 32:8; Psalm 143:10; Psalm 40:8; Proverbs 3:5–6; and Psalm 37:3–6

When you are discouraged:
> 1 Samuel 30:6; Joshua 1:9; Isaiah 41:10; Isaiah 40:26–28; and 2 Corinthians 4:15–16

When you are disheartened:
> Joshua 1:5–9; Psalm 73:2; Psalm 73:17; and Psalm 73:24–26

When you are facing opposition:
> 2 Timothy 3:12; 2 Timothy 2:3; 1 Peter 4:12–13; 1 John 4:4; and Romans 8:31–32

When friends seem to let you down:
> 2 Timothy 4:16–17; Hebrews 12:2–3; Matthew 28:20; and Deuteronomy 32:27

When you are lonely:
> Isaiah 41:10; Hebrews 13:5–6; Acts 18:9–10; and Isaiah 43:2

When you ask if it is worth it:
> Matthew 25:21; 1 Corinthians 15:58; Galatians 6:9; and 2 Corinthians 4:17

The Effective Christian's Daily Bible Reading

Christians used by God have one thing in common: a daily walk with God. A Christian's daily walk is based upon the foundation of Bible reading and prayer. It has often been said, "The Book will keep you from sin, or sin will keep you from the Book."

Printed at the bottom of the page for each day is a segmented reading calendar that will allow you to read through the Old and New Testaments during the course of a year.

When considering whether or not to spend time in the Word of God, it is advisable to listen to the words of David, a man after God's own heart, who under the inspiration of the Holy Spirit wrote:

Psalm 119:105
"Thy word is a lamp unto my feet, and a light unto my path."

Psalm 119:9
"Wherewithal shall a young man cleanse his way? by taking heed thereto according to thy word."

May God's Word draw you closer to Him, and help you be the Christian He saved you to be.

One-Year Bible Reading Schedule

January

- [ ] 1   Gen. 1–3   Matt. 1
- [ ] 2   Gen. 4–6   Matt. 2
- [ ] 3   Gen. 7–9   Matt. 3
- [ ] 4   Gen. 10–12   Matt. 4
- [ ] 5   Gen. 13–15   Matt. 5:1–26
- [ ] 6   Gen. 16–17   Matt. 5:27–48
- [ ] 7   Gen. 18–19   Matt. 6:1–18
- [ ] 8   Gen. 20–22   Matt. 6:19–34
- [ ] 9   Gen. 23–24   Matt. 7
- [ ] 10   Gen. 25–26   Matt. 8:1–17
- [ ] 11   Gen. 27–28   Matt. 8:18–34
- [ ] 12   Gen. 29–30   Matt. 9:1–17
- [ ] 13   Gen. 31–32   Matt. 9:18–38
- [ ] 14   Gen. 33–35   Matt. 10:1–20
- [ ] 15   Gen. 36–38   Matt. 10:21–42
- [ ] 16   Gen. 39–40   Matt. 11
- [ ] 17   Gen. 41–42   Matt. 12:1–23
- [ ] 18   Gen. 43–45   Matt. 12:24–50
- [ ] 19   Gen. 46–48   Matt. 13:1–30
- [ ] 20   Gen. 49–50   Matt. 13:31–58
- [ ] 21   Ex. 1–3   Matt. 14:1–21
- [ ] 22   Ex. 4–6   Matt. 14:22–36
- [ ] 23   Ex. 7–8   Matt. 15:1–20
- [ ] 24   Ex. 9–11   Matt. 15:21–39
- [ ] 25   Ex. 12–13   Matt. 16
- [ ] 26   Ex. 14–15   Matt. 17
- [ ] 27   Ex. 16–18   Matt. 18:1–20
- [ ] 28   Ex. 19–20   Matt. 18:21–35
- [ ] 29   Ex. 21–22   Matt. 19
- [ ] 30   Ex. 23–24   Matt. 20:1–16
- [ ] 31   Ex. 25–26   Matt. 20:17–34

February

- [ ] 1   Ex. 27–28   Matt. 21:1–22
- [ ] 2   Ex. 29–30   Matt. 21:23–46
- [ ] 3   Ex. 31–33   Matt. 22:1–22
- [ ] 4   Ex. 34–35   Matt. 22:23–46
- [ ] 5   Ex. 36–38   Matt. 23:1–22
- [ ] 6   Ex. 39–40   Matt. 23:23–39
- [ ] 7   Lev. 1–3   Matt. 24:1–28
- [ ] 8   Lev. 4–5   Matt. 24:29–51
- [ ] 9   Lev. 6–7   Matt. 25:1–30
- [ ] 10   Lev. 8–10   Matt. 25:31–46
- [ ] 11   Lev. 11–12   Matt. 26:1–25
- [ ] 12   Lev. 13   Matt. 26:26–50
- [ ] 13   Lev. 14   Matt. 26:51–75
- [ ] 14   Lev. 15–16   Matt. 27:1–26
- [ ] 15   Lev. 17–18   Matt. 27:27–50
- [ ] 16   Lev. 19–20   Matt. 27:51–66
- [ ] 17   Lev. 21–22   Matt. 28
- [ ] 18   Lev. 23–24   Mark 1:1–22
- [ ] 19   Lev. 25   Mark 1:23–45
- [ ] 20   Lev. 26–27   Mark 2
- [ ] 21   Num. 1–2   Mark 3:1–19
- [ ] 22   Num. 3–4   Mark 3:20–35
- [ ] 23   Num. 5–6   Mark 4:1–20
- [ ] 24   Num. 7–8   Mark 4:21–41
- [ ] 25   Num. 9–11   Mark 5:1–20
- [ ] 26   Num. 12–14   Mark 5:21–43
- [ ] 27   Num. 15–16   Mark 6:1–29
- [ ] 28   Num. 17–19   Mark 6:30–56

March

- [ ] 1   Num. 20–22   Mark 7:1–13
- [ ] 2   Num. 23–25   Mark 7:14–37
- [ ] 3   Num. 26–28   Mark 8
- [ ] 4   Num. 29–31   Mark 9:1–29
- [ ] 5   Num. 32–34   Mark 9:30–50
- [ ] 6   Num. 35–36   Mark 10:1–31
- [ ] 7   Deut. 1–3   Mark 10:32–52
- [ ] 8   Deut. 4–6   Mark 11:1–18
- [ ] 9   Deut. 7–9   Mark 11:19–33
- [ ] 10   Deut. 10–12   Mark 12:1–27
- [ ] 11   Deut. 13–15   Mark 12:28–44
- [ ] 12   Deut. 16–18   Mark 13:1–20
- [ ] 13   Deut. 19–21   Mark 13:21–37
- [ ] 14   Deut. 22–24   Mark 14:1–26
- [ ] 15   Deut. 25–27   Mark 14:27–53
- [ ] 16   Deut. 28–29   Mark 14:54–72
- [ ] 17   Deut. 30–31   Mark 15:1–25
- [ ] 18   Deut. 32–34   Mark 15:26–47
- [ ] 19   Josh. 1–3   Mark 16
- [ ] 20   Josh. 4–6   Luke 1:1–20
- [ ] 21   Josh. 7–9   Luke 1:21–38
- [ ] 22   Josh. 10–12   Luke 1:39–56
- [ ] 23   Josh. 13–15   Luke 1:57–80
- [ ] 24   Josh. 16–18   Luke 2:1–24
- [ ] 25   Josh. 19–21   Luke 2:25–52
- [ ] 26   Josh. 22–24   Luke 3
- [ ] 27   Judges 1–3   Luke 4:1–30
- [ ] 28   Judges 4–6   Luke 4:31–44
- [ ] 29   Judges 7–8   Luke 5:1–16
- [ ] 30   Judges 9–10   Luke 5:17–39
- [ ] 31   Judges 11–12   Luke 6:1–26

April

- [ ] 1   Judges 13–15   Luke 6:27–49
- [ ] 2   Judges 16–18   Luke 7:1–30
- [ ] 3   Judges 19–21   Luke 7:31–50
- [ ] 4   Ruth 1–4   Luke 8:1–25
- [ ] 5   1 Sam. 1–3   Luke 8:26–56
- [ ] 6   1 Sam. 4–6   Luke 9:1–17
- [ ] 7   1 Sam. 7–9   Luke 9:18–36
- [ ] 8   1 Sam. 10–12   Luke 9:37–62
- [ ] 9   1 Sam. 13–14   Luke 10:1–24
- [ ] 10   1 Sam. 15–16   Luke 10:25–42
- [ ] 11   1 Sam. 17–18   Luke 11:1–28
- [ ] 12   1 Sam. 19–21   Luke 11:29–54
- [ ] 13   1 Sam. 22–24   Luke 12:1–31
- [ ] 14   1 Sam. 25–26   Luke 12:32–59
- [ ] 15   1 Sam. 27–29   Luke 13:1–22
- [ ] 16   1 Sam. 30–31   Luke 13:23–35
- [ ] 17   2 Sam. 1–2   Luke 14:1–24
- [ ] 18   2 Sam. 3–5   Luke 14:25–35
- [ ] 19   2 Sam. 6–8   Luke 15:1–10
- [ ] 20   2 Sam. 9–11   Luke 15:11–32
- [ ] 21   2 Sam. 12–13   Luke 16
- [ ] 22   2 Sam. 14–15   Luke 17:1–19
- [ ] 23   2 Sam. 16–18   Luke 17:20–37
- [ ] 24   2 Sam. 19–20   Luke 18:1–23
- [ ] 25   2 Sam. 21–22   Luke 18:24–43
- [ ] 26   2 Sam. 23–24   Luke 19:1–27
- [ ] 27   1 Kings 1–2   Luke 19:28–48
- [ ] 28   1 Kings 3–5   Luke 20:1–26
- [ ] 29   1 Kings 6–7   Luke 20:27–47
- [ ] 30   1 Kings 8–9   Luke 21:1–19

May

- [ ] 1   1 Kings 10–11   Luke 21:20–38
- [ ] 2   1 Kings 12–13   Luke 22:1–30
- [ ] 3   1 Kings 14–15   Luke 22:31–46
- [ ] 4   1 Kings 16–18   Luke 22:47–71
- [ ] 5   1 Kings 19–20   Luke 23:1–25
- [ ] 6   1 Kings 21–22   Luke 23:26–56
- [ ] 7   2 Kings 1–3   Luke 24:1–35
- [ ] 8   2 Kings 4–6   Luke 24:36–53
- [ ] 9   2 Kings 7–9   John 1:1–28
- [ ] 10   2 Kings 10–12   John 1:29–51
- [ ] 11   2 Kings 13–14   John 2
- [ ] 12   2 Kings 15–16   John 3:1–18
- [ ] 13   2 Kings 17–18   John 3:19–36
- [ ] 14   2 Kings 19–21   John 4:1–30
- [ ] 15   2 Kings 22–23   John 4:31–54
- [ ] 16   2 Kings 24–25   John 5:1–24
- [ ] 17   1 Chr. 1–3   John 5:25–47
- [ ] 18   1 Chr. 4–6   John 6:1–21
- [ ] 19   1 Chr. 7–9   John 6:22–44
- [ ] 20   1 Chr. 10–12   John 6:45–71
- [ ] 21   1 Chr. 13–15   John 7:1–27
- [ ] 22   1 Chr. 16–18   John 7:28–53
- [ ] 23   1 Chr. 19–21   John 8:1–27
- [ ] 24   1 Chr. 22–24   John 8:28–59
- [ ] 25   1 Chr. 25–27   John 9:1–23
- [ ] 26   1 Chr. 28–29   John 9:24–41
- [ ] 27   2 Chr. 1–3   John 10:1–23
- [ ] 28   2 Chr. 4–6   John 10:24–42
- [ ] 29   2 Chr. 7–9   John 11:1–29
- [ ] 30   2 Chr. 10–12   John 11:30–57
- [ ] 31   2 Chr. 13–14   John 12:1–26

June

- [ ] 1   2 Chr. 15–16   John 12:27–50
- [ ] 2   2 Chr. 17–18   John 13:1–20
- [ ] 3   2 Chr. 19–20   John 13:21–38
- [ ] 4   2 Chr. 21–22   John 14
- [ ] 5   2 Chr. 23–24   John 15
- [ ] 6   2 Chr. 25–27   John 16
- [ ] 7   2 Chr. 28–29   John 17
- [ ] 8   2 Chr. 30–31   John 18:1–18
- [ ] 9   2 Chr. 32–33   John 18:19–40
- [ ] 10   2 Chr. 34–36   John 19:1–22
- [ ] 11   Ezra 1–2   John 19:23–42
- [ ] 12   Ezra 3–5   John 20
- [ ] 13   Ezra 6–8   John 21
- [ ] 14   Ezra 9–10   Acts 1
- [ ] 15   Neh. 1–3   Acts 2:1–21
- [ ] 16   Neh. 4–6   Acts 2:22–47
- [ ] 17   Neh. 7–9   Acts 3
- [ ] 18   Neh. 10–11   Acts 4:1–22
- [ ] 19   Neh. 12–13   Acts 4:23–37
- [ ] 20   Esther 1–2   Acts 5:1–21
- [ ] 21   Esther 3–5   Acts 5:22–42
- [ ] 22   Esther 6–8   Acts 6
- [ ] 23   Esther 9–10   Acts 7:1–21
- [ ] 24   Job 1–2   Acts 7:22–43
- [ ] 25   Job 3–4   Acts 7:44–60
- [ ] 26   Job 5–7   Acts 8:1–25
- [ ] 27   Job 8–10   Acts 8:26–40
- [ ] 28   Job 11–13   Acts 9:1–21
- [ ] 29   Job 14–16   Acts 9:22–43
- [ ] 30   Job 17–19   Acts 10:1–23

July

☐	1	Job 20–21	Acts 10:24–48
☐	2	Job 22–24	Acts 11
☐	3	Job 25–27	Acts 12
☐	4	Job 28–29	Acts 13:1–25
☐	5	Job 30–31	Acts 13:26–52
☐	6	Job 32–33	Acts 14
☐	7	Job 34–35	Acts 15:1–21
☐	8	Job 36–37	Acts 15:22–41
☐	9	Job 38–40	Acts 16:1–21
☐	10	Job 41–42	Acts 16:22–40
☐	11	Ps. 1–3	Acts 17:1–15
☐	12	Ps. 4–6	Acts 17:16–34
☐	13	Ps. 7–9	Acts 18
☐	14	Ps. 10–12	Acts 19:1–20
☐	15	Ps. 13–15	Acts 19:21–41
☐	16	Ps. 16–17	Acts 20:1–16
☐	17	Ps. 18–19	Acts 20:17–38
☐	18	Ps. 20–22	Acts 21:1–17
☐	19	Ps. 23–25	Acts 21:18–40
☐	20	Ps. 26–28	Acts 22
☐	21	Ps. 29–30	Acts 23:1–15
☐	22	Ps. 31–32	Acts 23:16–35
☐	23	Ps. 33–34	Acts 24
☐	24	Ps. 35–36	Acts 25
☐	25	Ps. 37–39	Acts 26
☐	26	Ps. 40–42	Acts 27:1–26
☐	27	Ps. 43–45	Acts 27:27–44
☐	28	Ps. 46–48	Acts 28
☐	29	Ps. 49–50	Rom. 1
☐	30	Ps. 51–53	Rom. 2
☐	31	Ps. 54–56	Rom. 3

August

☐	1	Ps. 57–59	Rom. 4
☐	2	Ps. 60–62	Rom. 5
☐	3	Ps. 63–65	Rom. 6
☐	4	Ps. 66–67	Rom. 7
☐	5	Ps. 68–69	Rom. 8:1–21
☐	6	Ps. 70–71	Rom. 8:22–39
☐	7	Ps. 72–73	Rom. 9:1–15
☐	8	Ps. 74–76	Rom. 9:16–33
☐	9	Ps. 77–78	Rom. 10
☐	10	Ps. 79–80	Rom. 11:1–18
☐	11	Ps. 81–83	Rom. 11:19–36
☐	12	Ps. 84–86	Rom. 12
☐	13	Ps. 87–88	Rom. 13
☐	14	Ps. 89–90	Rom. 14
☐	15	Ps. 91–93	Rom. 15:1–13
☐	16	Ps. 94–96	Rom. 15:14–33
☐	17	Ps. 97–99	Rom. 16
☐	18	Ps. 100–102	1 Cor. 1
☐	19	Ps. 103–104	1 Cor. 2
☐	20	Ps. 105–106	1 Cor. 3
☐	21	Ps. 107–109	1 Cor. 4
☐	22	Ps. 110–112	1 Cor. 5
☐	23	Ps. 113–115	1 Cor. 6
☐	24	Ps. 116–118	1 Cor. 7:1–19
☐	25	Ps. 119:1–88	1 Cor. 7:20–40
☐	26	Ps. 119:89–176	1 Cor. 8
☐	27	Ps. 120–122	1 Cor. 9
☐	28	Ps.123–125	1 Cor. 10:1–18
☐	29	Ps. 126–128	1 Cor. 10:19–33
☐	30	Ps. 129–131	1 Cor. 11:1–16
☐	31	Ps. 132–134	1 Cor. 11:17–34

September

☐	1	Ps. 135–136	1 Cor. 12
☐	2	Ps. 137–139	1 Cor. 13
☐	3	Ps. 140–142	1 Cor. 14:1–20
☐	4	Ps. 143–145	1 Cor. 14:21–40
☐	5	Ps. 146–147	1 Cor. 15:1–28
☐	6	Ps. 148–150	1 Cor. 15:29–58
☐	7	Prov. 1–2	1 Cor. 16
☐	8	Prov. 3–5	2 Cor. 1
☐	9	Prov. 6–7	2 Cor. 2
☐	10	Prov. 8–9	2 Cor. 3
☐	11	Prov. 10–12	2 Cor. 4
☐	12	Prov. 13–15	2 Cor. 5
☐	13	Prov. 16–18	2 Cor. 6
☐	14	Prov. 19–21	2 Cor. 7
☐	15	Prov. 22–24	2 Cor. 8
☐	16	Prov. 25–26	2 Cor. 9
☐	17	Prov. 27–29	2 Cor. 10
☐	18	Prov. 30–31	2 Cor. 11:1–15
☐	19	Eccl. 1–3	2 Cor. 11:16–33
☐	20	Eccl. 4–6	2 Cor. 12
☐	21	Eccl. 7–9	2 Cor. 13
☐	22	Eccl. 10–12	Gal. 1
☐	23	Song 1–3	Gal. 2
☐	24	Song 4–5	Gal. 3
☐	25	Song 6–8	Gal. 4
☐	26	Isa. 1–2	Gal. 5
☐	27	Isa. 3–4	Gal. 6
☐	28	Isa. 5–6	Eph. 1
☐	29	Isa. 7–8	Eph. 2
☐	30	Isa. 9–10	Eph. 3

October

☐	1	Isa. 11–13	Eph. 4
☐	2	Isa. 14–16	Eph. 5:1–16
☐	3	Isa. 17–19	Eph. 5:17–33
☐	4	Isa. 20–22	Eph. 6
☐	5	Isa. 23–25	Phil. 1
☐	6	Isa. 26–27	Phil. 2
☐	7	Isa. 28–29	Phil. 3
☐	8	Isa. 30–31	Phil. 4
☐	9	Isa. 32–33	Col. 1
☐	10	Isa. 34–36	Col. 2
☐	11	Isa. 37–38	Col. 3
☐	12	Isa. 39–40	Col. 4
☐	13	Isa. 41–42	1 Thess. 1
☐	14	Isa. 43–44	1 Thess. 2
☐	15	Isa. 45–46	1 Thess. 3
☐	16	Isa. 47–49	1 Thess. 4
☐	17	Isa. 50–52	1 Thess. 5
☐	18	Isa. 53–55	2 Thess. 1
☐	19	Isa. 56–58	2 Thess. 2
☐	20	Isa. 59–61	2 Thess. 3
☐	21	Isa. 62–64	1 Tim. 1
☐	22	Isa. 65–66	1 Tim. 2
☐	23	Jer. 1–2	1 Tim. 3
☐	24	Jer. 3–5	1 Tim. 4
☐	25	Jer. 6–8	1 Tim. 5
☐	26	Jer. 9–11	1 Tim. 6
☐	27	Jer. 12–14	2 Tim. 1
☐	28	Jer. 15–17	2 Tim. 2
☐	29	Jer. 18–19	2 Tim. 3
☐	30	Jer. 20–21	2 Tim. 4
☐	31	Jer. 22–23	Titus 1

November

☐	1	Jer. 24–26	Titus 2
☐	2	Jer. 27–29	Titus 3
☐	3	Jer. 30–31	Philemon
☐	4	Jer. 32–33	Heb. 1
☐	5	Jer. 34–36	Heb. 2
☐	6	Jer. 37–39	Heb. 3
☐	7	Jer. 40–42	Heb. 4
☐	8	Jer. 43–45	Heb. 5
☐	9	Jer. 46–47	Heb. 6
☐	10	Jer. 48–49	Heb. 7
☐	11	Jer. 50	Heb. 8
☐	12	Jer. 51–52	Heb. 9
☐	13	Lam. 1–2	Heb. 10:1–18
☐	14	Lam. 3–5	Heb. 10:19–39
☐	15	Ezek. 1–2	Heb. 11:1–19
☐	16	Ezek. 3–4	Heb. 11:20–40
☐	17	Ezek. 5–7	Heb. 12
☐	18	Ezek. 8–10	Heb. 13
☐	19	Ezek. 11–13	James 1
☐	20	Ezek. 14–15	James 2
☐	21	Ezek. 16–17	James 3
☐	22	Ezek. 18–19	James 4
☐	23	Ezek. 20–21	James 5
☐	24	Ezek. 22–23	1 Peter 1
☐	25	Ezek. 24–26	1 Peter 2
☐	26	Ezek. 27–29	1 Peter 3
☐	27	Ezek. 30–32	1 Peter 4
☐	28	Ezek. 33–34	1 Peter 5
☐	29	Ezek. 35–36	2 Peter 1
☐	30	Ezek. 37–39	2 Peter 2

December

☐	1	Ezek. 40–41	2 Peter 3
☐	2	Ezek. 42–44	1 John 1
☐	3	Ezek. 45–46	1 John 2
☐	4	Ezek. 47–48	1 John 3
☐	5	Dan. 1–2	1 John 4
☐	6	Dan. 3–4	1 John 5
☐	7	Dan. 5–7	2 John
☐	8	Dan. 8–10	3 John
☐	9	Dan. 11–12	Jude
☐	10	Hos. 1–4	Rev. 1
☐	11	Hos. 5–8	Rev. 2
☐	12	Hos. 9–11	Rev. 3
☐	13	Hos. 12–14	Rev. 4
☐	14	Joel	Rev. 5
☐	15	Amos 1–3	Rev. 6
☐	16	Amos 4–6	Rev. 7
☐	17	Amos 7–9	Rev. 8
☐	18	Obad.	Rev. 9
☐	19	Jonah	Rev. 10
☐	20	Micah 1–3	Rev. 11
☐	21	Micah 4–5	Rev. 12
☐	22	Micah 6–7	Rev. 13
☐	23	Nahum	Rev. 14
☐	24	Hab.	Rev. 15
☐	25	Zeph.	Rev. 16
☐	26	Hag.	Rev. 17
☐	27	Zech. 1–4	Rev. 18
☐	28	Zech. 5–8	Rev. 19
☐	29	Zech. 9–12	Rev. 20
☐	30	Zech. 13–14	Rev. 21
☐	31	Mal.	Rev. 22

90-Day Bible Reading Schedule

Day	Start	End	✔	Day	Start	End	✔
1	Genesis 1:1	Genesis 16:16	❏	46	Proverbs 7:1	Proverbs 20:21	❏
2	Genesis 17:1	Genesis 28:19	❏	47	Proverbs 20:22	Ecclesiastes 2:26	❏
3	Genesis 28:20	Genesis 40:11	❏	48	Ecclesiastes 3:1	Song 8:14	❏
4	Genesis 40:12	Genesis 50:26	❏	49	Isaiah 1:1	Isaiah 13:22	❏
5	Exodus 1:1	Exodus 15:18	❏	50	Isaiah 14:1	Isaiah 28:29	❏
6	Exodus 15:19	Exodus 28:43	❏	51	Isaiah 29:1	Isaiah 41:18	❏
7	Exodus 29:1	Exodus 40:38	❏	52	Isaiah 41:19	Isaiah 52:12	❏
8	Leviticus 1:1	Leviticus 14:32	❏	53	Isaiah 52:13	Isaiah 66:18	❏
9	Leviticus 14:33	Leviticus 26:26	❏	54	Isaiah 66:19	Jeremiah 10:13	❏
10	Leviticus 26:27	Numbers 8:14	❏	55	Jeremiah 10:14	Jeremiah 23:8	❏
11	Numbers 8:15	Numbers 21:7	❏	56	Jeremiah 23:9	Jeremiah 33:22	❏
12	Numbers 21:8	Numbers 32:19	❏	57	Jeremiah 33:23	Jeremiah 47:7	❏
13	Numbers 32:20	Deuteronomy 7:26	❏	58	Jeremiah 48:1	Lamentations 1:22	❏
14	Deuteronomy 8:1	Deuteronomy 23:11	❏	59	Lamentations 2:1	Ezekiel 12:20	❏
15	Deuteronomy 23:12	Deuteronomy 34:12	❏	60	Ezekiel 12:21	Ezekiel 23:39	❏
16	Joshua 1:1	Joshua 14:15	❏	61	Ezekiel 23:40	Ezekiel 35:15	❏
17	Joshua 15:1	Judges 3:27	❏	62	Ezekiel 36:1	Ezekiel 47:12	❏
18	Judges 3:28	Judges 15:12	❏	63	Ezekiel 47:13	Daniel 8:27	❏
19	Judges 15:13	1 Samuel 2:29	❏	64	Daniel 9:1	Hosea 13:6	❏
20	1 Samuel 2:30	1 Samuel 15:35	❏	65	Hosea 13:7	Amos 9:10	❏
21	1 Samuel 16:1	1 Samuel 28:19	❏	66	Amos 9:11	Nahum 3:19	❏
22	1 Samuel 28:20	2 Samuel 12:10	❏	67	Habakkuk 1:1	Zechariah 10:12	❏
23	2 Samuel 12:11	2 Samuel 22:18	❏	68	Zechariah 11:1	Matthew 4:25	❏
24	2 Samuel 22:19	1 Kings 7:37	❏	69	Matthew 5:1	Matthew 15:39	❏
25	1 Kings 7:38	1 Kings 16:20	❏	70	Matthew 16:1	Matthew 26:56	❏
26	1 Kings 16:21	2 Kings 4:37	❏	71	Matthew 26:57	Mark 9:13	❏
27	2 Kings 4:38	2 Kings 15:26	❏	72	Mark 9:14	Luke 1:80	❏
28	2 Kings 15:27	2 Kings 25:30	❏	73	Luke 2:1	Luke 9:62	❏
29	1 Chronicles 1:1	1 Chronicles 9:44	❏	74	Luke 10:1	Luke 20:19	❏
30	1 Chronicles 10:1	1 Chronicles 23:32	❏	75	Luke 20:20	John 5:47	❏
31	1 Chronicles 24:1	2 Chronicles 7:10	❏	76	John 6:1	John 15:17	❏
32	2 Chronicles 7:11	2 Chronicles 23:15	❏	77	John 15:18	Acts 6:7	❏
33	2 Chronicles 23:16	2 Chronicles 35:15	❏	78	Acts 6:8	Acts 16:37	❏
34	2 Chronicles 35:16	Ezra 10:44	❏	79	Acts 16:38	Acts 28:16	❏
35	Nehemiah 1:1	Nehemiah 13:14	❏	80	Acts 28:17	Romans 14:23	❏
36	Nehemiah 13:15	Job 7:21	❏	81	Romans 15:1	1 Corinthians 14:40	❏
37	Job 8:1	Job 24:25	❏	82	1 Corinthians 15:1	Galatians 3:25	❏
38	Job 25:1	Job 41:34	❏	83	Galatians 3:26	Colossians 4:18	❏
39	Job 42:1	Psalm 24:10	❏	84	1 Thessalonians 1:1	Philemon 25	❏
40	Psalm 25:1	Psalm 45:14	❏	85	Hebrews 1:1	James 3:12	❏
41	Psalm 45:15	Psalm 69:21	❏	86	James 3:13	3 John 14	❏
42	Psalm 69:22	Psalm 89:13	❏	87	Jude 1	Revelation 17:18	❏
43	Psalm 89:14	Psalm 108:13	❏	88	Revelation 18:1	Revelation 22:21	❏
44	Psalm 109:1	Psalm 134:3	❏	89	Grace Day	Grace Day	❏
45	Psalm 135:1	Proverbs 6:35	❏	90	Grace Day	Grace Day	❏

january

The Undeserved Gift

Then said he to the multitude that came forth to be baptized of him, O generation of vipers, who hath warned you to flee from the wrath to come? Bring forth therefore fruits worthy of repentance, and begin not to say within yourselves, We have Abraham to our father: for I say unto you, That God is able of these stones to raise up children unto Abraham. And now also the axe is laid unto the root of the trees: every tree therefore which bringeth not forth good fruit is hewn down, and cast into the fire.
—LUKE 3:7–9

In the middle of a fiery denunciation of sin and a ringing call to repentance, John the Baptist said something wonderful that reveals the love and nature of our Heavenly Father. There were many among the Jewish people who did not truly worship and obey the God of their fathers, but who still thought they were fine because of their heritage. Yet, as John pointed out, no one is a Christian because of the faith of their parents or grandparents. It is only through individual and personal faith in the sacrifice of Jesus Christ that we become part of God's family.

The wonderful mercy and grace of God extends the offer of salvation freely to all who believe. Salvation is not limited to those with the right pedigree or family heritage—it is freely available to all. Salvation is not given to those who are good, but to those who acknowledge their sinfulness and need of a Saviour. Salvation is a demonstration of God's love because it is given to those who do not deserve it in any way.

At a time of year when many of us work diligently to meet new goals and develop new habits, it is refreshing to realize that, if we have trusted Christ as our Saviour, we are completely and unconditionally accepted by the Father—not because of what we have done or will do, but because of what Jesus did for us: "To the praise of the glory of his grace, wherein he hath made us accepted in the beloved" (Ephesians 1:6).

Today's Discipleship Principle: Rejoice today in the completely undeserved gift of salvation that God has provided through Jesus Christ.

What Shall We Do Then?

*And the people asked him, saying, What shall we do then? He answereth and saith unto them, He that hath two coats, let him impart to him that hath none; and he that hath meat, let him do likewise. Then came also publicans to be baptized, and said unto him, Master, what shall we do? And he said unto them, Exact no more than that which is appointed you. And the soldiers likewise demanded of him, saying, And what shall we do? And he said unto them, Do violence to no man, neither accuse any falsely; and be content with your wages.—*LUKE 3:10-14

The message that John the Baptist preached was a ringing call to repentance. He brought the people who came to hear him to a moment of decision—they could continue as they were, or they could recognize that the Messiah was coming and prepare to meet Him. A few verses earlier he had told them, "Bring forth therefore fruits worthy of repentance" (Luke 3:8). John was not telling them to earn repentance or salvation by their works. Ephesians 2:8–9 tells us, "For by grace are ye saved through faith; and that not of yourselves: it is the gift of God: Not of works, lest any man should boast." But John was calling them to show that what they declared with their mouths was real by their actions.

The people responded with an appropriate question: "What shall we do then?" For each group who asked, John described a course of action that would demonstrate that something major had changed in their hearts and was on display in their behavior.

As we begin a new year, many of us set goals for what we would like to accomplish. This passage is a good reminder to us, however, that one of the ways we should answer the question, "What shall we then do [this year]?" should be in developing habits and actions that reveal outwardly what God has done in our hearts inwardly.

Today's Discipleship Principle: As you prepare goals for this coming year, consider what God has done in your heart and ways He has been prompting you to demonstrate the fruit of a changed life.

Focus on Jesus

And as the people were in expectation, and all men mused in their hearts of John, whether he were the Christ, or not; John answered, saying unto them all, I indeed baptize you with water; but one mightier than I cometh, the latchet of whose shoes I am not worthy to unloose: he shall baptize you with the Holy Ghost and with fire: Whose fan is in his hand, and he will throughly purge his floor, and will gather the wheat into his garner; but the chaff he will burn with fire unquenchable. —LUKE 3:15-17

The ministry of John the Baptist quickly attracted a great deal of attention. People flocked to see and hear him, recognizing that God was doing something special. There was a great deal of expectation regarding the coming of the Messiah. Many of the people were aware of the prophecies given to Daniel concerning His coming, and the timing that marked the years from the decree to rebuild the temple until the arrival of the Messiah. Beyond those prophecies, the fact that their nation was captive to Rome led the people to long for a political deliverance (far more than the spiritual deliverance they so desperately needed), and they were eager to see that to happen.

It was only natural for people to wonder if John himself were the Messiah, but he quickly crushed that speculation. John did not want to be elevated—he wanted to elevate Jesus. So he humbly declared that he was not to be worshiped and that he was not even worthy to untie Jesus' shoes. How different that attitude is from so many Christians in our day! So often we are tempted to lift up ourselves in pride, rather than giving all the honor and glory to Jesus. Charles Spurgeon said, "It is a remarkable fact that all the heresies which have arisen in the Christian church have had a decided tendency to dishonor God and flatter man."

Today's Discipleship Principle: Every day we have an opportunity to lift Jesus up in the eyes of those with whom we interact. But it always requires that we take our focus off ourselves to do it.

Willing to Pay the Price

And many other things in his exhortation preached he unto the people.
But Herod the tetrarch, being reproved by him for Herodias his brother
Philip's wife, and for all the evils which Herod had done, Added yet this
above all, that he shut up John in prison. —LUKE 3:18-20

In January of 1956, Jim Elliot, Ed McCully, Roger Youderian, Pete Fleming, and Nate Saint died in the jungles of Ecuador trying to take the gospel to the Huaorani (Auca) tribe that had never before been reached. The story of their martyrdom echoed around the world. It was not until later that it became known that the missionaries had had guns and could have defended themselves but chose instead to die so that door to the gospel would not be closed. A few of their wives continued the mission work, and eventually many from that tribe were saved and a church was established.

Most of us have not yet had to suffer any serious repercussions for our faith. America has long enjoyed a level of religious freedom that is almost unknown in human history, but we are not promised that our faith will never cost us anything. Indeed, the Bible declares the opposite. From his prison cell in Rome where he was awaiting execution, Paul wrote to Timothy, "Yea, and all that will live godly in Christ Jesus shall suffer persecution" (2 Timothy 3:12).

If we are not willing to pay the price when things are relatively easy, how will we respond if real persecution becomes a reality? The early church experienced great power and wonderful results, but they also faced great opposition. They did not regard hardship as evidence that God had abandoned them or that they should adjust their message to avoid trouble. "And they departed from the presence of the council, rejoicing that they were counted worthy to suffer shame for his name" (Acts 5:41).

Today's Discipleship Principle: Our love for God should be so great that we are willing to suffer and even die rather than deny or betray Him.

A Spirit-Filled Life

Now when all the people were baptized, it came to pass, that Jesus also being baptized, and praying, the heaven was opened, And the Holy Ghost descended in a bodily shape like a dove upon him, and a voice came from heaven, which said, Thou art my beloved Son; in thee I am well pleased.
—LUKE 3:21–22

Because we have finite minds, we cannot fully grasp how it is possible that Jesus was both completely God and completely man at the same time. But this is what the Bible teaches us. It is important for us to understand that here on earth Jesus voluntarily laid aside some of His rights and privileges, yet He remained completely divine in every respect.

But while a divine Saviour who was sinless and perfect was necessary to provide the sacrifice for salvation, we could never hope to copy His perfection. That is why we must understand that Jesus was also a man who lived in the power of the Holy Spirit. That is a role model we can follow. In speaking of Jesus, John the Baptist made a powerful declaration: "For he whom God hath sent speaketh the words of God: for God giveth not the Spirit by measure unto him" (John 3:34). There was no limit to the power of the Holy Spirit on the life of Christ because there was nothing to hinder His work.

The Bible tells us that we can grieve and quench the Holy Spirit by the things we do or fail to do. While the Holy Spirit is God and as such has no limits on His potential power, our conduct determines the extent to which He is able to work in our lives. The Children of Israel failed to receive the full blessings that were available to them because of their sinfulness: "Yea, they turned back and tempted God, and limited the Holy One of Israel" (Psalm 78:41).

Today's Discipleship Principle: To live as Jesus did, we must be yielded to and filled with the Holy Spirit so that we can truly follow in His steps.

Led into Difficulty

And Jesus being full of the Holy Ghost returned from Jordan, and was led by the Spirit into the wilderness, Being forty days tempted of the devil. And in those days he did eat nothing: and when they were ended, he afterward hungered.—LUKE 4:1–2

There is a widespread idea today that if we are doing what we should, everything will work out wonderfully—we won't get sick, we won't have money trouble, and our families will enjoy peace and harmony. Yet the Bible paints a different picture. While there are blessings for obedience, the Christian life is far from being simple and painless. There are times when doing exactly what we should do leads us to difficulty and hardship. Jesus was not out of the will of the Father when the devil came to tempt Him. He was exactly where the Holy Spirit had led Him.

The temptation of Jesus happened at a time when He was physically weak and alone. There were no friends or family there to encourage Him; there was no human support at all. Yet in that moment, Jesus still had full confidence in His Father. The presence of the Holy Spirit gave Him all of the help and spiritual strength that He needed to deal with what was coming.

We are never alone, even if we are separated from all our family and friends. The Holy Spirit is still with us when things get tough. And in those moments, our faith is more important than ever. The devil knows this, and he attempts to get us to question God's goodness. One of his main tactics against us is to bring suffering in hopes that the pain and trouble will make us turn against God. "And Satan answered the LORD, and said, Skin for skin, yea, all that a man hath will he give for his life" (Job 2:4). But when we live with an awareness of the Holy Spirit, we realize that we are never alone.

Today's Discipleship Principle: The presence of trouble should drive us to trust God more, rather than causing us to doubt His love and care for us.

7

The Vital Importance of the Word of God

And the devil said unto him, If thou be the Son of God, command this stone that it be made bread. And Jesus answered him, saying, It is written, That man shall not live by bread alone, but by every word of God
—LUKE 4:3–4

The devil devised three specific plans to try to divert Jesus from the course His Father had set. In each case, Jesus responded the same way—by quoting a principle from the Bible that overrode the temptation and keeping His focus on what God wanted rather than what He wanted. We need to understand the way Satan works. He is happy for us to sin and violate God's law, but he is just as happy if he can get us to do good things in the wrong way.

There is nothing wrong with food. God wants us to eat and enjoy the things He has made to sustain our lives. There is nothing wrong with using miracle power to feed hungry people. We see miracles of feeding people throughout Scripture. So Satan's attack was subtle, attempting to get Jesus to meet a legitimate need for something that is good and necessary, but to do so without regard to God the Father's plan for Him. Jesus responded with the words of Moses regarding the manna that fed the Israelites in the wilderness (Deuteronomy 8:3) to make the point that spiritual life matters far more than physical life.

We need to have a personal, powerful, meaningful, daily relationship with the Bible. Job did not have much, if any, of the written word of God, but he said, "Neither have I gone back from the commandment of his lips; I have esteemed the words of his mouth more than my necessary food" (Job 23:12). When we focus on the temporal and physical, it is easy for Satan to draw us away from God's path and God's plan.

Today's Discipleship Principle: When we love God's Word and depend on it for our daily strength, we are prepared to resist temptation.

God, and God Alone

And the devil, taking him up into an high mountain, shewed unto him all the kingdoms of the world in a moment of time. And the devil said unto him, All this power will I give thee, and the glory of them: for that is delivered unto me; and to whomsoever I will I give it. If thou therefore wilt worship me, all shall be thine. And Jesus answered and said unto him, Get thee behind me, Satan: for it is written, Thou shalt worship the Lord thy God, and him only shalt thou serve.
—LUKE 4:5–8

Though there were many laws and instructions given to the Children of Israel to govern their daily lives, the most central were the Ten Commandments that God gave to Moses on Mt. Sinai. The first of those ten highlighted the nature of God and that He alone is to be worshiped. In the New Testament, Jesus would reiterate the importance of this command by declaring that loving God was the most important command of all.

When Satan tempted Jesus to receive the honor and glory of the world by worshiping Satan, Jesus refused, once again, quoting Scripture, but this time citing the command to give God first place in our hearts and lives.

Throughout their history, the Israelites had struggled with the worship of idols. In our more sophisticated times we no longer carve images of animals to pray to, but there are still many things to which people give their lives and devotion and time to the exclusion of love and worship of God. Jesus warned that in the end times proper love of God would be in short supply: "And because iniquity shall abound, the love of many shall wax cold" (Matthew 24:12). Rather than trying hard to do right and overcome temptation in our own strength, if we will love God first, we will be less likely to fall into sin.

Today's Discipleship Principle: If we love God the way that we should, we will not be tempted to follow the devil to gain praise and glory.

Real Faith and Presumption

*And he brought him to Jerusalem, and set him on a pinnacle of the temple, and said unto him, If thou be the Son of God, cast thyself down from hence: For it is written, He shall give his angels charge over thee, to keep thee: And in their hands they shall bear thee up, lest at any time thou dash thy foot against a stone. And Jesus answering said unto him, It is said, Thou shalt not tempt the Lord thy God.—*LUKE 4:9–12

God has given us many wonderful promises in His Word regarding His protection of His children. Many of us have experienced that protection first hand. I am so thankful for God's guarding and protection over my life as I travel, preach, and do His work. Without His protection, none of us could survive. "It is of the LORD's mercies that we are not consumed, because his compassions fail not" (Lamentations 3:22).

At the same time, there are people who do foolish things and claim that they have faith that nothing bad will happen. This is what Satan tempted Jesus to do in the third of the wilderness temptations. Satan wanted Jesus to presumptuously act outside of the will of the Father, and he even twisted and misapplied a Scripture passage (Psalm 91:11–12) to push the temptation.

God does not expect us to be presumptuous because we have access to divine resources and protection. It may be that God will rescue us if we do something foolish where He has not led us, but it is wrong for us to claim that we are acting in faith when we are not doing something God has directed in His Word.

There are times when faith demands a response from us that defies human explanation or ability. But that kind of response must be grounded in the Bible. No amount of feelings or declarations of our words can be a legitimate basis of faith. We are only living by faith when we are acting in obedience to what God has commanded.

Today's Discipleship Principle: We can always trust God to do exactly what He says—and we should. The Christian life must be lived by faith.

The First Sermon Jesus Preached

And he closed the book, and he gave it again to the minister, and sat down. And the eyes of all them that were in the synagogue were fastened on him. And he began to say unto them, This day is this scripture fulfilled in your ears. And all bare him witness, and wondered at the gracious words which proceeded out of his mouth. And they said, Is not this Joseph's son?
—LUKE 4:20–22

When Jesus returned to His hometown of Nazareth for the first time after He had started His public ministry, the people were eager to hear Him. The news of the miracles that He had performed in other places had reached them, and they were not sure what to expect. On the Sabbath day Jesus went into the synagogue and read from the prophecy of Isaiah of the coming of the Messiah. In no uncertain terms, Jesus declared that He was the fulfillment of that prophecy. The people were shocked to hear what Jesus said. He had grown up in their town and been thought of as the son of Joseph. The people did not recognize Him as the Messiah. In fact, by the time He finished His first sermon, they tried to kill Him by throwing Him off the mountain at the edge of town.

But there is a powerful lesson for us in the very beginning of Jesus' words. His declaration that the people were seeing and hearing the fulfillment of Scripture is a declaration that what God says will always happen. The promises of God always come true. He has never failed to do what He said, and we can rest assured that our generation will not be the first to trust the promises of the Bible in vain.

There is a great need in our day for God's people to take Him at His Word. The Bible makes no mistakes, and we should believe and do all that it says.

Today's Discipleship Principle: The example Jesus set for us in accepting the authority of the Bible is one we need to follow.

Genesis 25–26   //   Matthew 8:1–17   33

A God Who Helps

But I tell you of a truth, many widows were in Israel in the days of Elias, when the heaven was shut up three years and six months, when great famine was throughout all the land; But unto none of them was Elias sent, save unto Sarepta, a city of Sidon, unto a woman that was a widow. And many lepers were in Israel in the time of Eliseus the prophet; and none of them was cleansed, saving Naaman the Syrian. —LUKE 4:25–27

In His sermon in Nazareth, Jesus highlighted two stories from the Old Testament when God reached out in miraculous ways to meet the needs of people who were not Israelites. The stories of Elijah with the widow in Zarepath (1 Kings 17) and Elisha with Naaman (2 Kings 5) tell us something significant about the nature of our Heavenly Father: He acts in grace and mercy. There was no reason for these two foreigners to receive the miraculous power of God to meet their needs—except for His grace and mercy.

Nothing we can do will ever be worthy of God. Our best efforts fall hopelessly short of His standard. The prophet Isaiah declared, "But we are all as an unclean thing, and all our righteousnesses are as filthy rags; and we all do fade as a leaf; and our iniquities, like the wind, have taken us away" (Isaiah 64:6). It is not our goodness but His grace that brings us the hope and help that we so desperately need.

Jesus' message was not well received by the people of Nazareth. In fact they tried to kill Jesus at the end of His sermon. Often we do not like to think of God's grace as being undeserved because it makes us face the reality of our sinful failure and our inability to make our own way to God. But the real message of grace should fill our hearts with joy and gratitude. Ephesians 2:8–9 says, "For by grace are ye saved through faith; and that not of yourselves: it is the gift of God: Not of works, lest any man should boast."

Today's Discipleship Principle: Rejoice today in the knowledge that God's grace was freely given to you because He loves you so much.

A Life-Changing Message

And came down to Capernaum, a city of Galilee, and taught them on the sabbath days. And they were astonished at his doctrine: for his word was with power.—LUKE 4:31–32

After He was rejected by the people in His hometown of Nazareth, Jesus moved to the city of Capernaum, which became His ministry headquarters. There He continued His practice of going to the synagogue each week on the Sabbath day to teach the people. It was easy for them to recognize that what Jesus was preaching was different than what they had previously heard from other rabbis. The parallel account in Mark highlights this truth: "And they were astonished at his doctrine: for he taught them as one that had authority, and not as the scribes" (Mark 1:22).

It was a common practice in those days for the rabbis to teach more about the teachings of rabbis and the arguments they had over what various parts of Scripture meant, than to actually focus on the Word of God. Jesus was different. He was not interested in the opinions of man. He declared the truths that the Holy Spirit of God had inspired to be written down and explained how they applied to daily life and what God expected of His people.

There is enormous power and authority when we stand and, like the Old Testament prophets, simply say, "Thus saith the Lord." Our ideas and opinions do not carry the weight to bring conviction of sin to the hearts of the lost. Noted author and skeptic Mark Twain said, "It's not the parts of the Bible that I don't understand that bother me. It is the parts I do understand." Though the Bible may not be accepted or appreciated, its power cannot be denied. We need to tell the world what God has said. His Word, shared in His power, is the means He has given us to reach the lost.

Today's Discipleship Principle: When we tell people God's truth from His Word, we give them a message with the power to transform lives.

A Demon Comes to Church

And in the synagogue there was a man, which had a spirit of an unclean devil, and cried out with a loud voice, Saying, Let us alone; what have we to do with thee, thou Jesus of Nazareth? art thou come to destroy us? I know thee who thou art; the Holy One of God. And Jesus rebuked him, saying, Hold thy peace, and come out of him. And when the devil had thrown him in the midst, he came out of him, and hurt him not.
—LUKE 4:33–35

Demons are real, and they are active in our world today. Though it is a mistake to obsessively focus on the demonic, it is also a mistake to ignore it. The devil has many agents at work, and they have a real impact on the world. It was true in Jesus' day, and it is still true now (although sometimes they manifest themselves in different ways to a modern world).

There are some twenty different references in the Gospel of Luke to Jesus dealing with people who were possessed by demons. Several of these confrontations took place in synagogues—the equivalent in our day of churches. Not everyone who comes into church is a believer, and we need to be discerning as we deal with people. John wrote, "Beloved, believe not every spirit, but try the spirits whether they are of God: because many false prophets are gone out into the world" (1 John 4:1).

When the demon interrupted Jesus as He taught, the Lord responded by casting the demon out of the man. The point of this story is not that we should go around looking to cast out demons, but that the power of God is greater than the power of Satan. The devil is a created fallen angel, and though his strength is greater than ours, it pales in comparison to God's power. As Christians, we are indwelt by the Holy Spirit. When we yield to His power in our lives, we will overcome the devil: "…because greater is he that is in you, than he that is in the world" (1 John 4:4).

Today's Discipleship Principle: The power of God is able to overcome all of the work of the devil in our lives.

Genesis 31–32   //   Matthew 9:18–38

The God Who Heals

And he arose out of the synagogue, and entered into Simon's house. And Simon's wife's mother was taken with a great fever; and they besought him for her. And he stood over her, and rebuked the fever; and it left her: and immediately she arose and ministered unto them. Now when the sun was setting, all they that had any sick with divers diseases brought them unto him; and he laid his hands on every one of them, and healed them.
—LUKE 4:38–40

In the time of Jesus, they did not have the advanced medical care that we are blessed with in our day. As a result, even relatively simple diseases and infections could easily become life-threatening. The arrival of Jesus in a town meant that there was hope for people, no matter how sick they might have been or what their problems were. Peter's mother-in-law had such a serious fever that she had been completely incapacitated. A few words from Jesus, however, took away the fever and restored her strength.

It's not always God's will to heal. (For instance, God did not give healing to the Apostle Paul, although 2 Corinthians 12:8 tells us that Paul prayed earnestly for it.) But as Jesus went about healing people, He revealed the power of God that is able to heal. His was not the healing of "professionals" who go into town and hold a meeting, but never go to a hospital to heal the people there. Instead, it was the supernatural healing of God.

Sometimes God does choose to supernaturally heal His people, and He encourages us to pray for healing: "Is any sick among you? let him call for the elders of the church; and let them pray over him, anointing him with oil in the name of the Lord" (James 5:14). But whether or not it is God's will to give physical healing, the spiritual healing He has given through salvation is the greatest miracle ever.

Today's Discipleship Principle: The miraculous physical healing Jesus sometimes gave proved His power as God; the miraculous spiritual healing He always gives proves the power of His gospel.

Who Do You Trust?

And when it was day, he departed and went into a desert place: and the people sought him, and came unto him, and stayed him, that he should not depart from them. And he said unto them, I must preach the kingdom of God to other cities also: for therefore am I sent. And he preached in the synagogues of Galilee. —LUKE 4:42–44

The people in Capernaum would have been delighted for Jesus to stay with them. In fact, they begged Him not to leave when it was time for Him to go. They realized that they had benefited greatly by His presence. Yet even at the very beginning of His ministry, Jesus made it clear that the priority of His life and work would be to reach as many people as possible with the gospel. Jesus recognized that He had been given this mission by His Father and as a result, He planned His life around what God had in mind for Him to do: "And he that sent me is with me: the Father hath not left me alone; for I do always those things that please him" (John 8:29).

What was true of Jesus should be true of us as well. We should plan and shape our lives around what matters to God rather than what matters to us. And nothing is more central to God's purpose and will for our lives than telling others about salvation in Jesus Christ.

When the Jewish rulers called the disciples before them to try to make them stop preaching about Jesus, even the unbelieving rulers had to admit the effectiveness of God's people carrying out God's plan: "Saying, Did not we straitly command you that ye should not teach in this name? and, behold, ye have filled Jerusalem with your doctrine…" (Acts 5:28). Would to God that Christians today would fill their communities and spheres of influence with the gospel! It is the heart of Christ that we would sense an urgency ("I *must* preach") to share the good news of salvation.

Today's Discipleship Principle: God's plan to reach the world has not changed—it is still for His children to proclaim the gospel to everyone.

God's Plan to Build Churches

And it came to pass, that, as the people pressed upon him to hear the word of God, he stood by the lake of Gennesaret, And saw two ships standing by the lake: but the fishermen were gone out of them, and were washing their nets. And he entered into one of the ships, which was Simon's, and prayed him that he would thrust out a little from the land. And he sat down, and taught the people out of the ship.—LUKE 5:1–3

There are a lot of "experts" who give advice with different methods to build churches. They can tell you what kind of music will be most effective in drawing a crowd, how long the sermon should be, how bright the lights ought to be, and which people in the community you should invite. Yet far too often, they and those who listen to their advice forget the most important thing. God's plan to build churches is the plan that we find in the Scriptures—the preaching of His Word.

The crowds who came to hear Jesus were impressed by His miracles of healing and casting out demons, but most of all, they wanted to hear Him declare what God had to say. More important than our décor, our lighting, or our service times is the content of our message. Everything we do and say to reach people must be founded on the Bible. Not only that, but we should be careful of becoming frustrated or offended over trivial matters such as service times or classroom locations in a church. After all, it is the preaching of God's Word that matters most.

This was the directive Paul gave Timothy in his final letter to his young protégé: "I charge thee therefore before God, and the Lord Jesus Christ, who shall judge the quick and the dead at his appearing and his kingdom; Preach the word; be instant in season, out of season; reprove, rebuke, exhort with all longsuffering and doctrine" (2 Timothy 4:1–2).

We must allow the Bible to fill our hearts and minds, and then we must share what God has to say with the world.

Today's Discipleship Principle: The ministry to which God has called us must be based on the Bible if it is to change lives.

What God's Power Can Do

Now when he had left speaking, he said unto Simon, Launch out into the deep, and let down your nets for a draught. And Simon answering said unto him, Master, we have toiled all the night, and have taken nothing: nevertheless at thy word I will let down the net. And when they had this done, they inclosed a great multitude of fishes: and their net brake.
—LUKE 5:4–6

We don't know how old Peter was when Jesus called him to be a disciple, but we do know that he was a professional fisherman in business with his father and brother on the Sea of Galilee. We would assume that he had spent much of his life on the water or with his nets. Even today fishing is a major industry on the small lake in northern Israel, with many different kinds of fish being caught commercially. In Peter's day, most of the fishing was done at nighttime in small boats using nets that would be thrown into the water and dragged back into the boat over and over again throughout the night. It was a tiring and backbreaking way to make a living, but it was Peter's livelihood.

When Jesus finished his sermon delivered from the boat He had borrowed from Peter, He asked Peter to launch back out onto the sea. It had already been a discouraging night for Peter, as his best efforts had produced nothing, and now the time for fishing was past. Yet he was willing to obey Jesus and do something that had no hope of success according to human reasoning. He agreed to let down the net again "at thy word." His faith was in the word of the Lord.

In return for his obedience, Peter found himself hauling in the greatest catch of his life. God is able to do anything. His power has not weakened. But too often we go the way we think best, leaning on our own understanding rather than trusting and obeying the Lord. As a result, we miss seeing His power at work in our lives.

Today's Discipleship Principle: When we do what God tells us to do, we get what His power can produce rather than what we can do on our own.

Humility before Jesus

And they beckoned unto their partners, which were in the other ship, that they should come and help them. And they came, and filled both the ships, so that they began to sink. When Simon Peter saw it, he fell down at Jesus' knees, saying, Depart from me; for I am a sinful man, O Lord.
—LUKE 5:7–8

In all the times I have been fishing, I have never caught so many fish that their combined weight threatened to sink the boat I was in—let alone so many that it was too much for two boats to handle. But that was the position that Peter found himself in when he launched out into the deep at Jesus' command. When he saw the power of God on display in this unique way, Peter's response is instructive. He did not cheer and congratulate himself—he knelt and repented. Peter realized just how far short he had come of God's purpose.

Too many Christians are self-satisfied and somewhat proud of what God has done in their lives. It is easy for us to start thinking that we deserve His blessings and even think that the success we may experience is due to us rather than to Him. Nothing could be further from the truth. Paul asked the members of the church at Corinth who were tempted to be lifted up in pride, "For who maketh thee to differ from another? and what hast thou that thou didst not receive? now if thou didst receive it, why dost thou glory, as if thou hadst not received it?" (1 Corinthians 4:7).

We realize that we are saved by grace through faith alone apart from any merit we have, but sometimes we forget that our work for God must be done the same way. The more we see God at work, the more we should bow down in grateful humility, recognizing that it is His power rather than ours that brings results.

Today's Discipleship Principle: When we humble ourselves, God is able to work powerfully to bring glory to Himself in our lives.

Fishers of Men

For he was astonished, and all that were with him, at the draught of the fishes which they had taken: And so was also James, and John, the sons of Zebedee, which were partners with Simon. And Jesus said unto Simon, Fear not; from henceforth thou shalt catch men. And when they had brought their ships to land, they forsook all, and followed him."
—LUKE 5:9–11

One of the most important truths we can learn is that God has a purpose and plan for our lives. We are not cast randomly out into the world to struggle through as best we can. The God who created everything also designed a purpose for us. And in the pages of His Word He has revealed the vital truths that, if we follow them, will shape our paths.

Peter, James, and John had successful careers in the fishing business, but Jesus had something else in mind for them. He wanted them to be part of His work. Because they acknowledged His right to command their lives, they left behind everything they had known to follow Him.

A.W. Tozer wrote, "Most of our problems are not circumstantial. Most of our problems are perceptual. Our biggest problems can be traced back to an inadequate understanding of who God is."

There on the Sea of Galilee these fisherman had just seen an amazing demonstration of the power of God as both of their boats were filled to overflowing with fish. Yet it was in that moment of great success and a financial windfall beyond what they had dreamed that Jesus called them to abandon what they had known for a new course in life. They were willing to follow Him and start catching men, and the entire world was transformed as a result. The great need of our day is the same—people who are willing to be fishers of men.

Today's Discipleship Principle: When we understand who God truly is, we will be willing to devote our lives to following His commands.

Believing God's Power

And it came to pass, when he was in a certain city, behold a man full of leprosy: who seeing Jesus fell on his face, and besought him, saying, Lord, if thou wilt, thou canst make me clean. And he put forth his hand, and touched him, saying, I will: be thou clean. And immediately the leprosy departed from him. And he charged him to tell no man: but go, and shew thyself to the priest, and offer for thy cleansing, according as Moses commanded, for a testimony unto them. —LUKE 5:12–14

Leprosy was probably the most dreaded disease in Bible times. When someone contracted leprosy, his life as he had known it was over. He became an outcast, forced to leave home and family and exist on what he could beg from others. A leper was commanded to cry out, "Unclean, unclean" in warning whenever anyone approached to keep others from becoming infected. It was a lonely and painful existence.

Yet this leper had the faith to come to Jesus. Despite all that he had endured, this man still had faith in God, and he recognized the power of Jesus to heal his incurable disease. To him there was no question about Jesus' ability to heal, it was simply a matter of Him being willing to do so. That is why he said to Jesus, "If thou wilt, thou canst make me clean."

And what was Jesus' response? Not only was He willing to heal the man, but Jesus *touched* him as well. How many years had it been since the leper had felt a kind touch before the Lord reached out to him in mercy and love?

There are many things that we need God to do for us. Yet sometimes we fail to see His power simply because we do not believe that God is willing to help us—that He cares enough to touch *our* situation. We may believe that God did great things for others, but we do not believe in our hearts that He will do the same for us. But all things are still possible for those who believe.

Today's Discipleship Principle: Do not miss out on God's power in your life due to an absence of faith in His love for you.

Praying in the Wilderness

But so much the more went there a fame abroad of him: and great multitudes came together to hear, and to be healed by him of their infirmities. And he withdrew himself into the wilderness, and prayed.
—LUKE 5:15–16

Prayer was a vital resource to Jesus—so important that He frequently drew apart from others in order to have time to spend with His Father in prayer. There were many occasions when He gave up sleep or eating in order to pray. More than once Jesus interrupted His ministry, leaving behind people who were wanting to see and hear Him and be healed, to go alone to pray. If Jesus needed time to pray, how much more important is it for us to spend time with Him in prayer?

The vital necessity of prayer is a reality that is far too often ignored in our day. Though we pay lip service to the power of prayer, the lack of time we spend in prayer reveals that we are not truly convinced that God will hear and answer when we call out to Him. As a result, we deprive ourselves of so much that God is able to give to us, and both our relationship with Him and our work for Him suffer as a result. The poet and hymn writer William Cowper wrote:

> Restraining prayer, we cease to fight;
> Prayer makes the Christian's armor bright;
> And Satan trembles, when he sees
> The weakest saint upon his knees.

The strength to overcome the obstacles we face, the power to triumph over temptation, and the resources—both physical and spiritual—to do God's work are supplied through prayer. The strength we have in ourselves is far too little to meet the challenges we face. Each day should find us on our knees begging God to work in our lives. Only then will we be equipped to do great and mighty things for Him.

Today's Discipleship Principle: If we do not take the time to pray, we will lack the power and resources to do the work God places before us.

Bringing People to Jesus

*And it came to pass on a certain day, as he was teaching, that there were Pharisees and doctors of the law sitting by, which were come out of every town of Galilee, and Judaea, and Jerusalem: and the power of the Lord was present to heal them. And, behold, men brought in a bed a man which was taken with a palsy: and they sought means to bring him in, and to lay him before him. And when they could not find by what way they might bring him in because of the multitude, they went upon the housetop, and let him down through the tiling with his couch into the midst before Jesus.—*LUKE 5:17–19

W e know basically nothing about the four men who brought their paralyzed friend to Jesus. We don't know their professions or their degree of education. We don't know their hometowns or their family heritage. We don't even know their names. What we do know is that they had an overwhelming love for their friend and faith in Jesus. They believed that Jesus was able to heal this man who had no other hope, and as a result they were willing to go above and beyond what people would normally do in order to place their friend at Jesus' feet.

It must have been extremely difficult to get a paralyzed man confined to his bed onto the roof of the house where Jesus was. It could not have been easy to take apart the roof so they could lower him down to Jesus' feet. Their actions no doubt seemed outrageous to many of those watching. But they didn't care how difficult it was or what others thought. They wanted to get their friend to Jesus.

We, too, should have a heart-filled passion to bring our friends to Jesus. We should be consumed with the desire to reach the lost and bring them to Him—so much so that we are willing to overcome the obstacles of time restraints, rejection, or fear in order to introduce others to Christ.

Today's Discipleship Principle: There is nothing more important than sharing the gospel with lost men and women before it is too late.

A Demonstration of Divine Power

But when Jesus perceived their thoughts, he answering said unto them, What reason ye in your hearts? Whether is easier, to say, Thy sins be forgiven thee; or to say, Rise up and walk? But that ye may know that the Son of man hath power upon earth to forgive sins, (he said unto the sick of the palsy,) I say unto thee, Arise, and take up thy couch, and go into thine house.—LUKE 5:22–24

The message of Jesus was not well received by many of the religious leaders of His day. Despite the testimony of John the Baptist and the clear teaching of Jesus Himself, they did not accept the truth that Jesus was the Messiah and the Son of God. Just as the Pharisees did not go to Bethlehem to see the Messiah—even though they knew and were able to tell Herod that Jesus would be born there—so when He began His public ministry, they did not welcome or receive Him.

When the paralyzed man was let down through the roof to see Jesus, the Lord declared that he was forgiven. Yet that claim seemed outrageous to the Pharisees who were gathered to hear Jesus. They realized that only God has the power to forgive sins, so they knew Jesus was claiming to be God. To drive home the point He was making, Jesus asked a rhetorical question. Those who opposed Him knew it was easy to say that sins were forgiven, because there is no outward way to confirm that had happened. But to say "Arise" to a paralyzed man gives an immediate evidence of power that cannot be ignored.

The God we serve has all power, and He has offered to us something far more valuable and important than physical healing. Jesus came not primarily to raise up the sick, but to heal the wounds of sin and offer us forgiveness through His blood. That is Divine power on display.

Today's Discipleship Principle: There is nothing that better demonstrates God's love and power than His forgiveness of our sins.

Transformed Lives

And immediately he rose up before them, and took up that whereon he lay, and departed to his own house, glorifying God. And they were all amazed, and they glorified God, and were filled with fear, saying, We have seen strange things to day.—LUKE 5:25–26

When people truly meet Jesus, it is a transforming experience. The man who had been paralyzed and unable to walk immediately got up when Jesus told him to do so. This is a wonderful picture of our salvation. Prior to coming to Christ, we had no power or ability to do what was right according to God's standard. We were crippled by sin, unable to help ourselves in any way. But the power of Jesus to save changes everything.

We see another great illustration of this truth in the life of Lazarus. Jesus waited until His friend was dead and buried before traveling to Bethany. When He went to the grave, Jesus wept for the sorrow and grief of His friends and their loss. Then He commanded Lazarus to rise from the dead—and he did! The resurrection of Lazarus was a miracle that the enemies of Jesus could not explain. "But the chief priests consulted that they might put Lazarus also to death; Because that by reason of him many of the Jews went away, and believed on Jesus" (Luke 12:10–11).

Our lives are meant to be testimonies to the power and grace of God. There should be evidence that is clear to everyone around us that we are no longer the same as we were before we met Jesus. Too often, however, Christians settle into a pattern of living just like the world around them rather than walking in the new life they have been given. If we are going to have an impact on the world, we must show clear evidence that we have been given a life-changing gift infused with power that can only be attributed to God.

Today's Discipleship Principle: The way we live each day should be irrefutable evidence of God's power to change lives forever.

Jesus Looking for Sinners

And after these things he went forth, and saw a publican, named Levi, sitting at the receipt of custom: and he said unto him, Follow me. And he left all, rose up, and followed him. —LUKE 5:27–28

In the time of Christ, Israel was under the control of the Roman Empire. As was the custom in those days, much of the expense of keeping a military occupation force in a conquered land was expected to be borne by the residents of that land. The Romans had devised an ingenious system for their tax collection. They would contract with local citizens of the country who would be responsible for meeting a certain quota of taxes. As an incentive to them, these men, known as publicans, were allowed to keep everything they collected above that amount.

Of course, this system was rife with corruption. The publicans could charge whatever taxes they felt like charging, with the military might of Rome available to back up their assessments. The Jews who collaborated with the Romans in this way were hated by their countrymen. Though they were often very wealthy, they were despised, even barred from entering the synagogues for prayer and worship.

Yet when Jesus saw a publican named Levi hard at work lining his own pockets and funding the Roman occupation of Israel in the process, He did not shame or condemn him. Instead Jesus called Levi to leave his old life behind to follow Him.

It is tempting after we have been saved for a while to forget how desperately lost and wicked we were before we met Jesus. Even those of us who were saved as children had a corrupt sin nature and no hope without Him. The grace and mercy of God sent Jesus into the world to look for lost sinners—for us. This truth is our hope of salvation and our source of joy.

Today's Discipleship Principle: Give thanks today that even while you were a sinner far from Him, Jesus came in love to save you.

Who Is Salvation Meant For?

And Levi made him a great feast in his own house: and there was a great company of publicans and of others that sat down with them. But their scribes and Pharisees murmured against his disciples, saying, Why do ye eat and drink with publicans and sinners? And Jesus answering said unto them, They that are whole need not a physician; but they that are sick. I came not to call the righteous, but sinners to repentance.
—LUKE 5:29–32

Once Levi had made the decision to leave his profitable tax collection business to follow Jesus, he invited a large number of his friends and colleagues to come to a special dinner at his house so they could meet Jesus themselves. When Jesus went to this large gathering of hated and despised people it angered the religious leaders. They had no interest in spending time with sinners—oblivious to the fact that they were sinners too.

Even today there are many people who think, like the Pharisees did, that they are just fine in their current state. They have no realization that they are hopelessly lost apart from Jesus. They despise the message of the gospel because they do not recognize their sin-sick condition.

But salvation is only for the lost. Only those who are willing to recognize the reality that they are lost without Christ will be willing to receive His offer of salvation. And it is our responsibility to warn them.

There was considerable warning before Mount St. Helens erupted in Washington state in 1980. Officials warned residents to flee, but not all of them listened. An eighty-three-year-old man named Harry Randall Truman told an interviewer, "I don't believe the mountain will hurt me." He perished in the volcanic blast because he did not take his need for deliverance seriously. We must do our best to alert those around us of the danger facing their eternal souls before it is too late.

Today's Discipleship Principle: Take the time to find someone you can share the good news of salvation with today.

A Time to Fast and Pray

And they said unto him, Why do the disciples of John fast often, and make prayers, and likewise the disciples of the Pharisees; but thine eat and drink? And he said unto them, Can ye make the children of the bridechamber fast, while the bridegroom is with them? But the days will come, when the bridegroom shall be taken away from them, and then shall they fast in those days.—LUKE 5:33–35

The enemies of Jesus were constantly looking for accusations they could make against Him and His followers. Here they complained that Jesus' disciples did not fast regularly like they did and as the early followers of John the Baptist had done. This accusation was not made in good faith. The fasting of the Pharisees was not a heartfelt, serious attempt to seek God's face. Instead they had turned it into an outward show to impress others.

The kind of fasting to which God responds is the kind that is an expression of a sincere desire for His work in our lives that takes precedence over anything else. Dr. John Rice said, "Fasting is really putting God first when one prays, wanting God more than one wants food, more than one wants sleep, more than one wants fellowship with others, more than one wants to attend to business." Jesus told the Pharisees that in the future, once He was no longer with them, His disciples would indeed fast.

There are some situations that are so serious they require more than just regular prayers on our part. Jesus told His disciples this after he cast a demon out of a boy when they had not been able to do so. "And he said unto them, This kind can come forth by nothing, but by prayer and fasting" (Mark 9:29). We do not earn favor with God by fasting, but it does focus our hearts and minds on Him, and it does produce results in our lives.

Today's Discipleship Principle: When we are serious enough about our praying to fast, we can see God work in powerful ways in our lives.

Jesus and Nothing Else

*And he spake also a parable unto them; No man putteth a piece of a new garment upon an old; if otherwise, then both the new maketh a rent, and the piece that was taken out of the new agreeth not with the old. And no man putteth new wine into old bottles; else the new wine will burst the bottles, and be spilled, and the bottles shall perish. But new wine must be put into new bottles; and both are preserved—*LUKE 5:36–38

In the time of Christ, it was common for people to adopt bits and pieces of other religions into their own. The Romans often took the gods of conquered lands and adapted them to their own pantheon of deities they worshiped. We see the same trends in our day with the common teaching that all religious roads lead to the same destination. There is a popular bumper sticker featuring the symbols of a number of different religions to spell out the word "Coexist."

Jesus did not come to add a little bit to what had gone before. He certainly did not come to simply put a patch on the Old Testament sacrifice system (which was never meant to be a substitute for the ultimate sacrifice Christ Himself would provide). Instead He came with a radically transforming message of salvation—a salvation that did not depend on national identity, religious regulations, or a system of sacrifices and offerings. He came to provide the single, only hope of salvation through His own death, burial, and resurrection.

"Jesus saith unto him, I am the way, the truth, and the life: no man cometh unto the Father, but by me" (John 14:6). Anyone who wants to add to or take away from that message is teaching false doctrine. There are no other options for salvation. People who sincerely follow other doctrines are lost, despite the depth of their conviction. Jesus is and always will be the only hope of salvation.

Today's Discipleship Principle: Hold to the truth that Jesus is the only way to Heaven and share that same truth with others.

Don't Add to God's Commands

And it came to pass on the second sabbath after the first, that he went through the corn fields; and his disciples plucked the ears of corn, and did eat, rubbing them in their hands. And certain of the Pharisees said unto them, Why do ye that which is not lawful to do on the sabbath days?
—LUKE 6:1–2

The law that God gave to Moses for the observance of the Sabbath day instructed the Israelites very clearly that they were not to work, but to rest on that day: "But the seventh day is the sabbath of the LORD thy God: in it thou shalt not do any work, thou, nor thy son, nor thy daughter, thy manservant, nor thy maidservant, nor thy cattle, nor thy stranger that is within thy gates" (Exodus 20:10). Over the years, various rabbis and teachers added to the rules and regulations for keeping the Sabbath until by the time of Jesus there were at least thirty-nine different categories of activity that had been defined as work and forbidden—going far beyond what God had commanded.

When the Pharisees went to Jesus and condemned the disciples for gathering and eating food as they passed through a field on the Sabbath, they accused them of doing something that was unlawful. But in truth the disciples were not violating the law of Moses, only the regulations that had been added on top of the law.

There is a danger when we go beyond what God has said. While we must apply the principles of the Bible to situations that are not directly addressed, we should never say that God has forbidden something that He has not in fact forbidden. We are responsible to obey what God has said, and part of that obedience is not adding additional rules and systems beyond what He has given. That path leads to prideful bondage and failure to receive God's grace.

Today's Discipleship Principle: Take God's Word at face value, and do not attempt to add anything to it.

Don't Miss the Point

And Jesus answering them said, Have ye not read so much as this, what David did, when himself was an hungred, and they which were with him; How he went into the house of God, and did take and eat the shewbread, and gave also to them that were with him; which it is not lawful to eat but for the priests alone? And he said unto them, That the Son of man is Lord also of the sabbath. —LUKE 6:3–5

The Pharisees knew the law inside and out. They memorized much of the writings of Moses, and in addition, they were experts in the volumes of commentary and teaching on the law that had been written by various rabbis and scholars over the years. Yet for all their knowledge, they missed the point of what God had in mind with His commands. The keeping of the Sabbath is a great illustration of this. For the Pharisees, enforcing not just God's law but their additions to it had become the end rather than the means to something greater.

The Pharisees kept the Sabbath, but they lost the value the day was meant to have. In *The Life and Times of Jesus the Messiah,* Alfred Edersheim wrote, "The Sabbath law was not one merely of rest, but of rest for worship. The service of the Lord was the object of the Sabbath."

God is not interested in just our outward conformity to His Word. He is looking for the heart to be in joyful and willing compliance with the command so that we can reap the blessings of obedience. Jesus pointed out the error of the Pharisees when it came to the Sabbath day: "And he said unto them, The sabbath was made for man, and not man for the sabbath" (Mark 2:27).

The goal of God's laws is not that we are devoted to them, but that we are devoted to *Him* above all else. When we become obsessed with the command while losing sight of the God who gave it, we are missing the point.

Today's Discipleship Principle: Since all of God's commands are given for our good, we should joyfully obey whatever He says.

Exodus 23–24 // Matthew 20:1–16 53

A Tragic Lack of Love

And it came to pass also on another sabbath, that he entered into the synagogue and taught: and there was a man whose right hand was withered. And the scribes and Pharisees watched him, whether he would heal on the sabbath day; that they might find an accusation against him.—LUKE 6:6–7

Because sin came into the world and brought suffering and death with it, we live in a world filled with hurting people. The proper response to the pain that we see around us is love and compassion. This attitude filled the heart of Jesus, and it shaped the way He interacted with people. "But when he saw the multitudes, he was moved with compassion on them, because they fainted, and were scattered abroad, as sheep having no shepherd" (Matthew 9:36).

In contrast, when the Pharisees saw a man who suffered every day because his right hand had no strength, they felt no love or compassion for him. Instead, they simply viewed him as another tool they could use to launch an attack against Jesus. Rather than caring about this man's condition—which was serious and no doubt painful—they wanted to use the man's suffering to their own advantage against Christ. It almost seems as if they had staged the moment. They certainly used the moment to accuse Jesus.

Jesus, however, didn't see people through the lens of political value or liability to Himself. He simply loved people. While still following God's Old Testament commands concerning the Sabbath (not the added layers the Pharisees had given), Jesus cared for the needs of others.

While it is important that we do right, it is possible to comply with the principles and commands of Scripture while truly caring for the needs of others. Our hearts should be broken instead of cold and indifferent as the Pharisees were, and we should do whatever we can to help those in need.

Today's Discipleship Principle: Keep your heart soft and compassionate to the needs of those around you and you will respond as Jesus did.

february

Time to Do Good

Then said Jesus unto them, I will ask you one thing; Is it lawful on the sabbath days to do good, or to do evil? to save life, or to destroy it? And looking round about upon them all, he said unto the man, Stretch forth thy hand. And he did so: and his hand was restored whole as the other. And they were filled with madness; and communed one with another what they might do to Jesus.—LUKE 6:9–11

When Jesus healed a man with a crippled hand on the Sabbath day, He was confronted by Pharisees eager to accuse Him of breaking God's law. Jesus responded by asking them powerful questions: "Is it lawful on the sabbath days to do good, or to do evil? to save life, or to destroy it?"

The fact that it was the Sabbath did not change the moral imperative to do good. Remember that Jesus was not violating the Sabbath law given by God, but only the many layers of restrictions that teaching and tradition had added to what God actually said. Jesus never did anything that was contrary to God's law. And we should not forget that the ends do not justify the means. As Dr. Bob Jones, Sr. said, "It is never right to do wrong in order to get a chance to do right." But Jesus was not doing wrong. He was not violating the Sabbath commandment. He was instead using the day of rest as an opportunity to do something good.

We are always to be doing good. If you sense an impulse to speak a kind word of encouragement, to spend time in prayer, to reach out and let someone know you are thinking about them, or to meet a need, do it. You do not have to worry or wonder if it is God's will for you to do good. Paul reminds us, "For we are his workmanship, created in Christ Jesus unto good works, which God hath before ordained that we should walk in them" (Ephesians 2:10).

Today's Discipleship Principle: There is never a time when it is wrong to do something truly good for the sake of someone else.

Looking for Leaders

*And it came to pass in those days, that he went out into a mountain to pray, and continued all night in prayer to God. And when it was day, he called unto him his disciples: and of them he chose twelve, whom also he named apostles;—*LUKE 6:12–13

It is impossible to overstate the importance of prayer to Jesus. And by extension, His example should be a constant reminder to us of the need for us to spend time seeking God's face and crying out to Him for help. The entire night before He selected the twelve apostles, Jesus prayed alone. He recognized the choice of this "inner circle"—the men into whom He would pour His life over the next three years—would be critical.

Our world today is in urgent need of godly leadership. We see this in our homes, our churches, and our nations. Dr. Lee Roberson said, "Everything rises and falls on leadership," and he was right. The truth is that far too many Christians have abdicated their leadership responsibilities. It is not just pastors and people who are in full time vocational ministry that are leaders. Every one of us is a leader in some part of our lives. There are always people watching us and drawing conclusions (whether good or bad) from the way that we respond to life.

A vital part of leadership is ensuring that the things you teach and believe are communicated to the next generation. That is why Jesus spent a whole night alone in prayer before selecting the twelve men who would continue His work after He returned to Heaven. Paul instructed Timothy: "And the things that thou hast heard of me among many witnesses, the same commit thou to faithful men, who shall be able to teach others also" (2 Timothy 2:2).

Today's Discipleship Principle: In addition to being a godly leader and example in whatever role you play, look to train leaders for the future.

A Traitor to the Lord

Simon, (whom he also named Peter,) and Andrew his brother, James and John, Philip and Bartholomew, Matthew and Thomas, James the son of Alphaeus, and Simon called Zelotes, And Judas the brother of James, and Judas Iscariot, which also was the traitor.—LUKE 6:14–16

He was undoubtedly the most gifted military strategist of all of America's generals during the Revolutionary War. He was loved by his soldiers, and courageously led them into battle rather than remaining behind as many officers did. He rallied the American troops to victory in the crucial Battle of Saratoga even though he had been ordered to remain in his quarters. This man they called the "Black Eagle" was so feared by the Indian allies of the British that just the rumor he was coming was enough to lift the Iroquois' siege of Fort Ticonderoga. Yet we do not remember him for any of his heroic actions. We know him as Benedict Arnold—the man who betrayed his country.

Though we look down on traitors like Judas or Benedict Arnold, the sad reality is that too often we also join forces with the enemy. We tend to take sin casually, not realizing what it truly says about our loyalty and allegiance.

Paul wrote, "Know ye not, that to whom ye yield yourselves servants to obey, his servants ye are to whom ye obey; whether of sin unto death, or of obedience unto righteousness?" (Romans 6:16). We must never forget that even though our eternal salvation is settled forever, as long as we live here on Earth we are part of a spiritual battle. Satan will tempt to allure us to abandon our allegiance to the Lord, and though he no longer controls our lives, when we sin, we are doing his bidding.

One of the best ways we can express our loyalty to Christ is by refusing to side with the enemy when he tempts us to sin against our God.

Today's Discipleship Principle: Every sin a Christian commits is an act of treason against the Lord who gave His life for our salvation.

The Cost of Ministry

And he came down with them, and stood in the plain, and the company of his disciples, and a great multitude of people out of all Judaea and Jerusalem, and from the sea coast of Tyre and Sidon, which came to hear him, and to be healed of their diseases; And they that were vexed with unclean spirits: and they were healed. And the whole multitude sought to touch him: for there went virtue out of him, and healed them all.
—LUKE 6:17–19

It's hard for us to imagine with the conveniences of modern communication and transportation what it was like in Jesus' day. The news that a rabbi in Galilee was performing miracles and healing people no doubt took some time to spread. But because the news was so spectacular, when it did spread, it drew crowds—not just from across Israel but surrounding countries as well. Before long, there were massive crowds coming to hear Jesus and wanting to be healed of various diseases. We are not told how many people were in the "multitude" Luke describes, but Jesus healed every one of them.

Yet, the work that Jesus did took a physical toll on Him. Each person He healed in His ministry exacted a price. And over time, the costs of ministry started to add up. At one point Jesus took His disciples away from the people just to try to find time to rest and eat. "And he said unto them, Come ye yourselves apart into a desert place, and rest a while: for there were many coming and going, and they had no leisure so much as to eat" (Mark 6:31).

Any time we set out to do something of value for God's kingdom, we need to be aware of the impact it will have. Of course, when we count the cost, we should remember that our God is worth our all. But it is also wise to do what we can to plan some times for renewal—and, even when that is not available, to consciously depend on the strength God gives.

Today's Discipleship Principle: Effectively doing the work of the Lord carries a cost, but it is compensated in the strength God provides.

The Present Versus Eternity

And he lifted up his eyes on his disciples, and said, Blessed be ye poor: for yours is the kingdom of God. Blessed are ye that hunger now: for ye shall be filled. Blessed are ye that weep now: for ye shall laugh.—LUKE 6:20–21

Given our choice, none of us would select poverty, hunger, and weeping for our condition. We prefer to have enough money, food, and joy rather than sorrow—and there is nothing wrong with that. Yet at the same time we need to recognize that there is something far more important than temporal comfort and pleasure. In fact, there are many cases where it is the very things that we lack that bring us lasting and eternal blessings. The missionary martyr Jim Elliot said, "He is no fool who gives what he cannot keep to gain what he cannot lose."

God wants us to ask Him for things we want as well as our bare necessities; but we must remember to keep our focus on Him and what matters for eternity, rather than on things that only matter for a little while. When we do that, the problems of greed and covetousness will be eliminated, and we will be blessed as a result. The Christian whose affections are set on the eternal will avoid much temptation.

Paul wrote, "Not that I speak in respect of want: for I have learned, in whatsoever state I am, therewith to be content. I know both how to be abased, and I know how to abound: every where and in all things I am instructed both to be full and to be hungry, both to abound and to suffer need" (Philippians 4:11–12). All of us should strive for the spirit of contentment that acknowledges God's goodness and love in providing what He knows we need. Whatever difficulties we face now, we have the promise of God that He will both sustain us in this life and reward us in eternity. "For I reckon that the sufferings of this present time are not worthy to be compared with the glory which shall be revealed in us." (Romans 8:18).

Today's Discipleship Principle: If our focus is on the eternal, hardship, and lack in the present will not cause us to lose faith in God.

The Blessing of Suffering

Blessed are ye, when men shall hate you, and when they shall separate you from their company, and shall reproach you, and cast out your name as evil, for the Son of man's sake. Rejoice ye in that day, and leap for joy: for, behold, your reward is great in heaven: for in the like manner did their fathers unto the prophets.—LUKE 6:22–23

Charles Spurgeon had a powerful and effective ministry that began while he was still a teenager. There is no question that his incredible gifts and the enormous growth of the church that he pastored were testimony to the work that God did in and through his life.

Yet for most of his ministry, Spurgeon suffered greatly from gout and Bright's disease, and he died at just fifty-seven years of age. The enormous physical pain he endured could have driven him to question and doubt God, but instead it led Spurgeon to trust Him more. He said, "I am certain that I never did grow in grace one-half so much anywhere as I have upon the bed of pain."

Hardship, affliction, and suffering are not pleasant, but they are often the necessary tools God uses to shape us into the men and women He needs us to be for His work. Each trial offers us an opportunity to learn more of God's grace and depend more fully on Him for our needs to be met.

God promises to give us victory as we live the Christian life, but He does not promise to give us a life of ease that is free of suffering. In addition to realizing that our hardships can be used by God, we must also remember that they are not permanent. Psalm 30:5 says, "…weeping may endure for a night, but joy cometh in the morning." There is a day of joy and victory coming for every believer who is faithful even during times of testing and tears.

Today's Discipleship Principle: When times of suffering come, do not allow yourself to question God's love and care for you.

The Danger of Success

But woe unto you that are rich! for ye have received your consolation. Woe unto you that are full! for ye shall hunger. Woe unto you that laugh now! for ye shall mourn and weep. Woe unto you, when all men shall speak well of you! for so did their fathers to the false prophets.
—LUKE 6:24–26

Some of the most dangerous times any of us face in our Christian walk are the moments of victory and success. When it seems like everything is going our way, we are tempted to become proud and assume it is our doing than remembering that all that we do is accomplished only through God's grace and strength freely bestowed on us. This foolish pride in our success leads to a great fall. Proverbs 1:32 warns: "For the turning away of the simple shall slay them, and the prosperity of fools shall destroy them."

Rather than making us proud, success should make us humble and grateful. Andrew Murray wrote, "The humble man has learned the secret of abiding gladness. The weaker he feels, the lower he sinks, and the greater his humiliations appear, the more power and the presence of Christ are his portion." There is no real and lasting success possible apart from God's help, and there is no faster way for us to lose His blessing than to attempt to take the credit and glory for ourselves.

When Saul was anointed king over Israel, he was humble; but his position lifted up his view of himself, and he stopped caring about obedience to God. "And Samuel said, When thou wast little in thine own sight, wast thou not made the head of the tribes of Israel, and the LORD anointed thee king over Israel?" (1 Samuel 15:17). As a result of Saul's pride, the throne was taken from him and given to David.

When we experience God's blessings in our lives, we should be especially on guard against pride and especially faithful to give thanks to God.

Today's Discipleship Principle: When God blesses you with success in your life, humbly give thanks to Him rather than taking the credit.

Love Your Enemies

But I say unto you which hear, Love your enemies, do good to them which hate you, Bless them that curse you, and pray for them which despitefully use you. And unto him that smiteth thee on the one cheek offer also the other; and him that taketh away thy cloke forbid not to take thy coat also.—LUKE 6:27–29

During the Revolutionary War, a Baptist preacher from Pennsylvania who was a friend of George Washington made a seventy-mile trip on foot to Philadelphia. He came to plead for the life of Michael Wittman who had been sentenced to die for treason. Miller's initial request was refused. Washington said, "I cannot grant the life of your friend." Miller then told Washington that Wittman was not his friend, but rather a man who had opposed and obstructed his ministry at every opportunity. Washington said, "You walked seventy miles to save the life of an enemy? I will grant the pardon." Miller took Wittman home, no longer an enemy, but a friend.

As we live in a society that is becoming increasingly hostile to Christianity, we are going to have more opportunities to love our enemies. Loving them certainly does not mean that we stop proclaiming and defending the truth. A doctor performing surgery to remove a malignant tumor does not hate his patient, even though he is literally cutting him open with a knife.

We must be filled with the same love that Jesus showed to those who put Him on the cross. Jesus was not overpowered or caught off guard by the cross. He willingly gave Himself as a sacrifice for our sins. He said of His life, "No man taketh it from me, but I lay it down of myself. I have power to lay it down, and I have power to take it again. This commandment have I received of my Father" (John 10:18).

Today's Discipleship Principle: Demonstrating genuine love for those who oppose and attack us is the most Christlike thing we can do.

The Golden Rule

Give to every man that asketh of thee; and of him that taketh away thy goods ask them not again. And as ye would that men should do to you, do ye also to them likewise.—LUKE 6:30–31

Charles Spurgeon was the most famous preacher in the world during his lifetime. But there were many other well-known preachers with large churches in London. One of them was pastored by a man named Joseph Parker. At one point, Spurgeon ran a large orphanage to take care of children who had no parents, and Parker made a remark about the awful lives those children faced. The remark was reported publicly as a criticism of the conditions inside Spurgeon's orphanages.

A furious Spurgeon went to the pulpit and harshly criticized Parker. The sermon was, as were all of Spurgeon's sermons, printed in the papers, and London eagerly awaited the following Sunday to see how Parker would respond. Rather than refuting what Spurgeon had said, Parker simply announced to the packed auditorium that they were going to take up a special offering for Spurgeon's orphanages. The offering was so generous that the ushers had to empty the offering plates three times

Later that week Spurgeon arrived at Parker's office and said, "Parker, you have practiced grace on me. You have given me not what I deserved, you have given me what I needed."

Every day as we interact with others, we face the choice of how we will treat them. Will we respond in kind to attacks, criticism, and harsh words? Will we respond in kind, trying to get even and prove we cannot be taken advantage of? Or will we defer our anger, even if it is justified, and allow God to settle any scores that need to be made right? Paul wrote, "Dearly beloved, avenge not yourselves, but rather give place unto wrath: for it is written, Vengeance is mine; I will repay, saith the Lord" (Romans 12:19).

Today's Discipleship Principle: When we treat people the way we want to be treated, we are fulfilling the command to love our neighbors.

The Right Kind of Giving

For if ye love them which love you, what thank have ye? for sinners also love those that love them. And if ye do good to them which do good to you, what thank have ye? for sinners also do even the same. And if ye lend to them of whom ye hope to receive, what thank have ye? for sinners also lend to sinners, to receive as much again.—LUKE 6:32–34

Charles Gordon went to China as a volunteer to help lead the fight against the Taiping Rebellion and protect Western citizens from the rampages of the revolt. His great success in the field in charge of what came to be known as the "Ever Victorious Army" helped put down the rebellion and restore peace to the troubled land. Unlike many military leaders of his day, Gordon did not come from a wealthy family and had little in the way of resources. The grateful Chinese government commissioned a special gold medal for Gordon in honor of his service.

When Gordon returned to England, he found news of a great famine, and he wanted to do something to help. His medal from the Chinese government was the only thing of real value that he possessed. Gordon took the medal and hammered out the inscription carved into it so that it could no longer be identified. He then sent it anonymously to the treasurer of the fund raising effort along with this note: "This is the secret of bliss—to give away your medal!"

When we give without any expectation of return, that is when we are most blessed. Though God does reward us for our giving, that can never be the primary motivation. Instead, a proper appreciation for the grace God has given to us so freely should lead us to give with the same spirit of generosity—and with no strings attached. When we invest the resources God has entrusted to us in His work to help others, we are giving the way that God commands.

Today's Discipleship Principle: If we are giving only to get a return, we aren't really giving but rather trading.

Loving Others Like God Loves Us

But love ye your enemies, and do good, and lend, hoping for nothing again; and your reward shall be great, and ye shall be the children of the Highest: for he is kind unto the unthankful and to the evil. Be ye therefore merciful, as your Father also is merciful.—LUKE 6:35–36

When the Berlin Wall was erected in 1961, it divided the capital city of Germany in a way that reflected the division that had been forced on the conquered nation following World War II. West Germany remained part of the free world while East Germany was under the domination of the Soviet Union. Once the wall was in place, people could no longer escape the communist government simply by reaching Berlin. There was a great division that remained until the wall was brought down in 1989.

It is said that at one point during a particularly tense moment in East-West relations, in the 1970s, that a group from East Berlin decided to begin throwing bags of garbage over the wall in a symbolic protest against the West. After seeing the bags of garbage, some residents of the western part of the city decided on an appropriate response. They filled bags with food and medical supplies that were in short supply in the communist part of the city and flung them over the wall with a note that read, "Each gives what he has."

If we only extend love to a select few, we are not obeying the command of God, and we are not showing His love to a world that so desperately needs to see it. If we are to live as children of the King, then we must love as He loves. James wrote, "If ye fulfil the royal law according to the scripture, Thou shalt love thy neighbour as thyself, ye do well:" (James 2:8).

Today's Discipleship Principle: When we love those who do not love us and treat them with grace, we are reflecting the love of our Heavenly Father.

Measure for Measure

Judge not, and ye shall not be judged: condemn not, and ye shall not be condemned: forgive, and ye shall be forgiven: Give, and it shall be given unto you; good measure, pressed down, and shaken together, and running over, shall men give into your bosom. For with the same measure that ye mete withal it shall be measured to you again.—LUKE 6:37–38

The Scottish preacher Alexander Whyte recounted the story of a visit he paid to a prominent lawyer in Glasgow. He said that when he entered the office, the lawyer asked, "Do you have a message for an old sinner?" Whyte responded by telling the man the text for his sermon the next Sunday. "Who is a God like unto thee, that pardoneth iniquity, and passeth by the transgression of the remnant of his heritage? he retaineth not his anger for ever, because he delighteth in mercy" (Micah 7:18).

God would have every right to delight in justice. Sin is an awful, despicable, hateful thing in His eyes, and it is fully fitting for it to be punished. Yet, instead, God's love and grace are so wonderful that He *delights* in extending mercy to us. And He calls for us to do the same in our dealings with others.

God has established a principle of sowing and reaping in the world, and it extends to our relationships with others. If we are harsh and critical and judgmental, we cannot expect to receive mercy when we need it—and we certainly are going to need it at some point in our lives.

Just as God enjoys the opportunity to extend mercy to us, we should enjoy extending mercy to others so a forgiving and gracious spirit characterizes our lives. We should be merciful because it is the right thing to do, but if we need an additional incentive, there is the truth that we will receive from others what we give to them.

Today's Discipleship Principle: Realizing that we will reap what we sow should encourage us to be merciful in the way we treat others.

Motes, Beams, and Self-Reflection

And why beholdest thou the mote that is in thy brother's eye, but perceivest not the beam that is in thine own eye? Either how canst thou say to thy brother, Brother, let me pull out the mote that is in thine eye, when thou thyself beholdest not the beam that is in thine own eye? Thou hypocrite, cast out first the beam out of thine own eye, and then shalt thou see clearly to pull out the mote that is in thy brother's eye.—LUKE 6:41–42

The story is told of an old New England preacher who found that the clock in the back of his church would not keep the correct time. Even worse, it was not consistent. Sometimes it ran too fast and other times it was too slow. After his attempts to reset the clock failed, the preacher hung a sign over the clock that read: "Don't blame my hands—the problem is deeper than that."

Human nature is such that it is far easier and more comfortable for us to focus on the sins and shortcomings of others rather than our own. And, in truth, our tendency is to exaggerate the faults of others while minimizing our own. Yet that does not reveal that our spiritual condition is better, but rather that we are hypocrites who are willing to condemn others for things that are even smaller than those we allow in our own lives.

A harsh and judgmental spirit is an indication of a heart problem. The pride that makes us feel better when we assess others to be worse than ourselves will not survive a careful look into the Word of God. "But whoso looketh into the perfect law of liberty, and continueth therein, he being not a forgetful hearer, but a doer of the work, this man shall be blessed in his deed" (James 1:25).

Today's Discipleship Principle: Before pointing out the failings of others, look at your own heart carefully in the mirror of God's Word.

What's in the Heart

For a good tree bringeth not forth corrupt fruit; neither doth a corrupt tree bring forth good fruit. For every tree is known by his own fruit. For of thorns men do not gather figs, nor of a bramble bush gather they grapes. A good man out of the good treasure of his heart bringeth forth that which is good; and an evil man out of the evil treasure of his heart bringeth forth that which is evil: for of the abundance of the heart his mouth speaketh.
—LUKE 6:43–45

Among the many wild plants that beautify the Texas landscape is the agave. One of the largest varieties is the *agave americanus,* more commonly called the century plant. So named because it only blooms once—and while it doesn't actually take a hundred years, it usually takes twenty-five to thirty years.

When the plant reaches its full height and has completely developed, it sends a massive stalk high into the air, often reaching forty feet, before bursting out an array of yellow flowers. The key to the flowering of the century plant is what is out of sight, underground in the roots.

The same thing is true in our lives. What is in our hearts will eventually show up on the outside. We may be able to conceal it for a time, but eventually our thoughts, attitudes, desires, and priorities will bear fruit in our lives.

The key to bearing good fruit is not found in the fruit, but in the heart. Long before anything shows on the outside, the nature of the fruit is set by what is on the inside. That is why Solomon wrote, "Keep thy heart with all diligence; for out of it are the issues of life" (Proverbs 4:23). The visible fruit of our lives, whether good or bad, is determined by the inward life that others cannot see.

Today's Discipleship Principle: Make sure that your heart is in shape to produce good fruit when what is on the inside comes out.

Following Jesus

And why call ye me, Lord, Lord, and do not the things which I say?
—LUKE 6:46

If every person who talks about following Jesus and claims to be following Jesus were actually doing so, our world would be a very different place. Instead, a vast number of people pick and choose from a few isolated things that Jesus said or take their own interpretation of what Jesus said and do that. God's pattern is different. He commands obedience in all things. In His last conversation with the disciples before His crucifixion, Jesus said, "Ye are my friends, if ye do whatsoever I command you" (John 15:14).

It is said that on one occasion, a French army officer asked George Washington's mother what she had done to rear her son into such a fine man. Mrs. Washington replied, "I taught him to obey." There are many different aspects and duties of the Christian life, but they ultimately boil down to obedience. Only when we do what God says can we legitimately claim to be following Him. All of our declarations of love and submission can never substitute for the actual obedience Christ commands.

In Roman times, a ruler had absolute authority over his subjects and their lives. At a whim he could order people to be moved from one place to another. He even had the power of life and death, by executing anyone who displeased him. While God is not a capricious tyrant, He does have supreme authority. It is a contradiction to claim that He is Lord while at the same time disobeying what He says for us to do. If He is Lord (and He is) then He must be obeyed.

We do not get to decide how we should live and what we should do because our lives do not belong to us. It is hypocritical to call Jesus our Lord while stubbornly refusing to obey what He tells us to do.

Today's Discipleship Principle: There is nothing that can take the place of our submissive obedience to the Lord's commands.

Building on the Rock

*Whosoever cometh to me, and heareth my sayings, and doeth them, I will shew you to whom he is like: He is like a man which built an house, and digged deep, and laid the foundation on a rock: and when the flood arose, the stream beat vehemently upon that house, and could not shake it: for it was founded upon a rock. But he that heareth, and doeth not, is like a man that without a foundation built an house upon the earth; against which the stream did beat vehemently, and immediately it fell; and the ruin of that house was great.—*Luke 6:47–49

Because of the frequent earthquakes we have here in California, the design and material of a foundation is critically important. Each time we have built a new building for our church or the college, we have had architects and engineers do careful planning to ensure that the foundation is laid in such a way as to withstand the shaking of the ground that comes with an earthquake. It would be faster and cheaper to just start building on the surface rather than dig into the ground, pour concrete, and reinforce it with steel. But taking the shortcut is a recipe for disaster.

The same is true in our lives. It requires effort, sacrifice, and commitment to obey the commands of Christ. It means giving up the temporary pleasures sin offers and rejecting short-term expediency for the sake of eternal reward. It means that we value the things of God over the things of the world. It means that we stand for and do what is right even if no one else is willing to do so.

This kind of commitment is the foundation for a life that withstands the storms. The storms come to everyone—the difference in response and outcome is found in the foundation. When our lives are built on the very words of God, we can rest assured that the storms will not destroy our foundation.

Today's Discipleship Principle: The only way to succeed as a Christian is to base your life on the foundation of obedience to Jesus Christ.

Where to Turn for Help

Now when he had ended all his sayings in the audience of the people, he entered into Capernaum. And a certain centurion's servant, who was dear unto him, was sick, and ready to die. And when he heard of Jesus, he sent unto him the elders of the Jews, beseeching him that he would come and heal his servant.—LUKE 7:1–3

When President James Garfield was a teenager, he had little interest in the things of God. He was working on a towboat on a canal near his home, when a freak accident threw him off the boat and pulled him underwater. He caught hold of a rope that had caught on the lock of the canal, and dragged himself out of the water. In later telling the story, Garfield said, "I was convinced that God had saved my life; therefore, my life was worth saving. I resolved to go home, get an education, and be something else than a hand on a towboat."

When Garfield reached his home, he found his mother by the fireplace with her Bible on her knees. She was praying over and over, "O turn unto me, and have mercy unto me; give thy strength unto thy servant, and save the son of thine handmaid" (Psalm 86:16).

Life is more than we can manage in our own power and strength. God does not intend for us to live without His help. He is our source to face the trials and burdens of life. "I will lift up mine eyes unto the hills, from whence cometh my help. My help cometh from the LORD, which made heaven and earth" (Psalm 121:1–2).

It is wonderful when friends stand with us and encourage and support us in times of trouble, but that doesn't always happen as it should. Yet even if we have no one else, God will never abandon us, and we need no one else.

Today's Discipleship Principle: Too often we make God our last resort rather than turning to Him first for the help that we need.

How to Build a Testimony

And when they came to Jesus, they besought him instantly, saying, That he was worthy for whom he should do this: For he loveth our nation, and he hath built us a synagogue.—LUKE 7:4–5

An overwhelming majority of the Jews in Jesus' day hated the Romans. They had enjoyed a brief respite of freedom following the revolt led by the Maccabees only to be conquered a few years later by the mighty Roman Empire. There were constant conflicts between the Jewish people and the occupying forces. While the Romans allowed certain freedoms to the lands that they captured, they made it clear who was in charge and enforced the edicts of the empire at the point of the sword. Thousands of Roman soldiers were stationed in Israel as a daily reminder of Roman power.

Yet even among the despised occupying force, there were some men who distinguished themselves by their compassion for the Jewish people. One of them was a high-ranking officer, a centurion who had one hundred soldiers under his command. Rather than treating the Jewish people harshly as some of his peers no doubt did, he went so far as to construct a synagogue for Jewish worship. And when he found himself in need of Jesus' help, the Jewish people urged Jesus to work on his behalf. That is a powerful testimony and a challenge to all of us.

The primary image that the world sees of Jesus is that which is reflected in our lives. In large measure they form their opinion of God based on their opinion of us. And sadly there are too many times when our lives do not demonstrate God's love and holiness to the watching world. Mahatma Gandhi of India is quoted as saying, "I like your Christ. I do not like your Christians." May it never be said that we have done something to make people turn away from God.

Today's Discipleship Principle: Each day we either build or tear down the testimony that we have in the eyes of those around us.

The Power of One Word from God

Then Jesus went with them. And when he was now not far from the house, the centurion sent friends to him, saying unto him, Lord, trouble not thyself: for I am not worthy that thou shouldest enter under my roof: Wherefore neither thought I myself worthy to come unto thee: but say in a word, and my servant shall be healed.—LUKE 7:6-7

The great English missionary statesman Andrew Fuller was well known for preaching on faith. In one of his sermons he described a trip he made in response to an invitation to preach. He was traveling on horseback following a time of heavy rains. He came to a river that was flooded, and was uncertain whether he could cross without being swept away. A farmer who lived nearby saw him hesitating and said, "Go on sir, you are quite safe." Fuller rode out into the water, and though it rose nearly to his saddle, there was solid footing, and he made it safely across. He believed what the farmer told him and acted on it—and that is exactly what faith is.

When we say we believe God but do not do what He says to do, we are demonstrating not just disobedience, but a lack of faith. Why do Christians not give generously, witness faithfully, work diligently, and love deeply? In large measure, it is because we do not truly believe that what God says about the rewards for faith-filled obedience. We do not trust the Word of God as we should.

The commands of God come with all the power we need to obey them. God never tells us to do something without equipping us to do so. A single word from Jesus, "Come" was enough to allow Peter to walk on the water until he took his eyes off the Lord. Our lives should be focused on living in obedience to what God has said.

Today's Discipleship Principle: Faith is not to be something we just talk about—it is to be something we do.

What Does Jesus Think of Your Faith?

For I also am a man set under authority, having under me soldiers, and I say unto one, Go, and he goeth; and to another, Come, and he cometh; and to my servant, Do this, and he doeth it. When Jesus heard these things, he marvelled at him, and turned him about, and said unto the people that followed him, I say unto you, I have not found so great faith, no, not in Israel.—LUKE 7:8–9

When Dr. Curtis Hutson was pastor of the Forrest Hills Baptist Church in Georgia, the church held a campaign to promote attendance. The teacher of the third grade boys Sunday school class challenged his students, and told the class which normally averaged about ten boys that they should try to have twenty-five come for a big day. When that Sunday came, the classroom overflowed with pupils—there were too many to fit. Instead of twenty-five, there were more than fifty third-grade boys.

As Dr. Hutson told the story, the teachers were scrambling trying to find places for the unexpected crowd. Just then one of the regular attenders began to cry. When the teacher asked him what was wrong, he replied, "This is all my fault." "What's your fault?" the teacher asked. "I prayed for fifty instead of twenty-five," the boy said through his tears.

So many times we do not have the things we want or need simply because we lack the faith to ask God for them. While God is not a genie who makes our wishes come true, He has promised on His good name to hear our prayers and answer when we cry out for help. Jesus was amazed at the faith of a Roman centurion who believed that one word from Him would heal his servant because most of the Jewish people who had received God's promises did not live as though they believed them.

Today's Discipleship Principle: We should live with a real and genuine faith that believes and expects God to do the impossible.

Comfort for the Pain of Death

Now when he came nigh to the gate of the city, behold, there was a dead man carried out, the only son of his mother, and she was a widow: and much people of the city was with her. And when the Lord saw her, he had compassion on her, and said unto her, Weep not. And he came and touched the bier: and they that bare him stood still. And he said, Young man, I say unto thee, Arise. And he that was dead sat up, and began to speak. And he delivered him to his mother.—Luke 7:12–15

A man was praying with his pastor one morning after church. He had been dealing with temptation in his life and had been seeking counseling and accountability with the leaders of his church. On that morning, he prayed a prayer the pastor had heard many times before, asking God to remove temptation, "Lord, take the cobwebs out of my life." Just as he said this the pastor interrupted, "Kill the spider, Lord."

It's easy to fall into the cycle of clearing the cobwebs of life. Falling into sin's trap, giving up control to the devil, repenting, then beginning the cycle again. As Christians, God has given us power to break the cycle by killing the spider—self.

The devil is bent on bringing in temptation and sin to Christian's lives to wear down their strength and joy. When you become so bogged down with repeatedly falling into sin then repenting, you cannot experience the full blessings of a life lived in God's freedom.

God desires that you would purposefully die to self every day. Realize that your flesh doesn't control you and give complete control to God. As Ephesians 2 says, you are created in Christ for the purpose of fulfilling His will and living a life of holiness. God has a life of spiritual freedom and blessing planned for you. But first He desires that you die to self, to the old fleshly desires and wants, and live for God's desires.

Today's Discipleship Principle: When you die to self, you can truly be alive to God's richest blessings.

Numbers 1–2 // Mark 3:1–19

God with His People

And there came a fear on all: and they glorified God, saying, That a great prophet is risen up among us; and, That God hath visited his people. And this rumour of him went forth throughout all Judaea, and throughout all the region round about. —LUKE 7:16–17

John Edwin Watts-Ditchfield, who pastored for many years in England, told the story of a visit he paid to an elderly relative when he was a small boy. On the wall of her house was a framed work of embroidery that read: "Thou God seest me."

Watts-Ditchfield recalled that she told him, "When you are older, people will tell you that God is always watching you to see when you do wrong, in order to punish you. I do not want you to think of it in that way, but I want you to take the text home, and to remember all your life that God loves you so much He cannot take His eyes off you."

Though God had worked in mighty ways throughout the history of Israel, in the time of Christ the people had not seen or heard much of God for centuries. He had been silent until the arrival of John the Baptist. Once Jesus began His ministry and people were hearing about the miracles He was performing, there was a real sense of excitement. News quickly spread that God was present and at work, and people flocked to find out what was going on.

While in a human body, Jesus could only physically be in one place at a time. Now every believer has the Holy Spirit living within them, and God's presence is a continual reality in our lives. Yet, many Christians do not live in a way that reflects His presence. Rather than rejoicing in His love and nearness, we try to go it alone. Instead we should fully rely on Him, joyfully remembering that He is with us.

Today's Discipleship Principle: The measure of God's love for us is seen in His daily presence in our lives through the Holy Spirit.

Faith When Answers Are Delayed

And the disciples of John shewed him of all these things. And John calling unto him two of his disciples sent them to Jesus, saying, Art thou he that should come? or look we for another? When the men were come unto him, they said, John Baptist hath sent us unto thee, saying, Art thou he that should come? or look we for another?—LUKE 7:18–20

While God sometimes answers our prayers immediately, there are other times when we must keep our faith strong enough to keep praying until the answer comes. Evangelist D.L. Moody told the story of one of the most notorious infidels in Scotland who came to one of his meetings. Moody asked if he could pray for the man, and the infidel just laughed, saying that prayer did not work because God was not real. He heard Moody preach a few times, but did not respond to the gospel.

A few weeks later he came to hear Moody again. After the meeting, Moody asked him if anything had changed. The man laughed and said, "I told you your praying is false. God hasn't answered." Moody said later, "I relied on faith." The team kept praying, and a few more weeks passed. The infidel went to a service in his hometown and told the man preaching, "I am troubled. I don't have any peace and I want you to pray for me." God had worked through the prayers of Moody and his group, and the man put his trust in Jesus Christ.

Even the strongest faith may waver from time to time during difficult days, but we must not give up on God. He has never yet failed to keep His promises. Our faith is not based on what we see around us but on what He has declared He will do. We do not need anything for confirmation of His reliability beyond what we find in the Scriptures.

Today's Discipleship Principle: Do not ever let the circumstances you face make you doubt that God will keep His promises.

Offended by Jesus

And in that same hour he cured many of their infirmities and plagues, and of evil spirits; and unto many that were blind he gave sight. Then Jesus answering said unto them, Go your way, and tell John what things ye have seen and heard; how that the blind see, the lame walk, the lepers are cleansed, the deaf hear, the dead are raised, to the poor the gospel is preached. And blessed is he, whosoever shall not be offended in me.
—LUKE 7:21–23

Dr. J. Vernon McGee told the story of going out to eat with a group of pastors. He said, "As we entered one of the drive-in places in that area, a carhop approached us. She was wearing about her neck the largest cross that I have ever seen. The cross was jet black against her white uniform. I asked her why she was wearing such a large cross. Her reply was, 'Don't you think it's pretty?' I countered, 'Do you know what that cross means?' She said, 'No, I do not.' Then I asked her, 'Did you know that 1900 years ago Jesus Christ died on a cross for you and for me?' 'Huh?' she asked. Then I gave her the story of salvation. Her only answer was, 'Well, I saw it downtown and liked it, so I bought it for an ornament.' She said that it meant nothing more to her."

That the world downplays the message of the gospel and the cross is sad but not surprising. The great tragedy in our day is that some who profess to be Christians are downplaying the message we are commanded to proclaim to the world in order to be more acceptable to society. God calls us to something different: "Wherefore Jesus also, that he might sanctify the people with his own blood, suffered without the gate. Let us go forth therefore unto him without the camp, bearing his reproach" (Hebrews 13:12–13).

To one who loves Christ, the cross is not to be taken lightly. It is to be treasured and proclaimed to others.

Today's Discipleship Principle: Let us never be ashamed to publicly declare the message of salvation in Jesus Christ alone.

Boldly Serving God

And when the messengers of John were departed, he began to speak unto the people concerning John, What went ye out into the wilderness for to see? A reed shaken with the wind? But what went ye out for to see? A man clothed in soft raiment? Behold, they which are gorgeously apparelled, and live delicately, are in kings' courts. But what went ye out for to see? A prophet? Yea, I say unto you, and much more than a prophet.
—LUKE 7:24–26

John Wesley and his brother Charles were part of the Great Awakening that shook both England and America in a mighty move of God. In part because of their effectiveness, they faced a great deal of opposition to their preaching. Hecklers disrupted their sermons, and on at least one occasion a bull was released into the field to break up an open air meeting. Yet they continued on undaunted, despite the obstacles they faced. John Wesley wrote, "Give me one hundred men who fear nothing but sin and desire nothing but God, and I care not whether they be clergymen or laymen, they alone will shake the gates of Hell and set up the kingdom of Heaven upon the earth."

One of the greatest needs of our day is men and women who are not afraid to take a clear, firm, unapologetic, and open stand for Jesus Christ. The praise and approval of men is only fleeting at best, but the eternal reward of hearing, "Well done," from the Lord is worth whatever the cost in this world may be.

The courage of Christians has been little tested in recent decades in America, but the time is coming when we will be forced to choose between paying the price to take a bold stand for God or avoiding trouble by watering down our message. Only those who stand firm will receive the reward of faithful servants.

Today's Discipleship Principle: It may not be popular to take a stand for the Lord, but it is always the right thing to do.

Being Great in God's Eyes

This is he, of whom it is written, Behold, I send my messenger before thy face, which shall prepare thy way before thee. For I say unto you, Among those that are born of women there is not a greater prophet than John the Baptist: but he that is least in the kingdom of God is greater than he.—LUKE 7:27–28

The Scottish pastor Ian MacLaren recounted visiting an elderly lady in his church, and finding her weeping. When he asked her what was wrong, she told him that she felt she had not done enough for God with her life. She said, "I have washed dishes, cooked three meals a day, taken care of the children, mopped the floor, and mended the clothes. That is all I have done all my life, and I wanted to do something for Jesus."

MacLaren then asked her to tell him about her sons. Her three oldest boys were all on the mission field, two in China and one in Africa. The youngest was preparing to leave and join one of his brothers in the work. She had reared her sons to desire to serve God more than anything else. MacLaren told her, "And you say your life has been wasted in mopping floors, darning socks, washing dishes, and doing the trivial tasks. I'd like to have your mansion when we are called Home! It will be very near the throne!"

The world is focused on major events, large companies, vast sums of money, and notable accomplishments. God is focused on faithfulness. The standard by which He measures our lives is what we have done in relation to what we have been given and the attitude with which we do it. Jesus said, "But he that is greatest among you shall be your servant. And whosoever shall exalt himself shall be abased; and he that shall humble himself shall be exalted" (Matthew 23:11–12).

Today's Discipleship Principle: The world may not notice or care, but God never overlooks the faithful service of His children.

One Message, Two Responses

And all the people that heard him, and the publicans, justified God, being baptized with the baptism of John. But the Pharisees and lawyers rejected the counsel of God against themselves, being not baptized of him.
—LUKE 7:29–30

The powerful preaching of John the Baptist as he prepared the people for the coming Messiah drew large crowds of people. Yet even though the message they heard was the same, there were very different responses. Some gladly repented and were baptized, while others refused the message because they were unwilling to change from their self-righteous ways and acknowledge that they needed God's forgiveness for their sins.

If you take a bag of carrots and a half dozen eggs and put them together into a pot of boiling water, they have opposite reactions. The carrots will become soft and tender, while the eggs will harden. The same is true of the response to fire with wax and clay. The wax will melt, but the clay will harden. The difference is not found in the medium of these testings, but in the nature of the material. So it is with our hearts.

Some people endure great hardship and suffering in their lives, but their faith is made stronger and their spirit sweeter. Others endure very similar circumstances but become angry and bitter at God for allowing bad things to happen to them. The difference is determined by the condition of our hearts.

That is why it is so vital for us to make sure that we remain tender to the things of God. If we do not, spiritual tragedy and divine judgment will certainly follow. "Yea, they made their hearts as an adamant stone, lest they should hear the law, and the words which the LORD of hosts hath sent in his spirit by the former prophets: therefore came a great wrath from the LORD of hosts" (Zechariah 7:12).

Today's Discipleship Principle: Keep your heart soft toward the things of God, and you will respond to the events of life properly.

Grow Up

And the Lord said, Whereunto then shall I liken the men of this generation? and to what are they like? They are like unto children sitting in the marketplace, and calling one to another, and saying, We have piped unto you, and ye have not danced; we have mourned to you, and ye have not wept. —LUKE 7:31–32

We understand the process of growing up physically pretty well. Every parent knows what it is like to teach their children to walk, talk, and feed themselves. As they grow older, the natural process should be that they learn and develop to the point where they can live on their own. If parents are still cutting food into little bites and "flying" them on a fork into the mouth of a healthy twenty-five year old child, something is wrong. When a physical or mental disability hinders the process of development, we rightly regard it as a tragedy.

Just as it is normal for us to develop physically, we are called to grow up spiritually. The work that God has for us to do for His Kingdom requires that we develop and mature. Paul highlighted the tragedy of Christians who do not grow up when he wrote to the church at Corinth, "And I, brethren, could not speak unto you as unto spiritual, but as unto carnal, even as unto babes in Christ" (1 Corinthians 3:1).

If we are to grow, we are going to have to put in the effort to develop our spiritual "muscles." I read that the great cellist Pablo Casals was still practicing six hours per day even when he was ninety-five years old. When asked why he did that he replied, "I think I'm making progress."

Rather than settling down and thinking that we have arrived, we should be continuing to work and grow throughout our Christian lives. The lazy approach does not build either physical, mental or spiritual strength.

Today's Discipleship Principle: One of the greatest needs of our day is for God's people to grow up to spiritual maturity.

Understanding the World We Must Reach

For John the Baptist came neither eating bread nor drinking wine; and ye say, He hath a devil. The Son of man is come eating and drinking; and ye say, Behold a gluttonous man, and a winebibber, a friend of publicans and sinners! But wisdom is justified of all her children.
—LUKE 7:33–35

It is common for people to talk about the society of our day with its refusal to believe the truth, and its insistence that anything except genuine Christian faith must be met with not just acceptance, but approval as if this is something new. But in truth, there has never been a time since the Garden of Eden when the truth has been accepted. Rebellion against God's laws may take different forms and use different languages as time passes, but it is a consistent part of human history. This knowledge should shape the ways in which we interact with the world.

There are many in our day urging the church to adopt radical new approaches to reach the world. They insist that only by changing to keep up with the times can we be relevant to society and gain an audience for our message. Yet, the response to the preaching of Jesus and John the Baptist reveals that it is the sinful nature of man that hinders repentance and redemption. It is hard to imagine a greater contrast in styles of living and ministry than that between Jesus and John, yet a large number of the people refused to listen to either of them.

Their problem was not with the way in which the message was presented. Their problem was the message itself. The exclusive offer of salvation by grace through faith alone is deeply offensive to the lost world. While we should not be harsh or unloving, we should be clear in presenting the truth, and we should trust God for the results.

Today's Discipleship Principle: When it comes to reaching the world, God is far more interested in our faithfulness than our trendiness.

march

Grateful Sinners

*And, behold, a woman in the city, which was a sinner, when she knew that Jesus sat at meat in the Pharisee's house, brought an alabaster box of ointment, And stood at his feet behind him weeping, and began to wash his feet with tears, and did wipe them with the hairs of her head, and kissed his feet, and anointed them with the ointment.—*LUKE 7:37–38

Jesus was holy and perfect and sinless. He never excused sin or lowered its definition. He preached a message of repentance, telling people that the only way to have a relationship with God was through the forgiveness of sin. Yet despite the clarity of His message and His unwavering commitment to righteousness, sinners were drawn to His presence. Meeting Jesus does highlight the awfulness of our sin, but it also offers hope—the only hope that is available to a lost and dying world.

I read the story of a young girl who accepted Christ as her Saviour and applied for membership in a local church many years ago. Wanting to be sure she had indeed been saved, a deacon questioned her: "Were you a sinner before you received the Lord Jesus into your life?" he inquired. "Yes, sir," she replied. "Well, are you still a sinner?" "To tell you the truth, I feel I'm a greater sinner than ever." "Then what real change have you experienced?" "I don't quite know how to explain it," she said, "except I used to be a sinner running after sin, but now that I am saved, I'm a sinner running from sin!"

If we take even a single moment to reflect on our salvation, both on the enormous cost with which it was purchased, and the amazing grace that offered it to us freely, even though we did nothing to deserve it, we find ourselves kneeling along with this woman from Luke 7 at the feet of Jesus. No service or worship can ever repay the indescribable gift of forgiveness we have received from His nail-scarred hands.

Today's Discipleship Principle: As we remember the cost of our salvation, our hearts should be filled with gratitude and praise to God.

The Scope of Forgiveness

And Jesus answering said unto him, Simon, I have somewhat to say unto thee. And he saith, Master, say on. There was a certain creditor which had two debtors: the one owed five hundred pence, and the other fifty. And when they had nothing to pay, he frankly forgave them both. Tell me therefore, which of them will love him most? Simon answered and said, I suppose that he, to whom he forgave most. And he said unto him, Thou hast rightly judged. —LUKE 7:40–43

Marghanita Laski was a prominent author and critic in England during the last century. In addition to her artistic skills, she was noted for her opposition to religion. A leading voice for atheism, Laski promoted the lack of man's need for religion. Yet not long before her death, she is reported to have told a guest, "What I envy most about you Christians is your forgiveness; I have nobody to forgive me."

The great gift of God's forgiveness by grace through faith covers all of our sins. Some of us were saved at a young age before we had experienced the worst that the world had to offer. Others spent years in bondage, suffering deep consequences for their sin before finding freedom in Christ. But, in truth, both a child saved early and an adult saved late were both hopelessly lost, without any way to save themselves. They were equally destined to an eternity apart from God in Hell until Jesus intervened.

The concept of forgiveness is one we sometimes want to avoid giving too much attention to precisely because it strikes at the very heart of our pride. It makes us feel better to think that God did not have to forgive us of as much as He forgives others. But if we allow that pride, it undermines our gratitude for God's forgiveness and keeps us from loving Him as we should.

Today's Discipleship Principle: The best way to keep our love for God fervent is to keep our appreciation for His forgiveness of our sins.

Numbers 23–25 // Mark 7:14–37

Saving Faith

Wherefore I say unto thee, Her sins, which are many, are forgiven; for she loved much: but to whom little is forgiven, the same loveth little. And he said unto her, Thy sins are forgiven. And they that sat at meat with him began to say within themselves, Who is this that forgiveth sins also? And he said to the woman, Thy faith hath saved thee; go in peace.—LUKE 7:47–50

When the woman the Bible describes as "a sinner" came and washed Jesus' feet with her tears and poured an expensive ointment on Him, she was expressing something remarkable—her belief that even though she was rejected by the religious leaders of her day who wanted nothing to do with her, Jesus offered her hope for a different life than the one she had known. There is only one source of salvation and deliverance from sin, and she was placing her faith completely in Jesus. In response, He told her that she had received the salvation she desired.

W.H. Griffith Thomas wrote, "Faith is the acknowledgment of our own inability and His ability. Faith includes intellectual perception as well as spiritual reception—the assent of the mind and the assent of the heart." Everyone trusts in something. Even atheists rely on their faith that God does not exist. Far more important than the quality or nature of our faith is the *object* of our faith. It is only when we trust in Jesus that we find salvation.

As we continue growing in faith, it is natural for there to be times when our faith is not be completely certain. We see this in the response of the father of a demon-possessed boy to Jesus. "And straightway the father of the child cried out, and said with tears, Lord, I believe; help thou mine unbelief" (Mark 9:24). When we believe in Jesus with all that we have, God helps whatever unbelief remains so that we can receive what we most need from Him.

Today's Discipleship Principle: Only through faith can we find the salvation that Jesus promises to those who believe in Him.

Supporting God's Work

And it came to pass afterward, that he went throughout every city and village, preaching and shewing the glad tidings of the kingdom of God: and the twelve were with him, And certain women, which had been healed of evil spirits and infirmities, Mary called Magdalene, out of whom went seven devils, And Joanna the wife of Chuza Herod's steward, and Susanna, and many others, which ministered unto him of their substance."
—LUKE 8:1-3

One of my favorite stories of answered prayer comes from the early days of Dallas Theological Seminary. The school was in great financial difficulty and needed $10,000 to continue operating. Dr. H. A. Ironside convened a group of leaders and prayed, "Lord, You own the cattle on a thousand hills. Please help us in this time of need." That very day a check arrived in the mail for the $10,000 they needed. The note enclosed informed them that a rancher had sold some cattle and wanted to give part of the money to the Lord's work.

Though the Lord certainly does not need our help or resources—everything already belongs to Him—His plan is for His work to be funded by His people. Every Christian needs to be involved in supporting and helping God's work in the world. These gifts are not giving God something that He lacks, but rather investments that provide for the work to continue, and that produce fruit in our lives.

Paul pointed out this truth in the letter that he wrote to the church at Philippi to thank them for their financial support of his ministry. "For even in Thessalonica ye sent once and again unto my necessity. Not because I desire a gift: but I desire fruit that may abound to your account" (Philippians 4:16–17). When we fail to give as we should, not only do we rob God, but we also rob ourselves of an opportunity to be part of something great and eternal.

Today's Discipleship Principle: It is a privilege to make an eternal investment by using our resources to support God's work.

The Condition of the Heart

A sower went out to sow his seed: and as he sowed, some fell by the way side; and it was trodden down, and the fowls of the air devoured it. And some fell upon a rock; and as soon as it was sprung up, it withered away, because it lacked moisture. And some fell among thorns; and the thorns sprang up with it, and choked it. And other fell on good ground, and sprang up, and bare fruit an hundredfold. And when he had said these things, he cried, He that hath ears to hear, let him hear.—LUKE 8:5–8

One of the men credited with starting the "fitness craze" in America in the 1970s was best-selling author Jim Fixx. His book *The Complete Book of Running* spent eleven weeks as the number one book in America, and Fixx became a frequent media presence. He was hailed as an authority on the health benefits of exercise. But in 1984 Jim Fixx died of a massive heart attack after finishing a workout run. He was just fifty-two years old.

The condition of our physical heart is central to our health, but the condition of our spiritual heart is even more important, for it is central to our spiritual health. The parable that Jesus told of the sower who cast the same seed out onto four different kinds of soil and received dramatically different results, reveals that the difference in our lives is found in the condition of our hearts.

We may be able to conceal what is on the inside for a time, but when the harvest comes, the nature of our hearts will be revealed. God said to Moses, "O that there were such an heart in them, that they would fear me, and keep all my commandments always, that it might be well with them, and with their children for ever!" (Deuteronomy 5:29). When our heart is hardened, either by sin or distraction, to things of the Lord, we will bear little spiritual fruit. But when we humble ourselves before the Lord, He renews our heart.

Today's Discipleship Principle: By keeping our heart soft and tender to the things of God, we prepare our life for fruitful work for Him.

Understanding the Word

And his disciples asked him, saying, What might this parable be? And he said, Unto you it is given to know the mysteries of the kingdom of God: but to others in parables; that seeing they might not see, and hearing they might not understand.—LUKE 8:9–10

One of the most important archaeological discoveries in history was made in 1799 by a soldier in Napoleon's army fighting in Egypt. The French troops were tasked with building a fort when the man found a stone with written inscriptions in three different languages. Dating to some two hundred years before the birth of Christ, the Rosetta Stone unlocked secrets of the past. The discovery proved crucial to understanding ancient Egyptian hieroglyphics because it contained the same decree written in Egyptian hieroglyphics and Greek. By first translating the known language, historians were able to develop an understanding of the Egyptian language that had not been possible before.

The Bible is not a normal book. While it was penned by men, it is not their thoughts and impressions. Second Peter 1:21 says, "For the prophecy came not in old time by the will of man: but holy men of God spake as they were moved by the Holy Ghost." God has given us what we need to know in His Word. And He has given us the same Holy Spirit who inspired the writing of Scripture to help us understand what it says. Jesus said that one of the purposes of the Holy Spirit coming to live within us was so that "he will guide you into all truth" (John 16:13).

Not everything in the Bible is simple and easy to understand, but if we are diligent students of the Word, we can know what God expects from us. Paul highlighted the vital importance of the Bible in his final letter to Timothy. "And that from a child thou hast known the holy scriptures, which are able to make thee wise unto salvation through faith which is in Christ Jesus" (2 Timothy 3:15).

Today's Discipleship Principle: Everything we need to live the victorious Christian life is found in the pages of God's Word.

Numbers 35–36   //   Mark 10:1–31   91

Fruitful Christians

And that which fell among thorns are they, which, when they have heard,
go forth, and are choked with cares and riches and pleasures of this life,
and bring no fruit to perfection. But that on the good ground are they,
which in an honest and good heart, having heard the word, keep it, and
bring forth fruit with patience. —LUKE 8:14–15

The ministry of Robert William Dale who pastored in England in the 1800s was characterized by a deep concern for the lives of others. While on a trip through Europe, he wrote to his wife back in Birmingham, England. "Lake Lucerene is before me—the noblest scenery in all Europe. But I declare that there is nothing in this magnificent view which makes me feel half the thrill I have when I look down on the smoky streets of Birmingham. That thought that you and I together may, with God's help, save multitudes sends the blood through my veins with an exultation which the most magnificent views of earth cannot create."

God did not save us for our sakes alone, but for a purpose—to be fruitful in His work. Jesus told the disciples, "Ye have not chosen me, but I have chosen you, and ordained you, that ye should go and bring forth fruit, and that your fruit should remain: that whatsoever ye shall ask of the Father in my name, he may give it you" (John 15:16).

The Lord could have chosen angels to carry the gospel to the lost, or written messages in clouds or any number of other means, but His plan is for those who have received His salvation to share that hope of eternal life with others.

The key to being fruitful is found in the heart. If your heart is to be fruitful, it must be "good ground" which is soft and tender to the things of God and yielded to His purpose. The seed of the gospel then not only takes root in your heart, but it continues to bear fruit as you share its message with others.

Today's Discipleship Principle: An unfruitful Christian is missing out on God's purpose and calling for his life.

Hidden Lights

No man, when he hath lighted a candle, covereth it with a vessel, or putteth it under a bed; but setteth it on a candlestick, that they which enter in may see the light.—LUKE 8:16

The great missionary David Livingstone spent much of his life on the mission field in Africa. He heard a challenge from missionary Robert Moffat and dedicated his life to taking the gospel to those who had never heard it before. Livingstone wrote, "I am a missionary heart and soul. God had only one Son, and He was a missionary and a physician. In His service I hope to live. In it I wish to die." Livingstone did die in Africa. Before his body was returned to England to be buried with honors, the African people who had been reached by his ministry cut his heart out of his body and buried it there—because they said that is where it belonged.

The calling of God on our lives is to be lights in the darkness of the world around us. This requires a commitment on our part to be willing to be mocked, ridiculed, and perhaps even persecuted as we stand for the light of the truth in the growing darkness. Paul wrote, "But if our gospel be hid, it is hid to them that are lost: In whom the god of this world hath blinded the minds of them which believe not, lest the light of the glorious gospel of Christ, who is the image of God, should shine unto them" (2 Corinthians 4:3–4).

When we think of ourselves as lights to the world, we realize the responsibility of not doing anything that will keep the light from shining brightly or hide it from those who most need to see it. Whether it be sin that hinders our testimony or fear that keeps us from sharing the truth, we should determine to not allow anything to conceal the light we have been given. There may be consequences for sharing the gospel, but the reality of eternity should motivate us to be bright lights in the world.

Today's Discipleship Principle: There are few tragedies greater than that of a Christian who is hiding his light from the world.

Use It or Lose It

For nothing is secret, that shall not be made manifest; neither any thing hid, that shall not be known and come abroad. Take heed therefore how ye hear: for whosoever hath, to him shall be given; and whosoever hath not, from him shall be taken even that which he seemeth to have.
—LUKE 8:17–18

Though D.L. Moody was a greatly used evangelist, he had little formal education, and it frequently showed in his preaching. It is said that after he finished a sermon in London, a critic came and said, "You made several grammatical errors in your sermon today." Moody admitted with regret that his language was often faulty. Then looking the man in the eye he said, "I am using all the grammar I know for God. What are you doing with the grammar you know?"

The Lord has given every one of us differing talents and spiritual gifts for use in His work. His plan is that as each of us use those gifts together, the church will be built and strengthened: "But now hath God set the members every one of them in the body, as it hath pleased him. And if they were all one member, where were the body? But now are they many members, yet but one body" (1 Corinthians 12:18–20). Without each one doing what he can for the work, it will suffer and be hindered.

God is under no obligation to give us gifts in the first place, and if we refuse to use what He has entrusted to us, we run the risk of it being taken away. The knowledge that we only have our gifts and talents as a result of His grace should make us even more willing to use them in any way that we can for His glory.

The same is true of the truths which God has committed to us. When we know the truth, we are responsible to act on it. If we are not using what we know, there is no reason for God to reveal more to us, and we'll eventually lose our understanding even of what He has given to us.

Today's Discipleship Principle: Every day look for an opportunity to use the gifts and talents God has given you to make known His truth.

The Value of Obedience

Then came to him his mother and his brethren, and could not come at him for the press. And it was told him by certain which said, Thy mother and thy brethren stand without, desiring to see thee. And he answered and said unto them, My mother and my brethren are these which hear the word of God, and do it.—LUKE 8:19–21

A number of years ago a preacher went to the Champness Hall in Yorkshire, England, to hear the noted cellist and conductor Sir John Barbirolli lead the symphony. A friend sitting nearby looked out at the vast crowd in the great hall and asked the preacher, "When will we see the Champness Hall filled to capacity for a Christian service?" The pastor pointed to the members of the orchestra playing on the stage and said, "When we see eighty men willing to give absolute obedience to the will of Christ as these give to Barbirolli."

One of the most effective temptations Satan uses against Christians who want to do what is right is to try to get them to go their own way rather than obeying God. It is not necessary for him to get us to commit overtly sinful acts. If he can convince us to rely on our own judgment, it will not be long before we are completely off track, for our judgment cannot be trusted. The Lord is not looking for people to go their own way, but to go His way.

The commitment required to be a victorious Christian and true disciple of Jesus is simple—that we listen to and obey what God has commanded, just as Jesus did. "For even hereunto were ye called: because Christ also suffered for us, leaving us an example, that ye should follow his steps" (1 Peter 2:21). Only when we are living in obedience can we experience close fellowship with the Lord and the power of the Holy Spirit.

Today's Discipleship Principle: Unless we are yielded to the commands of God, we cannot truly say that we are following Jesus.

Confidence during Storms

Now it came to pass on a certain day, that he went into a ship with his disciples: and he said unto them, Let us go over unto the other side of the lake. And they launched forth. But as they sailed he fell asleep: and there came down a storm of wind on the lake; and they were filled with water, and were in jeopardy. And they came to him, and awoke him, saying, Master, master, we perish. Then he arose, and rebuked the wind and the raging of the water: and they ceased, and there was a calm.
—LUKE 8:22–24

The story is told that as the evangelist D.L. Moody was crossing Lake Michigan to return home after a preaching trip, a great storm came up. The winds and waves were so strong that the passengers began fearing for their lives. While some gathered in an urgent prayer meeting, Moody remained sitting calmly. When someone asked him why he wasn't joining in their prayers, Moody replied, "I have one sister in Chicago and one in Heaven and I don't care which I see tonight."

Christians are not promised a life without troubles or hardships. We are going to face storms as we journey through life. Companies go under, jobs vanish, children get sick, friends betray us. All of these things are part of living in a fallen world, and Christians are not exempt from these trials.

The difference for Christians is that we have someone to helps us. We have a loving Saviour to whom we can turn for help when we are in distress just as the disciples did when they feared their boat would sink. We have been given direct access to God as part of our standing as children of God. Hebrews 4:16 urges, "Let us therefore come boldly unto the throne of grace, that we may obtain mercy, and find grace to help in time of need." We can have confidence in storms when we use the resource of prayer.

Today's Discipleship Principle: When God allows us to experience the storms of life, He never abandons or forsakes us.

Where Is Your Faith?

And he said unto them, Where is your faith? And they being afraid wondered, saying one to another, What manner of man is this! for he commandeth even the winds and water, and they obey him. —LUKE 8:25

In Rome, one can visit the Scala Sancta, the twenty-eight marble steps that supposedly once led into Pilate's judgment hall in Jerusalem which Jesus used as He was taken to His trial before the Roman governor. According to tradition, they were moved to Rome in the early 300s and since that time, millions of people have climbed those steps on their knees as an act of penance. In 1511, it is said that Martin Luther was performing that ritual hoping to gain God's favor when the words of Romans 1:17 sprung into his mind: "For therein is the righteousness of God revealed from faith to faith: as it is written, The just shall live by faith." It was then he realized that salvation does not come through a church, but through faith in Christ's sacrifice for our sins.

Everyone believes in something. The question is not *if* we believe, but *what* we believe. The question Jesus asked of His disciples, "Where is your faith?" did not ask whether their faith existed, but what its foundation was. What are we believing? What are we basing our faith on? The only solid and unchanging foundation for true faith is found in the Word of God. "So then faith cometh by hearing, and hearing by the word of God" (Romans 10:17).

When Jesus stilled the storm, the disciples marveled at the power of Jesus because His words commanded the storm and it obeyed. The power of God is greater than any challenge or difficulty that we may face, and that power is made available to us through prayer. The Christian life cannot be lived successfully by those who misplace their faith. Place your faith in His written Word, and you can experience peace even in the midst of storms.

Today's Discipleship Principle: Only when we take God at His Word, and believe He will do as He says, will we live by faith.

Nothing in Common

And when he went forth to land, there met him out of the city a certain man, which had devils long time, and ware no clothes, neither abode in any house, but in the tombs. When he saw Jesus, he cried out, and fell down before him, and with a loud voice said, What have I to do with thee, Jesus, thou Son of God most high? I beseech thee, torment me not.
—LUKE 8:27–28

At the end of *Animal Farm,* George Orwell's classic parable about Communism, there is a scene in which the pigs, who have taken over running the farm after the humans were chased away, have a meeting with surrounding farmers. The other animals, watching from outside the farmhouse, make a shocking discovery: "The creatures outside looked from pig to man, and from man to pig, and from pig to man again; but already it was impossible to say which was which." Orwell's point was that the distinctions between the leaders of the revolution and those they had replaced had been blurred away.

We are not supposed to be like the world. The expression of the demons, "What have I to do with thee" literally means "We have nothing in common." There are no similarities between God and Satan, and the differences between their children should be plainly visible. James tells us what the fruit of a real walk with God is: "Pure religion and undefiled before God and the Father is this, To visit the fatherless and widows in their affliction, and to keep himself unspotted from the world" (James 1:27).

In our day when so many are trying to break down the distinctions between the church and the world in the name of being more effective in reaching people, we need a return to the realization that we should have nothing in common with the world. While we are to reach out to them in love, we are not to be like them.

Today's Discipleship Principle: Keeping your life separated from the world preserves your testimony and effectiveness for God's work

The Power of God

And Jesus asked him, saying, What is thy name? And he said, Legion: because many devils were entered into him. And they besought him that he would not command them to go out into the deep. And there was there an herd of many swine feeding on the mountain: and they besought him that he would suffer them to enter into them. And he suffered them.
—LUKE 8:30–32

A Roman legion was comprised of more than six thousand soldiers. The maniac of Gadera was possessed by so many demons they referred to themselves as, "Legion," yet they had no power against the Lord. Instead they came as beggars, asking not to be immediately sent to their final judgment but instead sent into the herd of pigs feeding nearby.

Dr. A.J. Gordon told of a visitor from England who traveled to see Niagara Falls with a pastor friend from America. When they arrived to view the mighty waterfall, the visitor said, "This must be the greatest unused power in the world." The pastor replied, "No. The greatest unused power in the world is the Holy Spirit of the living God." God has all power and all authority, and He has given His Holy Spirit to all who trust Him.

We have within us all the power we need to overcome temptation, to witness effectively, and to fulfill the commands of God. He has not left us without the resources we need to accomplish the tasks He has given us. Jesus grounded the Great Commission on His divine power and authority. "And Jesus came and spake unto them, saying, All power is given unto me in heaven and in earth. Go ye therefore, and teach all nations, baptizing them in the name of the Father, and of the Son, and of the Holy Ghost" (Matthew 28:18–19).

The great tragedy is that while we have the power of God available to us, we often neglect it or resist the work of the Holy Spirit in our lives. He desires to work mightily in and through us if we will simply yield to Him.

Today's Discipleship Principle: A Christian living and working in the power of God has no need to fear any force on earth.

Telling Jesus to Go Away

*Then they went out to see what was done; and came to Jesus, and found the man, out of whom the devils were departed, sitting at the feet of Jesus, clothed, and in his right mind: and they were afraid. They also which saw it told them by what means he that was possessed of the devils was healed. Then the whole multitude of the country of the Gadarenes round about besought him to depart from them; for they were taken with great fear: and he went up into the ship, and returned back again.—*LUKE 8:35–37

Sometimes we read of the great revivals of history and wish we could have been part of them. Imagine being in church and listening to Jonathan Edwards preach "Sinners in the Hands of an Angry God." Picture standing in a crowd of more than twenty thousand people listening to George Whitfield preach with passion at the start of the Great Awakening. Yet while we remember these great moves of God with nostalgia, if we were honest we would have to acknowledge that we don't know how we would have responded. For there are many times in Scripture, in history, and in our own lives when we regard God's moving as an interruption to our plans.

Before Jesus came, the demon-possessed man terrorized the people of Gadera. The demons gave him so much power that no one could control him. Others lived in fear of him attacking and perhaps injuring or even killing someone. You would think that they would have been delighted when they rushed out of town seeing him wearing clothes and in control of himself for the first time in years. Instead, these people told Jesus to go away. Even though Jesus had delivered a man under the control of Satan, because the people lost their herd of pigs, they saw Jesus' work as an interruption to their lives. God is Sovereign, and He has the right to arrange our lives and work in our hearts in any way that He sees fit. When we yield to His plans, we will experience His continued work.

Today's Discipleship Principle: Do not quench or hinder the work that God is trying to do in and through your life.

Everywhere Evangelism

Now the man out of whom the devils were departed besought him that he might be with him: but Jesus sent him away, saying, Return to thine own house, and shew how great things God hath done unto thee. And he went his way, and published throughout the whole city how great things Jesus had done unto him. —LUKE 8:38–39

Dr. John R. Rice told of going to hear the great evangelist Gypsy Smith. As Gypsy Smith preached on the importance of winning souls to Jesus, Dr. Rice determined in his heart that he would find someone that very day with whom he could share the gospel.

The speaker left the building after the message, and when the announcements and other business was concluded, Dr. Rice went outside and saw a man standing by his taxi. He walked over, intent on witnessing to the man. But when he asked about his salvation, the taxi driver replied, "I just became a Christian. A short little man came out the speaker's door and told me about Jesus." Gypsy Smith had practiced what he had been preaching.

We have many opportunities to give people the gospel that we miss because we are not always alert to those around us. Going through the day, many priorities compete for our attention. But everywhere we go, we are to be telling people about what Jesus has done for us.

The man Jesus freed from demon possession wanted to follow Him, but instead Jesus told him to return home and tell others what had happened. When Jesus later returned to the region, huge crowds came to hear Him—in no small measure because this one man obeyed the command of the Lord to share his testimony with those around him. It is good to have regular times to go out and share the gospel, but we should always be alert to those who need to hear how Jesus offers salvation.

Today's Discipleship Principle: Every person you meet has an eternal soul, and you may be the only one to tell them how to reach Heaven.

The Great Physician

And it came to pass, that, when Jesus was returned, the people gladly received him: for they were all waiting for him. And, behold, there came a man named Jairus, and he was a ruler of the synagogue: and he fell down at Jesus' feet, and besought him that he would come into his house: For he had one only daughter, about twelve years of age, and she lay a dying. But as he went the people thronged him.—LUKE 8:40–42

D r. W.A. Criswell told of a visit he paid to a missionary who worked with the lepers of Africa. For days they drove from settlement to settlement, and in each one the missionary would provide medical care and then Dr. Criswell would preach. Criswell said, "They had built a little church out of mud. The building was made out of mud, the pulpit was made out of mud, and the pews were made out of mud. I did my best through an interpreter to preach to them about our blessed Jesus. After the preaching was done, the lepers stood up in the congregation and sang this song:

> "The great physician now is near, the sympathizing Jesus.
> He speaks the drooping heart to cheer, O list' to the voice of Jesus.
> Sweetest note on seraph's song, sweetest carol ever sung,
> Sweetest note on mortal tongue, Jesus, blessed Jesus."

The primary purpose of Jesus' life and ministry was to be the Saviour of the world. But His great love and compassion for the needs of people led Him to often meet their physical needs as well. While these are not as important as our eternal needs, they do matter to our loving Heavenly Father.

We have every right to cry out to Jesus for help with any problem that we have, trusting both His love and His power to meet our needs. Ultimately He is the source for everything good that happens in our lives.

Today's Discipleship Principle: For every pain of life—physical, emotional, and spiritual—we have a Saviour who can meet the need.

Run to Jesus

*And a woman having an issue of blood twelve years, which had spent all
her living upon physicians, neither could be healed of any, Came behind
him, and touched the border of his garment: and immediately her issue
of blood stanched.* —LUKE 8:43-44

Though medical science was far less advanced in Jesus' day than it is
in ours, there were doctors then who did their best to treat patients.
But often the problems were beyond their ability to cure. This was the
case with an anonymous woman who had tried everything without being
helped. Yet when she heard of the miracles Jesus was performing, a faith
grew in her heart. She believed that if she could reach Jesus and touch His
clothing, she would be healed.

When difficulty comes into our lives, how often do we murmur
and complain, rather than trusting that God knows what He is doing.
Our lives are not filled with accidents and coincidences, but with divine
appointments. Even trouble and sickness can be used to draw us closer
to God. Robert Murray McCheyne said, "Sometimes in health the Word
does not touch the heart. The world is all. Its gaieties, its pleasures, its
admiration, captivate your mind. God sometimes draws you aside into
a sickbed, and shows you the sin of your heart, the vanity of worldly
pleasures and drives the soul to seek a sure resting-place for eternity in
Christ. O happy sickness that draws the soul to Jesus."

Our response to trouble reveals where our faith rests. When we turn
to the best that man can offer first, we show a world focus. When we
turn to our own efforts and try to work things out on our own, we show
a self focus. But when we turn to God first, pouring out our hearts to
Him and seeking His help, we show a faith focus, and that is the life that
God blesses.

Today's Discipleship Principle: Don't make prayer a last resort—run to
Jesus at the first sign of trouble.

Jesus Cares about You

And Jesus said, Who touched me? When all denied, Peter and they that were with him said, Master, the multitude throng thee and press thee, and sayest thou, Who touched me? And Jesus said, Somebody hath touched me: for I perceive that virtue is gone out of me. —LUKE 8:45–46

If you have ever walked through a dense crowd of people at an airport, a ballgame, or even at church, you know it is common to be jostled and bumped as others in close proximity gather together. Yet when Jesus was making His way to the home of Jairus who had asked for help for his daughter who was sick, He stopped when a woman who needed healing reached out to touch him intentionally. He noticed it because He felt the power go out of Him to meet her need. There are many lessons about faith and God's power in this story, but one of the most important is the love and compassion of Jesus for one individual woman among the great crowd.

To God, you and I are not part of a huge mass of humanity, but unique individuals of His creation, and He cares about what happens to us. David marveled that the great God of creation would care about individuals: "When I consider thy heavens, the work of thy fingers, the moon and the stars, which thou hast ordained; What is man, that thou art mindful of him? and the son of man, that thou visitest him?" (Psalm 8:3–4).

Because of our human limitations—in time, memory, and resources—we cannot process the needs of billions of other people, nor could we do anything to meet more than a tiny fraction of those needs. Yet God in His infinite strength and wisdom knows each one of us by name, and He cares about what happens to us. We are never alone and never forsaken by our loving Heavenly Father.

Today's Discipleship Principle: You are not an abstract or part of a crowd to God, but a singular individual He knows and loves.

In the Family by Faith

*And when the woman saw that she was not hid, she came trembling, and
falling down before him, she declared unto him before all the people for
what cause she had touched him, and how she was healed immediately.
And he said unto her, Daughter, be of good comfort: thy faith hath made
thee whole; go in peace—LUKE 8:47-48*

One of the most famous images from all the years of the White
House is a photo that shows President Kennedy seated at his desk
while his young son John plays underneath it. The famed "Resolute desk"
made from the timbers of a British ship was a gift from Queen Victoria
to President Rutherford B. Hayes in 1880. If you or I went to the White
House, however, we would not be allowed to just walk into the Oval
Office and crawl under the desk to play while the president worked. But
the family relationship made all the difference for John F. Kennedy, Jr.

God has given us the immense privilege of being adopted into His
family with the full rights and privileges that come with having Him as
our Father. "Beloved, now are we the sons of God, and it doth not yet
appear what we shall be: but we know that, when he shall appear, we
shall be like him; for we shall see him as he is" (1 John 3:2). Although we
have not received everything that will be ours as children of God, we
already have the authority to enter His presence and confidently present
our requests to Him.

This access is not because of our merit, but because of His amazing
grace applied to our lives in response to faith in Him. From the moment
of salvation, we are in God's family, and we should not be content to live
like orphans. Instead we should climb under His "desk" with complete
confidence that we belong.

Today's Discipleship Principle: Rejoice that salvation placed you in a
new family—and enjoy your privileges as a child of God.

Faith for the Impossible

While he yet spake, there cometh one from the ruler of the synagogue's house, saying to him, Thy daughter is dead; trouble not the Master. But when Jesus heard it, he answered him, saying, Fear not: believe only, and she shall be made whole.—LUKE 8:49–50

Charles Spurgeon told of an elderly lady in his church who was confronted by a skeptic over the story of Jonah being swallowed by a great fish. When he attempted to scientifically prove to her that it was impossible for such a thing to happen, her faith remained unshaken. Finally she replied, "Not only do I believe that Jonah was swallowed by a great fish just as the Bible says, but if the Bible said Jonah swallowed the fish, I would believe that too!"

There are too many times when we only believe what we can see and understand and explain rather than taking God at His word that He is not limited by the things that are within our grasp. Instead He is able to do everything that He has promised, no matter how far beyond our ability and understanding it may be. "But Jesus beheld them, and said unto them, With men this is impossible; but with God all things are possible" (Matthew 19:26).

The Christian who lives as if God is not able to meet his needs is insulting his Heavenly Father. Through God's grace we have been given the right and privilege to enter His presence and present our needs to Him. Yet too often we do not believe that God will actually do for us what He has promised to do. As a result, we fail to please Him with our lives. "But without faith it is impossible to please him: for he that cometh to God must believe that he is, and that he is a rewarder of them that diligently seek him" (Hebrews 11:6). When we face the impossible, we should not fear but believe that God is with us, that He is able to do anything, and that He will do what is right and according to His Word.

Today's Discipleship Principle: The God we serve is the God of the impossible, and we should claim His power for our daily lives.

When We Know Better than God

And when he came into the house, he suffered no man to go in, save Peter, and James, and John, and the father and the mother of the maiden. And all wept, and bewailed her: but he said, Weep not; she is not dead, but sleepeth. And they laughed him to scorn, knowing that she was dead.
—LUKE 8:51–53

Someone said there are two foundational facts of life: 1) there is a God, and 2) you are not Him. There is a lot of truth in those statements. Though we would not publicly declare that we know better than God and could arrange to make things work better than He is doing, in our hearts we sometimes think that is the case. When we do not understand how He is working, and then decide to go our own way instead, we are really falling prey to the temptation Satan first used in the Garden of Eden—that we would be happier if we chose for ourselves rather than following God. "For God doth know that in the day ye eat thereof, then your eyes shall be opened, and ye shall be as gods, knowing good and evil" (Genesis 3:5).

The reason that the devil keeps using this temptation is that it works so well. We do not like to acknowledge our failings and limitations. We like to think that we have the knowledge and wisdom to make good decisions apart from the guidance of the Bible and the Holy Spirit. Yet each time we go our own way in defiance of God, we place ourselves on the road to ruin.

Jeremiah observed, "O LORD, I know that the way of man is not in himself: it is not in man that walketh to direct his steps" (Jeremiah 10:23). In humility and faith we need to yield our lives to the direction and control of the God who always knows best.

Today's Discipleship Principle: Faith in God rests on the acceptance that He is always right and what He says can be trusted.

Death Has No Power

And he put them all out, and took her by the hand, and called, saying, Maid, arise. And her spirit came again, and she arose straightway: and he commanded to give her meat. And her parents were astonished: but he charged them that they should tell no man what was done.
—LUKE 8:54–56

One of the best statements on eternal life I have ever read came from evangelist D.L. Moody. He said, "Some day you will read in the papers, 'D.L. Moody of East Northfield is dead.' Don't you believe a word of it! At that moment I shall be more alive than I am now; I shall have gone up higher, that is all, out of this old clay tenement into a house that is immortal—a body that death cannot touch, that sin cannot taint; a body fashioned like unto His glorious body. I was born of the flesh in 1837. I was born of the Spirit in 1856. That which is born of the flesh may die. That which is born of the Spirit will live forever."

Death is a great fear in our world—for many people, the greatest fear that they have. Yet while there is sorrow in the death of a friend or loved one, for a believer, death no longer has the power to harm us. Jesus has all power, even the power over death. "Jesus said unto her, I am the resurrection, and the life: he that believeth in me, though he were dead, yet shall he live: And whosoever liveth and believeth in me shall never die" (John 11:25–26).

Death did everything in its power to hold Jesus in the grave, but it failed. The power of the tomb has been defeated once and for all, and can live in the authority and power given to us by the One who died and rose again to live forever. When a Christian dies, they simply move from one place of living to another, and the place where they move is a far better place to live—in the physical presence of Christ with no sin, death, or suffering.

Today's Discipleship Principle: For the Christian, death is simply the door that allows us to enter the presence of our loving Saviour.

Empowered Ministry

Then he called his twelve disciples together, and gave them power and authority over all devils, and to cure diseases. And he sent them to preach the kingdom of God, and to heal the sick. And he said unto them, Take nothing for your journey, neither staves, nor scrip, neither bread, neither money; neither have two coats apiece. —LUKE 9:1–3

God calls and commands His children to do His work in the world. The plan for reaching the lost and building the church requires God's people to do the work—but it is a work that can only be done effectively through His power. The final command of Christ that we commonly call the Great Commission is grounded and based on the authority that belongs to Jesus: "And Jesus came and spake unto them, saying, All power is given unto me in heaven and in earth. Go ye therefore, and teach all nations, baptizing them in the name of the Father, and of the Son, and of the Holy Ghost" (Matthew 28:18–19).

The authority of Jesus means that we do not face our battles and our work on our own. We can and must rely on the power and work of the Holy Spirit who lives within us for the ministry we are meant to do. We have no other hope of success. A.W. Tozer said, "I'm not afraid of the devil. The devil can handle me—he's got judo I never heard of. But he can't handle the One to whom I'm joined; he can't handle the One to whom I'm united; he can't handle the One whose nature dwells in my nature."

When we operate based on our own strength and resources, we can only accomplish what lies in our ability. But no matter how great those abilities may be, they are not remotely equal to God's calling. Only in His strength can we fulfill His mission.

Today's Discipleship Principle: If we rely on the power given to us rather than our own strength, our ministry for God will be effective.

The Limit of Our Responsibility

And whatsoever house ye enter into, there abide, and thence depart. And whosoever will not receive you, when ye go out of that city, shake off the very dust from your feet for a testimony against them. And they departed, and went through the towns, preaching the gospel, and healing every where.—LUKE 9:4–6

John Quincy Adams lost his bid for a second term in the White House and then did something no other former President has ever done. He ran for and won a seat in the House of Representatives, where he spent most of the rest of his life working to bring about the abolition of slavery. This position was not widely popular -when Adams began his efforts, and often he labored nearly alone. Yet he refused to be discouraged or dissuaded from doing what he believed was right. Once Adams was asked how he kept going in the face of repeated disappointments and setbacks. Adams replied, "Duties are ours. Results are God's." Though he did not live to see slavery ended, his faithful work helped bring about the result he worked so long to see.

Many times we take on the responsibility for how people respond to the truth. But the only thing for which God holds us accountable is faithfulness in declaring the message. When Jesus sent the disciples out for their first preaching mission apart from Him, He told them up front that some people would not receive the message.

When it seems that work for the Lord is in vain, we simply need to continue to be faithful in doing what He has commanded. Not everyone to whom we witness will get saved. Witness anyway. Not everyone we seek to disciple will continue to walk in the truth. Disciple anyway. Not everyone we love will respond with love in return. Love anyway. This is all that God holds us responsible to accomplish with our lives.

Today's Discipleship Principle: As long as we are faithful, we can leave the results of our ministry in God's hands.

What Happens When We Ignore the Truth

Now Herod the tetrarch heard of all that was done by him: and he was perplexed, because that it was said of some, that John was risen from the dead; And of some, that Elias had appeared; and of others, that one of the old prophets was risen again. And Herod said, John have I beheaded: but who is this, of whom I hear such things? And he desired to see him.
—LUKE 9:7–9

There is an old joke about a man who ignored an evacuation order given because of a coming flood. As the water began to rise, a rescue officer in a boat came by his house and told him to get in or he might drown. The man replied, "I'm fine. God will take care of me." When the water continued to rise, he was eventually forced to the roof of his house. A helicopter flew over and lowered a ladder, but he again refused. "God will take care of me." After he drowned, he asked God why He hadn't rescued him. "I sent you a boat and a helicopter," God responded. "What else did you want?"

Herod is a prime example of what happens when we choose to ignore the truth. Because John the Baptist preached against his sin, the evil king had the fearless prophet beheaded. But then he was very interested in meeting Jesus. Yet when Jesus was brought before Herod just before the crucifixion, their encounter did not turn out the way Herod had planned. "Then he questioned with him in many words; but he answered him nothing" (Luke 23:9).

There are times when we do not listen to what God has said because it convicts us or would require us to do something we do not want to do. Until we obey what we already know, we should not expect further guidance from God.

Today's Discipleship Principle: If we ignore what we already know is true, we have no basis for asking God to give us guidance and direction.

Sacrificial Ministry

And the apostles, when they were returned, told him all that they had done. And he took them, and went aside privately into a desert place belonging to the city called Bethsaida. And the people, when they knew it, followed him: and he received them, and spake unto them of the kingdom of God, and healed them that had need of healing. —LUKE 9:10–11

I heard about a church that had a sign out front which read: "We care about you." Underneath in smaller letters it said: "Sundays 10:00 AM only." The reality is that caring about people and ministering to them and meeting their needs requires effort and sacrifice on our part. There are no shortcuts to touching lives. If we are not willing to make the investment, even if it means sacrifices on our part, we will never make an impact on others.

At this point in the life and ministry of Jesus, He and the disciples were physically exhausted. The parallel account in Mark's Gospel gives us a pointed insight into the toll His ministry was taking on Jesus and His disciples: "And he said unto them, Come ye yourselves apart into a desert place, and rest a while: for there were many coming and going, and they had no leisure so much as to eat" (Mark 6:31). When you don't even have time to eat, your ministry schedule is full indeed!

Yet, in what was supposed to be a time of rest and relaxation, the needs of the people prompted Jesus to respond by giving up His free time so that He could teach and heal the people. For Jesus it was a question of priorities. He wanted to rest and needed to rest, but what the people needed mattered more to Him than His own needs.

There certainly are times when we need to rest, and we are unwise if we never plan for these times. But if we only minister when it is convenient and refuse to give of ourselves to others when we crave rest, we will miss opportunities to invest in those whom God has called us to serve.

Today's Discipleship Principle: To reach others for Jesus, we must, like Jesus, be willing to sacrificially invest in their lives.

Judges 1–3 // Luke 4:1–30

Send Them Away or Give Them to Eat?

And when the day began to wear away, then came the twelve, and said unto him, Send the multitude away, that they may go into the towns and country round about, and lodge, and get victuals: for we are here in a desert place. But he said unto them, Give ye them to eat. And they said, We have no more but five loaves and two fishes; except we should go and buy meat for all this people. For they were about five thousand men. And he said to his disciples, Make them sit down by fifties in a company.
—LUKE 9:12–14

A Christian businessman named Wallace Speers told of a strange encounter he had on the street one day. A young man who was unshaved and disheveled stopped him and said, "You look like a friendly man. Will you do something for me? There is no one in the world who cares if I live or die. Will you just think about me for a while? If I could believe someone was thinking about me as a human being it would mean more to me than money or anything." In a moment he melted back into the crowd and was gone. Speers said later, "I've been haunted by that man's loneliness ever since."

All around us there are people in urgent need of help and hope. Yet sometimes, like the disciples who saw the massive crowd, we view people as a source of annoyance and frustration. We want them to just go away rather than having to deal with helping them. The heart of Jesus was filled with compassion for the needs of the people, and He was willing to do whatever He could to meet those needs. The difference between Jesus and the disciples was not the need, but the way they viewed the people with the need. Jesus did not see people as obstacles in the way of His agenda; He saw them as individuals He could serve.

Today's Discipleship Principle: If we are to be like Jesus, we must care for the needs of others rather than regarding them as frustrations.

More than Enough

Then he took the five loaves and the two fishes, and looking up to heaven, he blessed them, and brake, and gave to the disciples to set before the multitude. And they did eat, and were all filled: and there was taken up of fragments that remained to them twelve baskets. —LUKE 9:16–17

D r. John R. Rice told the story of his oldest daughter, Grace, getting very sick. The doctor came to the house and discovered that she had diphtheria. He gave her medicine and put the house under quarantine. Dr. Rice and his wife decided to pray. They prayed together for just a few minutes, and were confident that God had heard them. That very day Grace began feeling better, and by the next morning she was feeling completely better. She could not go out because of the quarantine, but she played happily with her dolls until the doctor came and certified that she was completely free of the disease and lifted the quarantine.

God is not limited in any way. He has all power, all authority, and all resources. When we ask for His help, we should not be surprised when He not only answers our prayers but also gives us even more than we ask. God revealed Himself to Abraham by the name El Shaddai—the Almighty God (Genesis 17:1). He has never yet failed one of His children, and He will not fail us now.

The miracle of the feeding of the five thousand is one of the most important demonstrations of the power of Jesus. Unlike any of the other miracles, except for the resurrection, it is recorded in all four Gospels. Turning the lunch of one little boy into enough food for thousands of people is miraculous, but Jesus went even beyond that. He created so much extra that they filled twelve baskets with the leftovers. God is more than able to meet every need you have—and then some. When you face difficulty and need, do not look to your insufficiency and despair; look to Christ's sufficiency and rejoice.

Today's Discipleship Principle: The God we serve is more than enough for the challenges, needs, and struggles we face.

Jesus Is Everything

*And it came to pass, as he was alone praying, his disciples were with him: and he asked them, saying, Whom say the people that I am? They answering said, John the Baptist; but some say, Elias; and others say, that one of the old prophets is risen again. He said unto them, But whom say ye that I am? Peter answering said, The Christ of God.—*LUKE 9:18-20

Many years ago in a small town in Virginia, the newspaper printed the upcoming sermon topics for the local churches. A pastor named R.I. Williams phoned the editor to share that his sermon for the upcoming Sunday would be titled "The Lord Is My Shepherd." The editor asked, "Is that all?" To which the pastor replied, "That is enough!" When the paper arrived at his home he opened it to find the printed topic: "The Lord Is My Shepherd and That Is Enough."

Jesus is not just a good teacher, an ancient mystic, or an example for us to follow. He is not merely a man—although He was fully human. He is the very Son of God and the Messiah who had been promised through the centuries. He was sent into the world to be the Lamb of God who would take away the sins of the world. The perfectly sinless life that He lived was a demonstration of His divinity, as He lived in complete obedience to the law which no one had ever been able to do.

People in Jesus' day who thought of Jesus as one of the Old Testament prophets risen from the dead thought that was wonderful. But the truth of who He is—God Himself who came to be our Saviour—is even better.

The wonderful thing is that Jesus is not just our Saviour. God's plan and purpose for us is to be changed into His likeness. Romans 8:29 tells us, "For whom he did foreknow, he also did predestinate to be conformed to the image of his Son, that he might be the firstborn among many brethren." Through the power of the Holy Spirit we can become more like our wonderful Saviour.

Today's Discipleship Principle: In Jesus we have everything that we will ever need both for this world and the next.

Judges 9–10   //   Luke 5:17–39   115

The Cost of Salvation

*And he straitly charged them, and commanded them to tell no man that thing; Saying, The Son of man must suffer many things, and be rejected of the elders and chief priests and scribes, and be slain, and be raised the third day.—*LUKE 9:21–22

For almost four hundred years, the people of Oberammergau, Bavaria, Germany have been performing a play depicting the final week of the life of Jesus. According to tradition, they began this practice after their village was spared from the bubonic plague. Every ten years they stage a massive event featuring hundreds of performers, singers, and helpers.

There is a story that some years ago, the actor portraying Jesus fell down during the scene when he was carrying the cross to Calvary. An onlooker was so overcome in the moment that he ran forward to help lift the cross from the actor's back. Thinking it would be a stage prop, he only used one hand, but found he could not move the heavy wood. Afterward he met with the actor who told him, "I cannot look like Jesus unless I carry a real cross."

Salvation is freely provided by God's grace to all who believe, but it was certainly not free. The awfulness of sin and the eternality of Hell required a great price to be paid for salvation. "For it is not possible that the blood of bulls and of goats should take away sins" (Hebrews 10:4). No work of man could atone for sin, and thus the death of Jesus was required.

Nothing that happened to Jesus was accidental. It was God's plan from the beginning that Jesus would live a perfect life, be crucified, and then rise again. Jesus willingly came into the world knowing the price that would be required, and He willingly paid it. The Saviour regarded the cross as an absolute necessity because that was His mission.

Today's Discipleship Principle: Rejoice today in the love of God that sent Jesus to die on the cross to pay the price for our salvation.

april

Valuing the Eternal

And he said to them all, If any man will come after me, let him deny himself, and take up his cross daily, and follow me. For whosoever will save his life shall lose it: but whosoever will lose his life for my sake, the same shall save it.—LUKE 9:23–24

The first two English missionaries who attempted to reach the inhabitants of the New Hebrides islands in the South Pacific were killed and eaten by the cannibals only a few minutes after they arrived. For some time after that, no one else was willing to go there with the gospel. Finally, in 1858, John Paton and his wife determined to risk the dangers to reach the lost of those islands.

As they announced their plans to their church, one of the elder members of the congregation discouraged the effort, warning, "You will be eaten by cannibals!" John Paton responded, "Mr. Dickson, you are advanced in years now, and your own prospect is soon to be laid in the grave, there to be eaten by worms; I confess to you, that if I can but live and die serving and honoring the Lord Jesus, it will make no difference to me whether I am eaten by cannibals or by worms."

The world tells us that we should cling to our lives and do everything possible to defend them. But God's call for us is different. He values the eternal over the temporal, and He is not looking for people to be focused on this life. The goal of the Christian life is not to be safe and comfortable; it is to invest in the eternal, and that requires self-denial and sacrifice.

Taking up the cross to follow Jesus is a descriptive metaphor. Dr. Curtis Hutson used to say, "A crucified man has no plans of his own for the future." Rather than focusing on how we can get the most for ourselves, we should, like Jesus, focus on how we can give the most to others.

Today's Discipleship Principle: If we care about what God cares about and make it our priority, there will be great eternal rewards.

Judges 13–15   //   Luke 6:27–49

Live for What Matters

For what is a man advantaged, if he gain the whole world, and lose himself, or be cast away? For whosoever shall be ashamed of me and of my words, of him shall the Son of man be ashamed, when he shall come in his own glory, and in his Father's, and of the holy angels.—LUKE 9:25–26

In his prayer journal, the missionary martyr Jim Elliot wrote: "Father, take my life, yea, my blood if Thou wilt, and consume it with Thine enveloping fire. I would not save it, for it is not mine to save. Have it, Lord, have it all. Pour out my life as an oblation for the world. Blood is only of value as it flows before Thine altar." Indeed, Elliot backed up his written devotion with his very life when he and four other missionaries were killed by the spears of the Ecuadorian tribe they were trying to reach with the gospel. Yet, their death was instrumental in raising the awareness of Christians around the world to the many people still without knowledge of the gospel, and many new missionaries surrendered their lives to the Lord because of this event.

The world does not value the things of eternal value. The prevalent attitude is summed up in the popular bumper sticker: "He who dies with the most toys wins." But once we die, there is no value in the toys of this world. Even as we live, God is not interested in earthly trinkets. He paved the streets of Heaven with gold and made the walls out of precious stones. No amount of acquisition on our part is going to impress Him. Even worse, when we live only for the temporal, we miss out on the opportunity to do something lasting and important for Him.

Are you living for what matters most? Many Christians will be ashamed when they look back at their lives and realize how few of the things that occupied their time were of eternal value. On the other hand, no Christian will stand before the Lord and regret a single investment that was made into eternity.

Today's Discipleship Principle: If you spend your time, talent, and resources on what is eternal, your life will not be in vain.

A Glimpse of Glory

And it came to pass about an eight days after these sayings, he took Peter and John and James, and went up into a mountain to pray. And as he prayed, the fashion of his countenance was altered, and his raiment was white and glistering. And, behold, there talked with him two men, which were Moses and Elias: Who appeared in glory, and spake of his decease which he should accomplish at Jerusalem.—LUKE 9:28–31

When Jesus came to Earth to be our Saviour, He did not stop being God. The entire time He was here on Earth, He was both fully human and fully divine. Yet even though He was still God, Jesus did voluntarily lay aside the power and glory that was His, not thinking it was important enough to cling to for the sake of the mission of providing salvation for the lost. Paul describes the love and humility of Jesus this way: "But made himself of no reputation, and took upon him the form of a servant, and was made in the likeness of men" (Philippians 2:7).

For one brief moment during Christ's ministry, however, the true nature of Jesus was revealed as He was transfigured before Peter, James, and John. There, on what we call the Mount of Transfiguration, the veil was drawn back, and His glory shone through—but even that was only a glimpse of His full glory.

Of all the disciples, John was the closest to Jesus. He witnessed the Transfiguration, the miracles, and walked and talked with Jesus after the resurrection. Yet when he was given his vision of Heaven and things to come on the Isle of Patmos, John collapsed at the sight of the glorified Lord: "And when I saw him, I fell at his feet as dead. And he laid his right hand upon me, saying unto me, Fear not; I am the first and the last" (Revelation 1:17). The world pictures Jesus as soft and weak, but God shows Him to us as the conquering King of kings.

Today's Discipleship Principle: Seeing Jesus for who He really is will make us want to serve and glorify Him more than ever.

We Can't Stay on the Mountain

But Peter and they that were with him were heavy with sleep: and when they were awake, they saw his glory, and the two men that stood with him. And it came to pass, as they departed from him, Peter said unto Jesus, Master, it is good for us to be here: and let us make three tabernacles; one for thee, and one for Moses, and one for Elias: not knowing what he said.—LUKE 9:32–33

One of the most majestic sights in the United States is the great peaks of the Rocky Mountains. If you travel across the west, the tall mountains rise up and up. Many of them are covered with snow all year long because of their elevation. Yet, as beautiful as they are, it is because of that elevation and the resulting cold air and lack of soil and moisture that almost nothing grows on the tops of the mountains. There is what is called a "tree line" and once you get above that point, there is little plant or animal life. The mountains are lovely to look at and experience, but they are not a place to stay.

Peter was amazed by what he saw on the Mount of Transfiguration and wanted to just stay there. He was all for building structures and leaving the rest of the world behind. But God does not call us to withdraw from the world and isolate ourselves into tiny spiritual communities. He calls us to go meet with people where they are and reach out to them with the gospel. Peter's desire is understandable, but as the text from Luke tells us, it was based on a lack of understanding of God's plan.

There are times to rest and recharge our spiritual batteries. There are times to spend seasons alone with God. But if we spend our lives in renewing seclusion, we miss one of the great purposes God wants to do through those times of rest—rejuvenate us through worship so we are able to serve others. Most of our lives are to be lived among the people around us, loving and ministering to them as Jesus did.

Today's Discipleship Principle: Although mountaintop experiences are a blessing, most of the work of the Christian life is done in the valleys.

Focus on Jesus

While he thus spake, there came a cloud, and overshadowed them: and they feared as they entered into the cloud. And there came a voice out of the cloud, saying, This is my beloved Son: hear him. And when the voice was past, Jesus was found alone. And they kept it close, and told no man in those days any of those things which they had seen. —LUKE 9:34–36

For several years leading up to Roger Bannister's historic run in May of 1954 to complete a mile in under four minutes, many athletes had tried and failed to break that barrier. Yet after Bannister proved it could be done, several others succeeded. One of them was a runner named John Landry. He broke Bannister's record by more than a second.

Track officials quickly put together a race between the top two milers in the world. As they reached the last lap, Landry was leading, but he was worried about how close Bannister was. When he looked back over his shoulder to check on his competitor, Bannister passed him and won the race. A distraught Landry told a reporter from *Time* magazine, "If I hadn't looked back, I would have won!"

One of the great temptations we face in our Christian life is to worry about what other people are doing instead of keeping our focus on doing our best for God. When Jesus met Peter after the resurrection and told him about His plan for the rest of Peter's life, Peter immediately turned his attention to John. "Then Peter, turning about, seeth the disciple whom Jesus loved following; which also leaned on his breast at supper, and said, Lord, which is he that betrayeth thee? Peter seeing him saith to Jesus, Lord, and what shall this man do?" (John 21:20–21).

God is well able to take care of everyone else without any help from us. But we are not well able to continue our course as we should while we are distracted by evaluating the progress of others. We need to keep our eyes on Jesus.

Today's Discipleship Principle: If our focus is fixed on Jesus, then we will not be drawn off course easily.

Powerless Christians

And, behold, a man of the company cried out, saying, Master, I beseech thee, look upon my son: for he is mine only child. And, lo, a spirit taketh him, and he suddenly crieth out; and it teareth him that he foameth again, and bruising him hardly departeth from him. And I besought thy disciples to cast him out; and they could not.—LUKE 9:38–40

While Jesus was on the Mount of Transfiguration with Peter, James, and John, a distraught father brought his demon possessed son to the other disciples, but they couldn't help. This is especially sad because it had been just a few days, or perhaps at most a few weeks earlier—in this same chapter of Luke's Gospel—that Jesus had specifically empowered them to deal with this kind of problem. "Then he called his twelve disciples together, and gave them power and authority over all devils, and to cure diseases" (Luke 9:1) Yet despite what Jesus had said, they did not believe they could deal with the demonic power that confronted them, and as a result, the demon remained until Jesus returned.

The old preacher Vance Havner said, "Too many of us today are shaky about what we believe but not shaken by what we believe. Too many people assemble at God's house who don't really believe in the power of God. Having begun in the Spirit, we live in the flesh. Never has the church had more wire stretched with less power in it. As the hymn puts it, 'All is vain unless the Spirit of the Holy One comes down.'"

The challenges of the world that we face are too great for our own strength, but we are not meant to operate in our strength. The problem is not a lack of power on God's part, but our failure to tap into the power source He has given us. You can rest assured that whatever comes your way today, God has the resources to help you overcome it. Rather than looking at your problems and feeling insufficient, look to your Saviour and depend on His power.

Today's Discipleship Principle: If we are not operating in the power of the Holy Spirit, we will be not be able to meet the challenges of life.

Disappointing Jesus

*And Jesus answering said, O faithless and perverse generation, how long shall I be with you, and suffer you? Bring thy son hither. And as he was yet a coming, the devil threw him down, and tare him. And Jesus rebuked the unclean spirit, and healed the child, and delivered him again to his father.—*LUKE 9:41–42

When John Paton, the missionary to the New Hebrides islands was working to translate the Word of God into the language of the people he served, he wanted to be sure he conveyed the meaning accurately. As he was trying to come up with just the right word for *faith*, one of the native workers who had been converted and was helping Paton came into the house after a long day of toil and labor. Collapsing into a chair, he propped his feet up and declared how good it felt to sit down. When Paton heard him use his word that meant "lean your whole weight on," he realized he had found the best translation possible for *faith*.

When we do not lean our whole weight on what God has told us, we rob ourselves of power and blessing and the answers to prayer that we need. But there is more. We also rob those around us of the impact and influence we should have on their lives, depriving them of the help that they need. But there is still more. When we do not walk by faith, we disappoint the Lord. Refusing to believe His promises is an insult to His nature and character. Hebrews 11:6 tells us, "But without faith it is impossible to please him: for he that cometh to God must believe that he is, and that he is a rewarder of them that diligently seek him."

God has never broken a promise, yet all too often we listen to the voices of doubt and hesitate to act upon what God has told us in His Word. In truth, we can "lean our whole weight on" every word of promise God has ever given.

Today's Discipleship Principle: The Christian life can only be lived successfully as we walk by faith in what God has promised us.

Why We Do Not Hear from God

And they were all amazed at the mighty power of God. But while they wondered every one at all things which Jesus did, he said unto his disciples, Let these sayings sink down into your ears: for the Son of man shall be delivered into the hands of men. But they understood not this saying, and it was hid from them, that they perceived it not: and they feared to ask him of that saying.—LUKE 9:43–45

James Hamilton in his book *Directions* told a story from the days before refrigerators when icehouses furnished the means of cooling food in the summer months. Thick blocks of ice were cut from ponds and lakes and stored in buildings with thick walls, and covered with layers of sawdust to slow the melting process. Hamilton wrote: "One man lost a valuable watch while working in an ice house. He searched diligently for it, carefully raking through the sawdust, but didn't find it. His fellow workers also looked, but their efforts, too, proved futile. A small boy who heard about the fruitless search slipped into the icehouse during the noon hour and soon emerged with the watch. Amazed, the men asked him how he found it. 'I closed the door,' the boy replied, 'lay down in the sawdust, and kept very still. Soon I heard the watch ticking.'"

I find it instructive that Jesus needed to tell the disciples to listen and pay attention to what He said. You would think that having the Messiah with them would be enough to grab their focus, but the reality is that they—just as is often true of us—had other things on their minds than what Jesus was saying. We have been given the Word of God and the Holy Spirit, yet too often we ignore or forget what God has told us and seek some other kind of guidance for our daily lives. We should instead follow Christ's instructions to "Let these sayings sing down into your ears."

Today's Discipleship Principle: God's still, small voice can easily be drowned out by the world if we do not listen intently for Him.

Putting Down Pride

Then there arose a reasoning among them, which of them should be greatest. And Jesus, perceiving the thought of their heart, took a child, and set him by him, And said unto them, Whosoever shall receive this child in my name receiveth me: and whosoever shall receive me receiveth him that sent me: for he that is least among you all, the same shall be great.—LUKE 9:46–48

An English pastor of the 1700s, James Hervey, recounted a conversation that he had with a faithful layman in his church that gave him a new appreciation for the dangers of pride to the Christian life. They were talking about the things that hinder spiritual growth, and at one point Hervey said, "I believe the difficulty is our reluctance to renounce our sinful self." The old farmer looked at him for a few moments and then replied, "No, I believe the greatest difficulty is to renounce our righteous self."

We easily give in to the temptation of pride because it is such a comforting sin. There are many worldly activities that leave us filled with guilt if we indulge them, but the sin of pride soothes and uplifts us. It is, of course, a false comfort, but so often we fail to recognize that root of pride has taken hold in our heart, and has led us to think of ourselves more highly than we should. Again and again the disciples had a conflict over which of them would have the most important role in God's work. And again and again, Jesus instructed them in humility and service.

God is not interested in our high opinion of ourselves, for He knows us as we really are. If we insist on our honor and glory, we forfeit our access to His grace and He holds us at arm's-length. James wrote, "But he giveth more grace. Wherefore he saith, God resisteth the proud, but giveth grace unto the humble" (James 4:6). The only way to receive God's grace is to acknowledge that we are not deserving of it.

Today's Discipleship Principle: If we seek to make ourselves great, we will fail to receive the grace we need for victorious living.

Committed to the Cause

And it came to pass, when the time was come that he should be received up, he stedfastly set his face to go to Jerusalem, And sent messengers before his face: and they went, and entered into a village of the Samaritans, to make ready for him. And they did not receive him, because his face was as though he would go to Jerusalem. —LUKE 9:51–53

One of only twelve men to walk on the moon, Apollo 15's Colonel James Irwin, was a committed Christian. When he retired from NASA, he established the High Flight Foundation and traveled the world telling people about Jesus. Irwin could have been proud of his achievement, but instead he dedicated himself to service. He said, "As I was returning to earth I realized I was a servant, not a celebrity. So I'm here as God's servant on planet Earth to share what I've experienced that others might know the glory of God."

The Christian life requires commitment. We live in a day of people dabbling in this and toying with that before taking something else up as a hobby to divert their attention still further. The ministry of Jesus Christ was powerful in large part because it was focused. Jesus knew what was important, and He did not allow other things to get in the way of what God wanted Him to do on any particular day.

If we only do what is easy, we will not get much done. Pressures, obstacles, and setbacks are not necessarily a sign that we have strayed from God's purpose; often, they are the devil trying to derail us. But if every time we encounter an obstacle, we go a different direction, we won't make continued progress for the cause of Christ. If, however, we follow the example of Jesus, we will stay on task and hold fast to our commitment to do the will of the Father. If we want to succeed in His work, then we must "set our face" and keep moving forward.

Today's Discipleship Principle: If we are going to accomplish anything of value for God, we must be committed to follow it through to the end.

Compassion or Contempt?

And when his disciples James and John saw this, they said, Lord, wilt thou that we command fire to come down from heaven, and consume them, even as Elias did? But he turned, and rebuked them, and said, Ye know not what manner of spirit ye are of. For the Son of man is not come to destroy men's lives, but to save them. And they went to another village.—LUKE 9:54–56

Sometimes we find it hard to love people as we should. If they just weren't so troublesome, it would be a lot easier. There was a news report about an eight-year-old boy named Zachary who saved the life of his six-year-old sister Meghan. She was sucking on a piece of candy and it got stuck in her throat and she couldn't breathe. Zachary performed the Heimlich maneuver on her, just as he had seen it done on television. When a reporter visited to interview the young hero, he asked the boy what it felt like to have saved his sister's life. "I wouldn't do it again," Zachary said. "She's been a pain this week."

In Jesus' day, there was no love lost between the Jews and the Samaritans. Even Jesus' disciples held this cultural prejudice. When Jesus passed through without being welcomed, James and John wanted to see him destroy the Samaritans by fire from Heaven. But James and John had a complete misunderstanding of the point of Jesus' ministry. Jesus will eventually return to earth as a Judge, and there will be fire and judgment awaiting those who have rejected Him. But today the door of grace and salvation is still open.

There are many enemies of Christ and the gospel in our world today. But rather than cheering for their destruction, we should be praying for their deliverance. Compassion should be the over-arching emotion in our hearts, even toward those who oppose all that we believe.

Today's Discipleship Principle: When we treat even our enemies with kindness and compassion, we are truly living as Jesus did.

Selfless Living in a "Selfie" World

And it came to pass, that, as they went in the way, a certain man said unto him, Lord, I will follow thee whithersoever thou goest. And Jesus said unto him, Foxes have holes, and birds of the air have nests; but the Son of man hath not where to lay his head.—LUKE 9:57–58

Each year the *Oxford English Dictionary* selects a Word of the Year as a way of recognizing a new word that has entered the language and made an impact. In a rare decision, 2013 saw the unanimous selection of "selfie" as the Word of the Year. The ubiquitous smart phones with their cameras have sparked a craze of self-portraits. The *Oxford English Dictionary* publishers released a statement saying, "It seems everyone has posted a selfie somewhere on the Internet." There are few more apt metaphors for our society—including within much of the church—than our obsession with placing ourselves in the center of the picture.

The example of Jesus is different. While He deserves all the glory of the universe, He willingly gave up not just immeasurable riches but even basic comforts and necessities to follow the will of His Father in Heaven. How tightly we cling to our rights and privileges, and how unfair we think it is when things don't go exactly as we think they should! Our response to disruption in our plans and schedules says so much about who is in charge of our lives.

Henry Drummond said, "The entrance fee into the kingdom of heaven is nothing: the annual subscription is everything." Those who would follow Jesus must first count the cost and determine if they are willing to pay the price of selfless living. The footsteps of Jesus will not lead us to a path of ease. And if we are focused on what makes us happy and comfortable, we will find His path too hard to keep walking.

Today's Discipleship Principle: The only way to follow Jesus is to focus on Him rather than on ourselves.

Giving Up Everything for Jesus

And he said unto another, Follow me. But he said, Lord, suffer me first to go and bury my father. Jesus said unto him, Let the dead bury their dead: but go thou and preach the kingdom of God. And another also said, Lord, I will follow thee; but let me first go bid them farewell, which are at home at my house. And Jesus said unto him, No man, having put his hand to the plough, and looking back, is fit for the kingdom of God.
—LUKE 9:59–62

Though he was saved as a teenager, Charles Studd did little for the Lord until he went to hear D. L. Moody preach. The evangelist's fervor for the lost stirred something within his heart and he became a fervent soul winner. After surrendering to go to the mission field, Studd gave away his massive inheritance, much of it to George Müller's orphanage, and spent the rest of his life as a missionary in China, India, and Africa. One of C. T. Studd's most remembered quotes is, "If Jesus Christ be God and died for me, then no sacrifice can be too great for me to make for Him."

There is no way we can fully comprehend the sacrifices Jesus Christ made for our salvation. Leaving Heaven filled with the praises of angels and laying aside His glory to take on the limited body of a man, Jesus valued our redemption more than His privileges. He took our sins upon Himself and endured the separation from His Father on the cross, which was far worse than the physical suffering He experienced. Having done all that, He freely offers salvation to all who believe without any qualifications or merit.

How, then, could we possibly think any demand He makes of us is too great? Given what we deserve, we should already be suffering the torments of Hell; instead, we have eternal life. When He calls us to do that which we think of as a sacrifice, whether it be large or small, our heart should be one of total surrender and complete eagerness to obey.

Today's Discipleship Principle: Those who are not willing to give up what they hold most dear are not prepared to follow Jesus.

Praying for the Harvest

*After these things the Lord appointed other seventy also, and sent them two and two before his face into every city and place, whither he himself would come. Therefore said he unto them, The harvest truly is great, but the labourers are few: pray ye therefore the Lord of the harvest, that he would send forth labourers into his harvest—*LUKE 10:1–2

In 1792, largely because of the efforts of William Carey, churches in England united together and formed the Particular Baptist Society with the stated purpose of "Propagating the Gospel among the Heathen" and appointed Carey and John Thomas to go to India as their first missionaries. In a tearful prayer service as they prepared to leave, those who remained behind promised to pray. Andrew Fuller later described their parting with the analogy of miners going deep underground secured by those on the surface holding fast to strong ropes. Fuller said, "Before [Carey] went, we engaged that while he lived we should never let go the rope."

There are many good and necessary things that are part of reaching the lost, but the thing Jesus said should come first is our prayers. In a day when more missionaries are coming home than going out and many are leaving full time ministry, we need to be more faithful than ever to pray that God will provide the workers to bring in the harvest.

Often we focus on programs, training, and materials, and all of those have their place. But sometimes we fail to see the needs of workers for the harvest met because we have failed to pray. The need for workers is certainly not limited to foreign missions. There are many places in our own countries that lack a clear gospel witness.

It should break our hearts and drive us to our knees to think of the harvest lacking workers. And while we pray, we should ask God to make us part of the solution.

Today's Discipleship Principle: Before the white fields of harvest can be reached, we must be faithful to pray.

Believing God's Provision

Go your ways: behold, I send you forth as lambs among wolves. Carry neither purse, nor scrip, nor shoes: and salute no man by the way. And into whatsoever house ye enter, first say, Peace be to this house. And if the son of peace be there, your peace shall rest upon it: if not, it shall turn to you again.—LUKE 10:3–6

David Brainerd often endured great hardship in his efforts to take the gospel to the American Indians. In his diary, he recounted one mission trip during which an intense storm forced him to seek shelter inside the hollowed out remains of a large tree. As the storm raged outside, Brainerd sat inside praying for the lost. After a while, he began to be hungry, but it was too dangerous to go out to look for something to eat. Soon a squirrel came and deposited several nuts near where Brainerd sat. Brainerd wrote that as he ate the nuts, he realized that God had sent the squirrel just as He sent the ravens to feed Elijah.

The Lord's promises to provide for our needs are repeated over and over in Scripture. There is no shortage of resources on His part. He is just as able to meet our needs as He was to work in the lives of Abraham, Moses, David, Peter, and Paul. There is nothing we face that will challenge God in the slightest. He never has to call for backup or dig down deep into His reserves to provide anything that we need.

In addition to having everything at His disposal, God has repeatedly told us that He loves *us*—personally. He wants us to have good things to enjoy in our lives. Yet despite these truths, too often we focus on making it on our own, hoping to handle things ourselves without resorting to His help.

You and I serve a God who loves us and promises to provide for us. It is foolish and tragic, then, for us to live like orphans—never turning to our Heavenly Father in prayer or trusting in His provision.

Today's Discipleship Principle: If we truly believe the promises of God, it will change the way we approach every part of our lives.

Practicing Contentment

And in the same house remain, eating and drinking such things as they give: for the labourer is worthy of his hire. Go not from house to house. And into whatsoever city ye enter, and they receive you, eat such things as are set before you: And heal the sick that are therein, and say unto them, The kingdom of God is come nigh unto you.—LUKE 10:7–9

Though she lost her eyesight as an infant, Fanny Crosby used the gifts and abilities she had rather than spending her life wishing for what she lacked. She wrote her first poem at the age of eight:

> O what a happy soul am I!
> Although I cannot see,
> I am resolved that in this world
> Contented I will be;
> How many blessings I enjoy
> That other people don't!
> To weep and sigh because I'm blind,
> I cannot, and I won't.

Fanny went on to write the words to more than eight thousand hymns and devoted her life to helping and encouraging others.

The secret of contentment is not found in our possessions or our comfort, but in our attitude. There are many with vast wealth who are not content, and there are many with very little wealth who are. Contentment only comes from within. If we are constantly grasping for more and better things, we are declaring we do not trust God to care for us.

From a prison cell in Rome, Paul wrote, "Not that I speak in respect of want: for I have learned, in whatsoever state I am, therewith to be content. I know both how to be abased, and I know how to abound: every where and in all things I am instructed both to be full and to be hungry, both to abound and to suffer need" (Philippians 4:11–12).

Today's Discipleship Principle: Contentment springs from a faith that God will never fail to give us everything we truly need.

Carrying God's Kingdom to the World

But into whatsoever city ye enter, and they receive you not, go your ways out into the streets of the same, and say, Even the very dust of your city, which cleaveth on us, we do wipe off against you: notwithstanding be ye sure of this, that the kingdom of God is come nigh unto you. But I say unto you, that it shall be more tolerable in that day for Sodom, than for that city.—LUKE 10:10–12

In 1942, Dr. Charles Weigel was in a revival meeting in California. He spent the afternoon between services visiting a large rose garden. He said that when he got to church that evening, people remarked on the smell of the roses that he carried with him when he left the garden. He had not gone to the rose garden for that purpose, but spending time there had an effect on his life and then, by extension, on others as well. Weigel wrote his song, "A Garden of Roses Is Jesus" after that experience.

When Jesus sent seventy of His followers out in teams to preach the gospel, they were to say that God's kingdom was coming to the towns and villages that they visited. That kingdom was not an earthly kingdom to have its power displayed by armies and military might; it was a heavenly kingdom whose power would be displayed by simple men who had believed and followed Jesus and as a result were like Him.

The world today is in desperate need of seeing Christians who bear the mark of those who have been influenced by their time spent with Jesus. This is how the disciples turned the world upside down: "Now when they saw the boldness of Peter and John, and perceived that they were unlearned and ignorant men, they marvelled; and they took knowledge of them, that they had been with Jesus" (Acts 4:13). The power of Jesus' presence is no less in our day, but sometimes our time spent with Him is.

Today's Discipleship Principle: Everyone with whom we come in contact should be able to tell that they have met a follower of Jesus Christ.

No Need for Repentance?

*Woe unto thee, Chorazin! woe unto thee, Bethsaida! for if the mighty works had been done in Tyre and Sidon, which have been done in you, they had a great while ago repented, sitting in sackcloth and ashes. But it shall be more tolerable for Tyre and Sidon at the judgment, than for you.—*LUKE 10:13–14

The little towns around the Sea of Galilee saw most of the miracles that Jesus performed during His life and ministry. Multitudes of sick people were healed, thousands were fed from one little boy's lunch, demons were cast out, and blind people received their sight. There was no shortage of miraculous evidence to support the claim that Jesus made to be the Son of God and to highlight the importance of His message of repentance and faith. Yet many of those who saw the greatest evidence refused to believe the message because they thought that they were fine the way they were and had no need for repentance.

The gap between the way we view ourselves and the way God views us is vast. The pride in our hearts convinces us that we are really not that bad (there is always someone we can find who is worse to make us feel better about our own failings), and thus there is no need to turn to God for help. Yet our self-righteousness is both built on a false foundation and is an offense to a completely holy God. He knows all that we conceal from those around us, and even from ourselves.

Many times Christians have an exalted view of themselves. We see this highlighted in the warning given to the church at Laodicea: "Because thou sayest, I am rich, and increased with goods, and have need of nothing; and knowest not that thou art wretched, and miserable, and poor, and blind, and naked" (Revelation 3:17). Even as Christians, there are many times when we need to come to the Lord in humble repentance and ask Him to cleanse us of our pride.

Today's Discipleship Principle: When we see ourselves as God sees us, pride flees, and we recognize our need for His grace.

Pride and Humility

And thou, Capernaum, which art exalted to heaven, shalt be thrust down to hell. He that heareth you heareth me; and he that despiseth you despiseth me; and he that despiseth me despiseth him that sent me.
—LUKE 10:15–16

Though both George Whitefield and John Wesley were greatly used in the revival known as the Great Awakening, they had significant theological differences. As the story goes, when Wesley went to the memorial service for George Whitefield after the evangelist's death, he was confronted by a lady who agreed with Whitefield on those theological points and asked, "Mr. Wesley, do you think you shall see Mr. Whitefield in Heaven?" Wesley replied, "No." Thinking that he was referring to their disagreements, the lady said, "I was afraid you would say that." Then Wesley explained, "George Whitefield will be so near the throne of God, that men like me will never catch a glimpse of him."

How easily we yield to the temptation of pride. How quickly we forget that God *hates* pride. It is not by accident that on the list of sins that God hates, pride takes first place. "These six things doth the LORD hate: yea, seven are an abomination unto him: A proud look..." (Proverbs 6:16–17). It is part of our sinful nature to want to be exalted, but God will not tolerate pride in our hearts.

When our family traveled to Israel, we visited the ruins of the once thriving and prosperous city of Capernaum. Just as Jesus prophesied, the city that exalted itself and refused to listen to Him was brought low. The same holds true for every individual who chooses the path of pride over the way of humility—destruction always follows. The judgment of God is nothing to be trifled with. Instead we should view pride as God does and stamp out every appearance that it makes in our lives.

Today's Discipleship Principle: Only as we humble ourselves do we receive the grace of God for victory in our daily lives.

Why Rejoice?

And the seventy returned again with joy, saying, Lord, even the devils are subject unto us through thy name. And he said unto them, I beheld Satan as lightning fall from heaven. Behold, I give unto you power to tread on serpents and scorpions, and over all the power of the enemy: and nothing shall by any means hurt you. Notwithstanding in this rejoice not, that the spirits are subject unto you; but rather rejoice, because your names are written in heaven.—LUKE 10:17–20

When the disciples rejoiced at the victories they had seen in their work, Jesus pointed out to them that they were rejoicing in the wrong thing. The great reason we have for joy in our lives is not found in this world but in the next. Because of the gift of salvation we have received, we have the hope of eternal life that can never be taken away.

Matthew Henry said, "Joy and peace as believers arises chiefly from our hopes. What is laid out upon us is but little, compared with what is laid up for us (in glory); therefore the more hope we have the more joy and peace we have."

Victories in this world are good, but at best they are only temporary. Each sick person Jesus or the disciples healed still eventually died. But each person who heard and received the gospel received eternal life that could never be taken away. The main reason for our rejoicing should not be the short-term blessings we receive in this world. We should be thankful and give God praise when we see Him at work in our lives, but we must maintain our focus on the great gift of salvation.

Any temporal blessing we receive has a limited impact on our lives. But our names are written in Heaven forever, and our eternal destiny has already been sealed by God. This gives us cause to rejoice that is greater than any fleeting victory or benefit. And it gives us cause to rejoice that is longer than any earthly joy.

Today's Discipleship Principle: One of the biggest reasons for a lack of joy is a focus on this world rather than on eternity.

Hidden from the Wise

*In that hour Jesus rejoiced in spirit, and said, I thank thee, O Father, Lord of heaven and earth, that thou hast hid these things from the wise and prudent, and hast revealed them unto babes: even so, Father; for so it seemed good in thy sight. All things are delivered to me of my Father: and no man knoweth who the Son is, but the Father; and who the Father is, but the Son, and he to whom the Son will reveal him—*LUKE 10:21–22

On his twenty-fifth birthday, Ford Porter prayed, "Oh God, give me a ministry that will reach souls for Christ, encircle the world, and be carried on long after I am gone." In 1933, Porter wrote a tract called "God's Simple Plan of Salvation" that has been used around the world in many languages. To date, over half a *billion* of these tracts have been distributed, all with the message that God's plan of salvation is by grace through faith without anything else.

No one gets saved on the strength of their intellect or reasoning. No one gets saved on the basis of their merit or worth. Everyone who comes to God for salvation must come in simple faith, believing the promises of our Heavenly Father just as a child believes the promises of his earthly father. There is no other way of salvation, and those who insist on doing it according to their own wisdom find the only true door to Heaven hidden from their sight.

Those of us who have received the gift of eternal life have also received the command to take the good news to others. When we lay aside our self-reliance and rely instead on the power of God, our witnessing becomes effective. God has devised both the plan for our salvation and the plan for people to hear it, and we must follow it. Both salvation and God's plan to make it known are simple. We receive the gift of salvation by faith, and we are to make it known with humble dependance on the Holy Spirit.

Today's Discipleship Principle: Having received the gift of salvation through God's grace, we have the privilege of sharing it with others.

A Blessing Ignored?

And he turned him unto his disciples, and said privately, Blessed are the
eyes which see the things that ye see: For I tell you, that many prophets
and kings have desired to see those things which ye see, and have not seen
them; and to hear those things which ye hear, and have not heard them.
—LUKE 10:23-24

For much of history in many parts of the world, the Word of God was only available on a limited basis. Even today there are groups of people who do not have the Bible available in their own language. Yet in our nation with the Scriptures in bookstores, online, on mobile devices, and easy to find, far too many Christians ignore the blessing of the Bible, rarely reading and heeding what it says. King George V of England once wrote, "It is my confident hope that my subjects will never cease to cherish their noble inheritance in the English Bible, which is the first of national treasures. Its spiritual significance is the most valuable thing the world affords."

The wisdom of God that is meant to guide and direct our lives is found in the pages of the Bible. King Artaxerxes told Ezra, "And thou, Ezra, after the wisdom of thy God, that is in thine hand, set magistrates and judges, which may judge all the people that are beyond the river, all such as know the laws of thy God; and teach ye them that know them not" (Ezra 7:25). When we open that blessed Book, we hold in our hands what God has revealed.

It is sad not to have a copy of the Bible, but it is tragic to have the very Word of God and ignore it. If we do not know what God has decreed, or if we are not willing to do as He says, there is no possibility that we will walk in a way that is pleasing to Him. There are people around the world who have never heard the Word of God and Christians around the world who would love to have their own copy. May we who have it not ignore it.

Today's Discipleship Principle: It is tragic for God's children not to fill their hearts and minds with His Word to guide their daily lives.

Dealing with Sin

And, behold, a certain lawyer stood up, and tempted him, saying, Master, what shall I do to inherit eternal life? He said unto him, What is written in the law? how readest thou? And he answering said, Thou shalt love the Lord thy God with all thy heart, and with all thy soul, and with all thy strength, and with all thy mind; and thy neighbour as thyself. And he said unto him, Thou hast answered right: this do, and thou shalt live.
—LUKE 10:25–28

In 1944, during a massive storm, the *SS Richard Montgomery,* a ship loaded with thousands of tons of aerial fragmentation bombs, broke up and sank not far from the English coast. Despite the danger posed by the unexploded ordinance, the decision was made to leave it in place for fear of setting off a massive explosion. It would be more dangerous to try to remove the bombs than it was to leave them in place. For more than seventy years, the wreckage of that ship has been home to a lethal danger.

Every human being is born with a lethal danger within—a sin nature that we inherit passed down from Adam. But we are not just sinners by nature. We are also sinners by choice. When presented with the opportunity to do right or wrong, our inclination is toward the evil rather than the good. And because of the punishment for sin that God has decreed, our sin problem requires a solution. We cannot just hope it sinks out of sight under the water and stays there.

Sin must be dealt with, but we have no way to do that. The very best that we can do falls short of the perfection God demands. No one, other than Jesus Himself, has perfectly obeyed the two great commandments— to wholly love God and perfectly love others.

But because Jesus fulfilled the law and died in our stead, we can receive salvation through Him. It is only by accepting His sacrifice on our behalf that we can have salvation.

Today's Discipleship Principle: There is no hope for us to deal with sin, unless we accept the provision God has made for salvation.

2 Samuel 16–18   //   Luke 17:20–37

How to Make Things Right with God

But he, willing to justify himself, said unto Jesus, And who is my neighbour?—LUKE 10:29

The man whose question sparked perhaps the most famous of all of Jesus' parables—the story of the Good Samaritan—was not asking out of a sincere desire to know the truth. Instead, the Bible reveals that his motive was to make himself look better. So often we yield to the temptation to justify ourselves, thinking we (unlike others around us) are doing pretty good before God.

I read about a children's Sunday school teacher who taught her pupils from the parable of the Pharisee and the publican praying in the Temple. When she finished her lesson she called on one of her students to pray. The little boy said, "God, thank You that I'm not like that Pharisee!"

If we set out to justify ourselves, we can always find a reason why what we have done is not as bad as others, or an excuse that will rationalize or explain away our behavior. But God doesn't grade on a curve. He does not compare us to what others are doing, but rather to the perfect standard of His Son. And He is not deceived by our attempts to make ourselves look better. He sees us as we really are, and He will not accept any attempt to avoid responsibility on our part.

The only hope we have is to abandon our efforts to justify ourselves and instead rest on the finished work of Jesus Christ. It is sufficient for everything that we lack, and because of grace we have already received God's stamp of approval: "To the praise of the glory of his grace, wherein he hath made us accepted in the beloved" (Ephesians 1:6). When in our pride and self confidence we attempt to make things right with God, we always fail.

Today's Discipleship Principle: Since God sees through all our excuses, we should humbly confess our sins rather than justifying ourselves.

Refusing to Help

And Jesus answering said, A certain man went down from Jerusalem to Jericho, and fell among thieves, which stripped him of his raiment, and wounded him, and departed, leaving him half dead. And by chance there came down a certain priest that way: and when he saw him, he passed by on the other side. And likewise a Levite, when he was at the place, came and looked on him, and passed by on the other side.—LUKE 10:30–32

In March of 1964, a young woman named Kitty Genovese was attacked on her way home from work in New York City. Though many people saw or heard at least part of the attack (various news reports and investigations put the number between thirty-six and forty-nine), no one intervened, and only a few people called the police. The attack was carried out over the space of half an hour, and it is quite likely that Genovese's death could have been prevented if only someone had been willing to intervene. But no one was willing to do what it took to save her life. One of the bystanders even admitted to a reporter, "I didn't want to get involved."

All around us there are people who are facing far worse than physical death. The lost have no hope of salvation unless someone loves and cares for them enough to reach out to them with the gospel. Yet too often, like the priest and the Levite in the parable Jesus told, those who should be the first to help find reasons not to do so.

We are not told what motivated those two men to cross to the other side of the road. Perhaps they feared for their safety, or perhaps they simply didn't want to get their hands dirty. But whatever the case, they failed to step up and answer the challenge of helping someone in desperate need. When the Holy Spirit prompts your heart to help someone, especially by sharing the gospel with them, do it right away. Don't be guilty of refusing to get involved in the work God has placed in your path.

Today's Discipleship Principle: If those of us who are saved do not do our part to reach them, the lost have no hope for eternity.

He Gave Himself

But a certain Samaritan, as he journeyed, came where he was: and when he saw him, he had compassion on him, And went to him, and bound up his wounds, pouring in oil and wine, and set him on his own beast, and brought him to an inn, and took care of him.—LUKE 10:33–34

There is an ancient Persian legend about a great ruler who loved to disguise himself and wander among his people unrecognized. One night, dressed as a beggar, Shah Abbas met a poor workman who invited him to share his meager food. As they talked, the shah was impressed with the man's attitude and character. Night after night he returned to meet with the worker, until at last he determined to reveal himself. When he told the man that he was the ruler of the entire land, he expected a request for wealth or promotion. But the poor worker replied, "You have left your palace and glory to sit with me in the dark and share my poverty. You have given me your presence, and even you can give nothing more precious."

Salvation is freely offered to all who believe, but it was certainly not free for Jesus. Like the Good Samaritan in the parable, Jesus gave up what was rightly His in order to rescue and deliver us. While Jesus hung on the cross, the Pharisees mocked Him saying, "He saved others; himself he cannot save. If he be the King of Israel, let him now come down from the cross, and we will believe him" (Matthew 27:42). Though they were intending to deride and mock Jesus, they unknowingly expressed a profound truth. Jesus faced the choice of saving Himself or saving us—He could not do both. And He chose to be the sacrifice for the sins of the world. Only the gift of the Saviour made it possible for us to receive salvation.

Never stop giving thanks to Christ for His incredible sacrifice. He did not *send* us what we needed to be saved; He *came* and gave Himself.

Today's Discipleship Principle: Jesus owed us nothing, yet in mercy and love He gave Himself to be the ransom for our sins.

Showing Mercy

And on the morrow when he departed, he took out two pence, and gave them to the host, and said unto him, Take care of him; and whatsoever thou spendest more, when I come again, I will repay thee. Which now of these three, thinkest thou, was neighbour unto him that fell among the thieves? And he said, He that shewed mercy on him. Then said Jesus unto him, Go, and do thou likewise.—LUKE 10:35–37

Ira Sankey, D.L. Moody's great song leader, told the story of a British actress who was saved in a most unusual way. As she walked down the street one day, she heard a group singing in preparation for a Bible study. The song stuck in her mind and her heart, and she finally went and got a hymn book that had the song in it and sang it over and over until she had learned it by heart. In just a few days she had given her heart to Christ. She no longer had any desire for her former profession, but at the urging of the theater manager, she agreed to take the stage one more time. But rather than singing one of the popular songs of the day, she began singing the hymn that had been instrumental in drawing her to Jesus:

"Depth of mercy can there be,

Mercy still reserved for me?"

Every one of us who are saved have been the recipients of God's mercy. In turn, He commands us to show mercy toward others—but often that is a difficult command to keep. Even as we rejoice in our own escape from God's wrath, we tend to want to see others get what is coming to them. But James warns us, "For he shall have judgment without mercy, that hath shewed no mercy; and mercy rejoiceth against judgment" (James 2:13).

A merciful heart rests on the foundation of undeserved forgiveness. It is only when we remember the greatness of what we have been given that our heart is tender enough to give to others.

Today's Discipleship Principle: We did not receive the mercy of God solely for ourselves, but so that we could share it with others.

Weighed Down and Burdened

Now it came to pass, as they went, that he entered into a certain village: and a certain woman named Martha received him into her house. And she had a sister called Mary, which also sat at Jesus' feet, and heard his word. But Martha was cumbered about much serving, and came to him, and said, Lord, dost thou not care that my sister hath left me to serve alone? bid her therefore that she help me.—LUKE 10:38–40

In her book *The Hiding Place*, Corrie ten Boom told the story of asking her father about something he didn't think she was old enough to understand. She wrote: "He turned to look at me, as he always did when answering a question, but to my surprise he said nothing. At last he stood up, lifted his traveling case off the floor and set it on the floor. 'Will you carry it off the train, Corrie?' he said. I stood up and tugged at it. It was crammed with the watches and spare parts he had purchased that morning. 'It's too heavy,' I said. 'Yes,' he said, 'and it would be a pretty poor father who would ask his little girl to carry such a load. It's the same way, Corrie, with knowledge. Some knowledge is too heavy for children. When you are older and stronger, you can bear it. For now you must trust me to carry it for you.'"

Many times the burdens that we carry are self-imposed. We find ourselves weighed down, not because of the responsibilities and obligations we have, but because we have taken on things we should not. A prime example of this kind of burden is worry. Sometimes it is even service when we are placing greater importance on what we do for God than spending time with God. But whatever the source of our burdens, we are invited to lay them down at Jesus' feet and stop carrying the weight. "Come unto me, all ye that labour and are heavy laden, and I will give you rest" (Matthew 11:29).

Today's Discipleship Principle: Do not allow yourself to be encumbered by burdens you were never meant to carry.

Ordering Our Priorities

And Jesus answered and said unto her, Martha, Martha, thou art careful and troubled about many things: But one thing is needful: and Mary hath chosen that good part, which shall not be taken away from her.
—LUKE 10:41–42

The story is told that one day a man went into the bookstore owned by Benjamin Franklin in Philadelphia. After looking around, he identified a book he wished to purchase, but when the clerk told him the book cost one dollar, he objected. "That price is too high. Ask your boss if he will lower it." The clerk went to get Franklin, who after hearing the man's request said, "The book costs one dollar and a quarter." The man protested that he had been told one dollar and asked again for the price. Franklin replied, "A dollar and a half." The man asked why the price kept increasing. Franklin said, "Do you not see that you are wasting my time? The price of the book was one dollar. But because you are wasting my time, the price of the book has to go up."

None of us has enough time to do everything that could be done or that we would like to do. Many times we are faced with a choice between two good things, only able to do one of them. The key to making good decisions and spending our lives wisely is to order our priorities so that the best of our time, energy, and resources are devoted to the things that truly matter. The noted management guru Peter Drucker pointed out that most people are so busy trying to do things right that they fail to stop and consider whether they are doing the right things. We must work to remain in control of our schedules, keeping our focus on doing what will matter for eternity rather than frittering away our lives on the temporal.

This was the lesson that Jesus sought to teach Martha when she complained that Mary was wasting time at Jesus' feet. In reality, Mary was investing her time in what matters most.

Today's Discipleship Principle: A major part of wise living consists of spending our time and resources on the things that really matter.

A Unique Request

And it came to pass, that, as he was praying in a certain place, when he ceased, one of his disciples said unto him, Lord, teach us to pray, as John also taught his disciples.—LUKE 11:1

D r. John Rice told a story about prayer that highlights a trap many of us fall into. When their oldest daughter Grace was a little girl, the custom of their family was to gather at the table and pray before their meal. Dr. Rice said that he noticed a peculiar trait in his daughter. Just before he would finish his praying, she would begin saying, "Amen, Amen." He then said, "As I thought, I realized that I was just saying the same words day after day, and she said 'Amen' because she knew I was almost finished." Prayer is not just a ritual featuring meaningless repetition of words we say with our eyes closed. Prayer is pouring out our hearts before God.

Though Jesus taught the disciples many things during the three years they shared together, the only thing recorded in Scripture that they asked Him to teach them was to pray. As they traveled and ministered across the land, they watched Jesus pray again and again. Early in the morning, throughout the day, and late at night, they saw Jesus seeking His Father's face, and eventually they asked Him for instruction in the matter of prayer.

One of the greatest tragedies of our day is the lack of prayer on the part of Christians. While many people wouldn't think of eating without praying and we routinely pray at the beginning of church services, Sunday school classes, and meetings, there is a great lack of serious, intense, and fervent prayer. We're often willing to go about our responsibilities and even attempt the work of God without prayer. The power and provision of God flow into our lives in response to our prayers. And if we have not prayed as we should, we should not be surprised to find ourselves lacking those things.

Today's Discipleship Principle: The Christian life requires serious, continual, habitual prayer as a foundation for all that we do.

may

A Pattern for Prayer

And he said unto them, When ye pray, say, Our Father which art in heaven, Hallowed be thy name. Thy kingdom come. Thy will be done, as in heaven, so in earth. Give us day by day our daily bread. And forgive us our sins; for we also forgive every one that is indebted to us. And lead us not into temptation; but deliver us from evil.—LUKE 11:2-4

I heard of a preacher who used the analogy of a boat coming up to a dock for prayer. He described the process of pulling on a rope that is moored to the dock, and he pointed out that the person on the boat is pulling on the rope, but he isn't moving the dock or the shore—he is moving the boat to align itself with the fixed point. In the same way, prayer requires that we surrender and submit ourselves and our will to God's will. We're not using prayer to change God's will, but prayer helps to change our hearts to His will. There is no legitimate prayer that does not begin with a commitment to God's will rather than our own.

It is not by accident that Jesus began His instruction on prayer with a focus on God and His will: "Thy kingdom come. Thy will be done, as in heaven, so in earth." Our tendency is to focus on ourselves. The problem is that our knowledge and understanding is limited. Many times the things we want most from God are the opposite of what we actually need. If we insist on having our way, we do not allow God to do the work He wants to do in and through us. There is nothing wrong with asking God for what we want, but there is a great deal wrong with demanding and insisting on having our way.

Jesus did not just teach this theoretically—He practiced it. In His moment of greatest need, He prayed just as He taught us to pray: "Saying, Father, if thou be willing, remove this cup from me: nevertheless not my will, but thine, be done" (Luke 22:42).

Today's Discipleship Principle: When we pray the way Jesus instructed, we are positioned for God to work great things in our lives.

Importunity

And he said unto them, Which of you shall have a friend, and shall go unto him at midnight, and say unto him, Friend, lend me three loaves; For a friend of mine in his journey is come to me, and I have nothing to set before him? And he from within shall answer and say, Trouble me not: the door is now shut, and my children are with me in bed; I cannot rise and give thee. I say unto you, Though he will not rise and give him, because he is his friend, yet because of his importunity he will rise and give him as many as he needeth.—LUKE 11:5–8

Speaking on the importance of not giving up in prayer, R.A. Torrey said, "I prayed fifteen long years for the conversion of my oldest brother. When he seemed to be getting farther and farther away from any hope of conversion, I prayed on. My first winter in Chicago, after fifteen years of praying, never missing a single day, one morning God said to me as I knelt, 'I have heard your prayer.' Within two weeks he was in my home, shut in with sickness which made it impossible for him to leave my home for two weeks. Then the day he left, he accepted Christ over in the Bible Institute in Mr. Moody's office, where he and I went to talk and pray together."

The Lord could answer our prayers that are in line with His will immediately, and sometimes He does just that. But often we must pray over and over, sometimes even for years, before the answer arrives. This is not because God does not love us or because He does not hear our prayers the first time, but because He knows our need for character and consistency. When we continue to trust Him and pray faithfully even though we do not see Him at work, it strengthens our walk and our relationship with Him. When you do not see an answer to your prayers immediately, don't give up. Take a lesson from the friend in Jesus' parable, and continue praying with importunity.

Today's Discipleship Principle: Many of our prayers are not answered simply because we give up before the answer comes.

Asking, Seeking, and Knocking

And I say unto you, Ask, and it shall be given you; seek, and ye shall find; knock, and it shall be opened unto you. For every one that asketh receiveth; and he that seeketh findeth; and to him that knocketh it shall be opened.—LUKE 11:9–10

The Bible frequently uses the lives of Old Testament characters to teach and illustrate a New Testament truth. When it comes to the topic of being serious about our prayers, the prophet Elijah is given to us as an example. He was called to minister in a time of great spiritual darkness in the land. Under the wicked rule of Ahab and Jezebel, the people had turned away from God and were worshiping Baal. As a result, Elijah pronounced a judgment from God—a judgment that came in response to the prayers of the prophet.

Although we tend to think of the answers to Elijah's prayers as being exceptional, James 5:17 emphasizes that Elijah was a man just like us— with the same struggles we face. Yet he was faithful in earnest prayer, and it made a difference. "Elias was a man subject to like passions as we are, and he prayed earnestly that it might not rain: and it rained not on the earth by the space of three years and six months" (James 5:17).

Earnest praying is like asking, seeking, and knocking—you don't do it once and give up; you keep at it. It is not always asking once that gets the answer, but continued asking. It is not always seeking once that finds, but continued seeking. It is not always knocking once that gets the door opened, but continued knocking. Many times our prayers fail to be answered, not because we are asking for the wrong things, but because we stop praying. When our faith is not immediately rewarded with an answer, it is not time to give up on God and on our prayer, but to keep on praying until the answer comes.

Today's Discipleship Principle: Unless God clearly closes a door and leads you in a different direction, never give up on your prayers.

Trusting God's Love for Us

If a son shall ask bread of any of you that is a father, will he give him a stone? or if he ask a fish, will he for a fish give him a serpent? Or if he shall ask an egg, will he offer him a scorpion? If ye then, being evil, know how to give good gifts unto your children: how much more shall your heavenly Father give the Holy Spirit to them that ask him?—LUKE 11:11–13

The evangelist J. Wilbur Chapman told of a man who had been converted in one of his meetings who gave a wonderful illustration of God's love for us. The man had left home long before, turning his back on his family and the God they loved. His path led downward until he ended up as a beggar on the streets. The man said that he was begging at the Philadelphia train depot when he touched a man on the shoulder and asked for a dime. It was his own father, who seeing his son, cried out, "I have found you. I have found you! All that I have is yours." He said, "I stood there a tramp, begging my father for ten cents when for eighteen years he had been looking for me to give me all he was worth."

We did not get saved because we were worthy, but because God loved us enough to provide salvation for us through the sacrifice of His Son. And not only does He save us, but He places us in His family and gives us access to all of the privileges and benefits that come with being a child of God.

We do not come to God as a pauper imploring an uninterested prince for leftovers, but as a beloved child asking our Heavenly Father for what He delights to give us. Furthermore, we don't have to fear that we will ask for too much and anger God or that He will retaliate and give us something harmful. We ask in complete confidence that He loves us and will give us the absolute best thing for us. As our Heavenly Father, God delights to bless us in answer to our prayers.

Today's Discipleship Principle: Faith rests on the foundation of God's love for us—He will never abandon His children.

Rejecting God

And he was casting out a devil, and it was dumb. And it came to pass, when the devil was gone out, the dumb spake; and the people wondered. But some of them said, He casteth out devils through Beelzebub the chief of the devils.—LUKE 11:14–15

Despite all the evidence available from astronomy, the space program and history, the Flat Earth Society still exists, claiming hundreds of members. The group, which traces its roots back to the 1800s continues to promote the flat disk model of the earth that posits a world ringed by a wall of ice. No matter how many astronauts they talk to, no matter how many moon rocks they see, no matter how many pictures taken from space they are shown, they deny the reality in favor of clinging to their beliefs.

While we may be amused by people who believe the world is flat, many people in our world take the same approach to God—insisting that He does not exist, even though there is no shortage of evidence to the contrary. The very creation around us speaks to the need for a Creator. But people realize that acknowledging creation requires an accountability, so instead they cling to anything else, no matter how far-fetched it may be, rather than admitting that God is real.

This is not a new thing. Peter dealt with people who refused to acknowledge God: "For this they willingly are ignorant of, that by the word of God the heavens were of old, and the earth standing out of the water and in the water" (2 Peter 3:5). To be willingly ignorant is preferable to these people than admitting the existence of God and facing the fact that they will one day stand before Him and be judged.

As Christians, however, we have experienced the reality of God at work in our lives, and we should be not just telling but also showing those around us that He is real.

Today's Discipleship Principle: God is real whether people acknowledge Him or not, and our lives should give testimony to His work.

Unity in God's Family

And others, tempting him, sought of him a sign from heaven. But he, knowing their thoughts, said unto them, Every kingdom divided against itself is brought to desolation; and a house divided against a house falleth. If Satan also be divided against himself, how shall his kingdom stand? because ye say that I cast out devils through Beelzebub.—LUKE 11:16–18

In 1858, accepting his nomination as a candidate for the U.S. Senate, Abraham Lincoln sounded a theme that two years later would see him elected to the White House—the pressing need for national unity. Lincoln said, "'A house divided against itself cannot stand.' I believe this government cannot endure, permanently half slave and half free. I do not expect the Union to be dissolved—I do not expect the house to fall—but I do expect it will cease to be divided. It will become all one thing or all the other."

What is true for nations is true for churches and families as well. If we allow ourselves to be divided, the future is dark. While we may limp along for a little while, eventually the foundations will be undermined, and the church or family will fall. Knowing this truth, we must recognize that a large part of the reason for divisions between people in God's family who should be getting along is that we are not willing to put forth the effort and invest the work required to keep unity intact.

One of the strongest of all the New Testament churches was the church at Ephesus. And one of the primary reasons for their effectiveness was that they followed the admonition of Paul to keep their unity intact: "Endeavouring to keep the unity of the Spirit in the bond of peace" (Ephesians 4:3). The word used here for *endeavouring* is the Greek word for diligent exertion—serious, continued, careful effort put forth over a period of time. Since we know that a house divided cannot stand, we should be diligent in working to keep unity.

Today's Discipleship Principle: Unity does not just happen—it requires our investment and sacrifice, but it is worth it.

The Strength to Overcome

*But if I with the finger of God cast out devils, no doubt the kingdom of God is come upon you. When a strong man armed keepeth his palace, his goods are in peace: But when a stronger than he shall come upon him, and overcome him, he taketh from him all his armour wherein he trusted, and divideth his spoils. He that is not with me is against me: and he that gathereth not with me scattereth.—*LUKE 11:20-23

Satan completed and utterly defeated man, starting in the Garden of Eden and continuing throughout all of human history. He rules over the world with a power that the greatest dictators of history have never come close to attaining. Yet for all of his strength, his power and authority were destroyed by the Saviour who was even stronger. And that destruction was brought about by the very thing that appeared to be Satan's moment of greatest triumph—the death of Jesus Christ on the cross. Jesus was not overcome by Satan. He willingly laid down His life as part of God's plan for victory. And He forever defeated sin and the grave.

All of Satan's power was nothing compared to that of Jesus. He is the complete sum of power, and His appearance as the Lamb of God was only a facet of His nature. He is also the conquered Lion of Judah.

Revelation 5:5–6 gives us a glimpse into Heaven where we see Jesus as the overcoming Lion: "And one of the elders saith unto me, Weep not: behold, the Lion of the tribe of Juda, the Root of David, hath prevailed to open the book, and to loose the seven seals thereof. And I beheld, and, lo, in the midst of the throne and of the four beasts, and in the midst of the elders, stood a Lamb as it had been slain, having seven horns and seven eyes, which are the seven Spirits of God sent forth into all the earth."

Sometimes we look at our weakness and feel discouraged. The truth is, we *are* weaker than Satan. But it is also true that our God is greater!

Today's Discipleship Principle: Though we cannot defeat Satan in our strength, we have the strength of the Lion of Judah on our side

The Necessity of Replacement

When the unclean spirit is gone out of a man, he walketh through dry places, seeking rest; and finding none, he saith, I will return unto my house whence I came out. And when he cometh, he findeth it swept and garnished. Then goeth he, and taketh to him seven other spirits more wicked than himself; and they enter in, and dwell there: and the last state of that man is worse than the first.—LUKE 11:24-26

Any one who has done gardening knows the importance of getting the ground ready before you plant. If you simply chop holes into a grassy field and plant some seeds, your harvest is going to be puny—if there is any production at all. Instead you have to break up the ground, take out any rocks, and remove any weeds.

As important as preparing the ground is, however, this is not the only step. In fact, if you stop here, you still won't have a harvest. If you till and prepare the ground but then walk away and leave it, you will have a bumper crop of weeds. They will move right in and take over the whole plot. That is because it is just as important that you put in the seeds. If there are no seeds, there will be no harvest.

Our lives operate in the same manner. While it is right and important to remove sin, it is not enough. We must replace the bad with something good or eventually things will be worse than they were when we started.

This is true in every part of life. It is true for our habits. A vital part of breaking a bad habit is replacing it with a good one. That is the greatest protection against slipping back into our old ways. It is easy for us to focus only on the negative things that we need to avoid and lose sight of the positive things we need to be cultivating. Instead we need to be focused on putting good things in the place of the bad ones.

Thankfully, the Holy Spirit is willing to fill our lives with His presence and power (Ephesians 5:18). He requires, however, that we yield to Him.

Today's Discipleship Principle: If your life is filled with the Spirit of God, the devil will find he has little room to operate.

The Sign of Jonah

And when the people were gathered thick together, he began to say, This is an evil generation: they seek a sign; and there shall no sign be given it, but the sign of Jonas the prophet. For as Jonas was a sign unto the Ninevites, so shall also the Son of man be to this generation.—LUKE 11:29–30

The popular conception of the life and ministry of Jesus in the world today is of a kind teacher who set a good moral example for people. While He certainly was that, this view only captures a small part of His purpose and ministry. Jesus clearly and repeatedly proclaimed that judgment was coming. Jonah was sent to the city of Nineveh with the message that God's judgment was about to fall. So when Jesus referenced Jonah as a sign, His hearers understood that this was a warning to the people who refused to believe what He preached of impending judgment.

The fact that God has not yet brought destruction on the world is not evidence that judgment is not warranted or that it is not coming. It is evidence that God is gracious and merciful. The reality that so many in our day are trying to avoid is that one day each person will give account of himself to God. There will be no excuses, no passing of responsibility, or shifting of blame. The God who sees and knows everything will sit in judgment, and all will be brought before Him.

The reality of coming judgment should inspire and motivate us to be diligent in our efforts to reach people while there is still time. As the Apostle Paul, who fully invested his life in making the gospel known, wrote, "Knowing therefore the terror of the Lord, we persuade men; but we are made manifest unto God; and I trust also are made manifest in your consciences" (2 Corinthians 5:11).

The only hope the people of Nineveh had was in the warning that Jonah reluctantly delivered to them. Our world today needs to hear from us before it is too late.

Today's Discipleship Principle: Like Jonah, we are tasked to sound the alarm regarding the coming judgment of God on sin.

Let Your Light Shine

No man, when he hath lighted a candle, putteth it in a secret place, neither under a bushel, but on a candlestick, that they which come in may see the light. The light of the body is the eye: therefore when thine eye is single, thy whole body also is full of light; but when thine eye is evil, thy body also is full of darkness. Take heed therefore that the light which is in thee be not darkness.—LUKE 11:33–35

As a young boy growing up in Edinburgh, Scotland, Robert Louis Stevenson was fascinated with lights. Themes of light and dark would find frequent mention in his literary works. This fascination is probably understandable given that his father, two of his uncles, and his grandfather all worked in lighthouse design and construction.

One night Stevenson was watching a man who walked along the street to light the gas lights that illuminated the neighborhood through the night. He had a flame on a long pole, and one by one he lit the lamps along the sidewalk. Stevenson called out to his mother, "Come see the man poking holes in the darkness."

When we trusted Christ as our Saviour, we turned "from darkness to light, and from the power of Satan unto God" (Acts 26:18). But we still live in a dark world. The difference is that now we have the light everyone around us so desperately needs. God did not light us with His love and grace to hide us, but to set us on a candlestick to show the world what happens when someone trusts Him for salvation.

Although there is great darkness around us today, the great problem is not that the darkness is so great, but that our lights are so feeble and often hidden from the world. We need a return to the days when God's people put their faith on clear and unmistakable display, and spend their lives poking holes in the darkness.

Today's Discipleship Principle: If we do not shine as lights in the dark, the world has no other way to see the truth.

Clean from the Inside Out

And as he spake, a certain Pharisee besought him to dine with him: and he went in, and sat down to meat. And when the Pharisee saw it, he marvelled that he had not first washed before dinner. And the Lord said unto him, Now do ye Pharisees make clean the outside of the cup and the platter; but your inward part is full of ravening and wickedness.
—LUKE 11:37–39

I read about a little boy who was preparing to leave for his piano lesson. Before they left the house his mother wanted to make sure he was presentable when he got to his teacher. "Did you wash your hands?" she asked. "Yes, Mother," he replied. "Did you wash your face?" Yes, Mother," he said once more. "And did you wash behind your ears?" she continued. He hesitated for a moment and then said, "On her side I did."

The Pharisees in Jesus' day were not concerned with genuine holiness, but rather only cared about the outward appearance they presented to others. Those who only saw them in public would be quite impressed as they passed by with their elaborate garments, praying loudly as they went. But God saw their hearts, and He was not impressed because He knew that their outward religiosity hid inward evil.

It is possible to outwardly conform to the commands of Scripture for a time without truly desiring to love and follow God, but eventually what is on the inside will show up in our lives. If we want our conduct to be pleasing to God, rather than focusing on the external, we should begin by focusing on the heart.

This is why the psalmist prayed, "Search me, O God, and know my heart: try me, and know my thoughts: And see if there be any wicked way in me, and lead me in the way everlasting." (Psalm 139:23–24). When we sincerely ask God to search our hearts and thoughts, He will. And He will also lead us in a way that is truly pleasing to God.

Today's Discipleship Principle: The cleansing of our lives begins when we align our hearts with the things God wants us to love.

Ignoring What Really Matters

*But woe unto you, Pharisees! for ye tithe mint and rue and all manner of herbs, and pass over judgment and the love of God: these ought ye to have done, and not to leave the other undone. Woe unto you, Pharisees! for ye love the uppermost seats in the synagogues, and greetings in the markets. Woe unto you, scribes and Pharisees, hypocrites! for ye are as graves which appear not, and the men that walk over them are not aware of them.—*LUKE 11:42–44

In Lewis Carroll's *Alice's Adventures in Wonderland*, the following conversation takes place between Alice and the Cheshire Cat that reveals how our effort in life can be wasted: "Would you tell me, please, which way I ought to go from here?" "That depends a good deal on where you want to get to," said the Cat. "I don't much care where—" said Alice. "Then it doesn't matter which way you go," said the Cat. "So long as I get SOMEWHERE," Alice added as an explanation. "Oh, you're sure to do that," said the Cat, "if you only walk long enough."

It is easy for us to find that our lives are filled with activity, but not with productivity. We can find that our focus drifts from one thing to the next, and we look only at what is before us rather than having clear goals and destinations in mind.

The truly important things in life are often drowned out by the clamor of the urgent, and if we are not careful, we will find ourselves spending all our time and energy on things that are of very little true significance.

The Pharisees counted out the tiniest leaves in their herb gardens to be sure they were tithing in accordance with the law, yet at the same time they ignored the matters of the heart. As a result, Jesus condemned them for their lack of proper priorities.

Today's Discipleship Principle: It is not pleasing to God when we pick and choose what we would obey and ignore His commands that we do not find appealing.

Carrying the Load

Then answered one of the lawyers, and said unto him, Master, thus saying thou reproachest us also. And he said, Woe unto you also, ye lawyers! for ye lade men with burdens grievous to be borne, and ye yourselves touch not the burdens with one of your fingers. Woe unto you! for ye build the sepulchres of the prophets, and your fathers killed them.—LUKE 11:45–47

Christopher Wren was the premiere English architect of the seventeenth century, but even he sometimes faced clients who thought they knew more about construction than he did. In 1688 he was commissioned to design a building in Windsor, England. Wren devoted his considerable skill to the task, and created a stunning design for a building held up by a series of columns that left an open space on the first floor where business and trade could be conducted. The city leaders feared the columns would not be sufficient to support the structure of the upper floors, and they insisted Wren add additional columns. So, in the interior of the open area, Wren designed four more pillars. However, he intentionally had them constructed too short, so that they did not reach the ceiling above. They looked like the other columns, but bore no actual weight.

There are many people who have the outward traits of godliness, but are doing nothing to carry the load of doing the work of God's kingdom. They are perfectly content to tell others how they should manage and carry their loads, but they do not take on any responsibility or burden themselves.

God's design for the church does not include any decorative columns. Each one of us is called to not only carry our own weight, but to be helpful and an encouragement to others as well. Paul wrote, "Bear ye one another's burdens, and so fulfil the law of Christ" (Galatians 6:2).

Today's Discipleship Principle: Each one of us has a responsibility to do our part to further the work of God and encourage other Christians.

The Testimony of Blood

Therefore also said the wisdom of God, I will send them prophets and apostles, and some of them they shall slay and persecute: That the blood of all the prophets, which was shed from the foundation of the world, may be required of this generation; From the blood of Abel unto the blood of Zacharias, which perished between the altar and the temple: verily I say unto you, It shall be required of this generation.—LUKE 11:49–51

The early church father Tertullian wrote, "The blood of martyrs is the seed of the church." Throughout the history of God's work, there have been men and women who have been willing to take a stand for the truth even at the cost of their own lives. They would not deny the Lord even in the face of death, but remained faithful. In fact, the English word for *martyr* comes from the Greek word for *witness*—signifying those who were willing to give everything in witness of the truth.

Though America has long enjoyed great religious freedom, and most of us have never faced any serious consequences for our faith, that is not true in much of the rest of the world, and it may not remain true in our nation forever. Thousands of Christians are dying for their faith around the world, choosing to join the line of heroes who have stood for the ages instead of denying the Lord.

It is easy for us to be confident that we would stand firm when we have not been put to the test. Peter certainly had no doubt what he would do: "Peter answered and said unto him, Though all men shall be offended because of thee, yet will I never be offended" (Matthew 26:33). Yet that very night Peter denied even knowing who Jesus was.

We need to be firm in our commitment to Christ regardless of what consequences may come as a result. He is worthy of our all—even of our very lives.

Today's Discipleship Principle: Our faith must be built and strengthened before the challenge comes so that we can stand the ultimate test.

Hidden Sins

In the mean time, when there were gathered together an innumerable multitude of people, insomuch that they trode one upon another, he began to say unto his disciples first of all, Beware ye of the leaven of the Pharisees, which is hypocrisy. For there is nothing covered, that shall not be revealed; neither hid, that shall not be known. Therefore whatsoever ye have spoken in darkness shall be heard in the light; and that which ye have spoken in the ear in closets shall be proclaimed upon the housetops.
—LUKE 12:1–3

Charles Lindbergh was one of the most famous and admired men in the world. Following his solo flight across the Atlantic in 1927, he gained world renown. His fame only increased after the tragic kidnapping and death of his oldest child. People looked up to Lindbergh and admired him as a man of virtue and character. What they did not know—what was not revealed until nearly thirty years after his death—was that Lindbergh had seven illegitimate children scattered across Europe. With great shock Lindbergh's youngest daughter from his marriage wrote, "This story reflects absolutely Byzantine layers of deception on the part of our shared father."

The temptation to hide and cover our sin rather than dealing with it goes all the way back to the fig leaves Adam and Eve wore as they hid from God in the Garden of Eden. We will try almost anything to avoid having to admit that we have done wrong. And there are times when it seems like we are succeeding at getting away with sin. But that is merely an illusion. God does not always immediately bring to light what we have done and punish us as we deserve. Sometimes He gives us grace and forbearance to see if we will return to Him on our own. If we insist, however, on allowing our sin to remain, it will eventually become known.

Today's Discipleship Principle: The only way to deal with sin is not to hide it, but to repent and confess and forsake it quickly.

The Fear of the Lord

And I say unto you my friends, Be not afraid of them that kill the body, and after that have no more that they can do. But I will forewarn you whom ye shall fear: Fear him, which after he hath killed hath power to cast into hell; yea, I say unto you, Fear him.—LUKE 12:4–5

Known as the "Nine Day Queen," Lady Jane Grey was just fifteen years old when she was briefly placed on the throne of England before being deposed by Bloody Mary, who would later order her execution. Jane Grey never wavered in her faith, even when told that converting to Catholicism might spare her life. In a letter not long before her death, she wrote, "For my sins the body of Christ was broken, and his blood shed on the cross. I ground my faith upon God's word, and not upon the church. The faith of the church must be tried by God's Word, and not God's Word by the church; neither yet my faith." She feared disappointing God more than losing her own life, and her faith remains a shining example hundreds of years later.

The first and greatest commandment is that we love God above all else and all others (Matthew 22:37). The priority of loving God determines how we spend our lives—how we use our time, talents, and resources. If He is first, then we will be devoted to following His Word and obeying His will. But we are to not only love God, but to fear Him too—to remember that while He is a loving and gracious Father to His children, He also hates sin with a fiery wrath, and He will not allow it to go unchecked in our lives.

It is when we fear God as we should, that we will avoid sin. Proverbs 16:6 says, "By mercy and truth iniquity is purged: and by the fear of the LORD men depart from evil." When we understand the holiness and character of God, we fear failing Him more than anything else.

Today's Discipleship Principle: The Christian who has an accurate view of God loves Him supremely and fears Him reverently.

Consider the Sparrows

Are not five sparrows sold for two farthings, and not one of them is forgotten before God? But even the very hairs of your head are all numbered. Fear not therefore: ye are of more value than many sparrows.
—LUKE 12:6–7

George Müller was a man of great faith. For many years, he operated orphanages that cared for thousands of children. The work was completely supported by prayer. Müller did not believe in asking people to give money—so much so that on more than one occasion when people asked him what needs the orphanage had, he would tell them, "I told God what we need. Ask Him what you should do." Müller carried a great weight of responsibility, but he did not bear it alone. On his desk Müller kept a frame with this declaration: "It matters to Him about you."

The devil lies and tells us that God does not care about our situation. When we stop and think that there are some seven billion people living on earth, it is easy to feel like our lives may not attract God's attention. But in reality, He knows exactly where we are and everything about us—even the number of hairs on our heads. This is the God whose knowledge and wisdom is so infinite that He even keeps track of the most insignificant birds, and He loves us far more than the sparrows.

God never loses sight of us, or forgets what we are experiencing in our lives. When He does allow things to come into our lives that are painful and difficult, He measures carefully what we are able to bear. "There hath no temptation taken you but such as is common to man: but God is faithful, who will not suffer you to be tempted above that ye are able; but will with the temptation also make a way to escape, that ye may be able to bear it" (1 Corinthians 10:13). And 1 Peter 5:7 expressly tells us that we can give our cares to Jesus because He cares for us: "Casting all your care upon him; for he careth for you."

Today's Discipleship Principle: Rejoice today in God's knowledge and love for you right where you are.

The Great Shame of Being Ashamed of Jesus

Also I say unto you, Whosoever shall confess me before men, him shall the Son of man also confess before the angels of God: But he that denieth me before men shall be denied before the angels of God.—LUKE 12:8–9

In 1765 Joseph Grigg published a hymn that was taken from a poem he had apparently written as a ten-year-old boy. It began:

Jesus! and shall it ever be!
A mortal man ashamed of Thee?
Scorn'd be the thought by rich and poor;
O may I scorn it more and more!

In our society, it is becoming less and less socially acceptable to declare allegiance to Jesus Christ and to follow the teachings of the Word of God. The more our culture turns its back on Jesus, the more important it is for us to take a clear, uncompromising, and determined stand that we are His followers and that we proudly bear His name.

The early church faced opposition because of their insistence on preaching Jesus. The high priest insisted that they stop using His name: "Saying, Did not we straitly command you that ye should not teach in this name? and, behold, ye have filled Jerusalem with your doctrine, and intend to bring this man's blood upon us" (Acts 5:28). More than anything else, the religious leaders did not want Jesus' name proclaimed—but that is exactly what the disciples preached.

What our world needs is not better methods, but the original message. Our wisdom and philosophy will not change the world, but the Saviour will. "And daily in the temple, and in every house, they ceased not to teach and preach Jesus Christ" (Acts 5:42).

Today's Discipleship Principle: The name of Jesus that we carry is an identifying mark we must never be ashamed to claim before the world.

The Work of the Holy Spirit

*And whosoever shall speak a word against the Son of man, it shall be forgiven him: but unto him that blasphemeth against the Holy Ghost it shall not be forgiven. And when they bring you unto the synagogues, and unto magistrates, and powers, take ye no thought how or what thing ye shall answer, or what ye shall say: For the Holy Ghost shall teach you in the same hour what ye ought to say.—*Luke 12:10–12

Charles M. Alexander, who was the song leader for many of R.A. Torrey's great revival campaigns told of attending a service in Tennessee where people were praying for God's power on their lives. One of those who was loudest in prayers was known in the church for continual backsliding and going away from God. Alexander said that once, as that man prayed for "the filling of the Holy Spirit," a woman who was sitting nearby watching, knowing his pattern of hot and cold living prayed aloud, "Don't bother filling him, Lord. He leaks!"

The Holy Spirit who indwells our lives from the moment of salvation is given to us both as a guide for our lives and as a seal that God will never forsake us. But we must walk according to His guidance if we are to benefit from it. Paul wrote, "And be not drunk with wine, wherein is excess; but be filled with the Spirit" (Ephesians 5:18). This is a direction—not for a one-time event, but for a continuing action. We all "leak" and need to yield ourselves to Him to be filled again and again.

The Holy Spirit only guides and teaches those who are listening. Through our obstinance and refusal to obey, however, we can hinder His work in our lives and disappoint and sadden Him: "And grieve not the holy Spirit of God, whereby ye are sealed unto the day of redemption" (Ephesians 4:30).

Today's Discipleship Principle: A Christian who does not walk in the guidance and power of the Holy Spirit will find that his walk is not pleasing to God.

What Makes a Life

And one of the company said unto him, Master, speak to my brother, that he divide the inheritance with me. And he said unto him, Man, who made me a judge or a divider over you? And he said unto them, Take heed, and beware of covetousness: for a man's life consisteth not in the abundance of the things which he possesseth. —LUKE 12:13–15

In his classic story "How Much Land Does a Man Need?" Tolstoy tells of a greedy man, Pahom, who wanted a vast estate. He is offered what seems like the opportunity of a lifetime. For a small sum of money, he can have all the land he can travel around in one day's time. Beginning early in the morning, Pahom sets out, determined to claim the best land he finds and as much as he can. He stops to rest and eat only reluctantly, and pushes himself to cover more and more ground. Finally he makes a desperate rush to return to the starting point before sundown so that he does not forfeit his money and his land. He reaches the hill just as the sun sets and falls dead from exhaustion. Tolstoy concludes, "Pahom was dead! The Bashkirs clicked their tongues to show their pity. His servant picked up the spade and dug a grave long enough for Pahom to lie in, and buried him in it. Six feet from his head to his heels was all he needed."

All of us face the temptation to be covetous and to give our energy and attention to acquiring the things that we think will bring us happiness and contentment. But no amount of acquisition can substitute for peace in the heart. And the things of this world are only temporal. "For we brought nothing into this world, and it is certain we can carry nothing out" (1 Timothy 6:7).

Covetousness comes in many shapes and sizes. It can be a desire for wealth, or it can be a desire for power or position. But tangible or intangible, anything that only lasts in this life, is of fleeting value and is not worth neglecting the pursuit of what is truly important to obtain it.

Today's Discipleship Principle: A life focused only on the things of this world will never make a real impact for eternity.

The Peril of Prosperity

And he spake a parable unto them, saying, The ground of a certain rich man brought forth plentifully: And he thought within himself, saying, What shall I do, because I have no room where to bestow my fruits? And he said, This will I do: I will pull down my barns, and build greater; and there will I bestow all my fruits and my goods. And I will say to my soul, Soul, thou hast much goods laid up for many years; take thine ease, eat, drink, and be merry.—LUKE 12:16–19

In his book *Money for Nothing*, Edward Ungel recounts the results of his investigation into the lives of people who won large jackpots playing the lottery. He tells the tragic story of Abraham Shakespeare, who won $30 million in 2006. Shakespeare was hounded by relatives and acquaintances for money and found himself surrounded by new friends who offered to help him. One of them, Dorice Moore, convinced him to transfer his assets to her to "protect" them, not long before she ended his life. A few weeks before he was killed, Shakespeare told his mother that he wished he had never won.

While many people dream of getting rich, they fail to understand that wealth does not take away problems and temptations; it simply changes their nature and scope. In fact, while great wealth is often viewed as a blessing, it can be the means of destruction for those who refuse to heed the wisdom and instruction of God. "For the turning away of the simple shall slay them, and the prosperity of fools shall destroy them" (Proverbs 1:32).

Money is not evil, and having money is not wrong. Money is simply a tool that we should use for eternal purposes. The danger comes when our focus is taken away from the eternal by the temporal resources so many try so hard to obtain.

Today's Discipleship Principle: If our trust is in God rather than our own resources, money will not have an unhealthy hold on us.

Time to Give an Account

But God said unto him, Thou fool, this night thy soul shall be required of thee: then whose shall those things be, which thou hast provided? So is he that layeth up treasure for himself, and is not rich toward God.
—LUKE 12:20–21

In 1989, during filming for the television detective show B. L. Stryker, production assistants secured permission from the residents of a house in West Palm Beach, Florida, to stage a crash scene in front of the house. They warned the people that there was a possibility that there could be some damage to the lawn and the landscaping as a result, but were told to go ahead. At the last minute, a phone call from the irate owner of the house—who lived out of state in New York—halted their plans. The people living in the house were just renters, and did not have the right to authorize destruction of the property.

Everything that we have belongs to God. And one day we will face Him to give an account of how we have handled what He has entrusted to our care. This world is not meant to be our focus. All that we have will be left behind. As the old saying goes, "There are no pockets in a shroud." We never see the funeral hearse followed by a U-Haul truck. The life that is focused only on this world is a foolish life, and it will not produce eternal rewards.

The rich fool in the parable believed he was thinking about the future as he planned to store up resources and enjoy a life of ease and comfort. But in reality his thinking was deceitfully short term because he had no thought of eternity. In the end, he found that his life was over before he expected it to be.

We need to live each day with a consciousness that we are only stewards of God's blessings and invest our time, energy, and resources according to what matters most to Him.

Today's Discipleship Principle: When God calls us to give account, we should be ready to do so gladly because we have used our lives well.

Don't Worry

*And he said unto his disciples, Therefore I say unto you, Take no thought for your life, what ye shall eat; neither for the body, what ye shall put on. The life is more than meat, and the body is more than raiment. Consider the ravens: for they neither sow nor reap; which neither have storehouse nor barn; and God feedeth them: how much more are ye better than the fowls?—*LUKE 12:22–24

After Abraham Lincoln was elected president but before he took office, he was interviewed by the famous newspaper editor Horace Greeley. Greeley wanted information about the future and the looming threat of the Civil War. Lincoln responded with a story from his days as a lawyer. Lincoln said that he traveled on horseback from one court to another, and once after particularly heavy rain, found it difficult to cross the flooded streams. Nearing the Fox River, he stopped for the night. As he sat at supper, his dinner companion was a Methodist circuit riding preacher. Lincoln asked what he thought about crossing the Fox River in time of flood, and the old circuit rider replied, "I have one fixed rule regarding the Fox River—I never cross it until I come to it."

So much of our lives are spent worrying about the future. People fret over health, money, politics, environment, relationships, and more. Yet worry has never made any situation better. You will never see a stressed out bird making an appointment with a therapist. They trust their Maker, and He feeds them. And even though we intellectually realize God's care for even the smallest of animals, too often we fail to apply that same care to ourselves. The promises of God have not lost their power. Still we act as though we have no source of help and must figure everything out on our own. If we would invest the time and mental energy we spend worrying instead in remembering and meditating on God's promises, our trust would be strengthened.

Today's Discipleship Principle: Every time we worry we insult our loving Heavenly Father and deny His promises are true.

Worry Doesn't Make You Taller

*And which of you with taking thought can add to his stature one cubit?
If ye then be not able to do that thing which is least, why take ye thought
for the rest? Consider the lilies how they grow: they toil not, they spin not;
and yet I say unto you, that Solomon in all his glory was not arrayed like
one of these.* —LUKE 12:25–27

Just about every little boy who dreamed of growing up to be a basketball
player wanted to be taller. They looked up to those they saw on the
court and realized that almost all of them were above average in height.
But there are exceptions. Tyrone "Muggsy" Bogues had a long NBA career
as a professional basketball player, despite the fact that he stood only five
feet three inches tall. His rookie year, one of his teammates was Manute
Bol, who, at seven feet seven inches, was twenty-eight inches taller than
Bogues. Despite his lack of height, Bogues developed a complete game
that kept him in the league for fifteen years.

Whether we are tall or short, one thing is certain—worrying about it
won't change it even a fraction of an inch. The right course to take when
we have a challenge is to trust in the love and goodness of our Father in
Heaven, and believe that He will do what He has promised to care for us.

The world is filled with examples and illustrations of God's goodness
in the way that He has provided for the needs of all His creatures.
Jesus specifically pointed out the lilies and their care-free growth and
splendor—all because of the tender power of God.

Yet too often we think that somehow we are exceptions to His care,
and must figure things out on our own. But as the old saying goes, worry
is like a rocking chair. You may move back and forth and use up energy,
but you aren't getting anywhere. Worry doesn't change things—it only
takes away our strength.

Today's Discipleship Principle: Choosing to worry, rather than trust
God, only robs us of peace and joy without making things better.

How Great God's Love for Us Really Is

If then God so clothe the grass, which is to day in the field, and to morrow is cast into the oven; how much more will he clothe you, O ye of little faith? And seek not ye what ye shall eat, or what ye shall drink, neither be ye of doubtful mind. For all these things do the nations of the world seek after: and your Father knoweth that ye have need of these things.
—LUKE 12:28–30

Maybe you've heard the story of a teacher in math class presenting one of her students with this question: "Suppose your mother baked a pie, and there were seven of you—your parents and five children. What part of the pie would you get." The boy replied, "One sixth." "I'm afraid you don't know your fractions yet," the teacher said. "Remember that there are seven of you." "Yes," the boy said, "but you don't know my mother. She would say she didn't want any pie and cut it in six pieces."

There are times when a parent's love exceeds available resources and they are not able to do everything they would like to do for their children. That never happens with God. He never sees a problem or need in our lives that He is not able to meet. While He allows us to experience difficulties and struggles as part of our process of becoming more like His Son, nothing that happens to us takes Him by surprise or taxes His resources.

The world around us is filled with examples and illustrations of both God's power and His concern for even the smallest animals and plants that He made. When we think we are alone and must care for ourselves without His help, we are living just like the lost do. Instead, we should confidently trust that He will do what is best for us.

Today's Discipleship Principle: Because God is both all loving and all powerful, you can always trust Him to do what is best for you.

Where Is Your Treasure?

But rather seek ye the kingdom of God; and all these things shall be added unto you. Fear not, little flock; for it is your Father's good pleasure to give you the kingdom. Sell that ye have, and give alms; provide yourselves bags which wax not old, a treasure in the heavens that faileth not, where no thief approacheth, neither moth corrupteth. For where your treasure is, there will your heart be also.—LUKE 12:31-34

In the 1980s, workers renovating the old Lexington Hotel in Chicago, which had once been used by the gangster Al Capone for his headquarters, discovered a series of secret tunnels and passageways under the building. In addition to an underground shooting range, they discovered a sealed vault. Immediately there was great speculation regarding what riches might be hidden inside. Some thought that there might be bodies hidden there. In April of 1986, millions watched on live television as the vault was opened. But when the cameras were taken inside, all the vault contained was some garbage and a few empty bottles. There was no treasure in Al Capone's vault.

All around us people are hard at work laying up earthly treasures. While there is certainly nothing wrong with wise and careful planning for the future, we must never forget that this world is only a temporary stop and that we are meant to care about what is eternal.

Trusting in God rather than in what we are able to accumulate brings peace and frees us from fear. Spending our lives and our treasure on what is eternal ensures that when we reach Heaven we will not go empty handed.

The world cares about stuff in the here and now, but God wants to present us with eternal rewards. In fact Jesus said it was God's "good pleasure"—something in which He takes great delight—to give us the greatest riches, the kingdom of God.

Today's Discipleship Principle: If our resources are only spent on our own interests, it shows that our love for God is not what it should be.

Ready for His Return

Let your loins be girded about, and your lights burning; And ye yourselves like unto men that wait for their lord, when he will return from the wedding; that when he cometh and knocketh, they may open unto him immediately. Blessed are those servants, whom the lord when he cometh shall find watching: verily I say unto you, that he shall gird himself, and make them to sit down to meat, and will come forth and serve them.—LUKE 12:35–37

President John F. Kennedy was fond of historical anecdotes that he used to illustrate his speeches. One of his favorites dated back to the American Revolution. In 1780, with the fate of the country still hanging in the balance as the war with England continued, the Connecticut House of Representatives meeting was in session. Suddenly the sky darkened ominously, even though it was the middle of the day. Some feared it was a sign of coming judgment and called for the body to be adjourned. But the Speaker of the House, Colonel Davenport, rose and said, "The Day of Judgment is either approaching, or it is not. If it is not, there is no cause for adjournment. If it is, I choose to be found doing my duty. Therefore, I wish that candles be brought."

The reality that Jesus is coming back is one of the most powerful motivations that we have to do right and serve God. John wrote, "Beloved, now are we the sons of God, and it doth not yet appear what we shall be: but we know that, when he shall appear, we shall be like him; for we shall see him as he is. And every man that hath this hope in him purifieth himself, even as he is pure" (1 John 3:2–3).

The fact that Jesus has not yet returned does not change the fact that it could happen at any moment. Rather than lackadaisically waiting for His return, we should be diligently preparing to meet our Lord.

Today's Discipleship Principle: Every day we should live with the reality that Jesus is coming back, at the forefront of our thinking.

Overpowering the Enemy

And this know, that if the goodman of the house had known what hour the thief would come, he would have watched, and not have suffered his house to be broken through. Be ye therefore ready also: for the Son of man cometh at an hour when ye think not.—LUKE 12:39-40

As the Allied forces prepared for the invasion of Europe in 1944, they realized that the chances of success would be much higher if they could cloak the actual intended landing zones so the Nazis would be forced to defend the entire coast. An elaborate operation known as Operation Bodyguard was devised to sow confusion among the German high command about both the Allied strength and their intended target. They used double agents, allowed false-coded messages to fall into enemy hands, and even staged plywood tanks and planes. The operation was so successful that for weeks after the Normandy landing, Hitler refused to commit full reinforcements, believing that it was only a diversion and that the real attack was yet to come.

The awesome power of God is so great that He does not need to deceive the enemy in order to defeat him. It does not matter what Satan does, He cannot stop God's plan from being fulfilled.

Satan tried throughout history to destroy the Jewish people. When the time came for Jesus to be born, the devil intensified his efforts, but all to no avail. "He that committeth sin is of the devil; for the devil sinneth from the beginning. For this purpose the Son of God was manifested, that he might destroy the works of the devil" (1 John 3:8). We are on the winning side!

We do not need to understand everything about God's plan for the future to understand that it will take place. All we are commanded to do is to be faithful and prepared. The rest we can safely leave up to God.

Today's Discipleship Principle: There is nothing Satan or his minions can do to stop God from accomplishing His purpose in your life.

Faithful Where We Are

And the Lord said, Who then is that faithful and wise steward, whom his lord shall make ruler over his household, to give them their portion of meat in due season? Blessed is that servant, whom his lord when he cometh shall find so doing. Of a truth I say unto you, that he will make him ruler over all that he hath.—LUKE 12:42-44

Charles Spurgeon was the most famous preacher of his generation, regularly speaking to crowds of thousands each week in his church in London. His sermons were reprinted in the newspapers, and for many services, tickets were required for those who wished to attend. Yet he did not start out that way.

Spurgeon began his ministry in small and obscure villages, speaking to a handful of people at a time. He later said, "I am perfectly sure that, if I had not been willing to preach to those small gatherings of people in obscure country places, I should never have had the privilege of preaching to thousands of men and women in large buildings all over the land."

Often we say that if we had more money we would give more or if we had more time we would do more. Yet in reality, the test of our stewardship and faithfulness is not what we would do with greater resources and opportunities, but what we are doing right now with what we already have. A person who is selfish and stingy with a little would not change if he suddenly became wealthy. A teacher who does not prepare for a class of six would not automatically become diligent for a class of sixty or even six hundred.

Rather than seeking more, we should realize that we will give an account to God for our stewardship of what He has given us, and seek to use every day to the fullest to accomplish as much as we can for Him. "He that is faithful in that which is least is faithful also in much: and he that is unjust in the least is unjust also in much" (Luke 16:10).

Today's Discipleship Principle: God sees the faithfulness that man may not notice, and He always rewards those who are true to Him.

A Matter of Responsibility

And that servant, which knew his lord's will, and prepared not himself, neither did according to his will, shall be beaten with many stripes. But he that knew not, and did commit things worthy of stripes, shall be beaten with few stripes. For unto whomsoever much is given, of him shall be much required: and to whom men have committed much, of him they will ask the more.—LUKE 12:47–48

In his speech to the Harvard graduating class in 2007, Bill Gates revealed the impact his mother had on his life by encouraging him to do good for others. Gates said, "A few days before my wedding, she hosted a bridal event, at which she read aloud a letter about marriage that she had written to Melinda. My mother was very ill with cancer at the time, but she saw one more opportunity to deliver her message, and at the close of the letter she said: 'From those to whom much is given, much is expected.'"

Whatever we have is a gift from God. He has graciously given us life, talents, abilities, and resources to use in His Kingdom. These gifts, however, come with a requirement and an expectation—that we will put them to use. In the parable of the talents, Jesus talked about the condemnation that came to the servant who hid what he had been given to ensure it would not be lost. "His lord answered and said unto him, Thou wicked and slothful servant, thou knewest that I reap where I sowed not, and gather where I have not strawed" (Matthew 25:26).

God expects and has a right to demand a return on the investment He has made in our lives. Every one of us has opportunities to do things for Him that no one else does. Rather than wishing you had the opportunities or resources of others, wholeheartedly invest yourself in serving with what God has given you. You were uniquely gifted by God for His purposes, so put everything you have to work for Him.

Today's Discipleship Principle: Rather than wishing you had more resources, focus on using whatever God has given you for His glory.

A Cause of Division

*Suppose ye that I am come to give peace on earth? I tell you, Nay; but rather division: For from henceforth there shall be five in one house divided, three against two, and two against three. The father shall be divided against the son, and the son against the father; the mother against the daughter, and the daughter against the mother; the mother in law against her daughter in law, and the daughter in law against her mother in law.—*Luke 12:51–53

While Moses was on Mount Sinai receiving the Law from God, the people turned to Aaron and insisted that he make an idol they could worship. He carved a golden calf that they worshipped in place of Jehovah, despite the fact that He had just delivered them from bondage and slavery in Egypt. When Moses returned to the camp, he was angry at the lack of faithfulness of the people, and called for help in making things right. "Then Moses stood in the gate of the camp, and said, Who is on the Lord's side? let him come unto me. And all the sons of Levi gathered themselves together unto him" (Exodus 32:26).

The popular cultural ideal of Jesus as a weak, soft-spoken pacifist with only a message of love and harmony may appeal to the world, but it is far from the picture the Bible presents. The real Jesus Christ found in Scripture was as divisive as truth. He taught truth, stood for truth, and was the truth. Those who followed Him found that truth was not always popular with others.

If we are going to follow Christ in a sinful world, we should not expect popularity and praise. Increasingly, we are seeing those who hold to Bible truths of right and wrong being labeled as bigoted and intolerant. The world never wants their evil deeds exposed, and they react negatively to anyone who points out the difference between right and wrong. But we must stand for what is right regardless of the consequences.

Today's Discipleship Principle: Following Christ requires that we be willing to take a stand for truth even if it divides us from others.

june

Understanding the Times

And he said also to the people, When ye see a cloud rise out of the west, straightway ye say, There cometh a shower; and so it is. And when ye see the south wind blow, ye say, There will be heat; and it cometh to pass. Ye hypocrites, ye can discern the face of the sky and of the earth; but how is it that ye do not discern this time?—LUKE 12:54–56

On December 26, 2004, a massive earthquake in the Indian Ocean, the third largest ever measured by seismograph, sent tsunami waves crashing onto the shores of numerous countries. When the waters finally subsided, nearly a quarter of a million people were dead, and billions of dollars in homes, property, and businesses were tragically destroyed. Although most of the people had no warning of the coming danger, on several islands the population was completely spared. What made the difference? On the islands where people lived, they had followed tribal traditions to immediately flee away from the beach into the mountains when they felt the earthquake shake the ground. The people had passed down wisdom from one generation to the next that warned of the danger of flooding following an earthquake.

The Bible gives us clear indications of what the end times will be like, and God expects us to prepare ourselves accordingly. We are not meant to be blindly wandering through events, but rather wise to know what is coming so we will not be caught off guard. Explaining the end times to the church at Thessalonica, Paul wrote, "But I would not have you to be ignorant, brethren, concerning them which are asleep, that ye sorrow not, even as others which have no hope" (1 Thessalonians 4:13).

The condition of the world as we go forward is not getting better. And as a result, we will face new challenges and temptations in the days ahead. The key to being ready for what happens next is to be grounded in the Scriptures so we are not swayed by error.

Today's Discipleship Principle: A careful reading and study of the Word of God prepares us to understand the real implication of current events.

Sooner Is Better than Later

Yea, and why even of yourselves judge ye not what is right? When thou goest with thine adversary to the magistrate, as thou art in the way, give diligence that thou mayest be delivered from him; lest he hale thee to the judge, and the judge deliver thee to the officer, and the officer cast thee into prison. I tell thee, thou shalt not depart thence, till thou hast paid the very last mite.—LUKE 12:57–59

Though no one knows exactly who originated the expression, "A stitch in time saves nine," this proverb has been in print in one form or another since at least 1732 (and it appears to be even older than that). The concept of fixing a problem while it is small rather than waiting until it becomes larger seems so self-evident that it almost does not need expression. But the tendency of our fallen nature is to procrastinate and delay rather than taking on a challenge, and often that ends up with us facing much harsher consequences than we would have.

There is no merit in delaying doing something that is right and helpful. Whether in terms of healing a relationship, offering encouragement, or meeting a need, sooner is always better than later. While wise planning for the future is important, we must be careful not to fall into the trap of putting off doing things for others until some later date. The reality is that some opportunities are only available for a short time, and if we delay, they will disappear.

One of General George Patton's favorite sayings was, "A good solution applied with vigor now is better than a perfect solution applied ten minutes later." We certainly should not be constantly dashing around without any thought or plan for our lives, but we need to be active. Far more is lost by procrastination and delay than by fervent service for the Lord in the present moment.

Today's Discipleship Principle: If you delay doing good for others and for God's kingdom, you may miss the opportunity all together.

Give Heed to the Warning

There were present at that season some that told him of the Galilaeans,
whose blood Pilate had mingled with their sacrifices. And Jesus answering
said unto them, Suppose ye that these Galilaeans were sinners above all
the Galilaeans, because they suffered such things? I tell you, Nay: but,
except ye repent, ye shall all likewise perish. —LUKE 13:1–3

D.L. Moody told the story of a tragedy that occurred while he was in England on one of his preaching trips. In a small fishing town named Eyemouth after a week of bad weather, the fishing boats determined to set out when the sky finally cleared to make up for lost time. Moody said, "Before they started, the harbor-master hoisted the storm signal, and warned them of the coming tempest. He begged of them not to go; but they disregarded his warning, and away they went. Very few of those fishermen returned. In the church of which my friend was pastor, I believe there were three male members left. Those men were ushered into eternity because they did not give heed to the warning."

The message of Jesus was rejected by many in His day because they did not believe they needed to heed a warning of sin and the absolute requirement of turning to Him. The Pharisees and others thought they were just fine as they were, and that Jesus was only addressing the "sinners." They failed to recognize, or were unwilling to admit, that they needed the message just as much as anyone else.

Often we find it comforting to apply commands of Scripture or the messages we hear preached to the lives of others, rather than considering our own condition. This is a deadly error, because if we fail to see our own sin and repent of it, we will suffer the consequences. Every time we hear a warning, we should prayerfully consider if it applies to us and how we should respond.

Today's Discipleship Principle: The warnings and instructions of Scripture are just not for others—they are for us.

Not Just for Decoration

He spake also this parable; A certain man had a fig tree planted in his
vineyard; and he came and sought fruit thereon, and found none. Then
said he unto the dresser of his vineyard, Behold, these three years I come
seeking fruit on this fig tree, and find none: cut it down; why cumbereth
it the ground? And he answering said unto him, Lord, let it alone this
year also, till I shall dig about it, and dung it: And if it bear fruit, well:
and if not, then after that thou shalt cut it down.—LUKE 13:6-9

There is a world of difference between the Bradford pear tree and
the Bartlett pear tree. Both names sound similar, and at a casual
observation, they would appear to simply be different varieties of the
same kind of tree. They are not. The Bartlett pear is known for bearing
sweet, juicy fruit. In the spring, the Bradford pear tree is covered with
beautiful white blossoms that would seem to indicate a bumper crop of
pears. But the Bradford is a sterile hybrid that does not produce any fruit.
It looks like a pear tree, and if all you care about is appearance, it is fine.
But if you want pears, Bradford trees are a waste of time and space.

God's purpose for us as His children is not that we be decorative, but
that we be fruitful. Long before we were saved or even born, God had
a plan for us to serve Him and work in His Kingdom: "For we are his
workmanship, created in Christ Jesus unto good works, which God hath
before ordained that we should walk in them" (Ephesians 2:10).

All Christians, not just those in vocational ministry, are to be fruitful.
The work of the Holy Spirit in and through our lives will have a noticeable
impact on the way we speak, think, and act. Galatians 5:22-23 describes
the fruit that should be evident in our lives: "But the fruit of the Spirit
is love, joy, peace, longsuffering, gentleness, goodness, faith, Meekness,
temperance: against such there is no law."

Today's Discipleship Principle: The normal condition of an obedient
Christian is fruitfulness in every part of life.

Rejoicing in Our Deliverance

*And he was teaching in one of the synagogues on the sabbath. And, behold, there was a woman which had a spirit of infirmity eighteen years, and was bowed together, and could in no wise lift up herself. And when Jesus saw her, he called her to him, and said unto her, Woman, thou art loosed from thine infirmity. And he laid his hands on her: and immediately she was made straight, and glorified God.—*LUKE 13:10–13

Billy Bray was born into a poor mining family in Cornwall, England, in 1794. He followed his father into the mines, giving little thought to the future of his soul. But his near death in a mining accident prompted him to consider the gospel, and John Bunyan's book *Visions of Heaven and Hell* brought him to the Lord.

Though Bray had little education, he was excited about his faith and became a powerful preacher. He never lost the joy of his salvation. Bray said, "I shouted for joy, I praised Him with my whole heart for what He had done. They said I was a mad-man, but they mean I was a glad-man; and glory be to God, I have been glad ever since."

Too many Christians have gotten over their salvation. They are genuinely converted, saved from sin and eternal suffering in Hell, and part of God's family—and they act just as miserable, dejected, and worried as the lost who have no eternal hope. It shouldn't be that way! There is never a day, no matter how difficult our circumstances may be, when we do not have much for which to be thankful. The salvation we freely received was not given to us because we deserved it. It was a free gift of God's grace, and we should always be grateful to Him. As Billy Bray liked to say, "If they put me in a barrel, I'd shout 'glory' out the bunghole."

How long has it been since you paused to reflect on your salvation and give thanks to God for it? How long has it been since you glorified God to others for His grace and love in saving you?

Today's Discipleship Principle: Not a single day should pass without us giving glory and praise to God for our salvation.

The Glorious Kingdom of God

Then said he, Unto what is the kingdom of God like? and whereunto shall I resemble it? It is like a grain of mustard seed, which a man took, and cast into his garden; and it grew, and waxed a great tree; and the fowls of the air lodged in the branches of it. And again he said, Whereunto shall I liken the kingdom of God? It is like leaven, which a woman took and hid in three measures of meal, till the whole was leavened.—LUKE 13:18–21

In the 1600s, Louis XIV, the Sun King of France, took his father's hunting lodge at Versailles and began remodeling it into a massive palace. In 1682, Louis XIV moved the court there, and it became the official seat of government. Nothing but the best would do for the king and his court. No expense was spared as artisans from around the world were brought in to create sculptures and ornamentation for the royal family to enjoy. Thousands of pounds of gold and silver were used to trim fixtures and furniture throughout the massive building. Today millions of guests each year visit Versailles to marvel at the opulent splendor created by a king with virtually unlimited resources and power on display.

But all of those glories, and everything created by man, pales in comparison to the splendor of Heaven. God does not use gold for decoration He uses it like we use asphalt. His kingdom is not limited in any way, but rather reaches through time and space. Our limited minds cannot fully grasp the vast wonders of God and His kingdom, but we know it is far beyond anything we know, and He has made us part of it. "But as it is written, Eye hath not seen, nor ear heard, neither have entered into the heart of man, the things which God hath prepared for them that love him" (1 Corinthians 2:9).

Although we cannot comprehend the splendor of Heaven, we can look forward to it. And, as Colossians 3:1 instructs us, we can "seek those things which are above, where Christ sitteth on the right hand of God."

Today's Discipleship Principle: Since the greatest treasures are above, we should live this life with our eyes set on the next.

Does God Know You?

*Then said one unto him, Lord, are there few that be saved? And he said unto them, Strive to enter in at the strait gate: for many, I say unto you, will seek to enter in, and shall not be able. When once the master of the house is risen up, and hath shut to the door, and ye begin to stand without, and to knock at the door, saying, Lord, Lord, open unto us; and he shall answer and say unto you, I know you not whence ye are:—*LUKE 13:23–25

D r. Bill Rice recounted an experience he had while on a trip to Israel many years ago. From his hotel room he watched two Bedouin shepherds walking toward each other. Each was followed by a large flock of sheep. As the shepherds greeted each other and began to talk, the sheep milled around, grazing on the sparse grass. Within a few moments, the two flocks were so mixed together that Dr. Rice said he didn't see how they could ever get them separated. But when the conversation was over, each shepherd headed off, calling for his sheep to follow. In just a few moments the two flocks were perfectly grouped and each went on their way.

Jesus said, "My sheep hear my voice, and I know them, and they follow me: And I give unto them eternal life; and they shall never perish, neither shall any man pluck them out of my hand" (John 10:27–28). It is not enough for us to simply know of God, we must also have a personal relationship where we know Him and He knows us. Just as a sheep knows its shepherd, so we should recognize and be familiar with the voice of our Shepherd.

There are many people in our world who call Jesus "Lord" but have never become His own through salvation. When they stand before Him, they will be shocked to find that what they claimed was not real—and that God does not know them as part of His family. There is a difference between calling yourself a Christian and being born again through Jesus.

Today's Discipleship Principle: Without a personal, saving relationship with God through the blood of Jesus, we have no hope for the future.

The Reality of Hell

Then shall ye begin to say, We have eaten and drunk in thy presence, and thou hast taught in our streets. But he shall say, I tell you, I know you not whence ye are; depart from me, all ye workers of iniquity. There shall be weeping and gnashing of teeth, when ye shall see Abraham, and Isaac, and Jacob, and all the prophets, in the kingdom of God, and you yourselves thrust out.—LUKE 13:26-28

Harry Ironside told the story of the famous agnostic Robert Ingersoll who was known for his opposition to all religion, especially Christianity. Ingersoll announced a lecture in which he would prove that Hell did not exist—that it had been dreamed up by theologians to scare people into doing what they said. According to Ironside, just as Ingersoll was beginning, a drunken man in the audience stood up and called out, "Make it strong, Bob. There's a lot of us poor fellows depending on you. If you are wrong, we are all lost. So be sure you prove it clear and plain."

The world does not like to acknowledge the reality of Hell, because they do not want there to be any consequences for living however they like. But no amount of denial can change the reality that those who do not trust Christ as Saviour will spend eternity apart from God. Though Hell was not prepared for man, but for Satan (Matthew 25:41), it is the destination for those who cannot enter Heaven because their sins have not been taken away.

Hell is not metaphorical, but literal. The flames are real. The suffering is real. And the sentence is eternal. The world may not want to think about Hell, but we should. Because we have been spared that awful fate, we should do everything that we can to warn others of the danger of eternity apart from God. And we should do everything we can to tell them of Jesus' death, burial, resurrection, and gift of salvation.

Today's Discipleship Principle: Eternity in torment in Hell is the fate of the lost—and that should motivate us to do all we can to reach them.

God Is in Control

The same day there came certain of the Pharisees, saying unto him, Get thee out, and depart hence: for Herod will kill thee. And he said unto them, Go ye, and tell that fox, Behold, I cast out devils, and I do cures to day and to morrow, and the third day I shall be perfected. Nevertheless I must walk to day, and to morrow, and the day following: for it cannot be that a prophet perish out of Jerusalem.—LUKE 13:31–33

One of the greatest illustrations of the complete sovereignty of God is the life of Jesus. Everything that He did was done in God's timing, and though both religious and political leaders plotted against Him, no one could do anything to change the schedule for His life, death, and resurrection that God had planned. Herod's plot to kill Jesus was not a threat to Him, because the time of the crucifixion had not yet come. Even when it did, it was not the power of Roman legions but the purpose of God that put Jesus on the cross, as He told Pilate: "Jesus answered, Thou couldest have no power at all against me, except it were given thee from above: therefore he that delivered me unto thee hath the greater sin" (John 19:11).

What was true of Jesus' life is true of ours as well. God is fully in control. He has complete knowledge of everything that will happen—what is future and unknown to us is not to Him. This truth is so important for us to remember as we make our way through a worry-filled world. We do not have to know what is coming next to be confident that God will ultimately use all the circumstances of our life for His glory and for our good. We can take both good and bad with complete faith that God knows what He is doing. While we may be familiar with the words of Romans 8:28, we don't always remember the certainty of its promise: "And we know that all things work together for good to them that love God, to them who are the called according to his purpose."

Today's Discipleship Principle: Nothing that happens to you today will take God by surprise or annul His promises for your life.

A Rejected Invitation

O Jerusalem, Jerusalem, which killest the prophets, and stonest them that are sent unto thee; how often would I have gathered thy children together, as a hen doth gather her brood under her wings, and ye would not! Behold, your house is left unto you desolate: and verily I say unto you, Ye shall not see me, until the time come when ye shall say, Blessed is he that cometh in the name of the Lord.—LUKE 13:34–35

During his large evangelistic campaign in England in 1875, D.L. Moody preached a number of messages in London. In a sermon on why men reject God, Moody said, "Let any man get an invitation from Queen Victoria to go down to Windsor Castle, to some banquet; and there is not a man but would consider it a great honor to receive such an invitation. But only think of the invitation that I bring tonight! It comes from the King of kings. The marriage supper of the Lamb is going to take place, and God wants every man in this assembly to be present. I have missed a good many appointments in my time, but, by the grace of God, I mean to make sure of keeping that one."

The description Jesus gave to Jerusalem is one of the saddest epitaphs ever recorded: "Ye would not." The offer of salvation was presented by the Messiah Himself, yet the great majority of people refused to accept the invitation. They were looking for something other than what Jesus offered, and missed the greatest opportunity any person ever has. Rather than being sheltered and cared for by God Himself, the city and the people were eventually destroyed.

All of God's invitations carry the weight of a royal command that cannot be disobeyed without consequence. And most of them come with a time limit. Though God is patient and long-suffering, He will not wait forever for us to respond.

Today's Discipleship Principle: Opportunities that God presents to us must be seized while the door is still open.

Don't Delay Doing Good

*And, behold, there was a certain man before him which had the dropsy. And Jesus answering spake unto the lawyers and Pharisees, saying, Is it lawful to heal on the sabbath day? And they held their peace. And he took him, and healed him, and let him go; And answered them, saying, Which of you shall have an ass or an ox fallen into a pit, and will not straightway pull him out on the sabbath day?—*LUKE 14:2–5

D r. R.B. Ouellette related a lesson that his father taught him by example. He watched as his dad, who served faithfully for many years as a pastor, evangelist, and director of a rescue mission, was asked for prayer about a financial need by a man. After Dr. Ouellette's father prayed with him, he opened his wallet and gave him money to help meet the need. He later told his son, "I have learned that if I am prompted to help someone and don't do it right away, I usually don't ever do it."

We are not often in life presented with opportunities to help when it is convenient. Usually the greatest needs cross our paths at moments when we are busy, burdened, or in some difficulty ourselves. There are always reasons we can think of why it would be better to help later on. But those excuses often lead to inaction.

When Jesus was presented with a man who needed healing, Jesus didn't turn him away, saying, "Come again when it is more convenient for Me and the Pharisees won't accuse Me of breaking the Sabbath." He simply healed the man. Although the Pharisees accused Jesus anyway, He actually did not break the law. However, He was not bound by man's rigid traditions that had been built up around what God commanded, and He did not use the Sabbath as an excuse to avoid doing good to others. Instead, He used it as an example to us of the importance of meeting needs in the lives of others whenever and wherever we can.

Today's Discipleship Principle: Do not miss your chance to help someone in need by waiting for the perfect moment to do so.

The Shame of Self Promotion

And he put forth a parable to those which were bidden, when he marked how they chose out the chief rooms; saying unto them, When thou art bidden of any man to a wedding, sit not down in the highest room; lest a more honourable man than thou be bidden of him; And he that bade thee and him come and say to thee, Give this man place; and thou begin with shame to take the lowest room.—LUKE 14:7–9

In Aesop's fable "The Tortoise and the Ducks," he tells of a tortoise who envied those who could travel about and see the world. Taking pity on him, two ducks came up with a plan that would allow him to experience places he had never seen before. "We can help you to see the world," said the ducks. "Take hold of this stick with your mouth, and we will carry you far up in the air where you can see the whole countryside. But keep quiet or you will be sorry."

The tortoise was very glad indeed. He seized the stick firmly in his mouth, the two ducks took hold of it one at each end, and away they sailed up toward the clouds. Just then a crow flew by. He was very much astonished at the strange sight and cried: "This must surely be the King of Tortoises!" "Why certainly—" began the tortoise. But as he opened his mouth to say those foolish words he lost his hold on the stick, and down he fell to the ground.

There are some people whose only interest is self-promotion. They only take jobs that will bring them praise, and they only work hard when others are watching. Paul describes a different approach: "Not with eyeservice, as menpleasers; but as the servants of Christ, doing the will of God from the heart; With good will doing service, as to the Lord, and not to men" (Ephesians 6:6–7). When we live for the praise of men or seek their affirmation, we miss opportunities to serve the Lord at times and in places where no one else would know.

Today's Discipleship Principle: Rather than seeking to glorify ourselves, we should always be lifting up Jesus Christ.

How to Really Get Ahead

But when thou art bidden, go and sit down in the lowest room; that when he that bade thee cometh, he may say unto thee, Friend, go up higher: then shalt thou have worship in the presence of them that sit at meat with thee. For whosoever exalteth himself shall be abased; and he that humbleth himself shall be exalted.—LUKE 14:10–11

Before the 2001 football season, Notre Dame announced the hiring of George O'Leary, who had been the head coach at Georgia Tech, to lead their program. A few days after he was hired, a reporter discovered that while his biography claimed O'Leary was a three year letterman on the football team in college, he actually had not played in even one game. Then it was discovered that the master's degree O'Leary claimed on his resume was from a school that didn't even exist. O'Leary was fired by the school. In an apology statement he wrote, "In seeking employment I prepared a resume that contained inaccuracies regarding my completion of course work for a master's degree and also my level of participation in football at my alma mater." He went on to describe it as "a selfish and thoughtless act."

Many people are tempted to take shortcuts and try to promote themselves on the way up the ladder. But the only way to truly get ahead is to have God's help and blessing. "For promotion cometh neither from the east, nor from the west, nor from the south. But God is the judge: he putteth down one, and setteth up another" (Psalm 75:6–7).

To receive God's grace, we must be humble because "God resisteth the proud, and giveth grace to the humble" (1 Peter 5:5). If our goal is the praise of men and their approval, we should not expect God's help along the way. If our goal is to glorify Him, He will place us in the position to best accomplish that noble purpose.

Today's Discipleship Principle: If we humble ourselves, God will not have to bring us low, but can rather raise us up.

God Helps Those Who Help Others

Then said he also to him that bade him, When thou makest a dinner or a supper, call not thy friends, nor thy brethren, neither thy kinsmen, nor thy rich neighbours; lest they also bid thee again, and a recompence be made thee. But when thou makest a feast, call the poor, the maimed, the lame, the blind: And thou shalt be blessed; for they cannot recompense thee: for thou shalt be recompensed at the resurrection of the just.
—LUKE 14:12–14

Many people like to cite Bible "verses" that aren't actually in the Bible. According to several surveys, ones of the most often quoted of these "verses" is this: "God helps those who help themselves." While the Bible does teach individual responsibility and the importance of our effort and hard work in whatever we do, it does not teach that God is impressed with our work on our own behalf. Instead, it repeatedly teaches, as Jesus does in the above passage, that God is looking for those who are committed to helping and meeting the needs of others.

The Christian life is not meant to be self-focused. Our natural sinful tendency is to worry only about what we can get for ourselves, but the Divine tendency is to sacrifice for the needs of others. "For ye know the grace of our Lord Jesus Christ, that, though he was rich, yet for your sakes he became poor, that ye through his poverty might be rich" (2 Corinthians 8:9). The example that Jesus left for us was of compassion and ministry to those who were without value in the eyes of the world. The Lord could have chosen to be born in a palace, but instead was born in a stable. Rather than living among the elite of Jerusalem, he grew up in the despised town of Nazareth. And His ministry—like our lives should be—was focused on others.

Today's Discipleship Principle: If we are to truly live as Jesus did, then we must care about those that others overlook and discount.

The Folly of Excuses

And sent his servant at supper time to say to them that were bidden,
Come; for all things are now ready. And they all with one consent began
to make excuse. The first said unto him, I have bought a piece of ground,
and I must needs go and see it: I pray thee have me excused. And another
said, I have bought five yoke of oxen, and I go to prove them: I pray thee
have me excused. And another said, I have married a wife, and therefore
I cannot come.—LUKE 14:17–20

When people do not want to do something, they will use any excuse to justify their conduct. At one point the noted author O. Henry was having difficulty getting a royalty check that was due to him from a New York publishing house. He had been promised that it would come, but no payment arrived. Finally, he went to the office in person only to be told that the man who signed checks for the company had a sprained ankle. "Does he sign them with his feet?" O. Henry asked.

Rather than trying to avoid what we should do, we need to demonstrate character by taking on responsibility and seeing to it that we do all that we can and should do. This is true in our work for God and in every other part of our lives. There is no part of life where we should not be diligent and faithful. Those who rely on excuses may avoid work in the short term, but they rob themselves and others in the process.

The people in Jesus' parable made ridiculous excuses which emphasized their disinterest in attending the king's supper to which they had been invited. Contrast that, however, with David who, when his father instructed him to take food to his brothers, did not abandon his responsibilities or make excuses. "And David rose up early in the morning, and left the sheep with a keeper, and took, and went, as Jesse had commanded him" (1 Samuel 17:20). The path to accomplishment is never paved with excuses.

Today's Discipleship Principle: Instead of making excuses, do the work necessary to make progress in your life today.

The Urgency of the Gospel

So that servant came, and shewed his lord these things. Then the master of the house being angry said to his servant, Go out quickly into the streets and lanes of the city, and bring in hither the poor, and the maimed, and the halt, and the blind. And the servant said, Lord, it is done as thou hast commanded, and yet there is room. And the lord said unto the servant, Go out into the highways and hedges, and compel them to come in, that my house may be filled.—LUKE 14:21–23

On Sunday night, October 8, 1871, D.L. Moody was preaching at his church in Chicago on the topic, "What Shall I Do with Jesus?" At the conclusion of the sermon, he told the large crowd to take the text home and think it over. The following week he announced that he would preach on the cross, and ask them to answer the question. But that night the Great Chicago Fire swept across the city, destroying thousands of buildings, including Moody's church, and leaving some three hundred people dead.

"I have never since dared," Moody later said, "to give an audience a week to think of their salvation. If they were lost they might rise up, in judgment against me. I have never seen that congregation since. But I want to tell you of one lesson that I learned that night which I have never forgotten, and that is, when I preach, to press Christ upon the people then and there and try to bring them to a decision on the spot. I would rather have that right hand cut off than to give an audience a week now to decide what to do with Jesus."

Salvation is literally a matter of life and death—eternal life and death—and our presentation of the gospel to others should reflect that. While we never want to encourage insincere professions of Christ, we are instructed to "compel"—to urge—people to respond to the gospel. It is a matter of greatest urgency.

Today's Discipleship Principle: If we realize the certainty of Heaven and Hell, there is no room for casual witnessing to the lost.

Loving God Most of All

And there went great multitudes with him: and he turned, and said unto them, If any man come to me, and hate not his father, and mother, and wife, and children, and brethren, and sisters, yea, and his own life also, he cannot be my disciple. And whosoever doth not bear his cross, and come after me, cannot be my disciple.—LUKE 14:25-27

In his sermon "The Secret of Loving God," Charles Spurgeon highlighted the importance of taking a public stand for God and declaring our love for Him to the world with the story of his baptism: "I always look back, with deep gratitude, to the day when I was baptized. Up to that time, I was timid and fearful, and afraid to confess Christ; but after I went into the river, and was publicly baptized into His death, I lost all fear of man, and I think I can honestly say that I have never been ashamed to acknowledge my Lord from that day to this. The world has had many a cruel word for me from that day to this, and there is no love lost between us; I am done with the world as the world is done with me; I am crucified to the world, and the world to me."

The parallel account in Matthew's Gospel of Christ's words above is instructive: "He that loveth father or mother more than me is not worthy of me: and he that loveth son or daughter more than me is not worthy of me. And he that taketh not his cross, and followeth after me, is not worthy of me" (Matthew 10:37–38). These verses show us that our love for God should be so great that other loves pale so much in comparison so as to look like hatred.

When we love God above all else, that will inevitably show up in every area and relationship of our lives. Our love for God will determine how we use our time, what we allow and avoid, how we treat those around us, and what we are willing to give of ourselves for our Lord.

Today's Discipleship Principle: Our love for God should be so great that it is visible to everyone who knows or meets us.

Counting the Cost

For which of you, intending to build a tower, sitteth not down first, and counteth the cost, whether he have sufficient to finish it? Lest haply, after he hath laid the foundation, and is not able to finish it, all that behold it begin to mock him, Saying, This man began to build, and was not able to finish.—LUKE 14:28–30

During the days of Hudson Taylor, the China Inland Mission established a boarding school in China where young men could come and receive an education both in secular and spiritual matters. At one time, the school was headed by a Mr. Li, a conscientious worker. His diligence came to the attention of the Standard Oil Company, which was expanding their operation in China, and he was offered a position that would double his pay. He initially agreed to accept the job, but when he was told that it would require him to work on Sundays and miss the services at his church, Mr. Li declined the position. In response, the company offered to raise his salary further to three times what he had been making, and to give him Sundays off. But as Mr. Li prayed, he came to the decision that he needed to stay with his work for the Lord, despite the financial sacrifice. He wrote, "I am sorry I cannot come and work for your company. I have decided to work for God, and win the boys to Jesus Christ. I beg you a thousand pardons."

True service for God never comes without a price. Jesus knew the cost before He came to Earth to die for our sins, yet He gave Himself willingly.

It is true that all of the time, effort, and resources that we put into the Lord's work could be used for other purposes. But Jesus calls us to consider the eternal rather than the temporal and to be willing to make whatever sacrifices are required in order to live as He calls and commands us to live.

Today's Discipleship Principle: Only those who are willing to pay the cost are able to truly walk in Jesus' steps.

Clinging to Belongings

Or what king, going to make war against another king, sitteth not down first, and consulteth whether he be able with ten thousand to meet him that cometh against him with twenty thousand? Or else, while the other is yet a great way off, he sendeth an ambassage, and desireth conditions of peace. So likewise, whosoever he be of you that forsaketh not all that he hath, he cannot be my disciple.—LUKE 14:31-33

In 1888 Jonathan and Rosalind Goforth went to northern China to open a pioneer missionary work. They labored on the field for decades, being forced to flee from the Boxer Rebellion, and then returning to China and Manchuria where they stayed until Jonathan's blindness forced them to return to Canada in 1935. Over the years they made many sacrifices for their work, including the deaths of five of their eleven children. In her book, *How I Know God Answers Prayer,* Rosalind recounted her sorrow at returning home after a mission trip to find their home had been broken into and all their belongings stolen: "My dear, they were just things," her husband reminded her, and they continued on in the work.

The recognition of the temporary nature of our earthly possessions is vital to our faithful following of Jesus Christ. The materialistic culture that surrounds us encourages us to adopt the mentality that our belongings define our worth and status. Jesus calls us, however, to be willing to give up anything and everything in order to follow Him. While most of us will likely never be called on to make such extreme sacrifices, the point is that our value system—the things that we truly love—are revealed by that to which we cling most tightly.

Jesus calls us to follow Him, which means placing His commands above our own interests and desires, and being willing to pay the price to be His disciple. Without a willingness to forsake all, we cannot truly follow Christ.

Today's Discipleship Principle: When we cling to Jesus rather than the things of Earth, we will follow Him wherever He leads.

Staying Salty

Salt is good: but if the salt have lost his savour, wherewith shall it be seasoned? It is neither fit for the land, nor yet for the dunghill; but men cast it out. He that hath ears to hear, let him hear.—LUKE 14:34–35

In Bible times, salt was a valuable substance. In the Roman Empire, it was common for workers and soldiers to be paid in salt. In fact, our word *salary* comes from the Latin word for "salt money." The description of a lazy worker as "not worth his salt" traces back to that custom. Salt was valuable not only because it was rare, but because it was so important to food preservation and flavoring. Salt was sometimes collected in pools by bodies of water like the Mediterranean Sea, and more often was mined from the ground. But when salt was exposed to the elements, it would lose its sharp nature, and become simply a bland chemical that no longer produced any positive effect.

The world has a way of wearing away the "saltiness" of Christians. Over time we can become more like the world as the edges of our distinctiveness get ground down and we cease to stand apart as God calls us to do. God's intention is for His children to be distinct and different from the world in their love, their life, their language, and their labor. Titus 2:14 reminds us that Christ "…gave himself for us, that he might redeem us from all iniquity, and purify unto himself a peculiar people, zealous of good works."

There is enormous pressure in our day to stop clearly and plainly declaring the Word of God so as to avoid offending anyone's sensibilities or hurting their feelings. But God's Word has not changed. Sin is still sinful and God still hates it. Righteousness is still right and God still loves it. And our job is to be salt and light to the world. We must guard against losing the very distinctiveness that is to characterize our walk with God and work for God.

Today's Discipleship Principle: The more closely we cling to God and His Word, the more distinct from the world we will be.

A Complaint about Reaching Sinners

Then drew near unto him all the publicans and sinners for to hear him. And the Pharisees and scribes murmured, saying, This man receiveth sinners, and eateth with them.—LUKE 15:1–2

The Pharisees and religious leaders hated Jesus for many reasons. He pointed out their hypocrisy and refused to follow their additions to God's law, choosing instead to keep the law as God had given it. But of all the things that Jesus did that infuriated them, nothing sparked more outrage than the fact that Jesus loved "sinners." Of course the Pharisees were just as sinful as those they condemned, but their approach to those they held in contempt was to have nothing to do with them at all. They thought that by avoiding sinners at all costs, they were avoiding contamination.

Jesus never tolerated sin, but He was gracious and kind to sinners and was happy to spend time showing them the way of salvation. "The Son of man came eating and drinking, and they say, Behold a man gluttonous, and a winebibber, a friend of publicans and sinners. But wisdom is justified of her children" (Matthew 11:19). Jesus knew the need of sinners was not condemnation but repentance and salvation, and He interacted with them in a way that made them want to hear the message.

The world often views Christians as harsh and judgmental because we still believe in right and wrong and because we believe that right and wrong are defined by the Bible. We should never abandon the truth or compromise our message in order to reach the lost, but we should be compassionate and loving in our dealings with others so they know we care for their souls. There is still a Heaven and a Hell, and every person we meet needs God's salvation.

Today's Discipleship Principle: There is no such thing as a Christian who is too focused on reaching the lost with the gospel.

God Looking for Sinners

And he spake this parable unto them, saying, What man of you, having an hundred sheep, if he lose one of them, doth not leave the ninety and nine in the wilderness, and go after that which is lost, until he find it?
—LUKE 15:3–4

In 1987, Joy White took her infant daughter, Carlina, to the hospital in New York City because the child was running a fever. To her horror, someone snatched the baby girl from her hospital bed, and she disappeared. Police were unable to identify any suspects, and the case was never closed. But Joy White believed that her daughter was still alive. Twenty-three years passed, but she never gave up hope. Then in 2011, she received a call from the National Center for Missing and Exploited Children with the amazing news that her daughter had been found. The mother's love in her heart never failed, and her long search was finally rewarded.

All of us are born sinners apart from God, and we have no hope of rescuing ourselves. But in His boundless love and mercy, our Heavenly Father did not wait for us to seek Him—He sent His Son to seek for us. Jesus said, "I am the good shepherd, and know my sheep, and am known of mine. As the Father knoweth me, even so know I the Father: and I lay down my life for the sheep" (John 10:14–15).

The world likes to think that people are fine just as they are, but the Bible teaches that all of us are in desperate need of a Saviour. The reality is that we don't look for Him. "As it is written, There is none righteous, no, not one: There is none that understandeth, there is none that seeketh after God" (Romans 3:10–11). He must seek for us, that is exactly what Jesus did: "For the Son of man is come to seek and to save that which was lost" (Luke 19:10).

Today's Discipleship Principle: The measure of God's love for us is found in the fact that Jesus left Heaven to seek and to save us.

Making Heaven Happy

*And when he hath found it, he layeth it on his shoulders, rejoicing. And when he cometh home, he calleth together his friends and neighbours, saying unto them, Rejoice with me; for I have found my sheep which was lost. I say unto you, that likewise joy shall be in heaven over one sinner that repenteth, more than over ninety and nine just persons, which need no repentance.—*LUKE 15:5–7

William Cushing had a successful pastorate, but then one day he lost his voice. Determined that he still wanted to do something for God, Cushing began writing poems. He worked with Ira Sankey on a number of hymns that were greatly used in D.L. Moody's revivals. One day when he heard a report of those who had been saved in a meeting, Cushing rejoiced. He later said, "It seemed like such a glad day with the very bells of Heaven ringing in my soul. Then the words, 'Ring the Bells of Heaven,' at once flowed down into this waiting melody."

> Ring the bells of heaven! there is joy today
> For a soul, returning from the wild!
> See! the Father meets him out upon the way,
> Welcoming His weary, wand'ring child.
>
> Glory! glory! how the angels sing!
> Glory! glory! how the voices ring!
> 'Tis the ransomed army, like a mighty sea,
> Pealing forth the anthem of the free.

When the lost are saved, all of Heaven rejoices. The salvation of a sinner is the culmination of the work and sacrifice of Jesus, and we have the privilege of being part of this most important effort. "And all things are of God, who hath reconciled us to himself by Jesus Christ, and hath given to us the ministry of reconciliation" (2 Corinthians 5:18).

Today's Discipleship Principle: Nothing we can do on Earth brings more joy to Heaven than reaching the lost with the gospel.

Searching by Candlelight

Either what woman having ten pieces of silver, if she lose one piece, doth not light a candle, and sweep the house, and seek diligently till she find it? And when she hath found it, she calleth her friends and her neighbours together, saying, Rejoice with me; for I have found the piece which I had lost. Likewise, I say unto you, there is joy in the presence of the angels of God over one sinner that repenteth. —LUKE 15:8–10

If you've ever lost something valuable, you know how frustrating it can be to look for it. If it happens at night, you face a choice—you can either wait for the sun to come up, or you can find some kind of a light to help in your search. The decision is usually based on how valuable the lost object is. If it is something fairly minor, you may be content to wait for the sun to come up. But if what you have lost is something important to you, you will probably be down on your hands and knees with a flashlight, searching for it even in the darkness.

We need a renewed sense of the incredible value of the souls of men. Too often we relegate witnessing to an activity we do once a week, or even less frequently. But if we are aware of the reality of Heaven and Hell, we will not wait for convenient times and "good light" to witness. We will strike a match and go out into the darkness to find those who are lost. When Paul summed up his ministry in the city of Ephesus, he pointed out the around-the-clock nature of his effort: "Therefore watch, and remember, that by the space of three years I ceased not to warn every one night and day with tears" (Acts 20:31).

I believe that it is important to schedule specific times for sharing the gospel because the message we share is urgent enough that we should create time to share it. But I also believe that we should be seeking people out in the course of our daily living. Even when you are not engaged in a designated time for witnessing, look for opportunities to share the gospel.

Today's Discipleship Principle: Every Christian needs to be about the work of bringing light into the darkness to find the lost.

Job 1–2   //   Acts 7:22–43   205

Focus on the Father

And he said, A certain man had two sons: And the younger of them said to his father, Father, give me the portion of goods that falleth to me. And he divided unto them his living. —LUKE 15:11-12

J. Wilbur Chapman was often asked to speak in prisons as he traveled around the country in revival meetings. It is said that once he was at the prison in Joliet, Illinois, preparing to speak when the warden said, "Dr. Chapman, we have had twenty-four ministers here this year, and every one of them has preached on the Prodigal Son. Can you speak on something else?" Chapman looked at his Bible which was marked in Luke 15, and then stood to preach. But instead of focusing on the wayward son, Chapman talked about the loving father who never gave up on his child.

We call it the parable of the Prodigal Son, but Jesus told this story as the conclusion of a series of three parables aimed at revealing the nature of God's love toward the lost and the way people respond when others are saved. The world we live in has a distorted picture of God, and that has often infected the church as well. We need to return to the focus that the Bible places on our Heavenly Father and understanding of His nature and character.

This parable begins with what was, in the Middle Eastern culture of Jesus' day, an unbearable insult. Sons did not go to their fathers and demand to be given their inheritance. Yet rather than responding in kind, the father did as he was asked. And, as the rest of the story reveals, he never stopped loving his son or watching for his return.

All of us were born as sinners, enemies of God both by nature and by choice. We have no hope apart from God's love, but His love is overwhelming. "But God commendeth his love toward us, in that, while we were yet sinners, Christ died for us" (Romans 5:8).

Today's Discipleship Principle: Never doubt that God's amazing love for you is settled and certain regardless of what happens in your life.

When the Party Ends

And not many days after the younger son gathered all together, and took his journey into a far country, and there wasted his substance with riotous living. And when he had spent all, there arose a mighty famine in that land; and he began to be in want. —LUKE 15:13–14

When the Prodigal Son got to the far country, at first it seemed like everything was going exactly as he had planned. The rules that he had been forced to obey at home were gone, and he had the resources to do whatever he liked. But there came a day when the money ran out, and the party came to a quick end. Those he thought were his friends when he had money were nowhere to be found when he was broke.

Satan is a master deceiver, and the pictures he paints in temptation leave out the end of the story. If we choose to follow his way, there may be some short-term enjoyment, but the party always ends.

One of the best defenses we have against temptation is the realization that the pleasures of sin only last for a short time. Hebrews 11:24–25 tells us that Moses took this into consideration when he chose to forsake Egypt and identify himself with God's people: "By faith Moses, when he was come to years, refused to be called the son of Pharaoh's daughter; Choosing rather to suffer affliction with the people of God, than to enjoy the pleasures of sin for a season."

God's pleasures are not temporary, but eternal, and never leave us with the pain at the end. There may often be difficulties or obstacles that arise when we follow Him, but the trials are temporary and their results are eternal.

The difference between God's party and Satan's is that God's celebration will be eternal and unending. "And there shall be no night there; and they need no candle, neither light of the sun; for the Lord God giveth them light: and they shall reign for ever and ever" (Revelation 22:5).

Today's Discipleship Principle: If we rightly evaluate what is lasting against what is temporary, we will by faith choose the things of God.

Reaching the Bottom of the Barrel

And he went and joined himself to a citizen of that country; and he sent him into his fields to feed swine. And he would fain have filled his belly with the husks that the swine did eat: and no man gave unto him.
—LUKE 15:15–16

Though Sam Jones was raised by godly parents and grandparents, he turned to drink, and his brilliant and promising legal career was destroyed by his alcoholism. After he lost his job, he still refused to quit drinking. But a visit to his father's deathbed provoked a change. Jones later said, "I went to the bar and begged for a glass of liquor. I got the glass and started to drink and looked into the mirror. I saw my hair matted, the filth and vomit on my clothes, one of my eyes totally closed, and my lips swollen. And I said, 'Is that all that is left of the proud and brilliant lawyer, Sam Jones?' I smashed the glass on the floor and fell to my knees and cried, 'Oh God! Oh God, have mercy!' Something happened to old Sam Jones."

The following Sunday, Jones walked the aisle of his grandfather's church and announced his conversion, and the next week began preaching the gospel. Jones said, "I have been going round the country bragging about Jesus ever since." Sam Jones saw half a million people saved under his ministry. But it was not until he had lost everything that he was willing to turn to God.

Too many times we insist on continuing in our sin until we reach absolute rock bottom, instead we should quickly repent and turn to God. "Let the wicked forsake his way, and the unrighteous man his thoughts: and let him return unto the LORD, and he will have mercy upon him; and to our God, for he will abundantly pardon" (Isaiah 55:7).

Today's Discipleship Principle: We do not have to wait until we suffer tragedy and great loss before we turn to God.

The Insanity of Sinners

And when he came to himself, he said, How many hired servants of my father's have bread enough and to spare, and I perish with hunger! I will arise and go to my father, and will say unto him, Father, I have sinned against heaven, and before thee, And am no more worthy to be called thy son: make me as one of thy hired servants.—LUKE 15:17–19

D r. Curtis Hutson once preached a sermon from the story of the Prodigal Son titled "The Insanity of Sinners" because the Bible says that the young man "came to himself," which indicates he had not been in his right mind. Dr. Hutson said, "Every sinner is insane, because his judgments are out of order. Notice what he did. He put eternity in the background. He wasn't thinking about the future, only about the here and now. He thought he knew better than his father. Sinners sometimes feel they know what is better for them than God does."

Although we usually think of this parable in the context of evangelism (and that was the context in which Jesus gave it as well), this truth is just as applicable to saved sinners as it is to lost sinners. When we turn away from following God to go our own way, we are on the pathway to destruction. Yet despite knowing the clear warnings of Scripture about what happens if we sin and refuse to repent and turn back to God, Christians continue to yield to temptation, and then try to cover their sin rather than confessing and forsaking it.

The false concept that we can hide our sin from God dates back to the Garden of Eden when Adam and Eve tried to keep God from finding out that they had eaten the forbidden fruit. It has never yet worked in all of history, but people continue to try it rather than quickly making things right with God. Yet, all the while, they have a loving Heavenly Father who desires to welcome them back to a life of joyful obedience and close fellowship with Him.

Today's Discipleship Principle: If we tolerate sin in our lives, it is clear evidence that our thinking has been skewed and we are off course.

The Father Running to the Son

And he arose, and came to his father. But when he was yet a great way off, his father saw him, and had compassion, and ran, and fell on his neck, and kissed him.—LUKE 15:20

When people in Jesus' day heard Him tell the story of the Prodigal Son, they heard it through the lens of their culture. To the Jewish listeners, this story contains something unusual that we often don't think of. For a man of wealth and standing in that time to run was extremely rare. He would have servants to take care of his tasks and would dispatch one of them to care for urgent matters. Yet the father saw his son coming from a great distance and ran to meet him. This is a wonderful picture of the way God treats us.

We do not have to persuade God to save us—He delights in rescuing sinners from Hell and placing them into His family. He is even patient and allows us opportunities to respond to the gospel rather than quickly giving us the punishment that we deserve: "The Lord is not slack concerning his promise, as some men count slackness; but is longsuffering to us-ward, not willing that any should perish, but that all should come to repentance" (2 Peter 3:9).

The full measure of the love of God for us can only be understood through the lens of the cross. God was willing to cause His perfect and innocent Son to suffer for the sins of man so that we could be redeemed, and He delighted when our redemption was accomplished. "Yet it pleased the LORD to bruise him; he hath put him to grief: when thou shalt make his soul an offering for sin, he shall see his seed, he shall prolong his days, and the pleasure of the LORD shall prosper in his hand" (Isaiah 53:10).

Even once we are God's children, He welcomes His penitent prodigals with the love of a Father. As soon as we move toward Him in repentance, He runs toward us in restoration.

Today's Discipleship Principle: If we remember how much God loves us, it motivates us to do all that we can to please and honor Him.

Job 14–16   //   Acts 9:22–43

God's Acceptance of Sinners

And the son said unto him, Father, I have sinned against heaven, and in thy sight, and am no more worthy to be called thy son. But the father said to his servants, Bring forth the best robe, and put it on him; and put a ring on his hand, and shoes on his feet:—LUKE 15:21-22

Dr. H.A. Ironside told of an unusual experience he had while preaching in Washington state. He was staying with a family of sheepherders during lambing season. Ironside said, "One morning I was startled to see an old ewe galloping across the road, followed by the strangest looking lamb I had ever beheld. It apparently had six legs, and the last two were hanging helplessly as though paralyzed." His hosts explained that the lamb had been orphaned and they had a ewe who had lost her lamb to a snakebite. But the ewe had originally rejected the lamb because it was not her own.

Ironside went on, "So the herders skinned the lamb that had died and very carefully drew the fleece over the living lamb. This left the hind-leg coverings dragging loose. Thus covered, the lamb was brought again to the ewe. She smelled it once more and this time seemed thoroughly satisfied and adopted it as her own. It seemed to me to be a beautiful picture of the grace of God to sinners. We are all outcasts and have no claim upon His love. But God's own Son died for us, and now we who believe are dressed up in the fleece of the Lamb who died. God has accepted us in Him."

God does not accept us because of anything we have done, but because the perfect righteousness of Jesus Christ has been placed over our lives like a cloak that covers us completely. If we try to clothe ourselves with our righteousness, we find we are covered in only filthy rags (Isaiah 64:6), but when we trust in the shed blood of Jesus, we are clothed in the very righteousness of Christ.

Today's Discipleship Principle: Christians are dressed in the righteousness of Christ so we have full confidence in God's acceptance.

Job 17–19   //   Acts 10:1-23   211

july

Preparing for a Party

And bring hither the fatted calf, and kill it; and let us eat, and be merry:
For this my son was dead, and is alive again; he was lost, and is found.
And they began to be merry.—LUKE 15:23–24

Long before his son returned from the far country, the father of the prodigal was preparing for his return. We know this because he was not only watching for his son, but he had started feeding a special calf to make sure it would be ready for a celebration meal when the boy did come back. That was an expression of faith—the kind of faith we need to have when we pray. Hebrews 11:1 says, "Now faith is the substance of things hoped for, the evidence of things not seen." Even before we see it, we should believe that God will do what He promises and act on that belief.

There is an old saying, "Don't pray for rain and leave your umbrella at home." Too many times we do what we should in praying about our needs and burdens, but without truly believing that God will hear and answer. Instead of walking forward confidently and preparing for the answer, we live with fear and worry. The presence of that emotional and mental discomfort and stress reveal that we do not truly expect God to answer us—that our faith is weak.

In contrast to our often-weak faith, consider Abraham who received a promise from God for something that seemed impossible. Yet he was willing to completely uproot his life and family, move hundreds of miles away, and trust that God would fulfill His promise: "(As it is written, I have made thee a father of many nations,) before him whom he believed, even God, who quickeneth the dead, and calleth those things which be not as though they were" (Romans 4:17). Abraham did not believe because he saw, but rather he saw because he believed.

Today's Discipleship Principle: God has never yet broken a promise, and you can fully rely on Him to do all that He said He would do.

Justice vs. Mercy

Now his elder son was in the field: and as he came and drew nigh to the house, he heard musick and dancing. And he called one of the servants, and asked what these things meant. And he said unto him, Thy brother is come; and thy father hath killed the fatted calf, because he hath received him safe and sound. And he was angry, and would not go in: therefore came his father out, and intreated him.—LUKE 15:25–28

While we know we should be gracious and forgiving toward others, there are times when we want them to get what they deserve rather than receiving mercy. Of course we want mercy for *ourselves,* but sometimes we are unwilling to extend it to others.

Jonah was like that. When God called him to go to Nineveh and preach, he refused, because he knew that if they repented, God would forgive them. We know this from Jonah himself, as he vented his frustration to God for His mercy toward Nineveh: "But it displeased Jonah exceedingly, and he was very angry. And he prayed unto the LORD, and said, I pray thee, O LORD, was not this my saying, when I was yet in my country? Therefore I fled before unto Tarshish: for I knew that thou art a gracious God, and merciful, slow to anger, and of great kindness, and repentest thee of the evil" (Jonah 4:1 2).

The reality is that a desire for others to get what they have coming reveals a hardness in our hearts more than a commitment to justice. It is easy for us to fall into the trap of the Pharisees, thinking that we are doing pretty good as we are and don't really need God's grace and mercy. Yet the very best that we do falls far short of God's standard of absolute righteousness, and it is not our goodness but His grace that prevents our destruction. "Who is a God like unto thee, that pardoneth iniquity, and… delighteth in mercy" (Micah 7:18). Rather than proudly judging others who fall short, we should rejoice when they receive God's forgiveness.

Today's Discipleship Principle: We need to show others the same mercy and forgiveness that God extended to us when He saved us.

An Exalted View of Self

And he answering said to his father, Lo, these many years do I serve thee, neither transgressed I at any time thy commandment: and yet thou never gavest me a kid, that I might make merry with my friends: But as soon as this thy son was come, which hath devoured thy living with harlots, thou hast killed for him the fatted calf.—LUKE 15:29-30

It is easy for us to look around and think that we are better than those around us, and not as much in need of God's grace as they are. But while such proud thoughts are satisfying to our fallen nature, they are not in line with reality. Near the end of one of his best known poems, "To a Louse—On Seeing One on a Lady's Bonnet at Church," the Scottish poet Robert Burns wrote:

> O wad some Power the giftie gie us
> To see oursels as ithers see us!

If we truly saw ourselves as God sees us (for while we may deceive others, He always knows not only our actions but our thoughts), we would abandon any pretense of pride.

The problem we have is that rather than measuring ourselves against the standard of God's perfect holiness, we look to those around us and measure ourselves against them. It is easy to find areas in which we are superior (or at least can convince ourselves we are) and focus on those. The problem with this approach is that it is flawed and foolish. "For we dare not make ourselves of the number, or compare ourselves with some that commend themselves: but they measuring themselves by themselves, and comparing themselves among themselves, are not wise" (2 Corinthians 10:12).

Instead of thinking that we are better than others by looking horizontally, we need to look up and realize that we are just as much in need of God's grace and mercy as those around us.

Today's Discipleship Principle: Having a high view of ourselves keeps us from having a proper view of God.

Wasted Opportunities

And he said unto him, Son, thou art ever with me, and all that I have is thine. It was meet that we should make merry, and be glad: for this thy brother was dead, and is alive again; and was lost, and is found.
—LUKE 15:31–32

The great Scottish poet, historian, and teacher Thomas Carlyle lost his wife Jane unexpectedly after forty years of marriage. On her grave he had these words carved: "For forty years she was the true and loving helpmate of her husband, and by act and word unweariedly forwarded him as none else could in all of worthy that he did or attempted. She died at London, 21st April, 1866, suddenly snatched from him, and the light of his life as if gone out." Yet Carlyle's diary reveals that he had failed to fully appreciate his wife until she was gone. He wrote, "Cherish what is dearest while you have it near you, and wait not till it is far away."

There are many opportunities that are only available to us for a limited period of time, and if we fail to take advantage of them, we will miss out. The older brother of the prodigal son had lived at home with a generous father who had vast resources, and never benefited because he failed to take the opportunities that his status would have provided. The result was that he became bitter and blamed his father for his own failure to take what was freely offered.

So many times we do without the things that we want or even need because we do not pray as God has instructed for our needs to be met. James 4:2 reveals why we do not have many things which God would provide: "…ye have not, because ye ask not."

It is a tragedy if our needs are not met because we fail to take God at His Word. Jesus instructed us in Matthew 7:7, "Ask, and it shall be given you; seek, and ye shall find; knock, and it shall be opened unto you."

Today's Discipleship Principle: Take advantage of what God offers to provide through prayer by daily coming to Him with your needs.

Called to Give Account

And he said also unto his disciples, There was a certain rich man, which had a steward; and the same was accused unto him that he had wasted his goods. And he called him, and said unto him, How is it that I hear this of thee? give an account of thy stewardship; for thou mayest be no longer steward.—LUKE 16:1-2

In 1960, Bernie Madoff started a small stock trading company that quickly became a major player on Wall Street. Madoff would eventually become chairman of the NASDAQ exchange. He received investments from some of the wealthiest individuals and institutions in the country and offered a much higher rate of return than normal to his investors. In 1999, a financial analyst called his business practices into question, but the authorities did not take the charges seriously. It was not until 2008 that Madoff was finally arrested for defrauding billions of dollars from investors. Rather than investing the money that was entrusted to him, Madoff siphoned off much of it to fund his lavish lifestyle. After his conviction, Madoff was sentenced to 150 years in prison.

One day each one of us will stand before God as stewards called to answer for how we have handled the time, talent, and treasure that God has given to us: "So then every one of us shall give account of himself to God" (Romans 14:12). The reality is that everything we have belongs to God, and He holds us responsible for how we use it. While we certainly would not cheat others or steal from them, when we fail to use the resources God has given to us and invest them in the eternal work of His kingdom, we are defrauding Him. That thought should motivate us to diligence and faithful service, recognizing that He is fully aware of not only what we have done and not done, but of what we could have done if we had been willing to do so.

Today's Discipleship Principle: If we live with the realization of the day we will give account to God, we will live wisely.

Finding a Way Forward

Then the steward said within himself, What shall I do? for my lord taketh away from me the stewardship: I cannot dig; to beg I am ashamed. I am resolved what to do, that, when I am put out of the stewardship, they may receive me into their houses. —LUKE 16:3–4

All of us face situations in our lives at times when we do not immediately know what to do. Whether it is an unexpected job loss, a serious medical diagnosis, a crisis in a family relationship, or even a natural disaster, we have a moment (or sometimes several moments) when we simply are not sure how we should respond. Christians are not immune to trouble and difficulty, no matter what popular television preachers may say. We have many of the same struggles, burdens, tears, pains, hurts, and heartbreaks that the world has. The difference is that we have a resource that is not available to the world—faith in a faithful God.

Job was a wealthy man with a large family, but all that he had—his wealth, his children, and his own health—was taken away from him in a single day. On the worst day of his life, when he did not know what else to do, Job trusted God: "Then Job arose, and rent his mantle, and shaved his head, and fell down upon the ground, and worshipped, And said, Naked came I out of my mother's womb, and naked shall I return thither: the LORD gave, and the LORD hath taken away; blessed be the name of the LORD" (Job 1:20–21).

All of us face situations that are beyond what we can handle, but we never have to face those burdens alone. God is always ready and able to assist those who turn to Him for guidance and help. The problem is never that He does not know or cannot help, but that too often we try to make it on our own without seeking His face. When we find ourselves wondering, "What shall I do?" we are wise to turn to the Lord in trust and ask Him to show us the way forward.

Today's Discipleship Principle: When we are unsure of what to do, we should run to the Source of all wisdom and ask for help.

It Wasn't Raining When Noah Built the Ark

*So he called every one of his lord's debtors unto him, and said unto the first, How much owest thou unto my lord? And he said, An hundred measures of oil. And he said unto him, Take thy bill, and sit down quickly, and write fifty. Then said he to another, And how much owest thou? And he said, An hundred measures of wheat. And he said unto him, Take thy bill, and write fourscore.—*LUKE 16:5-7

The central character in the parable of the unjust steward that Jesus told seems like an unlikely candidate to receive praise from the Lord. He was not careful in his business dealings, and as a result he was on the brink of losing his job because he was costing his employer money. It was not for his carelessness, however, but for his response that this steward is praised. Looking ahead at what was coming, he used the authority given to him to arrange discounts for those who owed money to his boss so that they would be favorably inclined toward him in the future.

Many people fail to adequately prepare for the future. Instead of planning ahead, they just go from one day to the next with little thought of tomorrow. Sometimes people even call this approach living by faith. But faith is not blindly assuming that everything is going to work out somehow without us being involved. Faith is obeying what God has told us to do. And one of the things His Word instructs us to do is to look ahead and plan for the future. "A prudent man foreseeth the evil, and hideth himself: but the simple pass on, and are punished" (Proverbs 22:3).

There are times when we complain about what happens to us when we could have avoided the unpleasantness if we had simply been diligent in our planning and preparation. As the old saying goes, "It wasn't raining when Noah built the ark."

Today's Discipleship Principle: Wise planning for the future is an important part of our obedience to God's commands.

Using Wealth Wisely

And the lord commended the unjust steward, because he had done wisely: for the children of this world are in their generation wiser than the children of light. And I say unto you, Make to yourselves friends of the mammon of unrighteousness; that, when ye fail, they may receive you into everlasting habitations.—LUKE 16:8–9

Many people are surprised to learn that Jesus talked more about money than He did about Heaven and Hell—combined. There is a great emphasis in Scripture on how we use our money, and it is important that we understand God's viewpoint. The primary purpose of money is that we can do things that matter both in the immediate, and in the eternal realm as well. The devil tempts us to selfishly consider our own interests, but God calls us to care about more than just ourselves.

It is said that in England there is a tombstone with the following inscription:

> Here lies a miser who lived for himself
> He spent his whole life in gathering wealth
> Where he is now and how he fares
> Nobody knows and nobody cares.

Living selfishly robs us of eternal rewards and damages our relationships. Jesus taught that we are to use our resources to help others. This is an expression of our love and concern for them, but it also builds friendships and relationships that will make life better both for us and for those we help.

Our society is increasingly isolated. Many of the connections that once bound communities and neighborhoods together have been weakened, and the same thing has happened in many churches as well. The investments that we make in the lives of others draw God's people together in meaningful and powerful ways.

Today's Discipleship Principle: God gives us temporal resources that we can and should use wisely to produce eternal results and rewards.

Faithfulness in Both Large and Small Things

He that is faithful in that which is least is faithful also in much: and he that is unjust in the least is unjust also in much. If therefore ye have not been faithful in the unrighteous mammon, who will commit to your trust the true riches? And if ye have not been faithful in that which is another man's, who shall give you that which is your own?—LUKE 16:10–12

In 1899, a magazine editor named Elbert Hubbard, who needed to fill one additional page with copy, dashed off a brief essay in one hour that told the story of an unsung hero of the Spanish American War who had undertaken and completed the difficult task of delivering a message from President McKinley to a rebel leader in Cuba. "A Message to Garcia" was eventually reprinted more than forty million times, and its emphasis on being willing to serve faithfully challenged generations to do what they could even in tasks that seemed small.

The temptation that we face is to cut corners in small things, rather than taking them seriously and being faithful and diligent. As someone once said, "Even if the task is not worthy of you, diligence is." Those who claim they would be faithful if the job were more important or the financial sums involved were higher are not telling the truth. Faithfulness is a character trait that does not depend on circumstances but on what lies within our hearts and minds.

We have no basis to expect God to entrust more to us if we are not being faithful with what we already have. The things already given to us form a test of what we would do with larger opportunity. It is not what we claim with our mouths, but what we demonstrate with our deeds that measures our faithfulness. And it is not in the future but in the present that faithfulness must be shown.

Today's Discipleship Principle: Faithfulness does not begin with large tasks; if it is not present in small things, it does not exist at all.

The Choice between God and Money

No servant can serve two masters: for either he will hate the one, and love the other; or else he will hold to the one, and despise the other. Ye cannot serve God and mammon. —LUKE 16:13

Jesus could have correctly said that it is impossible to serve both God and the devil at the same time. He could have said that we could not serve both God and the world. Both of those statements are true, but that is not the truth that Jesus chose to highlight. The distinction that He drew was that it is impossible for us to serve both God and money. Money is not an evil in and of itself, but the desire and love of money leads to all kinds of sin.

There are two kinds of love for money that lead us to serve wealth rather than serving God. The first is the love for money itself—a desire to accumulate large sums to provide security or status. The second is the love for the things that money buys. We live in a materialistic society where value and worth are measured by having the latest toys, the newest gadgets, the best houses and cars, and the best of everything.

Interestingly, neither of these wrong approaches to money is limited to the rich. The poor are just as susceptible to this snare as the wealthy.

Paul warned Timothy of the dangers of falling in love with either money or the things that money can buy, and he had seen firsthand the damage that serving money does to those who had formerly been dedicated to God's work: "For Demas hath forsaken me, having loved this present world, and is departed unto Thessalonica…" (2 Timothy 4:10). The deceitfulness of money is that it promises we can serve it while still serving God, but that is false.

Today's Discipleship Principle: If we love God as we should, there will be no room for money to rule on the throne of our hearts.

Outside and Inside

And the Pharisees also, who were covetous, heard all these things: and they derided him. And he said unto them, Ye are they which justify yourselves before men; but God knoweth your hearts: for that which is highly esteemed among men is abomination in the sight of God.
—LUKE 16:14–15

One of the things the Pharisees hated most about Jesus was that He was not impressed with the elaborate outward rituals they had developed to convince people that they were holy. Jesus saw through the outward piety into their hearts, and condemned them for the evil they allowed to remain hidden from the sight of men. Charles Spurgeon said, "O what fools men are, to think they can do anything in secret. This world is like the glass hives wherein bees sometimes work: we look down upon them, and we see all the operations of the little creatures. So God looketh down and seeth all."

The reputation that we have before the world matters, and it is important that we maintain a good testimony. But if the outward appearance that others see is only "skin deep" and our heart does not match, God knows. And eventually those around us will as well. One of the things about sin is that it always grows and spreads. We may be able to keep it concealed for a time, but sooner or later it will come to the surface.

Ever since the Garden of Eden man has been trying to hide and cover sin. It hasn't ever worked, but we keep trying.

God's remedy for sin is not covering, but confession: "He that covereth his sins shall not prosper: but whoso confesseth and forsaketh them shall have mercy" (Proverbs 28:13). When we are rightly focused, caring more about what God sees than about what others may think, we will be quick to confess and forsake our sins.

Today's Discipleship Principle: Knowing that God sees our heart should lead us to seek His forgiveness rather than trying to cover our sins.

The Unfailing Word of God

The law and the prophets were until John: since that time the kingdom of God is preached, and every man presseth into it. And it is easier for heaven and earth to pass, than one tittle of the law to fail. —LUKE 16:16–17

When Alexander Duff was on his way to India to serve as a missionary, his ship sank near the shore. While Duff and his party were able to swim to safety on shore, all of his belongings, including the eight hundred books he had brought to study and use in teaching and preaching were lost. The next morning, walking along the beach Duff found one book had survived—his Bible. Though he lacked the other resources he had hoped to use in his work, Duff built a school on the sure foundation of the Word of God that educated thousands of young students and made a great impact on India.

The Word of God is powerful because God's nature and character ensure that it will never fail. In his prayer at the dedication of the temple in Jerusalem, Solomon said, "Blessed be the LORD, that hath given rest unto his people Israel, according to all that he promised: there hath not failed one word of all his good promise, which he promised by the hand of Moses his servant" (1 Kings 8:56).

The sad reality is that most of us have had painful first-hand experiences with someone not keeping the promises that they have made to us. It really hurts to find out that we cannot rely on someone we trusted, but that never happens with God. When we build our lives on His promises, we can have complete confidence that they will not fail.

Every part of God's Word is faithful and true and unfailing, because it is a reflection of Him. Promises are only as good as the people who make them. And that is why we can fully rely on everything the Bible says. The Christian life can be based on this sure foundation.

Today's Discipleship Principle: The Bible is worthy of our full faith and confidence, for as the Word of God, it never fails.

Overlooked Needs

There was a certain rich man, which was clothed in purple and fine linen, and fared sumptuously every day: And there was a certain beggar named Lazarus, which was laid at his gate, full of sores, And desiring to be fed with the crumbs which fell from the rich man's table: moreover the dogs came and licked his sores.—LUKE 16:19–21

I read about a remarkable study conducted at Princeton some years ago. A group of theology students (who did not know they were being studied) were assigned one at a time to go across campus to speak on the story of the Good Samaritan. The researchers had hired an actor to take up a spot along the route and pretend to be suffering from a physical illness when the students came by. The final touch was to tell the students that they were running late and needed to hurry.

Ninety percent of the students who were going to speak on the Good Samaritan ignored the suffering person they met on the way. The researchers reported, "Indeed, on several occasions, a seminary student going to give his talk on the parable of the Good Samaritan literally stepped over the victim as he hurried away!"

All around us there are people in need. These needs may be readily apparent, or they may require some careful looking and listening on our part to identify, but they are real. We are surrounded by hurting people, and we have a duty to reach out in love and compassion to help them when we can. Peter summed up the life and ministry of Jesus this way: "How God anointed Jesus of Nazareth with the Holy Ghost and with power: who went about doing good, and healing all that were oppressed of the devil; for God was with him" (Acts 10:38).

It is always right to do what we can to help, encourage, and bless those who are hurting. Many times they are nearer to us than we realize because we don't take the effort to look to the needs of those around us.

Today's Discipleship Principle: Don't miss your opportunities to help those in need.

Eternal Destinies

And it came to pass, that the beggar died, and was carried by the angels into Abraham's bosom: the rich man also died, and was buried; And in hell he lift up his eyes, being in torments, and seeth Abraham afar off, and Lazarus in his bosom. —LUKE 16:22–23

Every one of the more than seven billion people living on earth today has an eternal destiny that awaits them. This life is just a brief interlude that passes by very quickly. And it is only during this life that the choice can be made that determines whether eternity will be spent in Heaven or Hell.

The culture surrounding us treats truth as relative and does everything it can to ignore the truth of the coming judgment. But refusal to believe it does not change the truth. Lazarus was immediately taken up, and the rich man was immediately sent down. Those are the only two options—there is no intermediate state or Purgatory. There is no "soul sleep" or annihilation. Every person will consciously either endure torment or enjoy blessing for eternity.

That truth should be constantly on our minds. Each person we meet is headed toward eternity, and since life tomorrow is not promised to any of us, we need to be serious in our efforts to sound the warning while there is still time.

Heaven and Hell are real places, and if we grasp the severity of the consequences of failing to accept Christ as Saviour, we will be diligent in our efforts to win the lost: "Knowing therefore the terror of the Lord, we persuade men; but we are made manifest unto God; and I trust also are made manifest in your consciences" (2 Corinthians 5:11). There are many things that are good and valuable and even important, but salvation is the one critical decision that every person needs to make before it is too late.

Today's Discipleship Principle: Do not let today end without speaking to someone about their salvation and the truth of eternity.

A Place of Torment

And he cried and said, Father Abraham, have mercy on me, and send Lazarus, that he may dip the tip of his finger in water, and cool my tongue; for I am tormented in this flame.—LUKE 16:24

Hell is a real place. The fires of Hell are not metaphorical, but literal. Scripture tells us that it was originally prepared not for people, but for Satan. Jesus said, "Then shall he say also unto them on the left hand, Depart from me, ye cursed, into everlasting fire, prepared for the devil and his angels" (Matthew 25:41). The first rebellion against God was not by man but by the devil, and Hell is the result of that rebellion. Yet when men refuse to turn to God, they doom themselves to eternity in that awful place.

It is hard for us to think about people spending eternity in the torment of Hell. It seems unfair to our judgment and sensibility. Yet when we look from God's vantage point, and realize what is happening when someone rejects salvation by grace through faith in Christ alone— salvation purchased at such an enormous price—we see that Hell is a fitting and just judgment. "Of how much sorer punishment, suppose ye, shall he be thought worthy, who hath trodden under foot the Son of God, and hath counted the blood of the covenant, wherewith he was sanctified, an unholy thing, and hath done despite unto the Spirit of grace?" (Hebrews 10:29).

As children of God, we have a responsibility to those who are lost. God has called and commanded us to proclaim salvation through Jesus Christ to the world. The message that we have been given to share is the only hope of escape from Hell. Because of the seriousness of this message, we must make sharing it with others as faithful witnesses of the gospel the highest priority of our lives.

Today's Discipleship Principle: Remembering the awful reality of Hell motivates us to tell others how they can escape its torment through Jesus.

Consider the Long Term Results

But Abraham said, Son, remember that thou in thy lifetime receivedst thy good things, and likewise Lazarus evil things: but now he is comforted, and thou art tormented. And beside all this, between us and you there is a great gulf fixed: so that they which would pass from hence to you cannot; neither can they pass to us, that would come from thence.
—LUKE 16:25–26

In the early 2000s, the Atlanta Public School system was being held up as an example to the nation of how to improve student performance and test scores. The school superintendent, Beverly Hall, was chosen as the national superintendent of the year in 2009. But an investigation of the test scores revealed something disturbing—a pattern of changed answers on the tests. When the investigation was complete, it was revealed that at forty-four of Atlanta's fifty-six schools, nearly two hundred teachers and principles had worked together to erase wrong answers and replace them with correct ones so their students would appear to be improving on the tests. Eventually eleven of those most involved were convicted and sentenced to prison for their roles in the scandal.

Dr. Bob Jones, Sr. often said, "Don't sacrifice the permanent on the altar of the immediate." All of us face the temptation to do what is easy in the moment rather than considering the long-term results of our choices. But those should be the most important consideration—not what feels good today, but what will produce good results in the future. Though God offers forgiveness when we repent for wrong choices, forgiveness does not always undo the consequences of the choices we have already made. Nothing we do is without impact, both on our own lives and the lives of others, and we need to remember that as we make decisions.

Today's Discipleship Principle: When faced with decisions today, consider their long-term results before committing to a course of action.

A Plea for Soulwinning from an Unexpected Source

Then he said, I pray thee therefore, father, that thou wouldest send him to my father's house: For I have five brethren; that he may testify unto them, lest they also come into this place of torment.—LUKE 16:27–28

The notion that Hell is not a place to be feared has been with us for a long time. In a biography published in 1886 of the lawyer and noted public speaker Emery A. Storrs, we find this anecdote: "A young man once approached him with, 'Mr. Storrs, pardon me, but you are a man who has thought much upon all topics. I wish to ask you for your opinion of Heaven and Hell.' Fixing his keen eyes on the enquirer, Mr. Storrs answered 'When I think of the beauteous descriptions of the abode of the saints, and when I recollect that many noble witty, genial souls have died unregenerate, I must answer you, sir, that, while, doubtless, Heaven has the best climate, Hell has the best society.'"

I've heard similar answers while sharing the gospel with others. People who are not interested in receiving Christ as their Saviour may say, "I want to go to Hell and be with my buddies." Yet those who are actually in Hell have no pleasure in the company they are keeping. In the story Jesus told of Lazarus and the rich man, we see that though he had been an unrepentant sinner during his life, this man greatly desired that someone would go warn his five brothers not to follow him to that place of torment. If we could hear the citizens of Hell today, they would be crying out for us to warn their friends and loved ones of the eternal death facing those without Christ.

Today's Discipleship Principle: We should be just as concerned about keeping people out of Hell as those who are already there are.

The Bible Brings Conviction

Abraham saith unto him, They have Moses and the prophets; let them hear them. And he said, Nay, father Abraham: but if one went unto them from the dead, they will repent. And he said unto him, If they hear not Moses and the prophets, neither will they be persuaded, though one rose from the dead.—LUKE 16:29–31

There are many people suggesting new ways to reach people for the Lord, given the rapidly changing society in which we live. And while not everything that is new is wrong—I'm thankful for the enlarged opportunities to reach people with the gospel through new tools—there is a danger that we will become so enamored with techniques and programs and forget the true source of the power of our message. What we most need in our day is not a new method of reaching people, but faithfulness to the method God has given us to reach the world—the proclamation of the Word of God.

Paul pointed this out in 1 Corinthians 1:21, "For after that in the wisdom of God the world by wisdom knew not God, it pleased God by the foolishness of preaching to save them that believe." It is not through our clever techniques or manipulation that people are reached. It is not through amazing demonstrations of power that conviction comes. Even miracles would not be enough to persuade those who will not believe what the Bible says is true.

The responsibility for results does not rest on us. It is not our job to bring conviction of sin. That is the work of the Holy Spirit through the Word of God: "For the word of God is quick, and powerful, and sharper than any twoedged sword, piercing even to the dividing asunder of soul and spirit, and of the joints and marrow, and is a discerner of the thoughts and intents of the heart" (Hebrews 4:12). But it is our job to share the Word of God through which the Holy Spirit works.

Today's Discipleship Principle: We can trust the Word of God to have its effect on others if we are faithful to proclaim it.

What Did You Expect?

Then said he unto the disciples, It is impossible but that offences will come: but woe unto him, through whom they come! It were better for him that a millstone were hanged about his neck, and he cast into the sea, than that he should offend one of these little ones.—LUKE 17:1–2

Most of us have had the experience of putting money in a vending machine, only to have it fail to deliver the product we were expecting. Sometimes insult is added to injury when the machine not only fails to dispense, but also does not return the money we put into it in the first place. When we do not receive what we expect, it is a disappointing experience. But I've never seen anyone shaking or pounding on a vending machine after he got the candy bar he wanted. His expectations were fulfilled, and he was not surprised, so there was no reaction.

Jesus tells us that there are going to be difficulties and offenses that we must deal with in life. While it would be nice if people did what they promised and treated us with kindness and respect, that is not the normal course of human interaction. Day after day we can expect to be offended—and when we are, God still expects us to respond properly rather than retaliating. The actions or failures of others do not excuse carnal behavior on our part.

But there is another lesson for us in what Jesus said. Rather than being hyper-vigilant to respond every time someone offends us, our focus needs to be on being diligent about ensuring that we are not giving offense to others. Paul placed a high value on this, and in his testimony before Felix, he was able to say, "And herein do I exercise myself, to have always a conscience void of offence toward God, and toward men" (Acts 24:16). If we have expectations that we will never be offended, we'll be disappointed. But we still should be careful to never be a source of offence to others.

Today's Discipleship Principle: Take great care not to be an unnecessary source of offense in the lives of others.

Repeat Offenders

Take heed to yourselves: If thy brother trespass against thee, rebuke him; and if he repent, forgive him. And if he trespass against thee seven times in a day, and seven times in a day turn again to thee, saying, I repent; thou shalt forgive him. —LUKE 17:3–4

Henry Earl of Kentucky holds the dubious distinction of being the most arrested man in the world. According to news reports, he has been arrested more than 1,500 times. Since almost all of the charges have been minor, most of them related to public intoxication or disorderly conduct, Earl has rarely been sentenced to more than a few days in jail for each offense. Yet because of the massive number of arrests, Henry Earl has spent more than sixteen years of his life in confinement.

All of us have people in our lives who hurt us and do things to us that are wrong. God calls us and commands us to forgive them—not just the first time they do it, but over and over again. The pattern and model for forgiveness, even toward repeat offenders, is that set by the way God treats us: "And be ye kind one to another, tenderhearted, forgiving one another, even as God for Christ's sake hath forgiven you" (Ephesians 4:32). The truth is that we ourselves are in constant need of God's mercy and forgiveness.

Because we need forgiveness on an ongoing basis, often for the same offense against God, we must not fail to extend forgiveness to others. Of course this does not mean that we allow ourselves to suffer repeated injury, but we cannot obey God and refuse to forgive those who harm us, even if they are repeat offenders. While it is easier to cut people off and hold what they have done against them, in the end it harms us far more than it impacts the offender. When you find yourself weary of forgiving someone else for their repeated offenses, remember the ongoing forgiveness that God gives to you.

Today's Discipleship Principle: God's forgiveness and patience toward us is the example we are meant to follow with others.

The Request Jesus Refused to Answer

And the apostles said unto the Lord, Increase our faith. And the Lord said, If ye had faith as a grain of mustard seed, ye might say unto this sycamine tree, Be thou plucked up by the root, and be thou planted in the sea; and it should obey you.—LUKE 17:5–6

O ften during the three years Jesus spent teaching and training His disciples, Jesus was asked to do different things for them. His normal response was to meet their need, whether it was teaching on a particular topic or working a miracle like calming a storm on the Sea of Galilee. But in one instance, Jesus refused to answer the request of the disciples. When they asked for their faith to be increased, Jesus did not lay hands on them and impart faith to them. Instead He told them that even a tiny bit of faith—the size of a mustard seed—was enough to see a great miracle worked.

You see, the problem is not that we need more faith, but that we need to use the faith that we have. If you read the stories of Hebrews 11, you will see imperfect people. Noah, Abraham, Moses, and David all had times of significant sin failures in their lives. Why are these people honored for their faith? Because although they did have times of failure which they confessed to God and repented of, they also faced choices when they believed God and acted in obedience to what He told them to do.

We sometimes make the mistake of thinking we must be giants of faith before we can see God work. Instead we simply need enough faith to take the next step in obedience. It is only through action that we receive the benefits of a growing faith. If you have enough faith to pray, you have enough faith to see God work.

Today's Discipleship Principle: If you put the faith you have into action today, it will be enough to equip and enable you to honor and serve God.

Understanding a Servant's Role

But which of you, having a servant plowing or feeding cattle, will say unto him by and by, when he is come from the field, Go and sit down to meat? And will not rather say unto him, Make ready wherewith I may sup, and gird thyself, and serve me, till I have eaten and drunken; and afterward thou shalt eat and drink?—LUKE 17:7-8

O ur modern view of Christianity has been infected by society so that we often find ourselves thinking of our service to God as a buffet where we pick and choose what we do. That is not the biblical model of servanthood. In Jesus' day a servant was expected to do what he was told without exception. There was no choice in the matter or consideration for the preferences of the servant. The tasks were assigned, and they were expected to be carried out in full. God is not just our friend, but also our Lord and Master, and He has the right to full and complete obedience from us.

Someone illustrated this truth by drawing a contrast between two ship captains. If you have ever been on a cruise ship, you know that the captain and crew are dedicated to providing whatever is necessary for the passengers to have a pleasant experience. They are there to serve the passengers. Anyone who has been in the Navy, however, knows the captain in a very different role. The captain of a battleship expects every order to be carried out to the letter by those under his command.

The great missionary David Livingstone wrote, "God, send me anywhere, only go with me. Lay any burden on me, only sustain me. And sever any tie in my heart except the tie that binds my heart to Yours." Rather than insisting on getting our way and avoiding anything that might be unpleasant, we must yield ourselves fully to God's control.

Today's Discipleship Principle: Unless we are willing and ready to do everything that God commands, we cannot truly call ourselves His servants.

Reasonable Service

Doth he thank that servant because he did the things that were commanded him? I trow not. So likewise ye, when ye shall have done all those things which are commanded you, say, We are unprofitable servants: we have done that which was our duty to do.—LUKE 17:9–10

Throughout Scripture we see God commanding people to do things that seem foolish, unhelpful, or difficult. Yet in each case those who did as He instructed were rewarded for their faithful obedience. Noah built a large boat to prepare for a flood that had never happened before. Abraham bound his son Isaac to an altar, preparing to offer him as a sacrifice. Joshua commanded the priests carrying the ark to walk into the flooded Jordan River. At the instruction of Jesus, Peter got out of the boat and walked on the Sea of Galilee during a storm. None of these things makes sense to our reasoning, but when God speaks, we should obey without question or hesitation. (Of course this does not apply to people claiming God has told them to do things that are not in His Word.)

To our reasoning, it does not make sense to completely yield our lives to God and obey Him, even as we understand that doing everything He says is the bare minimum that is expected—our simple duty. Paul wrote, "I beseech you therefore, brethren, by the mercies of God, that ye present your bodies a living sacrifice, holy, acceptable unto God, which is your reasonable service" (Romans 12:1). Because of the great sacrifice with which our salvation was purchased, it is completely reasonable for us to give God total control of our lives. No sacrifice that we could ever make compares to the death of Jesus on the cross for our redemption. Nothing that God commands us to do as His servants is unreasonable, because we belong completely to Him.

Today's Discipleship Principle: Rather than being impressed with how much we have done for God, we need to keep our focus on how much He has done for us.

Healed on the Way

And as he entered into a certain village, there met him ten men that were lepers, which stood afar off: And they lifted up their voices, and said, Jesus, Master, have mercy on us. And when he saw them, he said unto them, Go shew yourselves unto the priests. And it came to pass, that, as they went, they were cleansed.—LUKE 17:12–14

Jesus has all power and authority, and He often demonstrated that during His ministry by healing those who were sick beyond the power of medicine in His day to heal. Few things were more dreaded than leprosy both because of the terrible impact it had on the person's life, and even more because it was so contagious. Once they were identified, lepers were cut off and cast out from society unless they were carefully examined by a priest and certified to be healed.

Normally when Jesus healed people it happened instantaneously. Usually He would either speak to the sufferer or sometimes touch them and they would be healed. In the case of the ten lepers, however, He took a different approach. When the men asked Jesus for healing, He told them to go to the priests for examination. (The Old Testament stated that before a leper could be pronounced cured, he must be examined by the priest for any signs of the disease.) Jesus did not immediately proclaim them healed. He did not lay His hands on them and pronounce them cured. Instead He told them to do what they would do if they had already been healed. It was only as they went in obedience that they were cleansed of their leprosy.

Many times we want God to lay out every step of His plan in detail and make sure we understand it before obeying. But God normally only lays out one step at a time. Psalm 119:105 says, "Thy word is a lamp unto my feet, and a light unto my path." Faith is not revealed when we see the entire picture, but when we act on what we have been told.

Today's Discipleship Principle: If we do not obey what God has already said, we have no reason to expect Him to give us further direction.

Grateful Sinners

And one of them, when he saw that he was healed, turned back, and with a loud voice glorified God, And fell down on his face at his feet, giving him thanks: and he was a Samaritan.—LUKE 17:15–16

A nimosity between the Jews and Samaritans in the time of Christ was a deep-seated contempt, really a hatred, stretched back hundreds of years. The Samaritans resented the way the Jews viewed them, and the Jews looked down on the Samaritans because of their heritage. Jewish people would walk miles out of their way to avoid going through a Samaritan town. Yet when Jesus healed the ten lepers, the one who returned to give thanks was a member of this despised group.

This man had no hesitation about bowing down before a Jewish rabbi and expressing his gratitude for the life-saving healing he had received. He didn't care about the divisions or the ancient arguments over where and how to worship God—he was just grateful for what had happened to him.

Too many times we forget that before our salvation, we were the enemies of God. We tend to be pretty impressed by ourselves, but God is not. The very best that we are able to do on our own is disgustingly filthy in His eyes because it is measured against His perfect holiness. "But we are all as an unclean thing, and all our righteousnesses are as filthy rags; and we all do fade as a leaf; and our iniquities, like the wind, have taken us away" (Isaiah 64:6).

To have the proper gratitude to God for His salvation, we must never forget that we were once wretched sinners with no hope apart from His grace. When we remember how desperate our condition was without Christ, we will be more prone to give God the glory for His mercy and grace toward us.

Today's Discipleship Principle: If we forget where we were and where we were headed before God saved us, we will not be grateful as we should.

"Where Are the Nine?"

And Jesus answering said, Were there not ten cleansed? but where are the nine? There are not found that returned to give glory to God, save this stranger. And he said unto him, Arise, go thy way: thy faith hath made thee whole.—LUKE 17:17–19

D r. H.A. Ironside recounted the story that once when he was about to begin his meal in a restaurant, a man approached and asked if he could join him. Ironside invited him to sit and as was his custom, then bowed his head in prayer. When he was finished praying and opened his eyes, the other man asked, "Do you have a headache?" Ironside replied, "No, I don't." The man then asked, "Well, is there something wrong with your food?" Ironside said, "No, I was simply thanking God as I always do before I eat." The man said with some contempt, "Oh, you're one of those, are you? Well, I want you to know I never give thanks. I earn my money by the sweat of my brow and I don't have to give thanks to anybody when I eat. I just start right in!" Ironside replied, "Yes, you're just like my dog. That's what he does too!"

Though all sin is wrong and bears consequences, there are few sins more damaging to our lives than ingratitude. Romans 1:21 places it at the beginning of the downward slope away from God: "Because that, when they knew God, they glorified him not as God, neither were thankful; but became vain in their imaginations, and their foolish heart was darkened."

If we think that we have little or nothing for which to be thankful, we have a skewed view of the world, ourselves, and God's kindness to us. All that we have is a result of God's goodness and grace. Nothing that we have is truly our own, and without Him, we would have no help or hope for the future. But God has given us His great salvation, and every day He gives us His presence, grace, and untold blessings besides.

Today's Discipleship Principle: It is impossible to be an obedient and fruitful Christian without being a thankful Christian.

Missing the Kingdom of God

*And when he was demanded of the Pharisees, when the kingdom of God should come, he answered them and said, The kingdom of God cometh not with observation: Neither shall they say, Lo here! or, lo there! for, behold, the kingdom of God is within you.—*LUKE 17:20–21

The Jewish people of Jesus' time wanted one thing more than almost anything else—freedom from the occupying Roman Empire. They viewed all of the prophecies of the coming of the Messiah through the lens of a political leader who would bring about a restoration of the freedom and prominence that Israel had enjoyed under David and Solomon nearly one thousand years earlier. They were not focused on the spiritual teaching of Jesus and His emphasis on the things of God. They were looking for outward physical deliverance rather than inward spiritual salvation. As a result, many of those who had the greatest opportunity ever for accepting Jesus completely missed it. The Kingdom of God was offered to them, but they rejected it.

Often even those of us who have trusted Christ as Saviour fail to grasp the full impact of what the Bible tells us about the Kingdom of God. We easily fall into the trap of focusing on the temporal, not realizing that the things God values are not the things the world around us holds dear. Obedience to Scripture requires that we give up what the world treasures to grasp the things God values. The kingdom of God is not about political power or financial success; it is about making Christ known in all the world.

F.B. Meyer wrote, "Earthly thrones are generally built with steps up to them; the remarkable thing about the thrones of the eternal kingdom is that the steps are all down to them. We must descend if we would reign, stoop if we would rise, gird ourselves to wash the feet of the disciples as a common slave in order to share the royalty of our Divine Master."

Today's Discipleship Principle: If we do not have Christ reigning as King in our hearts, we will miss out on being part of His Kingdom work.

The Sudden Return of Jesus

And he said unto the disciples, The days will come, when ye shall desire to see one of the days of the Son of man, and ye shall not see it. And they shall say to you, See here; or, see there: go not after them, nor follow them. For as the lightning, that lighteneth out of the one part under heaven, shineth unto the other part under heaven; so shall also the Son of man be in his day.—LUKE 17:22–24

The timing of Christ's first coming was laid out in detail by the prophet Daniel. The decree by the Persian ruler Cyrus to rebuild the Temple in Jerusalem started the clock ticking, and Jesus entered Jerusalem on what we commonly call Palm Sunday—right on the schedule God had revealed to the prophet hundreds of years before.

Christ's Second Coming, an event for which we still wait, is just as certain and sure as was His first coming, but we are not given a time line for this event. Instead we are commanded to be ready for Him to return at any moment so that we will not be ashamed.

John Henry Jowett wrote, "Said a mother to me one day concerning her long-absent boy: 'I lay a place for him at every meal! His seat is always ready!' May I not do this for my Lord? May I not make a place for Him in all my affairs—my choices, my pleasures, my times of business, my season of rest? He may come just now; let His place be ready!"

Those who are eagerly anticipating the return of Jesus will receive a special reward from Him when He appears: "Henceforth there is laid up for me a crown of righteousness, which the Lord, the righteous judge, shall give me at that day: and not to me only, but unto all them also that love his appearing" (2 Timothy 4:8). Just as we would eagerly watch for the return of a loved one, we should watch for the return of Christ with eager anticipation.

Today's Discipleship Principle: Every day should be lived with both an awareness that Jesus could return and a longing in our hearts that it will be today.

The Days of Noah

But first must he suffer many things, and be rejected of this generation. And as it was in the days of Noe, so shall it be also in the days of the Son of man. They did eat, they drank, they married wives, they were given in marriage, until the day that Noe entered into the ark, and the flood came, and destroyed them all.—LUKE 17:25–27

The Flood that destroyed all of mankind except for those in the ark in Noah's day remains a powerful reminder of the holy hatred God has for sin. The fact that the Flood was completely unexpected says so much about human nature. In the verses above, Jesus tells us that people continued their routines right up to the very day that Noah went into the ark and the rain began. Yet we also know that for more than one hundred years Noah had proclaimed to those around him the warning that God's judgment was coming. They received the warning. They simply refused to heed it.

We are living in a similar day. The judgment of God came on the world not primarily because they were so wicked (there is plenty of wickedness in our day) but because they refused to repent. If the notably evil city of Nineveh was spared because they responded to Jonah's warning (Jonah 3:10) and the city of Sodom would have been spared if there had been at least ten righteous people there (Genesis 18:32), there is little doubt that if the people had responded to Noah, God's hand of judgment would have been stayed.

There are many lessons that could be drawn from this teaching, but one of the most important for us is the reality that it is a mistake to think that because God has not yet carried out judgment He will never do so. Instead of continuing on in our careless routines, we need to believe what He says.

Today's Discipleship Principle: Let us be quick to heed warnings from the Spirit of God and His Word and turn to Him for forgiveness.

Man Proposes, God Disposes

Likewise also as it was in the days of Lot; they did eat, they drank, they bought, they sold, they planted, they builded; But the same day that Lot went out of Sodom it rained fire and brimstone from heaven, and destroyed them all. Even thus shall it be in the day when the Son of man is revealed.—LUKE 17:28–30

Walter Knight recounted the story of an old Scottish woman who made her living by going from house to house across the countryside selling thread, buttons, and shoestrings. It was her custom that, when she came to an unmarked crossroad, she would toss a stick into the air and go in the direction the stick pointed when it landed. One day a farmer standing nearby saw her throw a stick in the air numerous times. "Why do you toss the stick more than once?" he asked. "Because," replied the woman, "it keeps pointing to the left, and I want to take the road on the right." She kept throwing the stick into the air until it pointed the way she wanted to go.

Many times we are tempted to ignore what God has directed because it conflicts with our plans and desires. James issued this warning to those who make their plans for the future without considering God. "Whereas ye know not what shall be on the morrow. For what is your life? It is even a vapour, that appeareth for a little time, and then vanisheth away. For that ye ought to say, If the Lord will, we shall live, and do this, or that" (James 4:14–15). Submission to God's will is not demonstrated by saying, "Lord willing" at the end of every sentence, but by submitting our plans to His revealed will. Though the Bible does not specifically address every situation we will face, it does give principles we must follow if we want to do God's will. We should enter each day and approach each decision with a sincere desire to know and follow the will of God and to obey what He has revealed in His Word.

Today's Discipleship Principle: Trusting God's will for the future is evidenced when we obey His Word and base our decisions on it.

The Danger of Turning Back

In that day, he which shall be upon the housetop, and his stuff in the house, let him not come down to take it away: and he that is in the field, let him likewise not return back. Remember Lot's wife.—LUKE 17:31-32

The Christian life is meant to be lived in only one direction—forward. Yet we are constantly tempted to look back to the world and the things that we left behind when we trusted Christ as Saviour. The danger is that if we keep looking back, sooner or later we will find a way to go back, regardless of the consequences.

This is not new, because the same danger faced Abraham and Sarah who followed God by faith to a land where they had never been: "And truly, if they had been mindful of that country from whence they came out, they might have had opportunity to have returned" (Hebrews 11:15). Rather than looking longingly to the past, we should keep our eyes fixed on Jesus.

Charles Spurgeon used this metaphor of mountain climbing for our progress in the Christian life. "The Christian life is very much like climbing a hill of ice. You cannot slide up. You have to cut every step with an ice ax. Only with incessant labor in cutting and chipping can you make any progress. If you want to know how to backslide, leave off going forward. Cease going upward and you will go downward of necessity. You can never stand still. If you begin to slip on the side of a mountain of ice, the first slip may not hurt if you can stop and slide no further. But alas, you cannot so regulate sin! When your feet begin to slide, the rate of the descent increases, and the difficulty of arresting this motion is incessantly becoming greater. It is dangerous to backslide in any degree, for we know not to what it may lead."

If we spend our time looking back to the things of the world, it will not be long before we go back to the world.

Today's Discipleship Principle: Keep your eyes fixed on Jesus, and you will keep walking by faith.

august

Living for Eternity

Whosoever shall seek to save his life shall lose it; and whosoever shall lose his life shall preserve it.—LUKE 17:33

Polycarp was one of the leaders of the early church. It seems that he was a personal disciple of the Apostle John, who ordained Polycarp to be the pastor of the church at Symnra. After years of faithful service, a great persecution arose against those in the church who refused to offer incense to Caesar. Polycarp was threatened with death if he would not recant his faith in Christ alone. The old Christian replied, "Eighty and six years I have served Him, and He has done me no wrong. How then can I blaspheme my King and Savior? You threaten me with a fire that burns for a season, and after a little while is quenched; but you are ignorant of the fire of everlasting punishment that is prepared for the wicked." The sentence of execution was carried out, but Polycarp's faith was not extinguished.

While none of us are eager to be martyred for our faith, we should all be willing to give our lives rather than deny the Lord. The real test most of us face is not whether to make the ultimate sacrifice or turn away from God to preserve our lives, but whether or not to make the small sacrifices of doing right when doing wrong would be more convenient or profitable in the short run. We may not be faced with the decision of if we will deny Christ at the point of the sword, but sometimes we face a decision of whether or not we will deny Him at the point of a friendship or a business dealing that demand compromise. If our faith is not strong enough to overcome small temptations and give us the victory over the world that God promises to us, we should not think that it will be strong enough to withstand a more serious test. The answer to the question of what we would do if our faith were put to the ultimate test is found in what we love the most—ourselves and our temporary lives or God and His eternal life.

Today's Discipleship Principle: If our lives are more precious to us than our love of Jesus, we will never serve Him faithfully as we should.

Christ Brings Division

I tell you, in that night there shall be two men in one bed; the one shall be taken, and the other shall be left. Two women shall be grinding together; the one shall be taken, and the other left. Two men shall be in the field; the one shall be taken, and the other left.—LUKE 17:34–36

Donald Barnhouse pastored in Philadelphia during World War I, and a young soldier who had been converted during the war asked him for advice on how to avoid falling back into his old lifestyle. Barnhouse suggested that he simply make his commitment to Christ public. He said, "You will not have to give up improper friends if you do—they will give you up." When the soldier got off the train at the station, he met a young lady he had known before. When she asked how he was doing he replied, "The greatest thing that could possibly happen to me has happened." When she asked if he had gotten engaged he replied, "No, it's better than that. I've trusted the Lord Jesus Christ as my Saviour." She quickly ended the conversation and went on her way. He had a similar conversation with another pre-war friend, and soon found that those he had known before who would pull him back into ungodly living stopped coming around.

The message of Jesus is a message of peace with God through salvation. It is not, however, a message of immediate peace on earth, nor will there be such peace until Jesus returns to rule the world. Jesus said, "Think not that I am come to send peace on earth: I came not to send peace, but a sword" (Matthew 10:34). It would be nice if being a good Christian meant that everyone would automatically like us and respond kindly to us, but the reality is the opposite. This vile world is no friend to grace, and if we are to follow Jesus, there will be those who will refuse to come with us.

Today's Discipleship Principle: It is impossible to be friends with the world and a faithful follower of Jesus Christ.

Recognizing the Signs

And they answered and said unto him, Where, Lord? And he said unto them, Wheresoever the body is, thither will the eagles be gathered together.—LUKE 17:37

When you drive down a country road and see a number of buzzards circling in the air, it doesn't take special insight to understand that there is probably a dead animal nearby that has attracted their attention. We would be shocked if we drove past to discover them enjoying a particularly beautiful display of flowers in a field. That is because we know what buzzards eat and what draws their interest, so when we see them we understand what it signifies. God expects us to have the wisdom and insight to approach the world in the same way.

We should not just casually pass through life without any understanding of the events we see happening around us. Instead we should look at them through the lens of God's Word and through the lessons of history to grasp the implications of what we see. Every nation, every church, and every family needs people with this skill. First Chronicles 12:31 speaks of "...the children of Issachar, which were men that had understanding of the times, to know what Israel ought to do...."

The Bible often speaks of the Christian life as a war, and no soldier who sleepwalks through his days without paying attention to his surroundings can expect to survive, let alone be victorious. We need to be wise, alert, and focused on what is happening, so we can plan for the future and anticipate the return of Christ based on what we see. The Lord does not leave us without the means to evaluate circumstances and events and avoid trouble that we do not need to experience. Colossians 4:5 instructs us, "Walk in wisdom toward them that are without, redeeming the time."

Today's Discipleship Principle: Looking at life through the pages of Scripture helps us understand the meaning of the events we see.

Pray or Else

*And he spake a parable unto them to this end, that men ought always to pray, and not to faint;—*LUKE 18:1

We live in an age of substitutes. You can go to the store and buy hamburgers that don't have any meat in them. You can buy clothing that has no natural materials. You can even get plastic and metal replacement parts for bad knees, hips, and shoulders. In many cases the substitutes that we've come up with work as well as (or at least almost as well as) the originals. But there are some things that cannot be replaced. For the Christian, prayer is one of those things. There are only two choices for the believer—either we pray, or we will faint.

Life is not meant to be lived in our own strength, and if we make that attempt, it is doomed to failure. One hymnist said it this way:

> Prayer is the Christian's vital breath,
> The Christian's native air,
> His watchword at the gates of death;
> He enters Heav'n with prayer.

God's plan for our lives as His children revolves around our communication with Him. We hear from Him through His Word, and He hears from us when we pray. Most religions throughout history have relied on a group of priests or religious leaders to go to their gods on behalf of the people. But Christianity offers a different approach. Because God adopts us into His family when we place our faith in Jesus Christ as our Saviour, He invites us to come directly to Him with our petitions.

God places all of His resources behind His promises to provide for our needs, yet many Christians do without for the simple reason that they do not pray.

Today's Discipleship Principle: A Christian who does not pray—faithfully, diligently and regularly—is a Christian headed toward defeat.

The Power of Importunity

*Saying, There was in a city a judge, which feared not God, neither regarded man: And there was a widow in that city; and she came unto him, saying, Avenge me of mine adversary. And he would not for a while: but afterward he said within himself, Though I fear not God, nor regard man; Yet because this widow troubleth me, I will avenge her, lest by her continual coming she weary me.—*LUKE 18:2–5

In his sermon on importunity in prayer, Andrew Murray noted that God's way of working in our lives is patterned after His creation. Murray said, "All nature has been so arranged by God that in sowing and reaping, as in seeking coal or gold, nothing is found without labor and effort. What is education but a daily developing and disciplining of the mind by new difficulties presented to the pupil to overcome? The moment a lesson has become easy, the pupil is moved on to one that is higher and more difficult."

The illustration Jesus used to teach the importance of faithful and persistent prayer was that of a judge who cared only for himself, and not for the cases brought before him. Although God is nothing like this judge in character, Jesus used this story to teach us about God and prayer. If even a hardhearted judge without any concern for the needs or claims of others could be moved to action by the repeated pleas of a powerless widow, how much more readily and willingly will God respond when His beloved children cry out to Him for help?

It is true that God does not always answer our prayers immediately, but that is not because of a lack of either the will or the resources to help. Instead He knows that our faith needs to be strengthened through times of adversity, and that if we receive an answer after prolonged prayer, we will appreciate it much more when it comes.

Today's Discipleship Principle: Prayers according to the will of God should never cease until the answer we are pleading for has come.

Trusting God's Justice

And the Lord said, Hear what the unjust judge saith. And shall not God avenge his own elect, which cry day and night unto him, though he bear long with them?—LUKE 18:6-7

Perhaps the greatest example in Scripture of the proper response to injustice is found in the life of Joseph. Though he was cruelly treated by his own brothers, who sold him into slavery only as an alternative to killing him outright, and spent years in prison when he was falsely accused by Potiphar's wife, Joseph's attitude remained one of faith. He did not take matters into his own hands and seek revenge, even when presented with the opportunity to do so when God raised him to a high and powerful position in Egypt. Joseph recognized that God had been at work even during the painful events of his life, and he was willing to trust God to settle any scores that needed to be made right.

The desire to seek revenge is natural, but as God's children we are called to trust God to bring justice. Romans 12:19 instructs, "Dearly beloved, avenge not yourselves, but rather give place unto wrath: for it is written, Vengeance is mine; I will repay, saith the Lord."

It is interesting that even in Heaven, John saw in his vision those who had been martyred for their faith and heard them crying out for God to execute vengeance: "And when he had opened the fifth seal, I saw under the altar the souls of them that were slain for the word of God, and for the testimony which they held: And they cried with a loud voice, saying, How long, O Lord, holy and true, dost thou not judge and avenge our blood on them that dwell on the earth?" (Revelation 6:9–10).

All of us will be disappointed or mistreated at some point. In those moments of pain and anguish, we face the choice of trusting God or trying to get even. It is not wrong to desire justice, but it is wrong not to trust God for it.

Today's Discipleship Principle: If we truly trust God, our faith will extend to not trying to get even with those who do us wrong.

The Tragic Absence of Faith

I tell you that he will avenge them speedily. Nevertheless when the Son of man cometh, shall he find faith on the earth?—LUKE 18:8

One day, perhaps very soon, Jesus will return to this world. And while He was with His disciples, He told us what He would be looking for on His return—faith.

It is impossible to overstate the importance of faith in our lives. It is the fundamental essential for everything in Christianity. We are saved by faith. We walk by faith. We obey by faith. Hebrews 11:6 even says we can't please God without it: "But without faith it is impossible to please him: for he that cometh to God must believe that he is, and that he is a rewarder of them that diligently seek him."

Yet the question that Jesus asked about finding faith carries a definite negative connotation in its construction. The way He asked it reveals that in most cases He expects the answer to be "No." It is tragic that so many of God's children live solely on their own strength and resources rather than relying on God and obeying His Word. Faith brings us into alignment with God's purpose and plan for our lives, because true faith is always based on what He says.

Why do so few have faith? While there are many reasons, the fundamental problem is that we do not treat the Bible as we should. God's Word is the source and foundation of our faith. Romans 10:17 says, "So then faith cometh by hearing, and hearing by the word of God."

If we are to be the exceptions to the negative expectation, if we are to be the people who will be found faithful when the Lord returns, then we must be people of the Bible. When God's Word fills our hearts, our thoughts, and our mouths, we will live faithfully in accord with what it teaches.

Today's Discipleship Principle: If our lives are not filled with faith, they will not be pleasing to Jesus upon His return.

A Proper View of Self

And he spake this parable unto certain which trusted in themselves that they were righteous, and despised others:—LUKE 18:9

The author and humorist Mark Twain was not a Christian, and his disregard for faith and the things of God were well-known. One of the things that Twain hated the most, and that helped turn him away from being saved, was the hypocrisy of professing Christians whom he saw. Though that does not excuse his sinful refusal of salvation, it should serve as a warning to all of us that our conduct does have a great impact on those around us. It is said that on one occasion a prominent businessman who claimed to be a Christian but was known for unscrupulous dealings told Twain, "Before I die I mean to make a pilgrimage to the Holy Land. I will climb Mount Sinai and read the Ten Commandments aloud at the top." Twain responded, "I have a better idea. You could stay in Boston and keep them."

The temptation to feel like we are doing well—or at least better than those around us—is so comforting that we often find ourselves giving in to it even though we should know better. When we evaluate our lives, however, by the measure and standard of the expectations and commands of a perfectly holy God found in His Word, we quickly realize that we fall far short.

God uses the metaphor of a mirror to describe the Bible: "For if any be a hearer of the word, and not a doer, he is like unto a man beholding his natural face in a glass: For he beholdeth himself, and goeth his way, and straightway forgetteth what manner of man he was" (James 1:23–24). Instead of looking around for others to whom we can compare ourselves so that we feel better, we need to allow the Scriptures to perform their cleansing and correcting work in our lives.

Today's Discipleship Principle: Rather than measuring ourselves by those around us, we need to hold up Jesus as the absolute standard.

The Pride of the Pharisees

Two men went up into the temple to pray; the one a Pharisee, and the other a publican. The Pharisee stood and prayed thus with himself, God, I thank thee, that I am not as other men are, extortioners, unjust, adulterers, or even as this publican. I fast twice in the week, I give tithes of all that I possess. —LUKE 18:10–12

The Pharisees in Jesus' day were experts in two things: They were diligent in following the traditions, customs, and rules that they had added to the Word of God, especially in public. (Following the things the Bible actually said was somewhat optional.) And they were diligent in judging and condemning all those who did not measure up to their regulations. The irony is that though they had memorized the first five books of the Bible and at least outwardly tried to present themselves as complying with all that God had commanded, they completely missed the point. The root of their problem, as we so often find in our day, was in their pride. They were relying on their own efforts and righteousness to gain acceptance from God without realizing how far short they fell of His perfection.

When Paul wrote to the church at Rome, he described his anguish over the refusal of his Jewish brothers and sisters toward Christ. This especially grieved Paul since he himself had once been a Pharisee, persecuting the church and thinking he was pleasing God by doing so. He described their efforts like this: "For they being ignorant of God's righteousness, and going about to establish their own righteousness, have not submitted themselves unto the righteousness of God" (Romans 10:3).

The desire to make ourselves righteous is not new—it goes back to Cain bringing an offering of what he produced rather than an animal sacrifice (Genesis 4:3–5). Without question, the primary reason this approach is so appealing is that it feeds our pride to think that we can gain standing with God on our own.

Today's Discipleship Principle: Since our righteousness will never be good enough, we must rest in Jesus' righteousness and abandon our pride.

What Blocks Our Prayers Most

And the publican, standing afar off, would not lift up so much as his eyes unto heaven, but smote upon his breast, saying, God be merciful to me a sinner. I tell you, this man went down to his house justified rather than the other: for every one that exalteth himself shall be abased; and he that humbleth himself shall be exalted.—LUKE 18:13–14

Following the assassination of President William McKinley in 1901—the third president to be killed in office—the Secret Service was given the responsibility of protecting the president's life. Agents were detailed to guard the leader of our nation around the world, a responsibility that continues to this day. One of the most important tools the Secret Service uses to guard the president is their ability to limit access to the occupant of the Oval Office. People are not allowed to just walk in and see the president whenever they want.

In contrast, God offers us the ability to freely enter His presence as His children. Yet even though that offer is available, we can cut ourselves off from His grace if we allow pride to lift up our view of ourselves and keep us from being humble. This is why 1 Peter 5:5 admonishes us, "Likewise, ye younger, submit yourselves unto the elder. Yea, all of you be subject one to another, and be clothed with humility: for God resisteth the proud, and giveth grace to the humble."

Like a parent holding a child whose face is covered in filth at arm's length until they can be cleaned up, God views our pride as putrid and disgusting, and it leads Him to resist our prayers. Though our standing as His children cannot be changed, our relationship with Him is dramatically damaged when we hold pride in our hearts.

Prayer and pride simply cannot coexist in our lives. And in most cases, a prideful Christian feels so self-sufficient that he or she neglects even the act of prayer.

Today's Discipleship Principle: Pride blocks our prayers from being heard and robs us of the grace God offers to freely provide.

Don't Turn Anyone Away

And they brought unto him also infants, that he would touch them: but when his disciples saw it, they rebuked them. But Jesus called them unto him, and said, Suffer little children to come unto me, and forbid them not: for of such is the kingdom of God.—LUKE 18:15–16

It's hard for us to understand the reaction of the disciples when parents brought their young children to Jesus for a blessing. Rather than welcoming them with open arms, they rebuked these parents who dared to bother the Lord with their babies. During the time of Christ, children, especially the very young, were not considered important or valuable. It appears that the disciples thought that the ministry of Jesus would be hindered if He stopped to bless these children who they thought would not benefit from it because they were so young. Jesus' response was different. He corrected the disciples and welcomed the children with open arms. In fact, He went on to use their innocence as an illustration of the process of salvation.

In this story we see a vitally important spiritual principle—we should never turn away anyone who wants to come to Jesus. The truth is that God calls us to reach sinners with the gospel, and if we obey that command, we will end up meeting and working with people who we could faithlessly assume won't come to Jesus and whose lives are falling apart.

The gospel is not meant for those who already have everything together, but for those who recognize their need. Jesus said, "But go ye and learn what that meaneth, I will have mercy, and not sacrifice: for I am not come to call the righteous, but sinners to repentance" (Matthew 9:13). We have the privilege of sharing the good news, and we need to not limit the scope of our outreach.

Today's Discipleship Principle: Jesus never turns away those who come to Him in faith, and we should make them welcome as well.

Come as a Child

Verily I say unto you, Whosoever shall not receive the kingdom of God as a little child shall in no wise enter therein. —LUKE 18:17

I read a wonderful story that took place during the massive German bombing of England during World War II. The Blitz took a terrible toll, not just on military targets, but on civilians as well. The unguided bombs often fell in residential neighborhoods. One night when their building was struck by a bomb, a father and his young son ran outside for fear the building would collapse. Seeing a bomb crater nearby, the father jumped in seeking shelter from the continuing attack. He called for his son to follow, but the terrified boy said, "I can't see you." "But I can see you," the father responded. "Jump!" The boy leaped into the arms of his father and to safety.

Faith is not based on our strength, our wisdom or anything about us. Like little children, we must place our faith in God alone and depend on Him completely. We are often so focused on what we can see that we fail to receive what God offers to those who trust His resources rather than their own. The Christian life cannot be lived as God intends apart from faith. "Therefore we are always confident, knowing that, whilst we are at home in the body, we are absent from the Lord: (For we walk by faith, not by sight:)" (2 Corinthians 5:6–7).

There are times when we are not able to do everything we would like to do for our children, but there is no limit to what God is able to do for us. Yet we find it difficult to rely on Him, because we forget that we are His children, and as such have the right to claim all that He has promised. It is simple faith that opens the storerooms of Heaven and unleashes the power of God in our lives. We need only go to Him in humble dependence and ask for what we need.

Today's Discipleship Principle: When we think our faith is based on us rather than on God, we are headed for trouble.

A Misplaced Sense of Confidence

And a certain ruler asked him, saying, Good Master, what shall I do to inherit eternal life? And Jesus said unto him, Why callest thou me good? none is good, save one, that is, God. Thou knowest the commandments, Do not commit adultery, Do not kill, Do not steal, Do not bear false witness, Honour thy father and thy mother. And he said, All these have I kept from my youth up.—LUKE 18:18–21

There is a vast gulf between the number of people who profess to be Christians and the number of people who have actually received salvation by grace through faith. Many of them have confidence in their standing with God, but it is sadly misplaced. Jesus said, "Many will say to me in that day, Lord, Lord, have we not prophesied in thy name? and in thy name have cast out devils? and in thy name done many wonderful works?" (Matthew 7:22). The wealthy leader who went to Jesus seeking assurance of his standing with God thought that everything was fine. He was not asking because he thought he had a need, but to confirm what he already thought about his spiritual condition.

Charles Spurgeon said of this person, "This young man lacked knowledge. He did not know the spirituality of the law. He had never been taught that the law concerns our glances, our thoughts, and our imagination. He supposed he had kept the law because he had not committed any act of adultery, or of theft—nor had he spoken the thing that was not true. He did not know that an unchaste glance, or a causeless hatred, or a covetous desire breaks the law of God and betrays the sin that lurks in the breast. The question showed that he did not know that salvation is not by doing, but by believing—not by our works, but by a simple trust in Jesus."

Today's Discipleship Principle: If your faith is solely in the finished work of Jesus then your salvation is fully settled and secure.

Nothing but Jesus

Now when Jesus heard these things, he said unto him, Yet lackest thou one thing: sell all that thou hast, and distribute unto the poor, and thou shalt have treasure in heaven: and come, follow me. And when he heard this, he was very sorrowful: for he was very rich.—LUKE 18:22-23

In 1859 Charles Blondin became an international sensation when he made the first of what would eventually be more than three hundred crossings above Niagara Falls on a tightrope. When people became accustomed to his feat, Blondin began adding even more difficulty by carrying various objects, including a camera to take pictures and a stove on which he cooked an omelet which he then lowered to passengers on a ship below. Perhaps nothing matched his feat of carrying his manager Harry Colcord across the falls on his back.

Blondin, who stood only five feet, five inches tall and weighed just 140 pounds, carefully balanced the man in place and said, "Look up, Harry…you are no longer Colcord, you are Blondin. Until I clear this place, be a part of me—mind, body, and soul. If I sway, sway with me. Do not attempt to do any balancing yourself. If you do we will both go to our death." The two men successfully made their way to safety across the roaring falls below because Colcord completely trusted Blondin.

When Jesus called us to follow Him, He meant that we would fully yield ourselves to Him. The Christian life is not about us—it is all about Jesus. Paul wrote, "I am crucified with Christ: nevertheless I live; yet not I, but Christ liveth in me: and the life which I now live in the flesh I live by the faith of the Son of God, who loved me, and gave himself for me" (Galatians 2:20). The selfish pride that tempts us to rely on our own strength and resources robs us of what Jesus provides when we yield ourselves fully to Him. Nothing can be allowed to come between the Lord and us.

Today's Discipleship Principle: To follow Jesus we must be willing to completely abandon ourselves and rest solely on Him.

Hindrances to Salvation

*And when Jesus saw that he was very sorrowful, he said, How hardly shall they that have riches enter into the kingdom of God! For it is easier for a camel to go through a needle's eye, than for a rich man to enter into the kingdom of God.—*Luke 18:24–25

There are many reasons that people do not accept God's free gift of salvation, but perhaps the most common of all is the insistence on making our own way—trusting our works, our resources, our abilities, and our efforts rather than relying on the finished work of Christ alone. The example Jesus used was of the difficulty rich people faced in being saved. It is not wealth that keeps men from Heaven but a reliance on riches rather than on God's grace that keeps them from recognizing their need of a Saviour.

The basic prerequisite for someone to get saved is for them to first realize that they are lost. "When Jesus heard it, he saith unto them, They that are whole have no need of the physician, but they that are sick: I came not to call the righteous, but sinners to repentance" (Mark 2:17).

In our day this is especially prevalent with our society's emphasis on self-esteem and making people feel good about themselves no matter what. (I read of a high school in Texas where students whose grades qualified them for the National Honor Society were not allowed to wear the stoles signifying that accomplishment so those who had not made the grades wouldn't feel bad.) But it is not kind to make people feel good about themselves instead of telling them that we all need a Saviour.

God doesn't grade on a curve, and nothing that we have or can do is worthy of merit in His sight. The Lord instructed the rich ruler to sell all that he had and give it away—not so that he could buy salvation, but so that his heart and what he truly loved would be exposed.

Today's Discipleship Principle: Effectively sharing the gospel with others requires helping them understand their lost condition without Christ so they can be saved.

The Great Miracle of Salvation

And they that heard it said, Who then can be saved? And he said,
The things which are impossible with men are possible with God.
—LUKE 18:26–27

Most people in the world who think about eternity believe that their destiny is determined by themselves—what they do or do not do, how they act toward others, or whether or not in the end their good deeds outweigh the bad things they have done. But if we understand what the Bible says about the perfection of God and the standard of His unchanging holiness, we quickly see that any salvation that depends on our own works and efforts is an utter impossibility.

In the time of Christ, great wealth was seen as a sign of God's special blessing (and in many places it is still the same today), so when Jesus said that it was hard for rich people to be saved, it came as a shock to His hearers. Their assumption seems to have been that if these favored people would find salvation difficult to attain no one else stood a chance. But Jesus pointed out to them that salvation itself is a miracle of God. It is not about what we do but about what God does in response to our faith in the death, burial, and resurrection of His Son.

The reality is that none of us have any hope of salvation on our own. No accomplishment, atonement, or achievement that we can reach offers any means of acceptance in His sight. Romans 3:23 says, "For all have sinned and come short of the glory of God." The word used for *sin* literally means" to miss the mark," like an archer shooting at a target and completely missing. In truth, we don't even come close to the righteousness of God.

No one can save themselves, no matter how hard they try. That is why salvation is a miracle of God—one He offers to perform to anyone who will place their faith in Him.

Today's Discipleship Principle: Rejoice today in your own salvation and then take time to share the good news with someone else.

Blessings Now and Later

Then Peter said, Lo, we have left all, and followed thee. And he said unto them, Verily I say unto you, There is no man that hath left house, or parents, or brethren, or wife, or children, for the kingdom of God's sake, Who shall not receive manifold more in this present time, and in the world to come life everlasting.—LUKE 18:28–30

Some people act like serving God is all about sacrificing and being miserable, as though it was a dreadful and painful thing to follow in the footsteps of Jesus. But Jesus painted a difficult picture. There are sacrifices and struggles, but they pale in comparison to the blessings that we receive, both in eternity as well as in this life.

Those who desire eternal joy must recognize the necessity of serving God in this life. His work is not grievous to those who love Him. Jesus said, "Take my yoke upon you, and learn of me; for I am meek and lowly in heart: and ye shall find rest unto your souls. For my yoke is easy, and my burden is light" (Matthew 11:29–30).

Dr. John R. Rice recounted his decision to enter the ministry this way. "Down at the Pacific Garden Mission, singing and doing personal work, one night I more or less volunteered myself to be a preacher on the basis of Romans 12:1–2, 'present your bodies a living sacrifice,' and the call of Isaiah 6 in which he said, 'Here am I, send me.' I wanted nothing better than to win souls and have welling up in my heart continually the glad joy I felt at that moment. I looked through the vista of future years and saw the time when 'they that be wise shall shine as the brightness of the firmament; and they that turn many to righteousness as the stars for ever and ever.'" When Christ calls us to follow Him, He is not calling us to a life of misery but a life of joy and blessing. While we will be called to forsake some things in following Jesus, it is only that we may have room to receive His blessings.

Today's Discipleship Principle: Every day there are blessings to be found for those who serve the Lord with gladness and with willing hearts.

Fulfilled Prophecy and God's Faithfulness

Then he took unto him the twelve, and said unto them, Behold, we go up to Jerusalem, and all things that are written by the prophets concerning the Son of man shall be accomplished.—LUKE 18:31

There's an old saying that goes like this: "If they ask for a date, don't give a number. If they ask for a number, don't give a date. If they insist on both, mumble softly." That is not how God gave prophetic declarations. He didn't mumble. In fact, the Bible is filled with declarative prophetic statements. These are not vague generalities designed to conceal failure through a lack of precision. God foretold specific incidents and details of the life of Jesus hundreds or even thousands of years in advance. And every one of those declarative statements was proved true down to every tiny detail.

These prophecies of the Old Testament were given to validate the claim of Jesus to be the Messiah. The gospel writers frequently talk about events as fulfilling particular prophetic declarations, citing the prophets who made them so that everyone would know that Jesus was the promised Saviour. The fact that He was born when and where the Bible said He would be, that He lived and ministered as the Bible said He would, and that He died, was buried, and resurrected exactly as foretold is evidence that He is the promised Son of God.

But these fulfilled promises also offer us confidence for the future. The same God who spoke those events that came to pass makes promises to us in His Word—and every one is just as certain and sure as those that have already been fulfilled. Peter tells us that the Bible is given to us to believe: "Whereby are given unto us exceeding great and precious promises…" (2 Peter 1:4).

Today's Discipleship Principle: Because God has never broken a promise in the past, we can place full confidence in every promise for the future.

The Holy Spirit and the Word of God

For he shall be delivered unto the Gentiles, and shall be mocked, and spitefully entreated, and spitted on: And they shall scourge him, and put him to death: and the third day he shall rise again. And they understood none of these things: and this saying was hid from them, neither knew they the things which were spoken.—LUKE 18:32–34

The temptation is for us to condemn the disciples for their failure to understand what Jesus told them about His upcoming crucifixion. He plainly said that He was going to Jerusalem where He would be put to death and then resurrected, but they didn't get the point. Before we judge them too harshly, however, we should remember that there are often things in the Bible that we struggle to understand—and we even have the great advantage of the indwelling Holy Spirit to help us understand what the Word of God teaches.

Charles Spurgeon said, "Commentators and expositors are very useful, indeed, but the best expositor is always the author of a book, himself. If I had a book which I did not quite understand, it would be a very great convenience to me to live next door to the author, for then I could run in and ask him what he meant. This is just your position, Christian! The book will sometimes puzzle you, but the divine Author, who must know His own meaning, is always ready to lead you into its meaning!"

One of the main roles of the Holy Spirit in our lives is to help us understand the Bible. Jesus said, "Howbeit when he, the Spirit of truth, is come, he will guide you into all truth: for he shall not speak of himself; but whatsoever he shall hear, that shall he speak: and he will shew you things to come" (John 16:13).

Today's Discipleship Principle: Because we have the Holy Spirit, we have everything we need to understand what God tells us in the Scriptures.

Blind Beggars Crying for Mercy

And it came to pass, that as he was come nigh unto Jericho, a certain blind man sat by the way side begging: And hearing the multitude pass by, he asked what it meant. And they told him, that Jesus of Nazareth passeth by. And he cried, saying, Jesus, thou Son of David, have mercy on me.—LUKE 18:35–38

If you've ever visited a third world country, you know how persistent needy beggars can be. They don't take the first "no" for an answer. They follow you down the street, asking for help. And while a few of them may be professional beggars, using the kindness of others as a way to avoid work, many of them are truly in desperate need. That sense of desperation gives an urgency to their requests. They do not merely *want* help—they *need* it.

The blind beggar outside Jericho was not shy about making his needs known. He was calling out at the top of his lungs, begging Jesus to stop and help him. He knew full well that he was blind and that he had no hope apart from this miracle-working teacher he had heard so many people talk about as they passed his place by the side of the road. He received mercy because he knew his need and cried out for it.

Too often we fail to realize our utter dependence on God. We wrongly think we don't need God's help. The stern warning to the church at Laodicea includes this description of their self-deception: "Because thou sayest, I am rich, and increased with goods, and have need of nothing; and knowest not that thou art wretched, and miserable, and poor, and blind, and naked" (Revelation 3:17).

We need God's grace, mercy, and strength just as much as Christians to live for Him as we did when we were lost and in need of salvation. This is what Jesus meant when He said, "Blessed are the poor in spirit: for theirs is the kingdom of heaven" (Matthew 5:3).

Today's Discipleship Principle: When we see ourselves in desperate need of God's grace and mercy, we will seek His face with intensity.

What Do You Want Most?

*And they which went before rebuked him, that he should hold his peace: but he cried so much the more, Thou Son of David, have mercy on me. And Jesus stood, and commanded him to be brought unto him: and when he was come near, he asked him, Saying, What wilt thou that I shall do unto thee? And he said, Lord, that I may receive my sight.—*LUKE 18:39–41

As a young man, David Livingstone was challenged when he heard the missionary Robert Moffat talk of seeing the campfires of a thousand villages where the name of Jesus had never been heard. He committed his life to taking the gospel to Africa, and he became one of the greatest missionaries in history. Though Livingstone gained great fame as an explorer, he cared about reaching the lost above all else, and he preached the gospel everywhere he went.

After Livingstone died, his body was returned to England where it was buried with great honor in Westminster Abbey. But before the African men who had trusted Christ as their Saviour through Livingstone's ministry prepared his body for shipment, they cut out his heart and buried it beneath a tall tree near his final camp. His heart, they explained, belonged in Africa.

When Jesus asked the blind beggar what he most wanted the Lord to do for him, he did not need to consider or weigh his options. There was one thing that he desired above all else, and he plainly asked Jesus for it.

There is enormous power found in a focused life—where instead of dashing heedlessly from one thing to the next we are focused on something that truly matters. Paul was able to say, "Brethren, I count not myself to have apprehended: but this one thing I do, forgetting those things which are behind, and reaching forth unto those things which are before, I press toward the mark for the prize of the high calling of God in Christ Jesus" (Philippians 3:13–14).

Today's Discipleship Principle: When God is what we love more than anything else, our lives will be devoted to His service.

Faith Impacts Others

And Jesus said unto him, Receive thy sight: thy faith hath saved thee. And immediately he received his sight, and followed him, glorifying God: and all the people, when they saw it, gave praise unto God.—LUKE 18:42–43

The core of Napoleon's army was an elite force known as the Old Guard. These veteran soldiers were selected from those who had shown the most skill and courage in battle. The members of "The Immortals" as they were known across Europe took great pride in their reputation that they had never lost a battle. The story goes that at one point when the enemy forces were gaining ground, Napoleon told his trumpeter to sound retreat. The young man drew himself up to his full height and replied, "I don't know that bugle call!" Instead he played the charge. The men, thinking reinforcements were on the way moved forward with new spirit and won the battle.

We most often think of faith as a personal matter, and it is that. But it is more—our faith, or our lack of faith, impacts those around us in powerful ways. When one man refuses to give in to doubt, others are encouraged to believe. When one woman refuses to give in to temptation, others are encouraged to do right. When one church is attempting to do great things for God, other churches are challenged to renew their efforts to reach the lost and make disciples.

The Christian life is not meant to be lived in isolation. Paul reminds us, "For none of us liveth to himself, and no man dieth to himself" (Romans 14:7). Everything that we do has an impact on those around us. When we are faithful and see God work in our lives, it honors and glorifies Him, and it serves as an inspiration and example to others of what He is able to do for them if they will walk in faith-filled obedience. When we take a step of faith, we have the incredible opportunity to glorify God, not only by our own faith but also by the impact its results will have on others.

Today's Discipleship Principle: By walking in faith, we not only please God with our lives, but we encourage others to do the same.

A Desire to See God

*And Jesus entered and passed through Jericho. And, behold, there was a man named Zacchaeus, which was the chief among the publicans, and he was rich. And he sought to see Jesus who he was; and could not for the press, because he was little of stature. And he ran before, and climbed up into a sycomore tree to see him: for he was to pass that way.—*LUKE 19:1-4

In 2009, police in Utah received several phone calls reporting a car that was driving erratically. When an officer got close to the vehicle, the driver pulled to a stop, jumped out and ran inside a nearby house. The guilty driver was just seven years old! When police entered the home, the boy was explaining to his father that he had taken the keys and driven off in the car because he did not want to go to church that morning.

There are times when our relationships with God are not what they should be and we have no desire for His presence. But when we are walking in fellowship with Him, there is nothing sweeter than the sense that He is near to us.

The main thing that comes between us and intimate fellowship with God and with other Christians is sin. Whether it is a sin that we are clinging to and do not want to give up or guilt that we should no longer be carrying because we have confessed and forsaken a sin in the past, there is a real division that comes in our relationship with God because of sin. This has been true ever since the Fall in the Garden of Eden: "And the LORD God called unto Adam, and said unto him, Where art thou? And he said, I heard thy voice in the garden, and I was afraid, because I was naked; and I hid myself" (Genesis 3:9–10).

It is possible that Zacchaeus only wanted to see Jesus out of curiosity. Certainly he had heard of Christ's miracles, and he may have just wanted a glimpse. But it's also possible that his heart was becoming tender toward his need for God. In any case, his desire to see Jesus led to his faith in Christ.

Today's Discipleship Principle: If our hearts are not eager for time spent with God and His people, it is a sign that something is wrong in our lives.

A Saviour Who Seeks Sinners

And when Jesus came to the place, he looked up, and saw him, and said unto him, Zacchaeus, make haste, and come down; for to day I must abide at thy house. And he made haste, and came down, and received him joyfully.—LUKE 19:5-6

The defining characteristic of the life and ministry of Jesus Christ was His great burden for people. He felt a deep sympathy for them, and, even when others did not care, Jesus did: "But when he saw the multitudes, he was moved with compassion on them, because they fainted, and were scattered abroad, as sheep having no shepherd" (Matthew 9:36).

Jesus had the compassion to reach out to everyone, especially to those who were looked down on and despised. When He saw Zacchaeus perched in a tree, He called to him. Even though as a tax collector Zacchaeus was hated by the people, he was not despised by Jesus. Christ cared for the lost man, and offered him salvation.

In his book *The Soul Winner's Fire,* Dr. John Rice wrote about the evangelist Gipsy Smith who saw many trust Christ under his preaching: "A preacher's heart is far more important than his head. It is heart preaching that has power, not head preaching. In Kansas City after the service an old preacher came into the room where Gipsy was sitting. Thousands were being blessed and hundreds saved. The older minister placed his hands upon the evangelist's head and felt about it. 'I am trying to find the secret of your success,' he said. 'Too high! Too high! My friend, you are too high,' Gipsy said. 'The secret of whatever success God has given me is not up there but down here,' and he placed his hand upon his heart! Gipsy Smith never had a day's schooling from men, yet he preached to the multitudes for sixty years. As he preached, I saw tears course down his cheeks, and my own heart was stirred, warmed and blessed."

Today's Discipleship Principle: If we are truly to be like Jesus, then we must have His compassion to reach the lost with the gospel.

Salvation Changes Things

And when they saw it, they all murmured, saying, That he was gone to be guest with a man that is a sinner. And Zacchaeus stood, and said unto the Lord; Behold, Lord, the half of my goods I give to the poor; and if I have taken any thing from any man by false accusation, I restore him fourfold.—LUKE 19:7–8

Though we are told almost nothing about Zacchaeus and his life, what we know from history and the culture of the time tells us that he was a man to whom money was very important. The Romans often used local citizens to collect the taxes they imposed on conquered nations. These men were called publicans, and those who chose this occupation were hated by their countrymen who saw them as collaborators with the enemy. Even worse, because they worked on what was basically a quota system and were allowed to keep all that they collected above that amount, many of them were corrupt and extremely wealthy because of the hard work of others. Money mattered to them more than loyalty to their country or fairness to their people.

Yet when Zacchaeus met Jesus, he immediately underwent a remarkable transformation. He did not, of course, get saved by giving away money. But, as an expression of his gratitude for salvation and an indication of his new priorities, he publicly declared a generous offering to meet the needs of the poor. Further he was willing to go the extra mile in making things right with anyone he had taken advantage of in his office as publican. Meeting Jesus truly changed the life of Zacchaeus.

When a person trusts Christ as Saviour, things change in their life. The change is not always as immediately obvious as it was with Zacchaeus, but change is always the result of salvation. "Therefore if any man be in Christ, he is a new creature: old things are passed away; behold, all things are become new" (2 Corinthians 5:17).

Today's Discipleship Principle: Our lives should give clear evidence to the fact that we have truly experienced God's transforming salvation.

Walking with Jesus
Pursuing Sinners

*And Jesus said unto him, This day is salvation come to this house, forsomuch as he also is a son of Abraham. For the Son of man is come to seek and to save that which was lost.—*LUKE 19:9-10

A lice Knight told the story of an elderly lady in New York City in the 1800s who made her living washing clothes. She was known as Sophie the Scrubwoman, and everyone who met her soon knew that she loved Jesus. She was often seen going about witnessing to those she met. One day she was seen witnessing to a wooden Indian that stood outside a cigar store. When someone pointed it out to her, she replied, "I didn't know I was talking to a wooden Indian about Christ. My eyesight is very bad. But talking to a wooden Indian about Christ is not as bad as being a wooden Christian and never talking to anybody about the Lord Jesus!"

If we are going to truly be followers of Jesus, we must shape our lives and priorities in the same way that He did. His constant purpose—always at the front of His mind and actions—was to bring the message and hope of salvation to those who were lost. It did not matter if they were rich or poor, spiritual leaders or pagans, Jesus told people about salvation everywhere He went. He shared the truth of the gospel with those who were respected and those who were despised. It was His overwhelming passion and purpose, and it shaped everything that He did.

Because Christ was perfect, every trait of His is worthy of our following. But what was most important to Him must also be our priority if we are to walk in His steps. Christ's heartbeat was to reach sinners with the gospel. If we can ignore the urgent need of the lost and dying world around us, our hearts are not in tune with His.

Today's Discipleship Principle: It is impossible to truly be like Jesus without a pressing burden for reaching those who are lost.

God's Schedule or Ours?

And as they heard these things, he added and spake a parable, because he was nigh to Jerusalem, and because they thought that the kingdom of God should immediately appear.—LUKE 19:11

George Matheson experienced great hardship in his life. He showed enormous academic promise as a young man and was preparing for the ministry when he lost his eyesight. His fiancée was unwilling to marry a man who was blind and broke off their engagement. Matheson never married, but he faithfully pastored for many years in Scotland and preached for Queen Victoria when she visited her castle at Balmoral. Today he is best remembered for a poem he wrote on the day of his sister's wedding which we know as the hymn "O Love that Will Not Let Me Go."

Matheson wrote, "We commonly associate patience with lying down. We think of it as the angel that guards the couch of the invalid. Yet there is a patience that I believe to be harder—the patience that can run. To lie down in the time of grief, to be quiet under the stroke of adverse fortune, implies a great strength; but I know of something that implies a strength greater still: it is the power to work under stress; to have a great weight at your heart and still run; to have a deep anguish in your spirit and still perform the daily tasks. It is a Christ-like thing! The hardest thing is that most of us are called to exercise our patience, not in the sickbed but in the street."

One of the reasons that people rejected Jesus as the Messiah was that He had not come to establish an immediate earthly kingdom. They had no interest in waiting for the timing that God had ordained—they wanted deliverance immediately. And in insisting on their timing for what Jesus should provide, they missed the salvation from sin that He offered. Too often we fail to submit our will to God's timing for our lives, and when we do, we always miss the gifts God desires to give us now.

Today's Discipleship Principle: When we are impatient we are declaring that we think we know better than God how our lives should go.

Working Till Jesus Comes

He said therefore, A certain nobleman went into a far country to receive for himself a kingdom, and to return. And he called his ten servants, and delivered them ten pounds, and said unto them, Occupy till I come.
—LUKE 19:12–13

Harry Ironside's father died when he was a young boy, so he went to work at an early age to help support the family. He got a job with a shoe cobbler who was a devout Christian man. Ironside's task was to pound the leather for the bottom of the shoes after they were soaked and cut into shape so they would dry. It was a long and tedious task. There was another cobbler in town who skipped that step, using wet leather for the soles. Once Ironside asked him about it, and he pointed out that though the quality was less, it created return business because his customers had to come back for repairs.

When Ironside suggested this measure to his boss, he rejected it—not for financial reasons but for spiritual ones. Ironside wrote, "Mr. Mackay stopped his work and opened his Bible. 'Harry,' he said, 'I do not cobble shoes just for the four bits and six bits that I get from my customers. I expect to see every shoe I have ever repaired in a big pile at the judgment seat of Christ, and I do not want the Lord to say to me in that day, 'Dan, this was a poor job. You did not do your best here.' I want Him to be able to say, 'Well done, good and faithful servant.'"

God has commanded us to be diligent in our work. This is true whether we are at work in the church, on the job, or at home. Every task is worthy of our faithful labor, and we are called to do it all as unto the Lord. Ephesians 6:6 tells us we should fulfill all our duties, "Not with eyeservice, as menpleasers; but as the servants of Christ, doing the will of God from the heart." While the world has devalued diligence and effort, God still sees and rewards those who work faithfully.

Today's Discipleship Principle: All of our work in every part of life is meant to be done to bring glory to God.

Time to Give an Account

But his citizens hated him, and sent a message after him, saying, We will not have this man to reign over us. And it came to pass, that when he was returned, having received the kingdom, then he commanded these servants to be called unto him, to whom he had given the money, that he might know how much every man had gained by trading.
—LUKE 19:14–15

George Bernard Shaw is widely regarded as one of the most influential writers of the English language. His dozens of plays and books made a huge impact on society. But Shaw had no use for God or religion, choosing instead to go his own way. It is said that near the end of his life, he was interviewed by a reporter who asked, "Mr. Shaw, if you could live your life over and be anybody you've known, or any person from history, who would you be?" "I would choose," replied Shaw "to be the man George Bernard Shaw could have been, but never was."

God has entrusted to each of us talents and opportunities, and He calls us to use these for His work. If we selfishly hoard what God has given us for our own pleasure or neglect opportunities that come our way because we do not want to invest the labor required to use them, we will be ashamed when we stand before God to give an account of our lives. Second Corinthians 5:10 tells us, "For we must all appear before the judgment seat of Christ…." This time of judgment is not to determine our salvation (that was settled when we trusted Christ) but our rewards or lack of them for how fully we have lived up to the potential that God entrusted to us to use in His work.

God does not give us talents and abilities solely for our own benefit. Each of us have different levels of gifts and resources, and there is coming a day when we will answer to God for how we have used the time and treasure that are His gifts. We are not free agents but servants and stewards.

Today's Discipleship Principle: If you live today in light of the coming accounting to God, you will not be ashamed when you stand before Him.

The Basis of Rewards

Then came the first, saying, Lord, thy pound hath gained ten pounds. And he said unto him, Well, thou good servant: because thou hast been faithful in a very little, have thou authority over ten cities. And the second came, saying, Lord, thy pound hath gained five pounds. And he said likewise to him, Be thou also over five cities. —LUKE 19:16–19

There is an old story about a missionary returning to America by boat after many years of faithful service in Africa. When the boat pulled into New York harbor, there was a huge crowd at the docks to welcome it. On that same vessel was former president Teddy Roosevelt, returning from his famous African safari. The crowds cheered and the band played as the people welcomed Roosevelt home. The missionary said that first he was somewhat disappointed to see the recognition given to the president while he received none, but then he had this thought: the President is home—you are not.

The world may never notice what we do for the Lord. In fact, the more faithful and diligent we are about His business the less popular we are likely to be. Yet God is not interested in whether we become famous and well liked by the world. He is watching to see whether we have made the most of the talents, resources, abilities, and opportunities He gives to us.

In God's eyes, small actions done out of love and service for Him matter a great deal. Nothing escapes His notice. Jesus said, "And whosoever shall give to drink unto one of these little ones a cup of cold water only in the name of a disciple, verily I say unto you, he shall in no wise lose his reward" (Matthew 10:42). Though we think of a drink as being a small thing, the Lord sees even those "little" things and marks them down on our record for when we stand before Him.

Today's Discipleship Principle: God is looking for faithfulness, not notoriety, when it comes to determining our rewards.

Hidden Gifts, Wasted Talents

And another came, saying, Lord, behold, here is thy pound, which I have kept laid up in a napkin: For I feared thee, because thou art an austere man: thou takest up that thou layedst not down, and reapest that thou didst not sow.—LUKE 19:20–21

Isidore Baline was born in Russia in 1888 and moved to the United States with his family in 1893. Living in abject poverty in New York City, every member of the family, including the children, was expected to work to contribute to their survival. The young boy had little formal education, and spent his early years on the streets. In his free time he taught himself to play the piano though he could only play in one key, and never learned to read music. Over the next sixty years, however, Irving Berlin wrote some 1,500 songs, including "God Bless America," and became one of the most famous and influential songwriters in American history.

All of us have reasons and excuses not to use the talents and abilities God has given to us. The temptation is to hope that someone else will step up so that we will not have to put forward the effort and exertion to accomplish what needs to be done. But failing to use what we have cheats both God's work and our own lives. The gifts and resources that we have are not there by accident. God has a plan for us to put them to use in His work.

Ephesians 2:10 tells us that God has planned specific good works for us to do in His name: "For we are his workmanship, created in Christ Jesus unto good works, which God hath before ordained that we should walk in them." No one else is as qualified to do for God the things He has ordained for you as you are. He knew before you were born what He wanted you to do, and purposely equipped you for those tasks. Do not bury the talents and gifts He trusted you to use.

Today's Discipleship Principle: Don't rob others and yourself of blessings by hiding the talents God has given to you—use them!

september

Even Small Things Matter

And he saith unto him, Out of thine own mouth will I judge thee, thou wicked servant. Thou knewest that I was an austere man, taking up that I laid not down, and reaping that I did not sow: Wherefore then gavest not thou my money into the bank, that at my coming I might have required mine own with usury?—LUKE 19:22–23

The British statesman and philosopher Edmund Burke said, "No man ever made a greater mistake than he who did nothing because he could only do a little." Small things matter, and even if we cannot do a great deal, God expects us to do what we can.

Indeed, small things can make a big difference. A few years ago the English government made one change to their tax collection letters— adding a single sentence—and it increased the clearance rate from 57 percent to 86 percent. The change, suggested by a consultant whose book is called *The Small Big,* encouraged people to pay by telling them that most other people were doing so. It doesn't seem like a big thing, but it brought in over 500 million pounds in delinquent tax revenue.

The temptation is for us to focus on the big things, and give them our time and attention while ignoring what seem to be small matters. But there are no little things in God's kingdom. If we overlook the little things, we miss great opportunities to accomplish things that will matter a lot in the future. "For who hath despised the day of small things? for they shall rejoice, and shall see the plummet in the hand of Zerubbabel with those seven; they are the eyes of the LORD, which run to and fro through the whole earth" (Zechariah 4:10).

Over and over in Scripture we see small things—a shepherd's staff, a sling, a boy's lunch—used by God in powerful ways. We should do our best with whatever we have been given and trust Him to work according to His will in our lives.

Today's Discipleship Principle: Even the smallest tasks and responsibilities are worthy of our diligent effort and attention.

Use It or Lose It

And he said unto them that stood by, Take from him the pound, and give it to him that hath ten pounds. (And they said unto him, Lord, he hath ten pounds.) For I say unto you, That unto every one which hath shall be given; and from him that hath not, even that he hath shall be taken away from him. —LUKE 19:24–26

The story of Samson is one of the great tragedies in the Bible. Samson was uniquely empowered by God to fight against the Philistines and deliver the Israelites. He used his great strength to win mighty victories on the battlefield, but his weakness of character led to his downfall. Samson's desire for Delilah led him to reveal to her the secret of his strength, and she brought in a barber to shave off his hair that had never been cut as part of the Nazarite vow. When his hair was cut (which was the last part of his fully breaking his Nazarite vow), his strength was gone. "And she said, The Philistines be upon thee, Samson. And he awoke out of his sleep, and said, I will go out as at other times before, and shake myself. And he wist not that the LORD was departed from him" (Judges 16:20). Samson had been given supernatural strength by God, but because he allowed it to be taken from him, it did not remain available.

There are opportunities that come to us only once. If we do not respond, we will lose them. Someone said, "The opportunity of a lifetime must be seized in the lifetime of the opportunity." There is a principle in play that works in every area of life. If we are faithful and diligent with what we already have, our opportunities will increase. If we are not diligent in what God has already given us, we have no good reason to think we should be trusted with more. The way to advance in God's eyes is not to wait around for a major opportunity but to be faithful in small things day after day.

Today's Discipleship Principle: We cannot expect God to increase our resources and responsibilities unless we are faithful with what we already have.

The Command of a King

And it came to pass, when he was come nigh to Bethphage and Bethany, at the mount called the mount of Olives, he sent two of his disciples, Saying, Go ye into the village over against you; in the which at your entering ye shall find a colt tied, whereon yet never man sat: loose him, and bring him hither. And if any man ask you, Why do ye loose him? thus shall ye say unto him, Because the Lord hath need of him. —LUKE 19:29–31

Though British monarchs had been entertained by performers and musicians for centuries, the tradition of a formal performance before the head of state is agreed to have begun in 1848 when Queen Victoria attended "The Merchant of Venice" at Windsor Castle. The Royal Command Performance became a tradition carried on by successive monarchs through the years, and the invitation to perform for a king or queen is not really a request—it is a command.

God does not ask us to do things, but rather tells us what He expects. He is the great King and has every right to command us to do whatever He chooses. We do not have the right to refuse, because we do not belong to ourselves but to Him. "What? know ye not that your body is the temple of the Holy Ghost which is in you, which ye have of God, and ye are not your own? For ye are bought with a price: therefore glorify God in your body, and in your spirit, which are God's" (1 Corinthians 6:19–20).

When Jesus sent his disciples to get the colt upon which He would ride into the city on what we refer to as Palm Sunday, He anticipated that people may ask them why they would untether a colt and lead him away. So Jesus gave them a fully-sufficient answer: "Because the Lord hath need of him."

Everything that God commands is our responsibility to perform. God is high and lifted up, beyond our ability to understand. It is not ours to reason or bargain with Him, but rather to obey completely.

Today's Discipleship Principle: We cannot say "No" to Jesus and rightly claim that He is Lord of our lives.

The Prophesied King

And they brought him to Jesus: and they cast their garments upon the colt, and they set Jesus thereon. And as he went, they spread their clothes in the way. And when he was come nigh, even now at the descent of the mount of Olives, the whole multitude of the disciples began to rejoice and praise God with a loud voice for all the mighty works that they had seen;
—LUKE 19:35–37

Hundreds of years before the birth of Jesus, God gave the prophet Zechariah a prophetic message regarding the nature of Christ's arrival: "Rejoice greatly, O daughter of Zion; shout, O daughter of Jerusalem: behold, thy King cometh unto thee: he is just, and having salvation; lowly, and riding upon an ass, and upon a colt the foal of an ass" (Zechariah 9:9). What we call the Triumphal Entry into Jerusalem on Palm Sunday was exactly what Zechariah had described.

The picture that the world has of our Saviour is a distorted one. Many see Jesus as a revolutionary, working against the power structures of His day. Others view Him as a teacher of peace and non-violence. Some look at Him as a deluded man who claimed Divinity. But Jesus Christ is the very Son of God, and He is the one who has been appointed to rule and reign over the entire world. That was not the purpose of His first coming, but those remaining prophecies will be fulfilled when He returns.

Because of the obedience of Jesus Christ to the will of His Father, God has ordained that all creation will one day acknowledge Him as the rightful ruler: "That at the name of Jesus every knee should bow, of things in heaven, and things in earth, and things under the earth; And that every tongue should confess that Jesus Christ is Lord, to the glory of God the Father" (Philippians 2:10–11). But those of us who know Him as our Saviour and Lord should already bow the knee to Jesus and give Him the glory He is due.

Today's Discipleship Principle: Jesus is far more than an example, a teacher, or a prophet. He is the King of kings and Lord of lords.

Uncontained Praise

Saying, Blessed be the King that cometh in the name of the Lord: peace in heaven, and glory in the highest. And some of the Pharisees from among the multitude said unto him, Master, rebuke thy disciples. And he answered and said unto them, I tell you that, if these should hold their peace, the stones would immediately cry out. —LUKE 19:38–40

Because we live in a world that has been cursed by sin, we cannot fully comprehend how the original creation worked together in perfect harmony to praise and glorify God. There are still traces of His design that can be found by those with eyes to see. David wrote, "The heavens declare the glory of God; and the firmament sheweth his handywork" (Psalm 19:1). The things we see in the natural world are only a shadow of what once was and what one day will be.

All that God made was designed to praise Him: "Let every thing that hath breath praise the LORD. Praise ye the LORD" (Psalm 150:6). But the height of God's creation was man, and it is our special purpose and duty to sound forth His praises. Truly, we have much for which to be thankful. The grace of God freely given to us is worthy of eternal and unending praise, and that is just the beginning of the benefits we receive from our loving Father in Heaven.

Just as it was when Jesus rode into Jerusalem in His triumphant entry and the Pharisees criticized those who praised Him as the Messiah, if you and I praise Him as we should there will probably be some who think it too extreme—but it is not. No amount of praise from our lips can ever be enough. No words of thanks and gratitude can express what we owe to Him, but we should take every opportunity to tell others the wonderful things God has done for us. The praise of a grateful heart cannot be contained. It overflows like a rushing spring that all can see and hear.

Today's Discipleship Principle: Do not make the stones cry out praise to God because you are silent about His greatness and glory.

The Weeping Saviour

And when he was come near, he beheld the city, and wept over it, Saying, If thou hadst known, even thou, at least in this thy day, the things which belong unto thy peace! but now they are hid from thine eyes.
—LUKE 19:41–42

In 1859 Swiss businessman Jean-Henri Dunant traveled to Italy to meet with the French Emperor Napoleon III in hopes of reaching an agreement on a business deal. The French Army was on the field in Italy, and Dunant arrived in Solferino at the end of a horrible battle. The Battle of Solferino left forty thousand soldiers dead or wounded on the field. At the time there was no organized effort to care for those injured in war. Seeing the great need, Dunant abandoned his commercial purpose and organized the local townspeople to provide relief for those wounded in battle.

When he returned home, Dunant wrote and self-published a book describing the horrors he had witnessed and the lack of response. In 1863, he was instrumental in the founding of what became the International Red Cross. Dunant also helped create and promote the Geneva Conventions which govern the treatment of combatants and civilians in times of war. He made a difference because he cared.

Jesus cared about people. He knew their needs and had compassion on them. He was not a harsh and cruel God, but a Saviour who wept for those He came to save and even for those who rejected Him. Often in the Gospels we see Jesus crying, not for Himself, but for others. As Isaiah 53:3 prophesied, "He is despised and rejected of men; a man of sorrows, and acquainted with grief...."

God calls us to look around us and open our eyes to the needs of those around us. Our hearts should break and be full of compassion just as Jesus' heart was.

Today's Discipleship Principle: If we are to be like Jesus, then our hearts must break for those who are lost and in need of salvation.

The Priority of Prayer

And he went into the temple, and began to cast out them that sold therein, and them that bought; Saying unto them, It is written, My house is the house of prayer: but ye have made it a den of thieves.—LUKE 19:45-46

It took Solomon seven long years of labor to complete the beautiful temple that would be the permanent home for the Ark of the Covenant. At the dedication for this magnificent building, Solomon led the people in a great service of sacrifice, praise, and worship. The Spirit of God filled the entire building in such a powerful way that the priests were unable to continue in His presence. At the conclusion of the service, Solomon prayed this prayer of dedication over the temple: "That thine eyes may be open upon this house day and night, upon the place whereof thou hast said that thou wouldest put thy name there; to hearken unto the prayer which thy servant prayeth toward this place" (2 Chronicles 6:20).

In New Testament times, each Christian is indwelled by the same Holy Spirit, and our bodies are referred to as the temple of God. And just as the Old Testament temple was meant to be a house of prayer, so too should our lives be characterized by constant, diligent, effective, passionate praying.

A.C. Dixon said, "When we rely upon organization, we get what organization can do; when we rely upon education, we get what education can do; when we rely upon eloquence, we get what eloquence can do, and so on. Nor am I disposed to undervalue any of these things in their proper place, but when we rely upon prayer, we get what God can do." If we want to see what God can do, we have only to pray and watch the results. As the temple of the Holy Spirit, it is our responsibility to see to it that our lives are clean both inside and out, and that our days are filled with prayer.

Today's Discipleship Principle: Nothing meaningful and lasting for God is ever accomplished apart from prayer.

Eager to Hear from Jesus

And he taught daily in the temple. But the chief priests and the scribes and the chief of the people sought to destroy him, And could not find what they might do: for all the people were very attentive to hear him.
—LUKE 19:47–48

According to a study conducted in 2014, almost 100,000,000 Americans attended at least one sports event for which they paid admission, with many of them going to more than one game. Millions more attended concerts, plays, and other performances. They spent billions of dollars to see and hear other people in action. On top of that, they watched games, contests, and shows both on television and online.

At the same time people are flocking to entertainment and sporting events, many churches are seeing their attendance dwindle. As a result many are suggesting new methods to attract crowds, trying to create an artificial sense of excitement and enthusiasm that will attract attention. Others are changing their messages, abandoning the Word of God for more "relevant" messages that will be better accepted by the world.

Instead we need to go back to what God directed us to do to reach the world. Jesus said, "And I, if I be lifted up from the earth, will draw all men unto me" (John 12:32). Rather than finding the latest method to build a crowd, we need to remember that our responsibility is to preach the truth.

Interestingly, although Jesus faced severe opposition to His message by those who didn't see their need for forgiveness, He never lacked for an audience. The common people heard Him gladly. Even in today's skeptical and cynical age, preaching that focuses on the Lord and His Word will have an effect. On the pulpit at the Pacific Garden Rescue Mission in Chicago is a reminder for those who speak to the men and women there to keep the message focused on what matters most. It simply reads, "We would see Jesus" (John 12:21).

Today's Discipleship Principle: If we make much of Jesus in our churches and in our lives, we will be effective in reaching people.

The Voice of Authority

And it came to pass, that on one of those days, as he taught the people in the temple, and preached the gospel, the chief priests and the scribes came upon him with the elders, And spake unto him, saying, Tell us, by what authority doest thou these things? or who is he that gave thee this authority?—LUKE 20:1–2

We are most familiar with the United States Supreme Court as an appellate body, hearing cases from lower courts and rendering a legal judgment that settles the matter. But under Article III, Section 2 of the Constitution, they also have original jurisdiction over certain cases, being the first (and last) court that hears the arguments. These cases are rare and generally involve disputes between two states. Most of those have been over boundary disputes or water rights. Whatever the Supreme Court says is the final decision—there is no appeal possible because of the authority they have been granted by the Constitution.

The Supreme Court may be the final authority on legal matters in America, but their authority pales in comparison to the ultimate authority of the Lord Jesus Christ. His authority is complete and unbounded, rising above all human power. "And Jesus came and spake unto them, saying, All power is given unto me in heaven and in earth" (Matthew 28:18). The Saviour does not need permission from anyone regarding anything that He wills or commands. He has the ultimate authority, and when He speaks, He is to be obeyed.

Jesus Christ is not only the ultimate authority, but as a result, He is the ultimate judge. "I charge thee therefore before God, and the Lord Jesus Christ, who shall judge the quick and the dead at his appearing and his kingdom" (2 Timothy 4:1). Realizing that we will one day give an account to the Lord who knows not just our actions but our very thoughts should motivate us to live in obedience to all that He says.

Today's Discipleship Principle: There is no appeal from the authority of Jesus Christ—it is both final and just.

Heed the Warning

And he answered and said unto them, I will also ask you one thing; and answer me: The baptism of John, was it from heaven, or of men? And they reasoned with themselves, saying, If we shall say, From heaven; he will say, Why then believed ye him not? But and if we say, Of men; all the people will stone us: for they be persuaded that John was a prophet. And they answered, that they could not tell whence it was.—LUKE 20:3–7

In 1982 a war broke out between England and Argentina over control of the Falkland Islands. During the fighting, the British destroyer *HMS Sheffield* was struck by an Exocet missile fired by an Argentine warplane. Six days later, despite the best efforts of the crew to patch the hole in the hull, heavy seas flooded and sank the ship. An investigation revealed that though radar had detected the incoming missile, because a plane had not been spotted, the warning was not immediately sounded and no evasive action was taken.

The great danger facing our society today is not primarily an absence of warning and truth, but rather the refusal to heed the warnings being received. This is true of the lost, who hear the message of salvation and reject it. And it is true of the saved, who read or hear the commands of God but refuse to obey them. The Bible is not filled with suggestions. It is not advice from God, but commandments given for our benefit.

The Pharisees tried to trap Jesus and questioned His authority to speak commands from God. They asked Him a trick question designed to give them reason to accuse Him. But Jesus undid their trap by asking them a question that revealed to them that they had refused to believe the message of John the Baptist before Him, even though they knew John was sent from God. Rejecting the truth was nothing new for them— simply a dangerous and destructive pattern of behavior. It will always prove to be the same for us.

Today's Discipleship Principle: Never disregard a spiritual warning which you know to be the truth from God's Word.

The Ingratitude of Man

Then began he to speak to the people this parable; A certain man planted a vineyard, and let it forth to husbandmen, and went into a far country for a long time. And at the season he sent a servant to the husbandmen, that they should give him of the fruit of the vineyard: but the husbandmen beat him, and sent him away empty. And again he sent another servant: and they beat him also, and entreated him shamefully, and sent him away empty.—LUKE 20:9–11

Ever since the Fall of mankind, people have been refusing to accept the gracious provision God has made for salvation through grace. In this story, which Jesus told to highlight the stubborn refusal of the Pharisees to acknowledge the truth of who He was, the focus at the beginning is on the man who planted the vineyard in the first place—a picture of God. We did not create this world in which we live or all the natural beauty and resources that make our lives possible, yet all too often we take them for granted, offering God no thanks or praise for all that He has done.

Our pride does not like to acknowledge that everything we have and are is the result of God's grace rather than our effort. We often are not thankful because we do not want to acknowledge that someone else is responsible. Yet ingratitude is the doorway that leads to downfall and destruction. "Because that, when they knew God, they glorified him not as God, neither were thankful; but became vain in their imaginations, and their foolish heart was darkened" (Romans 1:21).

The jobs, houses, cars, clothes, and any other blessings we enjoy—including spiritual blessings—are not the product of us creating a vineyard, but of God trusting us to work in His vineyard. We owe Him our gratitude for all that He has provided, and we should use these blessings to honor Him.

Today's Discipleship Principle: Not a day should pass without our hearts overflowing with thanks and praise to God for His blessings.

The Tragedy of Rejecting Jesus

And again he sent a third: and they wounded him also, and cast him out. Then said the lord of the vineyard, What shall I do? I will send my beloved son: it may be they will reverence him when they see him. But when the husbandmen saw him, they reasoned among themselves, saying, This is the heir: come, let us kill him, that the inheritance may be ours.
—LUKE 20:12–14

In 1833 the United States Supreme Court heard a most unusual case. A man named George Wilson was convicted and sentenced to die in the state of Pennsylvania. Influential friends appealed to President Andrew Jackson, and the president issued a pardon to Wilson. But the condemned man refused to accept the pardon.

The authorities were not certain how to proceed, and the case was appealed all the way to the highest court. In United States v. Wilson, the Supreme Court ruled, "A pardon is a deed, to the validity of which delivery is essential, and delivery is not complete without acceptance. It may then be rejected by the person to whom it is tendered; and if it is rejected, we have discovered no power in this court to force it upon him." George Wilson was hanged because he would not accept the pardon that was offered to him.

Every man and woman born on Earth is born under a death sentence. Jesus said, "He that believeth on him is not condemned: but he that believeth not is condemned already, because he hath not believed in the name of the only begotten Son of God" (John 3:18). They need to be warned to seek salvation while there is still time. God has graciously provided a way of escape from the coming judgment through the death, burial, and resurrection of Jesus Christ, but that pardon offered must be accepted for it to have effect.

Today's Discipleship Principle: God has trusted to us the most urgent task of warning the lost to accept His pardon before it is too late.

The Certainty of Judgment

So they cast him out of the vineyard, and killed him. What therefore shall the lord of the vineyard do unto them? He shall come and destroy these husbandmen, and shall give the vineyard to others. And when they heard it, they said, God forbid.—LUKE 20:15-16

The most famous sermon ever preached in America is undoubtedly Jonathan Edwards' "Sinners in the Hands of an Angry God." Edwards had preached the sermon in his own church with little effect, but on July 8, 1741, he delivered the message again at a church in nearby Enfield, Connecticut. The impact was immediate. Though Edwards read his message in a nearly monotone voice, the audience was gripped by such intense conviction that people began to openly weep and cry out to God for salvation even as Edwards preached.

He said, "Your wickedness makes you as it were heavy as lead, and to tend downwards with great weight and pressure towards Hell; and if God should let you go, you would immediately sink and swiftly descend and plunge into the bottomless gulf, and your healthy constitution, and your own care and prudence, and best contrivance, and all your righteousness, would have no more influence to uphold you and keep you out of Hell, than a spider's web would have to stop a falling rock."

God's people in our day need another awakening of the reality of God's judgment and awfulness of the place called Hell. This truth is not popular in our day, but it never has been. Lost and dying men do not want to be confronted with the fact that they will give an account to the God who created them.

For us as Christians, however, this reality should motivate us to diligent efforts to reach the lost. As Paul wrote, "Knowing therefore the terror of the Lord, we persuade men…" (2 Corinthians 5:11).

Today's Discipleship Principle: Take time today to warn someone of the eternal judgment that faces all those who reject Jesus Christ and to tell them of the salvation available through Jesus' blood.

A One-Sided Contest

And he beheld them, and said, What is this then that is written, The stone which the builders rejected, the same is become the head of the corner? Whosoever shall fall upon that stone shall be broken; but on whomsoever it shall fall, it will grind him to powder.—LUKE 20:17–18

For decades the Harlem Globetrotters basketball team traveled across the country and even around the world. Night after night they played another team known as the Washington Generals. And night after night, the Globetrotters always won. Thousands of games played between the two teams always ended with the same result. Some nights the score would be closer than others, but the ultimate outcome was never in doubt. People didn't go to the games to see who would win, but rather to be entertained and amused as the result they always knew was coming unfolded.

In our society there are many who speak out and stand in opposition to God. Militant atheists continue their efforts to have every mention and trace of Him removed from public life. They loudly proclaim that God does not exist and trumpet their defiance of Him. When they actually see Him in person, however, their response will be different—they will fall at His feet and acknowledge His authority. "For it is written, As I live, saith the Lord, every knee shall bow to me, and every tongue shall confess to God" (Romans 14:11).

Though the Christian life is filled with continuing spiritual conflict, the ultimate outcome of the contest has already been decided. God is the victor. None can stand against Him. Even Satan himself will one day be forced to kneel before God, and all who have refused His free offer of salvation will join their leader on their knees before the God they rejected. The struggle between God and man is truly a one sided contest.

Today's Discipleship Principle: Our God is the triumphant victor with all power and we can trust Him to fight and win every battle.

Listening for the Wrong Reason

And the chief priests and the scribes the same hour sought to lay hands on him; and they feared the people: for they perceived that he had spoken this parable against them. And they watched him, and sent forth spies, which should feign themselves just men, that they might take hold of his words, that so they might deliver him unto the power and authority of the governor.—LUKE 20:19–20

James Taylor was a big fan of the preacher John Wesley. He was a frequent attender when Wesley preached, especially at outdoor venues. Taylor did not go because he was a believer eager to be inspired and uplifted by the message. Instead he went because he was a scoffer, and he enjoyed hurling insults—and sometimes rotten vegetables—at the preacher and the crowd.

Just before his wedding in 1738, however, James Taylor went to hear Wesley again, intending to mock as was his habit. But that day Wesley was preaching from Joshua 24 on the topic "As for Me and My House, We Will Serve the Lord." The Holy Spirit used that text and the impending wedding to bring conviction to James Taylor (grandfather of the famed missionary to China, Hudson Taylor) and he was saved.

Many times we hear the Word of God, but are listening for the wrong reasons. We are tempted to apply the truths we hear to others rather than taking the message to our own hearts and lives. We are tempted to doubt whether the Bible really applies to every situation in our lives. We are even tempted to doubt whether or not what God says is true. Instead we should be like the Bereans and be careful listeners and students of the Word. "These were more noble than those in Thessalonica, in that they received the word with all readiness of mind, and searched the scriptures daily, whether those things were so" (Acts 17:11).

Today's Discipleship Principle: We need to hear the Word of God with open hearts and minds and accept it for the eternal truth that it is.

God Comes First

Is it lawful for us to give tribute unto Caesar, or no? But he perceived their craftiness, and said unto them, Why tempt ye me? Shew me a penny. Whose image and superscription hath it? They answered and said, Caesar's. And he said unto them, Render therefore unto Caesar the things which be Caesar's, and unto God the things which be God's.—LUKE 20:22–25

When Jesus' enemies were trying to trap Him into giving them a reason to turn Him over to the Roman authorities as a traitor, they focused on the responsibilities of citizens and subjects of the Roman Empire, particularly regarding paying taxes. If Jesus supported paying the tribute, the Jewish patriots would turn against Him; if, on the other hand, He said not to pay, the Romans would be outraged. Jesus avoided the trap by pointing out that we have responsibilities to both civil government and to God—and that God always must come first.

An American preacher named Samuel Davies visited England prior to the Revolutionary War. He visited with notable religious leaders, including the Wesley brothers, and was even invited to preach before King George III. During the message, it is said that the king began talking to his wife about something Davies had said. The bold preacher stopped his message and then said, "When the lion roars, the beasts of the forest tremble; when Jehovah speaks, let the kings of the earth keep silence before him."

It is not possible for human authorities to change what God has decreed, although that does not stop them from trying. And it is not within the realm of human authority, which is appointed by God, to compel people to go against God's law. We do have a responsibility to "render unto Caesar" but it is subordinate to our duty to "render to God." It is never right to violate His commands, no matter what a human government may say.

Today's Discipleship Principle: While we fulfill all of the responsibilities of life, including citizenship, we must never forget that God comes first.

Ignoring the Word Always Leads to Error

Then came to him certain of the Sadducees, which deny that there is any resurrection; and they asked him, Saying, Master, Moses wrote unto us, If any man's brother die, having a wife, and he die without children, that his brother should take his wife, and raise up seed unto his brother.
—LUKE 20:27–28

In September of 1862, General Robert E. Lee led the Army of Northern Virginia into Maryland in hopes that victories in the North would encourage other nations to recognize the Confederacy and put pressure on the Union to end the war. Lee laid out an ambitious and risky strategy, dividing his army into three units and sending them different directions in hopes of catching the Union Army under General McClellan off guard.

Lee's detailed battle plan, Special Order 191, told exactly what he planned to do. Mistakenly, one copy was left behind and discovered by a Union corporal. Yet despite receiving full details of the Rebel plans, General McClellan delayed, waiting almost a full day before responding. He had all the information he needed, but because of his delay the Battle of Antietam failed to be the victory it could have been. Historians still debate the reasons for McClellan's failure to act on the information he was given, but there is no question about the negative result.

The Lord has given us all that we need for the Christian life in His Word. When we fail to believe and act on the truth of the Bible, we always go astray. We forfeit the possibility of victory when we fail to take advantage of the wealth of information provided for us. God has given us the knowledge of the enemy's plan of attack and how we can defeat him: "Lest Satan should get an advantage of us: for we are not ignorant of his devices" (2 Corinthians 2:11).

Today's Discipleship Principle: If we do not take seriously what God has told us in His Word, our lives will be filled with error.

Contending with God

There were therefore seven brethren: and the first took a wife, and died without children. And the second took her to wife, and he died childless. And the third took her; and in like manner the seven also: and they left no children, and died. Last of all the woman died also. Therefore in the resurrection whose wife of them is she? for seven had her to wife.
—LUKE 20:29–33

The Sadducees of Jesus' day were proud of their intellectual accomplishments. They viewed themselves as superior to the common people, thinking their education and adoption of elements of the Greek and Roman societies elevated them above others. Yet when they attempted to trap Jesus, as they did in Luke 20, they found themselves hopelessly tangled in their own arguments. The best that they could come up with did not challenge or stress Him in the slightest.

God is far above us, and it is the height of folly to imagine that we can contend with Him. James Weldon Johnson's poem "The Prodigal Son" begins with these lines:

> Young man—
> Young man—
> Your arm's too short to box with God.

The only proper response to the Lord is to bow before Him in submission, recognizing His Divine authority. Job said, "I know it is so of a truth: but how should man be just with God? If he will contend with him, he cannot answer him one of a thousand" (Job 9:2–3).

Human knowledge has increased greatly in the past few decades. Year after year new discoveries are made, bringing advances that man has never known before. Yet all of those are old news to God. Nothing ever occurs to Him, surprises Him, or forces Him to rework His plans. God is far beyond anything we can imagine.

Today's Discipleship Principle: The only proper response to the Lord of the Universe is humble obedience in every part of life.

No More Death

And Jesus answering said unto them, The children of this world marry,
and are given in marriage: But they which shall be accounted worthy to
obtain that world, and the resurrection from the dead, neither marry, nor
are given in marriage: Neither can they die any more: for they are equal
unto the angels; and are the children of God, being the children of the
resurrection.—LUKE 20:34–36

In 1899, poor health forced D.L. Moody to end his evangelistic campaign in Kansas City and return to his home in Massachusetts. Moody told his family, "I'm not discouraged. I want to live as long as I am useful, but when my work is done, I want to be up and off." The next day Moody realized he was dying. He said, "Earth recedes, Heaven opens before me! It is beautiful. It is like a trance. If this is death, it is sweet. There is no valley here. God is calling me, and I must go."

Death is still with us, but its power over the Christian has already been defeated—and one day death will be gone forever. Because we have not known life without death, it's hard for us to picture what things will be like when it's gone and no one dies again.

The moment that Adam ate the fruit from the tree of the knowledge of good and evil, death entered into the world, just as God has warned would happen. From that moment on, every person who has been born has faced the certain prospect of dying. "And as it is appointed unto men once to die, but after this the judgment:" (Hebrews 9:27).

Many face that prospect with fear, but those of us who have trusted Christ as Saviour have the certain assurance that we will live forever, because the death, burial, and resurrection of Jesus ended the power of death to harm those who have placed their trust in Him. This knowledge brings comfort to our hearts.

Today's Discipleship Principle: We have already been given eternal life, and one day we will be removed from the presence of death forever.

The God of the Living

Now that the dead are raised, even Moses shewed at the bush, when he calleth the Lord the God of Abraham, and the God of Isaac, and the God of Jacob. For he is not a God of the dead, but of the living: for all live unto him.—LUKE 20:37–38

By some counts there are almost one thousand names and titles used for God in the Bible. Each of these descriptions tell us more about His nature and character. The expression Jesus used in Luke 20, calling Him "God...of the living" is a powerful one. There have been many deities worshiped by men throughout the years. But all of the worshipers of those false gods have perished. Only Christians have the assurance that because He is God not just of the past, but also of the present and future, we can look forward to eternal life.

God is the God of the living because He is also the God who conquered death. It was not enough for Jesus to die for us, but He also had to rise from the dead, proving His victory over the grave. It is the resurrection of Jesus that promises us eternal life. And without that resurrection, which ensures His promise that we too will be victorious over death, we have no basis for hope in either this life or the next. Paul wrote, "If in this life only we have hope in Christ, we are of all men most miserable" (1 Corinthians 15:19).

I read about a young preacher who was facing his first funeral service. Trying to be sure he would say what he should, he began searching the Bible to find what Jesus said at funerals. What he found was not a message of comfort, but triumph. Three times Jesus came in contact with dead people—and He brought all three back to life!

The future may be unknown, but it is nothing to fear. We know that ours is the God of the living, and we have hope because of His victory over the grave.

Today's Discipleship Principle: The triumph of Jesus over the grave allows us the blessing of certainty about the future.

The Son of David

And he said unto them, How say they that Christ is David's son? And David himself saith in the book of Psalms, The LORD said unto my Lord, Sit thou on my right hand, Till I make thine enemies thy footstool. David therefore calleth him Lord, how is he then his son?—LUKE 20:41-44

The promise that God made to David concerning the future of his family was given without qualification or limitation: "And when thy days be fulfilled, and thou shalt sleep with thy fathers, I will set up thy seed after thee, which shall proceed out of thy bowels, and I will establish his kingdom. He shall build an house for my name, and I will stablish the throne of his kingdom for ever" (2 Samuel 7:12–13). While some of that promise was fulfilled through Solomon, the unending rule could only be fulfilled by Jesus.

When Jesus came the first time, He was recognized by a number of the Jewish people as the fulfillment of the Old Testament prophecies regarding the Messiah. But many others rejected Him, despite His ability to trace His ancestry on both His mother's side as well as on Joseph's side (though of course He shared no blood relation to Joseph because of the virgin birth). The future ruler of Israel had to be the Son of David, and Jesus is.

None of the prophecies about the coming of the Messiah were unfulfilled in the birth, life, ministry, death, or resurrection of Jesus. Yet there remain many prophecies for the future, including the physical reign of Jesus Christ on Earth. The New Testament again and again points out the fulfillment of prophecy, not only to validate the office and work of Jesus, but to give us faith and confidence for the future. The same God who promised an heir to David and delivered, has given us certain and unshakable promises we can trust.

Today's Discipleship Principle: Because of God's faithful promises regarding the first coming of Christ, we can have full confidence in His second coming.

The Snare of Approval

Then in the audience of all the people he said unto his disciples, Beware of the scribes, which desire to walk in long robes, and love greetings in the markets, and the highest seats in the synagogues, and the chief rooms at feasts; Which devour widows' houses, and for a shew make long prayers: the same shall receive greater damnation.—LUKE 20:45–47

One of the clearest pictures of the lengths to which people will go in order to gain approval from others—and the consequences— is found in the history of the early church. The book of Acts records the story of the wonderful generosity of Barnabas, who sold his land and gave the money to the apostles to meet the needs of the poor of the church. His example of compassion and giving rightly earned him great appreciation. A man named Ananias along with his wife Sapphira decided that they too wanted the praise Barnabas got, but they were not willing to match his generosity.

When they sold their property, Ananias brought part of the money, but presented it to Peter as if they were giving everything to God. They wanted the credit for great sacrifice without actually making the full sacrifice. Peter was alerted to the scheme and confronted Ananias. He did not condemn the failure to give everything, but rather the deception. He said, "Whiles it remained, was it not thine own? and after it was sold, was it not in thine own power? why hast thou conceived this thing in thine heart? thou hast not lied unto men, but unto God" (Acts 5:4).

Both Ananias and Sapphira perished because they were more interested in gaining the praise of men than they were seeking the approval of God, to the point they were willing to lie to get it. Whenever our great desire is to be thought well of by others, we are on the path to trouble. Seeking praise leads us to cut corners and lower our standards, and frequently lures us into sin.

Today's Discipleship Principle: Only God's approval is lasting and meaningful and worthy of our pursuit.

A Small Gift with a Big Impact

And he looked up, and saw the rich men casting their gifts into the treasury. And he saw also a certain poor widow casting in thither two mites. And he said, Of a truth I say unto you, that this poor widow hath cast in more than they all: For all these have of their abundance cast in unto the offerings of God: but she of her penury hath cast in all the living that she had.—LUKE 21:1-4

D r. George Truett told of a church meeting where he had been asked to assist with a fund raising campaign for a church that had been struggling financially because the people would not give. He said, "It was the slowest and most reluctant giving I have ever encountered." When he finished his exhortation and the pledges were taken, they had less than half the money needed. Dr. Truett said that an elderly couple in the back then volunteered to sell their house to make up the difference—they had been offered exactly the amount remaining that needed to be raised for it the day before. But in less than five minutes, the previously stingy congregation rallied to pledge the entire amount so the couple could keep their home. The sacrifice of that couple motivated them to give.

When we realize that all we have belongs to God, it is impossible to justify refusing to give. Sometimes we make the excuse that we do not give because of our lack. But in reality, even small gifts have a big impact. The Lord is far more concerned about the condition of our hearts than the size of our offering.

This is the lesson Jesus sought to teach the disciples as He pointed out to them the poor widow who gave every coin she owned into the temple treasury. Before her, wealthy men had given large sums of money, but, in truth, theirs were "gifts" that cost them little in the way of sacrifice. But this widow evidenced true love and faith because, although her gift was small, it was sacrificial.

Today's Discipleship Principle: The measure of our generosity is not found in the amount of the gift, but in the sacrifice of the gift.

The End Result of Disobedience

*And as some spake of the temple, how it was adorned with goodly stones
and gifts, he said, As for these things which ye behold, the days will come,
in the which there shall not be left one stone upon another, that shall not
be thrown down.*—LUKE 21:5–6

Charles Spurgeon told of a man who came to him and said that he
had been a Christian for forty years but had never been baptized.
Spuregon said, "I felt grieved that he had so long been disobedient to a
known duty, and I proposed to him that he should be baptized at once.
It was in a village, and he said that there were no conveniences. I offered
to go with him to the brook, and baptize him, but he said, 'No; he that
believeth shall not make haste.' Here was one who had wilfully disobeyed
his Lord, for as many years as the Israelites in the wilderness, upon a
matter so easy of performance; and yet, after confessing his fault he was
not willing to amend it, but perverted a passage of Scripture to excuse
him in further delay."

When we do what God says, we receive the reward of obedience.
When we choose instead to go our own way, we receive the penalty of
disobedience. In almost every case the problem is not one of knowledge,
but of will. It is usually not that we do not know what we should do,
but that for one reason or another we do not want to do what God says.
Instead we choose to go our own way.

Both the Bible and history are filled with examples of the tragic
results of persistent disobedience to God—including the destruction of
Jerusalem that Jesus prophesied in the verses above. God is not impressed
with our rationalizations and excuses for failing to do what He says. He
does not grade on a curve. Nothing less than full and complete obedience
is what He deserves and what He demands.

Today's Discipleship Principle: God's law cannot be flouted and
disobeyed without serious consequences.

Guarding against Deception

And they asked him, saying, Master, but when shall these things be? and what sign will there be when these things shall come to pass? And he said, Take heed that ye be not deceived: for many shall come in my name, saying, I am Christ; and the time draweth near: go ye not therefore after them. —LUKE 21:7–8

In December of 1985, thousands of people living in and around Washington D.C. received exciting news in the mail from a company called Flagship International Sports Television. They were told that they had been selected to receive free tickets to the upcoming Washington Redskins and Cincinnati Bengals football game. All they had to do was show up at the Washington Convention Center where after a free brunch they would not only receive their tickets but also be entered into a drawing for free tickets to that year's Super Bowl as well. Roughly one hundred people responded to the offer, but when they arrived at the convention center they were arrested by U.S. Marshals and Washington D.C. police officers. The notices had been sent to criminals with outstanding warrants whom the police had been unable to find.

Satan has been using deception against God's children and lost people alike ever since the Garden of Eden. He does it because it works. "In whom the god of this world hath blinded the minds of them which believe not, lest the light of the glorious gospel of Christ, who is the image of God, should shine unto them" (2 Corinthians 4:4). He presents offers that look tempting on the surface but conceal death and destruction within. As Dr. John R. Rice used to say, "All Satan's apples have worms." God gives us the duty and responsibility to be alert to what is going on around us so that we are not taken in and led into sin because we are deceived.

Today's Discipleship Principle: God wants His children to be wise and discerning so that they are not ensnared by deception.

Fearless Living in Fearful Times

But when ye shall hear of wars and commotions, be not terrified: for these things must first come to pass; but the end is not by and by. Then said he unto them, Nation shall rise against nation, and kingdom against kingdom: And great earthquakes shall be in divers places, and famines, and pestilences; and fearful sights and great signs shall there be from heaven.—LUKE 21:9-11

The message of Jesus to His disciples (and to us) regarding the future was not that everything was going to be fine and that there would be no problems to worry about. Instead He said that there would be wars, natural disasters, and all kinds of trouble. Yet despite that grim prospect, He commanded them not to be gripped by fear. Many times we view fear as caused by our circumstances, but in truth fear is found in our hearts, not in what we see around us.

Peter learned this lesson well. When Herod began to persecute the church to stop the spread of the new religion, he first killed James, and then he arrested Peter and put him in prison, intending to kill him as well. The church stayed up all night praying the night before Peter was to be executed. But as for Peter, he went to sleep! In fact he was sleeping so soundly that when the angel came to rescue him, he had to give Peter a good whack to wake him up. "And, behold, the angel of the Lord came upon him, and a light shined in the prison: and he smote Peter on the side, and raised him up, saying, Arise up quickly. And his chains fell off from his hands" (Acts 12:7).

Our confidence and lack of fear is not found in the knowledge that nothing will ever go wrong, but in the faith that God is in control. Whether He delivers us by a miracle or welcomes us to Heaven, He makes no mistakes.

Today's Discipleship Principle: Life is filled with difficulty and trouble, but our circumstances can never cause us to fear unless we allow it.

An Opportunity to Witness

But before all these, they shall lay their hands on you, and persecute you, delivering you up to the synagogues, and into prisons, being brought before kings and rulers for my name's sake. And it shall turn to you for a testimony.—LUKE 21:12–13

When Mary came to the throne of England in 1553, her greatest desire was to see the nation returned to her Catholic faith. She launched a wave of persecution against those who would not profess allegiance to Rome that killed hundreds, leaving her with the name "Bloody Mary." Two of the victims martyred by Queen Mary were Nicholas Ridley and Hugh Latimer. Both had preached fearlessly under the reign of Henry, but Mary regarded them as heretics.

After a brief show trial, they were condemned to be burned at the stake. As the watching crowd stood by, the two men went to their fate. The executioners used green wood which would burn slowly to prolong the suffering of the condemned men. As he waited for death Latimer called out, "Be of good comfort, Mr. Ridley, and play the man! We shall this day light such a candle by God's grace, in England, as I trust never shall be put out."

None of us enjoy enduring hardship or suffering, but God regards these tests as both necessary and valuable: "That the trial of your faith, being much more precious than of gold that perisheth, though it be tried with fire, might be found unto praise and honour and glory at the appearing of Jesus Christ" (1 Peter 1:7). In addition to strengthening our character, trials present us with an opportunity to show to all around us that faith is real. Our faith is not just meant for the church and home, but for the hospital, the unemployment line, and the cemetery. Whatever hardships or even the threat of persecution and death, we may face, let us be found faithful.

Today's Discipleship Principle: Every difficult circumstance of life is an opportunity to demonstrate that our faith is real.

A Settled Heart

Settle it therefore in your hearts, not to meditate before what ye shall answer: For I will give you a mouth and wisdom, which all your adversaries shall not be able to gainsay nor resist.—LUKE 21:14–15

The great issues of life are all determined in the heart. When our hearts are right, our outward attitude and conduct will be as well. When our hearts are wrong, it will come through. Jesus warned His disciples of the need to have their hearts settled before the days of trouble came. Many times we fail to meet a test or resist a temptation because we have not previously settled our hearts regarding a matter. The time to choose to do right is before the challenge comes, not when we are facing it.

Consider Daniel who was ripped away from his home and family as a young boy and taken hundreds of miles away from home. He was placed into a carefully designed program meant to take his devotion away from his nation and his God and turn him into a loyal subject of the Babylonian Empire. They changed his name, his clothing, his schooling, and even tried to change his diet.

The Babylonians' program had a great success rate among others, but it did not work on Daniel, because Daniel's heart was settled: "But Daniel purposed in his heart that he would not defile himself with the portion of the king's meat, nor with the wine which he drank: therefore he requested of the prince of the eunuchs that he might not defile himself" (Daniel 1:8).

When we are put to the test, what we love most is revealed. Most of the other Hebrew young men who were taken to Babylon apparently went along with the program of their captors, but Daniel and three of his friends did not. They loved the God of their fathers more than they loved comfort or success or even life itself.

Today's Discipleship Principle: If your heart is fixed on God, nothing will be able to deter you from following Him faithfully.

Patience in Hard Times

And ye shall be betrayed both by parents, and brethren, and kinsfolks, and friends; and some of you shall they cause to be put to death. And ye shall be hated of all men for my name's sake. But there shall not an hair of your head perish. In your patience possess ye your souls.—LUKE 21:16–19

One of the most important traits of the Christian life is patience. We live in a hurry up world. It takes too long to cook a meal, so we have microwaves. It takes too long to go to the bank, so we make deposits with our phones. It takes too long to develop a skill, so we have apps to help us along. Yet nothing of lasting value can ever be accomplished unless we are willing to invest the time, diligence, and effort to achieve it—and the lack of patience is one of the greatest enemies of doing things that matter.

Patience is most put to the test when we encounter difficulties and tests that seem to have no end. That is when we have the greatest opportunity to demonstrate our faith in action as we faithfully work and wait to see what God will do.

Difficult times are also when we have opportunity to develop patience. It was to weary, persecuted believers that James wrote, "My brethren, count it all joy when ye fall into divers temptations; Knowing this, that the trying of your faith worketh patience. But let patience have her perfect work, that ye may be perfect and entire, wanting nothing" (James 1:2–4). And in the verse following, James encouraged these Christians to seek the wisdom of God in the midst of their trials: "If any of you lack wisdom, let him ask of God, that giveth to all men liberally, and upbraideth not; and it shall be given him" (James 1:5).

Jesus did not leave His disciples with the mistaken idea that as long as they were following God, all would be well. He told them that days were coming in which *because* they followed God they would face difficulty. Yet he encouraged them to endure those times with patient faith.

Today's Discipleship Principle: Be willing to patiently wait on God, even when you do not understand what He is doing.

The Knowledge to Prepare for the Future

And when ye shall see Jerusalem compassed with armies, then know that the desolation thereof is nigh. Then let them which are in Judaea flee to the mountains; and let them which are in the midst of it depart out; and let not them that are in the countries enter thereinto. For these be the days of vengeance, that all things which are written may be fulfilled.
—LUKE 21:20–22

In 1876, a wealthy businessman named Charles Taze Russell became convinced that the Lord would return to Earth in April of 1878. He sold his businesses—worth millions of dollars in today's money—and used the money to fund various publications promoting this doctrine. Russell began preaching and teaching that time was short, and that people must repent. Many believed Russell. Some even put on white robes and went and stood on hillsides on the appointed day, certain that the Lord was about to return. Of course Jesus did not come back then. Russell wasn't just wrong on the date itself; his entire doctrine was built on a false basis—that it is possible to know exactly when the Rapture will take place.

The Bible instructs us instead to be wise, using the time that we have to the fullest for God. We will not know the moment of His return, but we certainly can and should understand the events that are unfolding around us and what they mean. Jesus warned His hearers who would still be alive when the Roman army came to subdue Jerusalem some forty years later that they should not expect Divine deliverance, but should flee from the coming violence of war. The plan of God is not for us to know His schedule for the end time events, but it is also not for us to be ignorant of what we see happening about us. We need to be careful students of the Scriptures to grasp what is happening, and what is coming next.

Today's Discipleship Principle: God has given us in His Word everything that we need to know to prepare for the future.

october

Failing Because of Fear

And there shall be signs in the sun, and in the moon, and in the stars; and upon the earth distress of nations, with perplexity; the sea and the waves roaring; Men's hearts failing them for fear, and for looking after those things which are coming on the earth: for the powers of heaven shall be shaken. —LUKE 21:25–26

During World War II, American military hero General George Patton was interviewed following the successful invasion of Sicily. The dashing Patton was renowned for always being on the attack. When the interviewer praised his courage, General Patton replied, "Sir, I am not a brave man. The truth is, I am an utter craven coward. I have never been within the sound of gunshot or in sight of battle in my whole life that I wasn't so scared that I had sweat in the palms of my hands."

The difference between Patton and others was not that he was never afraid, but that he was not controlled by his fears. In his autobiography Patton wrote, "I learned very early in my life never to take counsel of my fears."

The Bible does not promise us that nothing bad will ever happen to us or that things will always be easy. Instead it tells us that there will be trouble and pain. But it does promise that we can have victory over our fears. The first step is to recognize the source of fear. "For God hath not given us the spirit of fear; but of power, and of love, and of a sound mind" (2 Timothy 1:7).

Fear does not come from God. But the Holy Spirit gives us what we need to overcome our fears and do what He has called us to do without regard as to whether or not we understand how things will work together. That is His responsibility, and in faith we conquer our fear by relying on God to do all things well.

Today's Discipleship Principle: We will all sometimes be afraid but we never have to be controlled by our fears.

A Glorious Appearing

And then shall they see the Son of man coming in a cloud with power and great glory. And when these things begin to come to pass, then look up, and lift up your heads; for your redemption draweth nigh. —LUKE 21:27-28

The Irish evangelist Dr. Henry Guinness used this illustration of the Second Coming: "I heard *The Messiah* with great delight last evening. Now if a man had asked me after the performance had proceeded a couple of hours how long I thought it would continue, I would have answered, 'About five minutes.' 'But,' the man might have expostulated, 'how can that be? It is in full swing, has been going on for two hours, and I see no reason why it should not continue for two hours longer. How do you know it will be over in five minutes?' Then I should have answered him, 'Because I have the score.'"

There are even more promises in the Bible regarding the Second Coming than there are about the first appearing of Jesus. In the 270 chapters of the New Testament, scholars find more than three hundred references to the return of the Lord. We may not see many signs of hope in our world. It may seem like things are getting darker and darker, and there is nothing good to which to look forward. But we have the "score"—the document that tells us how it all ends.

For the Christian, the days may be dark, but there is a bright light at the end of the book where the Bible tells us that Jesus is going to come back. There have now been almost two thousand years since Jesus returned to Heaven, but the promise made that day will be kept: "…this same Jesus, which is taken up from you into heaven, shall so come in like manner as ye have seen him go into heaven" (Acts 1:11). We have the promises of God to count on for the future, so we can be certain that the Lord will return.

Today's Discipleship Principle: When you feel overwhelmed about events unfolding around you, remember we haven't yet reached the final chapter—but we already have a record of how it ends.

Fig Trees and the Kingdom

And he spake to them a parable; Behold the fig tree, and all the trees; When they now shoot forth, ye see and know of your own selves that summer is now nigh at hand. So likewise ye, when ye see these things come to pass, know ye that the kingdom of God is nigh at hand.—LUKE 21:29–31

In the time of Christ, the Mount of Olives which Jesus often crossed going to and from Jerusalem had many fig trees. They were a staple of the Jewish economy, providing one of the major cash crops on which the people depended. One of the signs of the coming summer season, which Jesus used to illustrate future events, was when the leaves emerged on the fig trees. These were the last trees to bud in the late spring, so when the leaves appeared it clearly indicated that the change of seasons was at hand.

The plan of God for the future is settled and certain, but He has not chosen to reveal His timing to us. Jesus said, "But of that day and hour knoweth no man, no, not the angels of heaven, but my Father only" (Matthew 24:36). Many have set specific dates for the Lord's return in violation of His Word, but they have all been proven wrong. Some of us remember the smash best-selling book from years ago called *88 Reasons Why the Rapture Will Be in 1988*. Millions of copies were sold, but the follow up called *89 Reasons Why the Rapture Will Be in 1989* did not sell nearly as well.

The point of the parable of the fig tree is not to set a date for the Lord's return, but to remind us that it is certain, as summer is always followed by the appearing of the leaves, and that it will not be long delayed. Remember that God's timing is not ours, and what seems many years to us is but a moment to Him.

When we remember that Christ could return at any moment, it both gives us hope and motivates us to be ready.

Today's Discipleship Principle: The truth of the Second Coming should affect the way we live every single day.

Truly Unshakable

Verily I say unto you, This generation shall not pass away, till all be fulfilled. Heaven and earth shall pass away: but my words shall not pass away. —LUKE 21:32–33

From the time of Aristotle until the 1800s, the belief in spontaneous generation of life was widespread. Leading scientists actually believed that living things could come from dead matter. The teaching was so commonly accepted that few even thought of challenging it. Then the great scientist Louis Pasteur conducted a series of experiments that conclusively demonstrated that life did not spring from dead matter. By sterilizing and sealing his test subjects, Pasteur showed that despite what had long been confidently believed, life only comes from other living things, just as God described in His Word.

Over and over throughout history the things that many, or even most, people believed that are contrary to Scripture have been proven false. Seemingly solid scientific and historical knowledge has been shaken as new discoveries have undermined what was previously thought to be certain. Those who trust in the Word of God never have that problem. Though what God said has been challenged by skeptics and doubters through the centuries, it has never wavered and never been proved false.

The Word of God is a reflection of the nature and character of God. It never changes, and it is never in error. There are no mistakes in Scripture, and no one who trusts in the Word of God needs fear that there will be a day when it proves not to be true. That is the basis on which our faith rests—and it is solid and trustworthy. "Nevertheless the foundation of God standeth sure, having this seal, The Lord knoweth them that are his. And, Let every one that nameth the name of Christ depart from iniquity" (2 Timothy 2:19). Faith is only as good as the object of belief, and faith in the Bible is never in vain.

Today's Discipleship Principle: No one has ever gone wrong by believing what God says, for His Word is always faithful and true.

On Guard

And take heed to yourselves, lest at any time your hearts be overcharged with surfeiting, and drunkenness, and cares of this life, and so that day come upon you unawares. For as a snare shall it come on all them that dwell on the face of the whole earth. Watch ye therefore, and pray always, that ye may be accounted worthy to escape all these things that shall come to pass, and to stand before the Son of man.—LUKE 21:34–36

According to the Greek historian Herodotus, when Cyrus marched on the city of Babylon, he was unable to breach the walls or defeat the defenses of the great city. Unsure of how to proceed, he withdrew the main body of his force, leaving a token siege around Babylon. Finally he came up with a plan. The great Euphrates River flowed through Babylon, providing it with a source of fresh water that allowed them to hold off enemy armies.

Cyrus moved far enough away from the city so his workers could not be seen and then began digging great basins near the river. The work took months, but when everything was finally ready, they breached the river banks and diverted the flow of water away from the river bed. Under the cover of darkness when the drop in the water level was not seen, the army was able to creep under the wall of the city in the nearly dry river bed and conquer the strong citadel.

We must never let down our guard. There is never a day that passes without the threat of an attack from Satan. Peter warned, "Be sober, be vigilant; because your adversary the devil, as a roaring lion, walketh about, seeking whom he may devour" (1 Peter 5:8). I imagine that when the Holy Spirit inspired him to write those words, Peter remembered the night when his guard was down and he denied the Lord three times (Matthew 26:69–75). Thank God for His grace that restores us when we do fall, but it is better to never let down our guard.

Today's Discipleship Principle: The devil is seeking to destroy your life today and he will succeed if you let down your guard.

The Traitor

*Then entered Satan into Judas surnamed Iscariot, being of the number of the twelve. And he went his way, and communed with the chief priests and captains, how he might betray him unto them. And they were glad, and covenanted to give him money. And he promised, and sought opportunity to betray him unto them in the absence of the multitude.—*LUKE 22:3–6

During the second Persian invasion of Greece by Xerxes, the vastly outnumbered Greeks led by King Leonidas of Sparta held the narrow pass at Thermopylae where they were able to hold off the Persians who could only attack in small groups. For two days the Greek forces held firm, until a local Greek man named Ephialtes led the Persians to a path that allowed them to attack the Greeks from behind. Leonidas and most of his men perished because they had been betrayed.

There is a war taking place in our world between light and darkness, between good and evil, between God and Satan. Every one of us who are saved has a duty and responsibility to perform in this war, yet too often we find ourselves fighting for the wrong side. James 4:4 points out that we often make friends of the enemy: "Ye adulterers and adulteresses, know ye not that the friendship of the world is enmity with God? whosoever therefore will be a friend of the world is the enemy of God."

The church is not making the impact it should on the world in large part because too many Christians are not engaged in the battle. There is no place in God's plan for non-combatants. Every Christian is called to resist Satan and stand for truth: "Fight the good fight of faith…" (1 Timothy 6:12). Even worse there are some who are helping the enemy. Though we do not like to think that way, when we allow unconfessed and continuing sin in our lives, we are siding with the enemy. We cannot truthfully profess loyalty to Christ while privately making friends with sin.

Today's Discipleship Principle: When we allow sin to remain in our lives, we are betraying the Lord who saved us.

Omniscience and Providence

*And he said unto them, Behold, when ye are entered into the city, there shall a man meet you, bearing a pitcher of water; follow him into the house where he entereth in. And ye shall say unto the goodman of the house, The Master saith unto thee, Where is the guestchamber, where I shall eat the passover with my disciples? And he shall shew you a large upper room furnished: there make ready.—*LUKE 22:10-12

In his book *Prayer, Asking and Receiving,* Dr. John R. Rice told the story of his decision to go to Bible college. Times were hard, and his family had no money to pay for his tuition. After praying for God to meet the need, Dr. Rice rode his horse to a small bank to see if he could borrow the money for the first semester until he could get a job at the school to pay it back. The banker simply asked how long he needed the money and approved the loan. A man standing nearby protested that the banker had just told him he was unable to make six month loans due to the bad economy. The banker explained that John Rice had done him a favor (Dr. Rice had helped him with his peach trees), and he was making the loan. Dr. Rice knew that this was an answer to his prayer. Even the favor performed sometime earlier was something God already knew that He would use to answer the later prayer.

God knows what we need before we need it, and He knows how those needs will be met. We do not often see His plan revealed ahead of time. Usually it is only in looking back that we are able to see how God arranged every detail to accomplish His purpose and provide for us. God never fails His children.

David wrote, "And they that know thy name will put their trust in thee: for thou, LORD, hast not forsaken them that seek thee" (Psalm 9:10). God has never faced a challenging problem. He already knows the solution even before we seek His help.

Today's Discipleship Principle: Because God has all knowledge and all power, we can fully trust Him in every situation.

A Meal to Anticipate

And when the hour was come, he sat down, and the twelve apostles with him. And he said unto them, With desire I have desired to eat this passover with you before I suffer: For I say unto you, I will not any more eat thereof, until it be fulfilled in the kingdom of God. —LUKE 22:14–16

W hat we commonly call the Last Supper was the observance of Passover by Jesus and His disciples in Jerusalem the night before Jesus was crucified. Though He had told the disciples that He would die in Jerusalem, they did not really understand what was about to happen. But with full knowledge of the plan that His Father had set in place even before the creation of the world, Jesus celebrated the feast that commemorated the deliverance of Israel from Egypt and foreshadowed His death as the Lamb of God who came to take away the sins of the world.

In the Jewish culture of Jesus' day there was a wonderful feast that accompanied the celebration of a wedding. Friends and family would gather and spend time together enjoying a special meal—one they had looked forward to since the wedding had been announced months before. Though they did not know exactly when it would happen, they eagerly anticipated the announcement of the arrival of the bridegroom.

The Bible uses this as a picture of what will happen after Jesus returns. There will be a great feast, and it is one that not only we, but also the Lord Himself is eagerly looking forward to celebrating: "And he saith unto me, Write, Blessed are they which are called unto the marriage supper of the Lamb. And he saith unto me, These are the true sayings of God" (Revelation 19:9).

We have a dinner appointment with our Saviour. Though we do not know exactly when it will be, we know it is certain. This truth should encourage us every day.

Today's Discipleship Principle: Our walk with God in this life is wonderful, but it pales in comparison to what is coming next.

The Price of Redemption

And he took the cup, and gave thanks, and said, Take this, and divide it among yourselves: For I say unto you, I will not drink of the fruit of the vine, until the kingdom of God shall come. And he took bread, and gave thanks, and brake it, and gave unto them, saying, This is my body which is given for you: this do in remembrance of me. Likewise also the cup after supper, saying, This cup is the new testament in my blood, which is shed for you. —LUKE 22:17–20

In France in the early 1960s a new form of crime emerged. Daring thieves began stealing valuable paintings and holding them for ransom. The so called "art-napping" trend followed the rise in the value of paintings during the 1950s. The owners of museums and collections were faced with a difficult choice. They could either pay for what was rightfully theirs in the first place, or perhaps lose it forever. Many of them paid to have their paintings returned, thinking that it was more important to have the masterpieces back than to have the money they would cost to recover.

We belonged to God by right of creation, but sin separated us from Him. Lost people have no hope of saving themselves. The only hope is for the price for our sins to be paid for us—but that price is far more than any amount of money. Peter wrote, "Forasmuch as ye know that ye were not redeemed with corruptible things, as silver and gold, from your vain conversation received by tradition from your fathers; But with the precious blood of Christ, as of a lamb without blemish and without spot" (1 Peter 1:18–19).

The enormity of our debt of sin demanded a steep payment—death. But Jesus willingly paid it for us. Romans 6:23 says, "For the wages of sin is death; but the gift of God is eternal life through Jesus Christ our Lord."

Today's Discipleship Principle: Every day of our lives should be lived in gratitude to the Lord for His sacrifice.

The Conflict of Pride

And there was also a strife among them, which of them should be accounted the greatest. And he said unto them, The kings of the Gentiles exercise lordship over them; and they that exercise authority upon them are called benefactors. But ye shall not be so: but he that is greatest among you, let him be as the younger; and he that is chief, as he that doth serve.
—LUKE 22:24–26

On the night before His crucifixion when Jesus was talking to the disciples about how He was looking forward to Heaven and explaining once again His role as the sacrifice for sin, the disciples were arguing over which of them should have the most prominent role in His kingdom. They were filled with pride and came into conflict. The Greek word translated *strife* indicates not just a conflict, but an eagerness to do battle.

At the root of all strife is the insistence that pride makes on having preeminence and having our own way: "Only by pride cometh contention: but with the well advised is wisdom" (Proverbs 13:10). It is hard for us to overcome pride because it appeals to us so much. Benjamin Franklin wrote, "There is perhaps no one of our natural passions so hard to subdue as pride. Beat it down, stifle it, mortify it as much as one pleases, it is still alive. Even if I could conceive that I had completely overcome it, I should probably be proud of my humility."

We do not often recognize pride in our own lives, though we easily detect it in others. Rather than humbling ourselves as God commands, we indulge our pride and feel much better about ourselves than we should. This inevitably brings us into conflict with those around us, and destroys the unity that should characterize Christians. When our focus is on ourselves rather than on God, we will find it easy to fall into the trap of pride.

Today's Discipleship Principle: One of the great indicators of pride in a Christian's life is frequent conflict with others.

The Serving Saviour

For whether is greater, he that sitteth at meat, or he that serveth? is not he that sitteth at meat? but I am among you as he that serveth. Ye are they which have continued with me in my temptations. And I appoint unto you a kingdom, as my Father hath appointed unto me; That ye may eat and drink at my table in my kingdom, and sit on thrones judging the twelve tribes of Israel.—LUKE 22:27–30

During World War II when England was under siege and it appeared that the Germans might invade at any moment, the British military urgently needed the support of the mine workers who dug out the coal that fueled the war effort. Winston Churchill met with the labor union leaders to urge them to encourage their men to work diligently. The gifted orator described the great parade that would be held in Picadilly Circus when the war was won. Churchill said that after the soldiers and airmen and sailors, the great line of workers would follow. "What did you do during the war?" they would be asked and the answer would be, "We were deep in the earth with our faces to the coal."

There is little fame or glory in this world for servants, but God sees those who are faithful even when they are not noticed by others. Even more He sees into our hearts and knows not only what we do but what motivates what we do. We may be very surprised at the Judgment Seat of Christ when people—perhaps who have even served near us—are rewarded for faithful, humble service about which we knew nothing.

Jesus, the Lord of Heaven and Earth, was willing to humble Himself and bow down as a servant. The example of Jesus washing the feet of the disciples in the Upper Room is more talked about than copied. Too many of His children are not willing to pick up the towel and serve. Instead we want to be noticed and receive service from others, but that is not the pattern Jesus set for us.

Today's Discipleship Principle: It is impossible to be like Jesus without being willing to humbly serve the needs of others.

A Target for the Devil

*And the Lord said, Simon, Simon, behold, Satan hath desired to have you, that he may sift you as wheat: But I have prayed for thee, that thy faith fail not: and when thou art converted, strengthen thy brethren. And he said unto him, Lord, I am ready to go with thee, both into prison, and to death. And he said, I tell thee, Peter, the cock shall not crow this day, before that thou shalt thrice deny that thou knowest me.—*LUKE 22:31–34

Before John Hinckley, Jr. shot President Ronald Reagan in March of 1981 in an assassination attempt, he was virtually unknown. Yet in the aftermath of the near killing of the president, a thorough investigation revealed that Hinckley had actually been working on an attack that would make him famous (he thought it would attract the attention of an actress) for quite some time. Photos of events held by the previous President, Jimmy Carter, revealed Hinckley in attendance. He had been looking for an opportunity to strike for some time, and he was ready to take it when it was presented.

Every Christian has a real, active, evil opponent who is always working against us and looking for an opportunity to strike. In our own strength we have no hope of defeating him. But God does not send us into this conflict alone. He gives us armor that is able to protect us from attack—and we need it. "Put on the whole armour of God, that ye may be able to stand against the wiles of the devil" (Ephesians 6:11).

Any day in which we do not put on our armor is a day when we are headed for defeat. The devil does not fight fair. He does not wait for us to get ready before he attacks. He does not give warning of his intentions. He uses every weapon at his disposal to bring us down.

That truth should make us sober, active, aware, and alert every day. It should make us conscious of and dependent on the presence and power of God.

Today's Discipleship Principle: Never forget that Satan is looking for an opportunity to destroy your life, character, and effectiveness for God.

The God Who Provides

And he said unto them, When I sent you without purse, and scrip, and shoes, lacked ye any thing? And they said, Nothing. Then said he unto them, But now, he that hath a purse, let him take it, and likewise his scrip: and he that hath no sword, let him sell his garment, and buy one.
—LUKE 22:35–36

In faith and obedience, Abraham took his promised son Isaac to Mount Moriah to offer him as a sacrifice as God commanded. He had waited and hoped and prayed for decades for the birth of a son who had been promised to him, but even with all that Isaac meant to him, Abraham did not hesitate to obey God. After Abraham built the altar and placed Isaac on it, God stopped Abraham, providing a ram for a sacrifice in a beautiful picture of Jesus serving as the substitute for our sins.

When the sacrifice of the animal was complete, Abraham rejoiced in what God had done: "And Abraham called the name of that place Jehovahjireh: as it is said to this day, In the mount of the LORD it shall be seen" (Genesis 22:13). The name Jehovah-Jireh has a dual meaning, both "God sees" and "God provides." Our good God not only sees our needs, but He stands willing and able to meet them as we cry out for His help.

Someone once described an atheist as, "A man with no invisible means of support." When we trust in God we are not foolish, but faithful. He has all of the resources available to go above and beyond any need we will ever face. When we are walking with Him and doing His will, we never need to fear going without our needs being met. The great burdens and struggles that challenge us do not tax His abilities. He never has to call for backup or dip into a reserve fund. He is abundantly able to provide all that we need. Our responsibility is to act in faith, believing He will provide.

Today's Discipleship Principle: God has never failed to keep His promises and provide for those who seek His face.

The Protection of Prayer

And he came out, and went, as he was wont, to the mount of Olives;
and his disciples also followed him. And when he was at the place, he
said unto them, Pray that ye enter not into temptation. And he was
withdrawn from them about a stone's cast, and kneeled down, and prayed,
—LUKE 22:39–41

O ne of the most famous human figures in Greek mythology was the
great warrior Achilles. His exploits were told by Homer in the Iliad.
Achilles had no equal on the field of battle and could not be defeated.
According to the legend, his mother had dipped him in the River Styx
when he was a baby. But since she held him by his foot, his heel was
not protected, and eventually Achilles died after being shot in the foot
with an arrow. Even today we speak of the "Achilles' heel" as a place
of vulnerability.

As Christians we do not believe in or need mystical waters or legends
to protect us—but we do have an enemy fighting against us on a daily
basis, and we do need God's protection. That protection is found in
prayer. Over the years I've counseled many Christians who have been
ensnared by sin. I've never yet met one who fell who was diligently and
regularly praying for protection from temptation. That is our greatest
defense, and yet it is one we all too often neglect.

We simply do not take Satan as seriously as we should. He is not a
comic figure with horns and a pitchfork. He is a powerful being created
by God who has turned that power to evil ends, and we have no hope of
fighting him in our own strength. Even "Michael the archangel, when
contending with the devil he disputed about the body of Moses, durst
not bring against him a railing accusation, but said, The Lord rebuke
thee" (Jude 1:9). We must pray.

Today's Discipleship Principle: A Christian who is not faithfully
praying is a Christian who is vulnerable to Satan.

Submission to the Will of God

Saying, Father, if thou be willing, remove this cup from me: nevertheless not my will, but thine, be done. And there appeared an angel unto him from heaven, strengthening him. And being in an agony he prayed more earnestly: and his sweat was as it were great drops of blood falling down to the ground.—LUKE 22:42–44

In the Garden of Gethsemane, on the night before His crucifixion, Jesus poured out His heart in prayer to His Father. He knew what He would face the next day. As agonizing as the physical suffering of the cross would be, it was nothing next to the burden of our sins that He would take on Himself. Yet even in that moment of great struggle, Jesus did not use prayer as a way to insist on what He wanted. His prayer was in complete submission to God's will. He wanted what His Father wanted more than what He wanted, even though He knew what the Father's will would cost Him.

Many people struggle with knowing how to make the right decisions and do what God wants. If we are to know His plan, then we must be willing to do it even if it is not what we would choose.

Additionally, the Christian who wants God's will must be a student of God's Word. On the subject of making decisions George Muller said, "I do not leave the result to feeling or simple impression. If I do so, I make myself liable to great delusions. I seek the will of the Spirit of God through, or in connection with, the Word of God. The Spirit and the Word must be combined. If the Holy Ghost guides us at all, He will do it according to the Scriptures and never contrary to them."

Although God's will sometimes leads us down paths that we would not choose for ourselves, as it did Christ, we can confidently go, knowing that His will for us truly is best and that He will give us the strength to do it.

Today's Discipleship Principle: If our will is subordinate to God's will, then our path will be pleasing in His sight.

Sleeping Christians

And when he rose up from prayer, and was come to his disciples, he found them sleeping for sorrow, And said unto them, Why sleep ye? rise and pray, lest ye enter into temptation.—LUKE 22:45–46

Church services in colonial America tended to be several hours long. Many churches had ushers who were equipped with long sticks that they could use to rouse sleepers during the sermons. A Puritan named Obadiah Turner recorded the story in his journal of one of these men named Allen Bridges who had placed a fox tail and a thorn on his stick. "On the last Lord's day, as he strutted about the meetinghouse, he did spy Mr. Tomlins sleeping with much comfort, his head kept steady by being in the corner, and his hand grasping the rail. And so spying, Allen did quickly thrust his staff behind Dame Ballard and give him a grievous prick upon the hand.

"Whereupon Mr. Tomlins did spring up much above the floor and with terrible force strike his hand against the wall; and also to the great wonder of all, profanely exclaim in a loud voice, 'Curse ye, woodchuck!' He was dreaming so it seemed that a woodchuck had seized and bit his hand. But on coming to know where he was, and the great scandal he had committed, he seemed much abashed, but did not speak. And I think he will not soon again go to sleep in worship."

We may laugh about people who fall asleep in church, especially if they wake up in such an amusing fashion. But there is nothing funny about Christians who are not alert to the threat of temptation and thus lethargic in prayer. Too often we simply do not realize the nature and seriousness of the threats we are facing in spiritual warfare. Like the disciples sleeping in the Garden of Gethsemane, we are oblivious to the danger approaching us and consumed with our own burdens. We should heed both the admonition and example of Christ and be faithful in prayer.

Today's Discipleship Principle: Spiritual alertness will lead to diligence and fervency in prayer.

Betraying Jesus

And while he yet spake, behold a multitude, and he that was called Judas, one of the twelve, went before them, and drew near unto Jesus to kiss him. But Jesus said unto him, Judas, betrayest thou the Son of man with a kiss?—LUKE 22:47–48

For two thousand years, the name Judas has been synonymous with betrayal and shame. We condemn the man who after three years as a disciple—walking everywhere with Jesus and hearing and seeing Him work, heal and pray—was willing to betray Him for just thirty pieces of silver. The outward Judas was a perfect disciple.

In the Upper Room when Jesus announced that He was going to be betrayed by one of the men there, the other disciples did not question the loyalty of Judas. Even when Judas left them to go to the Pharisees to lead them to Jesus, the others did not understand that he was a traitor. "For some of them thought, because Judas had the bag, that Jesus had said unto him, Buy those things that we have need of against the feast; or, that he should give something to the poor" (John 13:29). But despite his outward appearance as a faithful man, Judas was not. And eventually that became clear to everyone.

The effect of sin in our hearts is corrosive. It eats away at us from the inside, and even if we manage to conceal it from the world for a time, as Judas did, it is only hidden and not dealt with. Like an undiscovered cancer that grows and grows, sin destroys everything it touches.

Knowing this, is it not surprising that we so easily think we can manage our sin and keep it at an "acceptable" level? That never works. We need to regard sin with hatred and fear, realizing that any sin we allow in our lives is a monstrous betrayal of Jesus. We need to sincerely ask God to search our hearts and confess and turn from any sin that He reveals.

Today's Discipleship Principle: Every time we choose to sin we are turning our backs on the Saviour who gave His life for our salvation.

Light and Darkness

Then Jesus said unto the chief priests, and captains of the temple, and the elders, which were come to him, Be ye come out, as against a thief, with swords and staves? When I was daily with you in the temple, ye stretched forth no hands against me: but this is your hour, and the power of darkness.—LUKE 22:52–53

In the Garden of Gethsemane, the Light of the World was confronted under the cover of darkness. The contrast could not be greater. At the very beginning of creation God brought light into the world, and created a distinction between light and darkness: "And God said, Let there be light: and there was light. And God saw the light, that it was good: and God divided the light from the darkness" (Genesis 1:3–4). The division was present at the beginning, and it became even more pronounced with the entry of sin into the world.

God wants His children to be separated from the darkness. It is an indication of the power of our sin nature that we find the darkness so attractive. It appeals to us to think that what we are doing can be concealed from others, yet we must remember that nothing is concealed from God. His eyes are not shaded by the dark, and He sees not only our actions but our intentions and motives as well. The knowledge that God sees all that we do should be a powerful motivator to us to walk in obedience.

As new creatures in Christ we have nothing in common with the darkness any more. Paul pointed this out in a series of rhetorical questions as he taught the Corinthian church the importance of separation from the world: "Be ye not unequally yoked together with unbelievers: for what fellowship hath righteousness with unrighteousness? and what communion hath light with darkness?" (2 Corinthians 6:14). As children of light we have a responsibility to stand firm against the power of darkness.

Today's Discipleship Principle: If we are following Jesus, we will have a desire to avoid darkness and walk in God's light.

The Company You Keep

And when they had kindled a fire in the midst of the hall, and were set down together, Peter sat down among them. But a certain maid beheld him as he sat by the fire, and earnestly looked upon him, and said, This man was also with him. And he denied him, saying, Woman, I know him not.—LUKE 22:55–57

Jesse's father, a Baptist preacher, died when Jesse was just three years old. Jesse grew up idolizing his older brother Frank, even following his brother into battle during the Civil War when Jesse was still just sixteen years old. They served in the notorious guerrilla force under William Quantrill, fighting more against civilians than soldiers on the other side. When the war ended, many of those who served together in the military formed a criminal gang and began robbing banks, trains, and stagecoaches. It was not long before Jesse, still in his twenties, became the leader of one of the most famous gangs in American history. His life of crime continued until he was killed by one of his own men who wanted the reward that had been placed on Jesse James.

The people with whom we spend most of our time have a powerful influence on us. If we are sitting by the enemy's fire on a regular basis, it will not be long until we begin to seek their approval and acceptance more than God's. We may have good motives and not want to be pulled down, but the power of influence cannot be overcome with good intentions. Paul warned, "Be not deceived: evil communications corrupt good manners" (1 Corinthians 15:33).

Many good Christians have been led astray because they allowed the main influences in their lives to be those who were not friends of God. If Peter had not been warming himself at the fire of those who hated Jesus, he would not have been tempted to deny the Lord.

Today's Discipleship Principle: The most powerful influence in most people's lives are those with whom they spend the most time.

The Rooster's Sermon

And about the space of one hour after another confidently affirmed,
saying, Of a truth this fellow also was with him: for he is a Galilaean.
And Peter said, Man, I know not what thou sayest. And immediately,
while he yet spake, the cock crew. And the Lord turned, and looked upon
Peter. And Peter remembered the word of the Lord, how he had said unto
him, Before the cock crow, thou shalt deny me thrice. And Peter went out,
*and wept bitterly.—*LUKE 22:59-62

I have had the privilege of visiting Jerusalem on multiple occasions. Just outside the wall of the Old City, there is a small church known as the Church of Saint Peter in Gallicantu. Built over what is believed to have been the house of the high priest Caiaphas where Jesus was taken to be tried, the ancient church has been rebuilt and destroyed numerous times through history. Underground there are prison cells where the Lord may have spent the night before His crucifixion. The most striking feature you see when you approach the church is a golden rooster that rises from the dome—a reminder of the moment when Peter heard the cock crow and felt conviction in his heart for denying that he knew Jesus, just as Jesus had told him would happen.

The brash Peter was completely self-confident. When Jesus told him that he would deny Christ three times, Peter confidently declared himself ready to die for the Lord: "Peter said unto him, Though I should die with thee, yet will I not deny thee. Likewise also said all the disciples" (Matthew 26:35). Yet when the test came, Peter failed.

We do not judge Peter too harshly for each of us have failed to take the stand we should for Jesus. How deep the conviction that comes to us when we hear our "rooster" remind us that we have sinned. How sweet the restored fellowship when we confess and return to God.

Today's Discipleship Principle: If we do not heed the warnings of the Word of God, we must taste the bitter tears of repentance.

Striking the Saviour

And the men that held Jesus mocked him, and smote him. And when they had blindfolded him, they struck him on the face, and asked him, saying, Prophesy, who is it that smote thee? And many other things blasphemously spake they against him.—LUKE 22:63–65

We rightly recoil in horror when we read the account of created men striking the Creator, taking the very hands that He formed and using them to beat Him. It was a gruesome and blasphemous act, and those involved are worthy of the condemnation and judgment they face for doing so. Yet even as we sit in judgment of them, do we not sometimes ignore the consequences of the sin that we so readily and willingly tolerate in our hearts and lives? We think of our own sin as a small and meaningless thing, but to God it is a horrible insult to the precious Saviour who purchased us with His own blood.

There is a casualness about sin in the hearts of many Christians today that is destructive. Rather than attacking sin and defeating it, we tolerate it and make compromises with it. Just as the Israelites did when they entered the Promised Land, we settle for something short of the victory that God has provided, and our lives are crippled as a result. Sin does not stay contained. It grows and spreads until it takes over everything. Only by confessing and forsaking sin can we have victory over it.

When you are tempted to sin, remember the suffering of Christ. Remember that He died to redeem you from bondage to sin. And remember that the pain He endured at the hands of the Roman soldiers was inflicted because of sin. When you and I sin today, we are disregarding the sacrifice Jesus made for us. But when we resist temptation through His power, we demonstrate our gratitude for the cross. May we not make light of sin when it cost Jesus so great a price.

Today's Discipleship Principle: Each time we sin we reveal a lack of love and appreciation for the blood of Jesus Christ.

The Very Son of God

And if I also ask you, ye will not answer me, nor let me go. Hereafter shall the Son of man sit on the right hand of the power of God. Then said they all, Art thou then the Son of God? And he said unto them, Ye say that I am. And they said, What need we any further witness? for we ourselves have heard of his own mouth.—LUKE 22:68–71

Skeptics often claim that Jesus did not say He was the Son of God but that this claim is simply a deliberate misreading of the Scriptures. This is not true, however, as Jesus repeatedly declared that He was sent from God, that God was His Father, and that He was one with God.

The Jewish leaders who hated Jesus and wanted to put Him to death understood clearly that Jesus claimed He was the Messiah and the Son of God. Of one of these occasions, John 5:18 records, "Therefore the Jews sought the more to kill him, because he not only had broken the sabbath, but said also that God was his Father, making himself equal with God."

Charles Spurgeon said, "If we err concerning the Deity of Christ, then we err everywhere. The gospel that does not preach a Divine Savior is no gospel at all; it is like a ship without a rudder, the first opposing wind that blows will drive it to destruction, and woe are the souls that are trusting to it! Only the shoulders of the almighty God can ever carry the enormous weight of human guilt and human need."

Jesus was a man, but He was far more than that. He was at the same time completely God. "For in him dwelleth all the fulness of the Godhead bodily" (Colossians 2:9). Jesus is to be exalted, worshiped, praised, and adored. We can never hold Him too highly in hearts and minds, for He is God. All of our best efforts to praise Him fall short of what He deserves. He alone is worthy of all glory and honor and praise.

Today's Discipleship Principle: We need a renewed sense of awe and wonder at the amazing grace of our Divine Saviour.

No Fault in Jesus

*And they began to accuse him, saying, We found this fellow perverting the nation, and forbidding to give tribute to Caesar, saying that he himself is Christ a King. And Pilate asked him, saying, Art thou the King of the Jews? And he answered him and said, Thou sayest it. Then said Pilate to the chief priests and to the people, I find no fault in this man.—*LUKE 23:2–4

D r. W.A. Criswell began his ministry in a small town in Oklahoma. He would often preach on Saturdays to the crowds gathered at the farmer's market or at the courthouse. One day as he preached, Criswell asked the people why they were not attending church. He later said, "That was a rhetorical, question, and then I added, 'If you can give any good reason why you separate yourself from the people of God and why you don't go to church, come up here and tell us why don't you go.'" To his shock, person after person began to line up and pour out their complaints about what they had experienced in churches.

Criswell said that he went home weeping. He was filled with sorrow at what he had witnessed. Then he said that as he thought about it and prayed, he realized something important. "They had much to say against the preacher, much to say against the deacon, much to say against the church, much to say against the people, but I happened finally to realize not one, not one in all of that throng, not one ever said a word against the Lord Jesus Christ. I find in Him no fault at all."

We have a perfect Saviour. Only a sinless, spotless Lamb could be the sacrifice for the sins of the world, for otherwise Jesus would have had to pay for His own sins rather than ours. No matter how He is examined, no one ever finds fault with Jesus. He is perfect in character—He never sinned although fully human; but He is also perfect in love—He gave His life for us as God.

Today's Discipleship Principle: Give thanks today for the flawless Saviour who gave His life as ransom for your sins.

Passing the Buck

And they were the more fierce, saying, He stirreth up the people, teaching throughout all Jewry, beginning from Galilee to this place. When Pilate heard of Galilee, he asked whether the man were a Galilaean. And as soon as he knew that he belonged unto Herod's jurisdiction, he sent him to Herod, who himself also was at Jerusalem at that time.—LUKE 23:5-7

The famously blunt and plain-spoken Harry Truman was a relatively obscure senator from Missouri when President Franklin Roosevelt tapped him to be his running mate for his fourth term. The men only met twice in the eighty-two days between Roosevelt taking the oath of office in January and his death in April. Suddenly Truman was thrust into a position of great responsibility. Meeting with reporters shortly after he had been sworn in, Truman said, "Boys, if you ever pray, pray for me now. I don't know if you fellas ever had a load of hay fall on you, but when they told me what happened yesterday, I felt like the moon, the stars, and all the planets had fallen on me."

World War II was winding down, but Truman was faced with leading the nation to final victory over Germany and Japan. Truman quickly learned that while there were many to advise him, there had to be a place where decisions were made and responsibility taken. He put a sign on his desk that read "The Buck Stops Here."

The temptation to pass the buck has been with us ever since the Garden of Eden. Adam blamed Eve and Eve blamed the serpent. Similarly, Pilate passed Jesus to Herod, who then passed Jesus back to Pilate, neither man anxious to take the politically complicated trial surrounding Jesus—an obviously innocent man. Instead of looking for ways to avoid responsibility and accountability, we need to be diligent and faithful in our efforts.

Today's Discipleship Principle: If we accept responsibilities rather than trying to shift them to others, we can do great things for God.

The Silence of the Saviour

And when Herod saw Jesus, he was exceeding glad: for he was desirous to see him of a long season, because he had heard many things of him; and he hoped to have seen some miracle done by him. Then he questioned with him in many words; but he answered him nothing. And the chief priests and scribes stood and vehemently accused him.—LUKE 23:8–10

There is an interesting contrast in the story of the response of Jesus to the two leaders who examined Him on the day of His crucifixion. Jesus interacted with Pilate, answering his questions and pointing out that it was His submission to God's plan and not the soldiers of Rome that had brought Him to the cross. "Jesus answered, Thou couldest have no power at all against me, except it were given thee from above: therefore he that delivered me unto thee hath the greater sin" (John 19:11).

Yet when He was sent to Herod, Jesus did not respond to the king at all. Herod wanted Jesus to put on a demonstration for him, like a magician entertaining an audience. But the evil king had already had an opportunity to receive the truth from John the Baptist. Instead of repenting however, he responded by cutting off the head of the prophet who had the courage to criticize him for his immoral behavior. Since Herod had already rejected the truth, he did not receive any further instruction.

God owes us nothing, but He does present us with the opportunity to respond to Him. He does not promise, however, to continually extend those opportunities if we refuse to respond. It is a matter of stewardship. There is no reason to expect more from God if we are not using what we already have. "If therefore ye have not been faithful in the unrighteous mammon, who will commit to your trust the true riches?" (Luke 16:11).

Today's Discipleship Principle: If we do not respond to the truth we already have, we have no reason to expect further truth.

Worthy of Death

And Pilate, when he had called together the chief priests and the rulers and the people, Said unto them, Ye have brought this man unto me, as one that perverteth the people: and, behold, I, having examined him before you, have found no fault in this man touching those things whereof ye accuse him: No, nor yet Herod: for I sent you to him; and, lo, nothing worthy of death is done unto him.—LUKE 23:13–15

In ancient times, there were many governments that imposed a death penalty for certain offenses. Under the Code of Hammurabi, there were twenty-five different capital crimes. The law given by God to Moses listed a number of offenses for which the guilty party, after examination and with evidence, was to be put to death. The people in Jesus' day were familiar with the Roman practice of publicly executing those who had violated Roman law. The various legal codes had different standards for what constituted a capital crime and what was required for a conviction, but none of them prescribed the death penalty unless the crime was serious.

When God created man, He only issued one law to Adam and Eve in the Garden, but it was a serious one—it was a capital offense to break it: "But of the tree of the knowledge of good and evil, thou shalt not eat of it: for in the day that thou eatest thereof thou shalt surely die" (Genesis 2:17). Ever since Adam ate the forbidden fruit, every person who has been born has been under a sentence of death. Because of the serious nature of sin, this is a punishment that fits the crime.

The only person who has ever lived who was not worthy of death was Jesus Christ. Under the most careful examination of those who hated Him, nothing could be found in Him that was a violation of the laws of God or man. Yet He gave His life in our place.

Today's Discipleship Principle: Jesus, who was perfect and sinless, died in our place, removing the penalty of death from us forever.

The Call for Crucifixion

And they cried out all at once, saying, Away with this man, and release unto us Barabbas: (Who for a certain sedition made in the city, and for murder, was cast into prison.) Pilate therefore, willing to release Jesus, spake again to them. But they cried, saying, Crucify him, crucify him.
—LUKE 23:18–21

The life and ministry of Jesus gave ample demonstration of the truth of His claim to be the Messiah, and of His divinity. The miracles that He worked were impossible to explain apart from the power of God. Yet despite the truth of His teaching and the signs that were given, many of the Jewish people did not believe in Him. This was especially true for the religious leaders. Jesus did not fit into their model of what they wanted the Messiah to be, and so they rejected Him. Worse, they called for Him to be killed.

While we rightly condemn their failure to recognize and bow to the Lord, we must realize that we too share the sin nature that places us in opposition to God. We are not an exception to the common condition of man. Paul wrote, "Because the carnal mind is enmity against God: for it is not subject to the law of God, neither indeed can be" (Romans 8:7). God did not reach out to us in grace because we were worthy but because of His love for even those who were His enemies. As Romans 5:8 tells us, "But God commendeth his love toward us, in that, while we were yet sinners, Christ died for us."

The opposition that Jesus faced and those who cried out for His death was not because they were a particularly evil group of people. They were just like us—sinners—only they had not been touched by God's grace. Without that grace, we too would be crying "Crucify Him." But because of His grace, we rejoice in His love.

Today's Discipleship Principle: Even after salvation we must constantly guard against our hearts wandering from or hardening toward our Saviour.

Courage or Cowardice?

And he said unto them the third time, Why, what evil hath he done? I have found no cause of death in him: I will therefore chastise him, and let him go. And they were instant with loud voices, requiring that he might be crucified. And the voices of them and of the chief priests prevailed. And Pilate gave sentence that it should be as they required.—LUKE 23:22–24

Edmund G. Ross of Kansas had only been in the United States Senate for two years when he faced one of the most important decisions of his life. President Andrew Johnson had been impeached by a Congress filled with those who opposed his position on reuniting the nation following the Civil War. Thirty-six votes were needed to convict Johnson and remove him from office, and the vote counters knew they had thirty-five certain votes for conviction. They put enormous pressure on Ross to be the deciding vote, but he insisted on hearing all of the evidence before reaching a conclusion.

When the day came, Ross voted "not guilty," and by one vote Johnson retained his office. Of the crucial moment when he cast his vote Ross later said, "I looked into my open grave. Friendships, position, fortune, and everything that makes life desirable to an ambitious man were about to be swept away by the breath of my mouth, perhaps forever." Ross lost his Senate seat in the next election and was ostracized by those who had once been his most ardent supporters. But he did what he believed was right, and history vindicated his decision.

There are times when doing right comes with a high price. Pilate was unwilling to pay that price and sentenced Jesus to be crucified. When we find ourselves in moments when the cost for making a right decision seems high, if we consider the price that Jesus paid for us, we will find strength and courage to do right. God does not promise us painless service, but He does promise rewards to those who are faithful.

Today's Discipleship Principle: If we are not willing to take a stand and pay the price, we will not do what is right when it matters most.

Carrying the Cross of Jesus

And as they led him away, they laid hold upon one Simon, a Cyrenian, coming out of the country, and on him they laid the cross, that he might bear it after Jesus. And there followed him a great company of people, and of women, which also bewailed and lamented him. But Jesus turning unto them said, Daughters of Jerusalem, weep not for me, but weep for yourselves, and for your children.—LUKE 23:26–28

Though Rembrandt van Rijn is best known to us as a painter, it is his drypoint etching "The Three Crosses" that many art scholars consider his finest work. The work depicts the Lord on the cross with the thieves on either side. Light from Heaven shines in the center of the picture, but the edges are dark. At the very edge of the picture stands a figure in the shadows representing the artist himself—which apparently was Rembrandt's recognition of the fact that his sin was responsible for the death of the Lord.

Under Roman law, soldiers could force anyone they encountered to carry burdens for them. When Jesus was unable to bear the weight of His cross because of the physical suffering He had already endured, soldiers picked a man named Simon out of the crowd and compelled him to carry the cross for Jesus. He became part of the crucifixion story simply because he was passing by at the moment Jesus was taken out of the city. In a very real sense, however, you and I are also part of the story.

It was your sin and my sin that resulted in the necessity of the cross. Jesus died for the sins of the world, but He also died for me. Though the crucifixion happened centuries before we were born, we were part of the events of that day, as Jesus died for our sins, just as much as those who stood there physically when Jesus died. And His payment for our sin is as sufficient as it was for those were physically crucifying Him.

Today's Discipleship Principle: If we see the cross without seeing ourselves in the picture, we have failed to grasp the point.

Jeremiah 18–19   //   2 Timothy 3

Christ's Prayer on the Cross

And there were also two other, malefactors, led with him to be put to death.
And when they were come to the place, which is called Calvary, there they
crucified him, and the malefactors, one on the right hand, and the other
on the left. Then said Jesus, Father, forgive them; for they know not what
they do. And they parted his raiment, and cast lots.—LUKE 23:32–34

In the four Gospels, we find recorded seven different things that Jesus
said while He hung on the cross. The very first of those is this powerful
prayer for forgiveness of those who were crucifying Him. Charles
Spurgeon said, "It was not a prayer for enemies who had done Him an ill
deed years before, but for those who were there and then murdering Him.
Not in cold blood did the Saviour pray, after He had forgotten the injury,
but while the first red drops of blood were spurting on the hands which
drove the nails; while yet the hammer was bestained with crimson gore,
His blessed mouth poured out the fresh warm prayer."

Christ's forgiveness for those who were in that moment crucifying
Him is an incredible revelation of the depth of God's love. He does not
love us because we are good or deserving, but because He is love and, in
love, paid the price for our sins. We need a renewed sense of appreciation
and gratitude for the salvation we have received. Especially for those of us
who have been saved for many years, the temptation is to take salvation
for granted and forget how much we needed it. "But he that lacketh these
things is blind, and cannot see afar off, and hath forgotten that he was
purged from his old sins" (2 Peter 1:9).

But Christ's prayer on the cross should also motive us who have
received the forgiveness of God to freely forgive others. Ephesians 4:32
says, "And be ye kind one to another, tenderhearted, forgiving one
another, even as God for Christ's sake hath forgiven you."

Today's Discipleship Principle: Never forget the amazing love of Jesus
that prayed for your salvation even on the cross, and never withhold
forgiveness from others.

The Necessity of Sacrifice

*And the people stood beholding. And the rulers also with them derided him, saying, He saved others; let him save himself, if he be Christ, the chosen of God. And the soldiers also mocked him, coming to him, and offering him vinegar, And saying, If thou be the king of the Jews, save thyself.—*LUKE 23:35–37

A s the enemies of Jesus were watching Him hang on the cross, they mocked Him, trying to add to His suffering and grief. Yet even in their hatred, they expressed a profound spiritual truth—Jesus Christ could not save both Himself and us. He made the choice, not being forced to the cross but willingly laying down His life as a sacrifice for our sins because of His love for us. There was no other way for salvation to be accomplished than through His sacrifice. It was essential to God's plan: "For ye know the grace of our Lord Jesus Christ, that, though he was rich, yet for your sakes he became poor, that ye through his poverty might be rich" (2 Corinthians 8:9).

Those of us who have benefited from the sacrifice of Jesus and received His grace have an obligation to live in the same manner. We must be willing to give up our rights, comforts, privileges, and possessions when called to do so by God if we are to be followers of Jesus. There is no service without sacrifice.

When David sinned by numbering the people and a great plague came, he wanted to offer a sacrifice to pray for God's mercy. He was offered the land for his sacrifice for free but declined: "And the king said unto Araunah, Nay; but I will surely buy it of thee at a price: neither will I offer burnt offerings unto the LORD my God of that which doth cost me nothing. So David bought the threshingfloor and the oxen for fifty shekels of silver" (2 Samuel 24:24).

Today's Discipleship Principle: If we are not willing to make sacrifices, we will never accomplish anything meaningful for God.

november

The Difference Is in the Heart

But the other answering rebuked him, saying, Dost not thou fear God, seeing thou art in the same condemnation? And we indeed justly; for we receive the due reward of our deeds: but this man hath done nothing amiss. And he said unto Jesus, Lord, remember me when thou comest into thy kingdom. And Jesus said unto him, Verily I say unto thee, To day shalt thou be with me in paradise.—LUKE 23:40–43

The contrast in response between the two thieves crucified with Jesus couldn't have been greater. One joined in the mockery directed at the Saviour, but the other recognized his sins and his need for mercy. He also recognized that the sinless Son of God was his only hope, and he cried out for mercy. Jesus heard and answered his prayer.

We are reminded through this passage that salvation is not something we earn. The thief on the cross could not, in his present state, be baptized or join a church or even make restitution for what he had stolen. Yet he cried out to Jesus with a penitent and faith-filled heart, and Jesus granted him immediate salvation.

Although we do not earn salvation, when we are saved, there will be evidence of what has happened in our hearts. The evangelist Gipsy Smith told of a man who was converted during his evangelistic campaign in South Africa. Smith said that the next morning, the new Christian knocked on the door of another man's house and showed him a watch. The man was surprised to see it, for though it had his initials on it and was definitely his, he had not seen it for eight years. He asked why the man had it, and the new convert replied, "I stole it. I was converted last night, and I have brought it back first thing this morning. If you had been up, I would have brought it last night!" Salvation always makes a difference in the heart.

Today's Discipleship Principle: Pause to consider where your life would be today if you had not trusted Christ, and thank God for the difference salvation has made in your life.

The Opened Veil

And it was about the sixth hour, and there was a darkness over all the
earth until the ninth hour. And the sun was darkened, and the veil of
the temple was rent in the midst. And when Jesus had cried with a loud
voice, he said, Father, into thy hands I commend my spirit: and having
said thus, he gave up the ghost. Now when the centurion saw what was
done, he glorified God, saying, Certainly this was a righteous man.
—LUKE 23:44–47

Though the Ark of the Covenant was a tangible symbol of God's presence among His people for most of the Old Testament, it was usually hidden. During the Exodus and the early days in the Promised Land it was carried by priests from one place to another. But after that, it was normally kept first in the tabernacle and later in the temple in a special place known as the Holy of Holies. No one was allowed to enter except for the high priest, and he could only do that once a year on Yom Kippur, the Day of Atonement.

But Jesus came not just to fulfill the law and be our salvation, but to provide a new way for man to access God. No longer would there be a veil concealing God's presence from His people. Now the way was open. As Jesus hung on the cross, the veil was torn apart by unseen hands from top to bottom, symbolizing that man could now enter the presence of God because of Jesus' blood.

Sadly, many Christians never take full advantage of the amazing blessing of the access to God's presence offered to us through grace. Hebrews 4:16 invites, "Let us therefore come boldly unto the throne of grace, that we may obtain mercy, and find grace to help in time of need." We have every right to approach God confidently, not because of our merit, but because of the sacrifice of His Son.

Today's Discipleship Principle: Do not fail to receive God's help because you do not enter His presence and seek His face.

The Borrowed Tomb

And, behold, there was a man named Joseph, a counsellor; and he was a good man, and a just: (The same had not consented to the counsel and deed of them;) he was of Arimathaea, a city of the Jews: who also himself waited for the kingdom of God. This man went unto Pilate, and begged the body of Jesus. And he took it down, and wrapped it in linen, and laid it in a sepulchre that was hewn in stone, wherein never man before was laid. —LUKE 23:50–53

According to one report, the most commonly borrowed item among people living in the United States today is a book. The second is jumper cables. Most of us have experience with borrowing something from a neighbor, family member, or friend. But I'm willing to confidently state that neither you nor anyone else you know has ever borrowed a grave. When we borrow a tool, money, or a book, we expect to return it. Yet for our physical bodies, the grave is a destination that will be in use until the Lord returns, and no one expects it to be returned.

Jesus was buried in a tomb carved out of rock that belonged to a man named Joseph. In first-century Palestine, people often purchased burial sites well before their death. But Jesus had no need to purchase a tomb, for He wasn't planning to stay in the grave.

David by inspiration of the Holy Spirit described the brief period before the resurrection when he wrote, "For thou wilt not leave my soul in hell; neither wilt thou suffer thine Holy One to see corruption" (Psalm 16:10). The Lord did indeed die on the cross, but death did not have power over Him.

One day, unless the Lord returns first, each of us will make one final trip to a cemetery or other resting place. But because Jesus only borrowed His tomb, that will not be our ultimate destination. Instead we will live forever with Him.

Today's Discipleship Principle: The same power that brought Jesus out of the grave is active and working in your life today.

The Death of Jesus

And that day was the preparation, and the sabbath drew on. And the women also, which came with him from Galilee, followed after, and beheld the sepulchre, and how his body was laid. And they returned, and prepared spices and ointments; and rested the sabbath day according to the commandment.—LUKE 23:54–56

It is popular among scoffers and those who do not accept the Word of God to propose alternate explanations for the resurrection. In the 1700s German rationalists proposed what came to be known as the "swoon theory" which suggested that Jesus merely fainted rather than actually died and then revived in the coolness of the tomb. This allowed them to provide a natural explanation for Jesus being seen by hundreds of people after His crucifixion.

The problem is that in addition to ignoring what the Bible clearly says, believing that Jesus did not die requires ignoring the thoroughness of the Romans in carrying out their executions. While it is certainly possible for people to survive for a day or two on a cross, the Romans did not casually declare someone dead. The soldiers knew that if a prisoner escaped the punishment, they would be forced to take his place. Jesus, the very Son of God, did indeed die. His followers did not go to the tomb Easter Sunday morning expecting to find Him gone, even though He had told them of the resurrection. They went with the burial spices that were used to anoint dead bodies in that day.

The faith that we have is based on the Word of God being true. The events happened as described. The Bible is not a collection of fables or oral traditions passed down. Human authors wrote what the Holy Spirit spoke, and we have the very words that God has preserved for us through the ages just as He promised. Jesus did die—but He did not stay dead.

Today's Discipleship Principle: Never lose your confidence in the death, burial, and resurrection of Jesus as the sure foundation of your faith.

Empty Tomb

Now upon the first day of the week, very early in the morning, they came unto the sepulchre, bringing the spices which they had prepared, and certain others with them. And they found the stone rolled away from the sepulchre. And they entered in, and found not the body of the Lord Jesus.
—LUKE 24:1–3

D r. Curtis Hutson told the story of two English unbelievers named Lyttleton and West who set out to undermine the faith of Christians. They decided that the two stories that would most damage the Christian religion if they could be disproved were the resurrection of Christ and the conversion of Paul on the road to Damascus. They agreed together that each take one story and spend a year gathering evidence to prove it was false.

At the end of the year, the two met back together. Lyttleton said, "After a year of investigation, I am convinced that the Bible story of the conversion of the Apostle Paul is true. I too have been converted." West replied, "I have discovered that the resurrection of Jesus Christ is a fact. Undeniable. I have received Him as my Saviour."

The reason no one can prove the story of the resurrection false is that it is entirely and completely true. Jesus died, was buried, and was resurrected just as He said would happen ahead of time. The very first time He went to Jerusalem after His ministry began, Jesus described what was coming: "Jesus answered and said unto them, Destroy this temple, and in three days I will raise it up" (John 2:19).

Though even His closest followers did not understand or believe what He was telling them until after it happened, Jesus did indeed come back to life. And it is His triumph over death and the grave that is our assurance that our faith is real and that our future with Him in Heaven is secure.

Today's Discipleship Principle: The greatest proof of the Christian faith is found in the empty tomb that Jesus left behind.

Seeking the Living among the Dead

And it came to pass, as they were much perplexed thereabout, behold, two men stood by them in shining garments: And as they were afraid, and bowed down their faces to the earth, they said unto them, Why seek ye the living among the dead?—LUKE 24:4–5

One of the most remarkable geographical features of the Holy Land is the Dead Sea. The lake is the lowest spot on the land surface of the planet, at some fourteen hundred feet below sea level. The salt and mineral content of the water is so high that nothing lives in it, and visitors are cautioned against swallowing even a mouthful of the water because of the danger of serious illness that can result. Though the Dead Sea is a source of chemicals used in makeup, health care, and commercial applications, it is not the place to go to look for living things.

The only source of true and lasting life is God, and yet many people, including some Christians, seek life in the things of the world rather than turning to Him. This search is always doomed to failure, because what they are looking for simply does not exist where they are looking. The world simply has nothing to offer that is lasting and meaningful. At best it only offers temporary pleasure and enjoyment that by its very nature is fleeting.

In contrast Jesus offers a life that overflows and cannot be taken away. As Jesus Himself said in John 10:10, "The thief cometh not, but for to steal, and to kill, and to destroy: I am come that they might have life, and that they might have it more abundantly." If we are seeking life, we must look to the only source where it can be found. This is one of the great lessons of the resurrection—that in Jesus alone we have the hope and promise of everlasting life.

Today's Discipleship Principle: The only way to find and enjoy abundant life is to seek the presence of the Lord.

Remember His Words

He is not here, but is risen: remember how he spake unto you when he was yet in Galilee, Saying, The Son of man must be delivered into the hands of sinful men, and be crucified, and the third day rise again. And they remembered his words, And returned from the sepulchre, and told all these things unto the eleven, and to all the rest.—LUKE 24:6–9

In the dark days of June 1940, following the collapse of France and the surrender of Belgium, Prime Minister Winston Churchill took the floor at the House of Commons in London to rally his shaken countrymen. He urged them not to give in to despair and laid out the plans England would undertake. Churchill concluded his speech by his now-famous words, "We shall fight on the seas and oceans, we shall fight with growing confidence and growing strength in the air, we shall defend our Island, whatever the cost may be, we shall fight on the beaches, we shall fight on the landing grounds, we shall fight in the fields and in the streets, we shall fight in the hills; we shall never surrender."

These powerful words from a gifted orator had a great impact on an entire nation. But the most carefully crafted speech from the most talented man pales in comparison to the power of the Word of God. The Lord has given us everything that we need in the Bible, but too often we do not remember what He has said. Psalm 119:11 says, "Thy word have I hid in mine heart, that I might not sin against thee," but we often don't keep His Word in our hearts.

Those who followed Jesus and heard Him teach in person still failed to remember what He had told them until they were reminded by the angels. It was only when they remembered His words that they were prepared to face the assignment they would be given to take the gospel to the world—and that is the same source of power we must have.

Today's Discipleship Principle: Bible reading and meditation are essential requirements for a victorious Christian life.

Refusing to Believe

It was Mary Magdalene, and Joanna, and Mary the mother of James, and other women that were with them, which told these things unto the apostles. And their words seemed to them as idle tales, and they believed them not. Then arose Peter, and ran unto the sepulchre; and stooping down, he beheld the linen clothes laid by themselves, and departed, wondering in himself at that which was come to pass.—LUKE 24:10–12

It's hard for those of us who have heard the story of the resurrection of Jesus all of our lives to fully grasp what it felt like to those who had mourned for three days and three nights over His death. The intensity of their loss was still fresh when the women who had gone to the tomb to anoint the body of Jesus but had met the angel who told them He was alive rushed in. Though the news they were bringing was good news indeed, the disciples thought it was too good to be true and refused to believe it. They were not comforted until later when Jesus Himself appeared to them. These disciples missed out on the joy that could have been theirs.

The promises of God are not empty words. They are sure and steadfast, and worthy of our full trust. When our faith fails and we refuse to believe what He says, we miss out on so much. The only sure foundation we have been given is not found in our feelings or in our circumstances but in the Word of God.

When we do not believe, we do not harm God, but we do harm ourselves. We lose the power to overcome the world when we lose our faith, and we miss out on our rewards. This is why Hebrews 10:35 admonishes, "Cast not away therefore your confidence, which hath great recompence of reward." Instead we should boldly and confidently act on and claim the promises of Scripture.

Today's Discipleship Principle: When we fail to believe the promises of God, we rob ourselves of both power and joy.

Relying on Reasoning Rather than Revelation

And, behold, two of them went that same day to a village called Emmaus, which was from Jerusalem about threescore furlongs. And they talked together of all these things which had happened. And it came to pass, that, while they communed together and reasoned, Jesus himself drew near, and went with them.—LUKE 24:13–15

In his message "Ten Reasons I Believe the Bible is the Word of God" Dr. R. A. Torrey said, "You will sometimes meet a pious old lady who tells you that she knows that the Bible is God's Word, and when you ask her for a reason for believing that it is God's Word she can give you none. She simply says: 'I know it is God's Word.' You say: 'That is mere superstition.' Not at all. She is one of Christ's sheep, and recognizes her Shepherd's voice from every other voice. She is one of God's children and knows the voice which speaks to her from the Bible is the voice of God."

The Bible contains more truth than could be learned in a thousand years of study. Yet, although our faith has solid historical, scientific, and archeological evidence and can stand the scrutiny of reason, it is not primarily through reason and research we that learn of the things of God.

If we do not believe by faith what the Holy Spirit has given us, we will never learn what God wants us to know. It is the combination of the Scriptures and the Spirit that open the truth of the Word to our hearts: "But the natural man receiveth not the things of the Spirit of God: for they are foolishness unto him: neither can he know them, because they are spiritually discerned" (1 Corinthians 2:14).

When it comes to faith, the mind is vital; but it is not enough alone. It must be joined with the heart so that we apply what we know and have learned and put it into practice.

Today's Discipleship Principle: The Lord is searching the hearts of His children to find those who are willing to live and walk by faith.

Recognizing Christ's Presence

*But their eyes were holden that they should not know him. And he said unto them, What manner of communications are these that ye have one to another, as ye walk, and are sad? And the one of them, whose name was Cleopas, answering said unto him, Art thou only a stranger in Jerusalem, and hast not known the things which are come to pass there in these days?—*LUKE 24:16–18

Maybe you've heard the story of the little boy who was visiting his grandmother's house when she asked him to go to the downstairs pantry and get a can of tomatoes she could use in making supper. He looked at the dark stairs leading down to the basement with some fear, and to comfort him she said, "Johnny, don't be afraid. Remember Jesus is in there." The little boy started into the darkness and then stopped and said, "Jesus if You're in there, could You just hand me the tomatoes?"

We know the spiritual truth that God is always with us in the person of the Holy Spirit who lives within each believer from the moment of salvation. One of the most beautiful of all the names of Jesus is Immanuel, which means "God with us." Yet the reality is that many Christians do not have a real sense of His presence as part of their daily lives. We go to work, go home, go to church, go about our errands as a matter of routine without stopping to consider that God is there with us.

We have Christ's promise "I will never leave thee, nor forsake thee" (Hebrews 13:5), but sometimes we forget to remember His presence. If we live with a real sense of God's presence, it changes us. The apostles were not powerful in their witness because of their great education or eloquence, but because of the time they spent with the Lord. "Now when they saw the boldness of Peter and John, and perceived that they were unlearned and ignorant men, they marvelled; and they took knowledge of them, that they had been with Jesus" (Acts 4:13).

Today's Discipleship Principle: Christ never leaves us or forsakes us, but we must be alert and aware of His presence.

God Is at Work

*And he said unto them, What things? And they said unto him, Concerning
Jesus of Nazareth, which was a prophet mighty in deed and word before
God and all the people: And how the chief priests and our rulers delivered
him to be condemned to death, and have crucified him.*—LUKE 24:19–20

The discovery of the Dead Sea Scrolls was a treasure for both students
of history and the Word of God. The ancient scrolls dated back to the
time of Christ and had been hidden safely in caves until their discovery
by local shepherds shortly after World War II. The scrolls contained some
entire Old Testament books and portions of all the others—except one.
The excluded book was Esther, which the Essenes who copied the scrolls
disapproved of because this book does not contain the name of God. Yet
though His name does not appear, the hand of God is visible on every
page in the story of the deliverance of the Jews from the plot of Haman to
destroy them. In fact, the book of Esther reveals the sovereignty of God in
working behind the scenes in our lives.

The reality is that God is always at work, whether or not we see and
understand His plan. And often it is in the moments of what appear to
be our greatest defeats that God is working His greatest triumphs. The
victory is never lost because God is not faithful, but it can be lost because
we lose heart and give up before it is won. "And let us not be weary in
well doing: for in due season we shall reap, if we faint not" (Galatians 6:9).

Those who were closest to Jesus during His ministry had faith in Him
as long as they saw Him, but once He was dead they found themselves
doubting what He had taught. They believed only what they could see.

When Jesus appeared to Thomas who had previously doubted His
resurrection but then believed, Jesus said, "Thomas, because thou hast
seen me, thou hast believed: blessed are they that have not seen, and yet
have believed" (John 20:29). It is belief without sight that is true faith.

Today's Discipleship Principle: The true demonstration of our faith is
when we cannot see evidence that God is working but trust Him anyway.

Misplaced Faith

But we trusted that it had been he which should have redeemed Israel: and beside all this, to day is the third day since these things were done. Yea, and certain women also of our company made us astonished, which were early at the sepulchre; And when they found not his body, they came, saying, that they had also seen a vision of angels, which said that he was alive.—LUKE 24:21–23

When Satan tempted Jesus, one of the things he tried to get the Lord to do was to presume upon God, going beyond what God had actually said and expect Him to work in ways He had not promised. "And saith unto him, If thou be the Son of God, cast thyself down: for it is written, He shall give his angels charge concerning thee: and in their hands they shall bear thee up, lest at any time thou dash thy foot against a stone" (Matthew 4:6). This promise, found in Psalm 91 is not a guarantee that God will rescue us if we jump off buildings, yet that is the way Satan tried to twist it. Jesus, however, rejected Satan's interpretation of this passage and responded, "It is written again, Thou shalt not tempt the Lord thy God" (Matthew 4:7).

Many times we struggle because we are expecting God to work in ways which He has not promised. Our society is filled with people proclaiming what they say are God's promises concerning health and wealth and the things of this world—but often what they confidently declare is not actually what God said. Faith that is based on anything other than God's Word will lead to trouble.

The two disciples Jesus talked to following His resurrection revealed that they had been looking for Jesus to overthrow the Romans and make Israel an independent nation again. But that is not what Jesus had been teaching them. They did believe God, but, because they believed He would do something different than He had said, their faith was disappointed.

Today's Discipleship Principle: It is critical that we properly understand the promises of God when we claim them in faith.

Jeremiah 51–52   //   Hebrews 9   353

Slow to Believe

And certain of them which were with us went to the sepulchre, and found it even so as the women had said: but him they saw not. Then he said unto them, O fools, and slow of heart to believe all that the prophets have spoken:
—LUKE 24:24–25

Perhaps the most famous of Aesop's fables is the story of the boy who cried wolf. A bored shepherd boy learned that he could break up the monotony of his day by crying out that a wolf was after the sheep. The townspeople would rush from their homes to drive off the intruder and protect the flock, only to find that there was no wolf. In time they lost their confidence in the boy, and one day when a wolf really did come and he cried for help, no one responded. He had given people a reason to be slow to believe what he said.

The Word of God in contrast is completely faithful and reliable. Solomon said, "Blessed be the LORD, that hath given rest unto his people Israel, according to all that he promised: there hath not failed one word of all his good promise, which he promised by the hand of Moses his servant" (1 Kings 8:56). Joshua, too, said, "…ye know in all your hearts and in all your souls, that not one thing hath failed of all the good things which the LORD your God spake concerning you; all are come to pass unto you, and not one thing hath failed thereof" (Joshua 23:14).

Strange, isn't it, that despite a six thousand year track record of being completely trustworthy, we are often slow to believe that God will do what He has promised? The reality is that God has never—not one time—failed to make good on His promises.

Our hesitancy to believe God reveals a lack of faith in our hearts. Too often, we are like the disciples in that we first fail to understand God's promises and then are slow of heart to believe what God has spoken.

Today's Discipleship Principle: Since God is always faithful to His promises, we should be quick to believe all that He says.

The Story of Jesus

Ought not Christ to have suffered these things, and to enter into his glory? And beginning at Moses and all the prophets, he expounded unto them in all the scriptures the things concerning himself.—LUKE 24:26-27

The Bible is completely accurate in all its historical, scientific, and geographical information, but that is not its primary purpose. The Bible is not just a collection of ancient stories. It is the inspired Word of God. When we approach it, we need to be looking for more than just information—we need to be looking for Jesus. For ultimately the Bible is the story of the Son of God. Every part of Scripture is about Him. Someone wrote:

> I find my Lord in the Bible
> Wherever I chance to look,
> He is the theme of the Bible
> The center and heart of the Book;
> He is the Rose of Sharon,
> He is the Lily fair,
> Wherever I open my Bible
> The Lord of the Book is there.

Jesus is both the theme and source of the Bible. John 1:1 says, "In the beginning was the Word, and the Word was with God, and the Word was God." When we speak of knowing the Lord on a deeply personal and intimate level, there is only one possible avenue of success. We must immerse ourselves in the Scriptures. Jesus said, "Search the scriptures; for in them ye think ye have eternal life: and they are they which testify of me" (John 5:39). We will never know Jesus unless we know the Bible, for that is the only book that was inspired by God to tell us about Him.

Today's Discipleship Principle: There is no way for us to truly know Jesus apart from finding Him in the pages of the Bible.

Abiding in His Presence

And they drew nigh unto the village, whither they went: and he made as though he would have gone further. But they constrained him, saying, Abide with us: for it is toward evening, and the day is far spent. And he went in to tarry with them.—LUKE 24:28-29

The Communist government of Romania hated Richard Wurmbrand because he would not stop preaching and telling others about Jesus. He was repeatedly arrested, beaten, tortured, and imprisoned because of his faithfulness. After his release, Wurmbrand wrote a number of books, including one called *With God in Solitary Confinement* which contains some of the more than three hundred sermons he prepared while he was isolated in a prison cell and cut off from all human contact.

The truth is that as children of God we are never truly alone. Even if those who should be closest to us turn against us, God never will. As David, who was forsaken by many who he had trusted, wrote, "When my father and my mother forsake me, then the LORD will take me up." The question is not whether God is there, but whether we are living with a serious, focused realization that He is there. That is the great lack that robs Christians of the joy and peace that comes by resting in God's presence.

The two disciples Jesus spoke with on the day of His resurrection did not recognize Him as the Saviour, but they knew they wanted Him to stay with them. It should be the great desire of our hearts to be in such close fellowship with Jesus that we are constantly aware that He is present. Paul wrote, "That I may know him, and the power of his resurrection, and the fellowship of his sufferings, being made conformable unto his death" (Philippians 3:10). The Christian life must be lived in close fellowship and communion with Jesus, for He is the source of our strength, hope, and victory.

Today's Discipleship Principle: Live with a real awareness of God's presence and closeness to you today.

Recognizing Jesus

And it came to pass, as he sat at meat with them, he took bread, and blessed it, and brake, and gave to them. And their eyes were opened, and they knew him; and he vanished out of their sight. —LUKE 24:30–31

Hannah dedicated her son Samuel to the service of God before he was born, and when he was very small, he went to live with Eli at the tabernacle. Samuel worked with the old priest and was exposed to the things of God on a daily basis. But he was still young, and when God spoke to him one night, Samuel did not recognize who was speaking: "Now Samuel did not yet know the LORD, neither was the word of the LORD yet revealed unto him. And the LORD called Samuel again the third time. And he arose and went to Eli, and said, Here am I; for thou didst call me. And Eli perceived that the LORD had called the child" (1 Samuel 3:7–8). Samuel had to be taught and trained to recognize and respond to the voice of God.

In contrast, the disciples had spent over three years with Jesus before He was crucified. Yet, when He appeared to two of them on the road to Emmaus after His resurrection, they did not recognize Him—because they did not remember His promises and were not expecting to see Him.

The Lord is still working in our world today. Though He no longer speaks audibly as He did before the written Word of God was completed and we do not seek His leading in dreams and visions, He is still active. It is our responsibility to be alert to His Spirit and aware to the opportunities that He brings us to be part of the work He is doing in our world. We do not need voices from Heaven to let us know that we should witness to the lost, comfort the sick and hurting, encourage those who are lonely, give to those who are in need, and pray continually, because God has already told us to do these things in His Word, and by His Holy Spirit, He reminds us of these commands as we go throughout our days.

Today's Discipleship Principle: If we do not feel like God is working in our lives, it is because we are not alert to His presence or listening to His voice.

Ezekiel 3–4   //   Hebrews 11:20–40   357

Stirred Up Hearts

And they said one to another, Did not our heart burn within us, while he talked with us by the way, and while he opened to us the scriptures? And they rose up the same hour, and returned to Jerusalem, and found the eleven gathered together, and them that were with them,—LUKE 24:32–33

Early in the second half of the 2013 Super Bowl between the Ravens and the Giants, most of the lights went out in the Mercedes-Benz Superdome in New Orleans where the game was being played. For more than half an hour, the players, fans, and coaches stood around, waiting for something to happen. Electric crews worked frantically to get the lights back on so the game could resume. Finally, full power was restored, and the game went on.

There are a lot of Christians and churches in our day who are much like that stadium while the lights were out. They are on the team—truly children of God—but they are standing around in the dark and not accomplishing much of anything.

What we need to overcome this spirit of lethargy and darkness is a renewed connection to our Divine source of power. Paul wrote to his young protégé Timothy, "Wherefore I put thee in remembrance that thou stir up the gift of God, which is in thee by the putting on of my hands" (2 Timothy 1:6). From time to time all of us need a renewed sense of God's power and presence and a stirring and revival of our hearts. This is what took place in the disciples' hearts as Jesus explained to them the Old Testament prophecies fulfilled by His life, death, and resurrection.

We do not have Jesus to talk to us personally as the two disciples did, but we have the indwelling Holy Spirit to quicken the Word of God in our minds and renew our hearts and spirits within us. If we will listen to His voice, we will find ourselves strengthened and encouraged for the work to which He has called us.

Today's Discipleship Principle: If your heart is not on fire for God, run to the Word and stir it up.

The Power of Testimony

Saying, The Lord is risen indeed, and hath appeared to Simon. And they told what things were done in the way, and how he was known of them in breaking of bread.—LUKE 24:34–35

After many years as an effective evangelist, Dr. Bob Jones, Sr. developed Alzheimer's late in his life. Before it was fully realized what was happening, he continued to preach, but he would often lose his place in a sermon. Those who heard those final few messages said that invariably, when he did not know what else to say, Dr. Jones would tell the story of his conversion as an eleven-year-old boy at a small country church near his family's home in Alabama. He may have forgotten almost everything else, but he remembered the moment he met Jesus.

The world has no rebuttal to the testimony of transformed lives. When we tell what we have heard it is one thing, but when we tell what we have experienced, it is something much more meaningful. After Jesus raised Lazarus from the dead and news of the miracle spread, Lazarus actually became the target of a deadly plot: "But the chief priests consulted that they might put Lazarus also to death; Because that by reason of him many of the Jews went away, and believed on Jesus" (John 12:10–11). Lazarus' life was a threat to those who didn't want to believe Jesus was God.

Every one of us who is saved has experienced a greater miracle than the raising of Lazarus. We have passed from death to eternal life, and our lives are first-hand, eyewitness testimonies to the power of the gospel. It is important that we know what the Bible says about salvation and can explain it to others and answer their questions. But we should not overlook the command Jesus gave to the man who had once been possessed by many demons: "Go home to thy friends, and tell them how great things the Lord hath done for thee" (Mark 5:19).

Today's Discipleship Principle: Share your testimony of God's working in your life with everyone you can—it is powerful.

Terror or Peace?

And as they thus spake, Jesus himself stood in the midst of them, and saith unto them, Peace be unto you. But they were terrified and affrighted, and supposed that they had seen a spirit.—LUKE 24:36–37

D. L. Moody said that just before He died, Christ made a will. To His disciples (and to us) Jesus left His peace. "Peace I leave with you, my peace I give unto you; not as the world giveth, give I unto you. Let not your heart be troubled, neither let it be afraid" (John 14:27). Then Moody said, "They say that a man cannot make a will now that lawyers cannot break. I will challenge them to break Christ's will. Let them try it. No judge or jury can set that aside. Christ rose to execute His own will. He left His peace and His joy for every true believer, and no power on earth can take it from him who trusts."

Though Jesus had promised lasting peace to His disciples four days earlier on the evening before He was crucified, when He appeared to them after His resurrection, they were in terror. They did not believe that Jesus had risen from the dead as He had said would happen, as the angels had told the women at the tomb, and as the two disciples who had just returned from Emmaus had said.

Here is the lesson from the disciples' fear: when we do not believe what God has said, we forfeit His peace. It is only through faith that we can maintain the peace of God in the face of the storms and tests of life. It is not from the outside—the difficult circumstances around us—that peace is stolen, but from the inside—weak faith in our hearts—that it is given away. The promises of God are backed by His faithfulness and complete power, and they never fail. So when we are facing trials and burdens, we can have God's peace instead of terror as long as we do not give it away in unbelief.

Today's Discipleship Principle: Nothing in the world can take the peace of Jesus away from us unless we give it up ourselves.

Why Are You Troubled?

And he said unto them, Why are ye troubled? and why do thoughts arise in your hearts? Behold my hands and my feet, that it is I myself: handle me, and see; for a spirit hath not flesh and bones, as ye see me have.
—LUKE 24:38–39

Many people in our world live with fear, worry, doubt, and consternation on a regular basis. There are long lists of different phobias and fears that effect people. Some of them are common—fear of snakes, spiders, and other insects are widespread. Others are less common, only effecting small numbers of people. For example:

> Catoptrophobia—The fear of mirrors.
> Pogonophobia—The fear of beards.
> Ligyrophobia—The fear of loud noises.
> Coulrophobia—The fear of clowns.
> Allodoxaphobia—The fear of opinions.
> Disposophobia—The fear of getting rid of possessions.

Fear is a natural part of life in a fallen world, but we do not need to allow it to control us. David spent much of his life facing people who were literally trying to kill him. More than once they nearly succeeded. In response to the threats he faced David declared, "What time I am afraid, I will trust in thee" (Psalm 56:3). The presence of fear is not a sin; it is an opportunity for us to turn to God in faith and rest in His promises.

On His last night with the disciples before His crucifixion, Jesus said, "Let not your hearts be troubled: ye believe in God, believe also in me" (John 14:1). The only real and lasting cure for fear is faith. Faith does not teach us that nothing ever goes wrong. Faith teaches us that nothing ever takes God off guard, that He works all things together as part of His plan for our lives, and that we can trust Him with the end result.

Today's Discipleship Principle: When our faith is strengthened, our fears will be diminished.

The Scars of Our Salvation

And when he had thus spoken, he shewed them his hands and his feet.
And while they yet believed not for joy, and wondered, he said unto them,
Have ye here any meat?—LUKE 24:40-41

The Bible tells us a great deal about the wonders and beauty of Heaven. It speaks of a place where no sin can enter, there is no night, and tears have been wiped away forever. Heaven will be completely perfect—except for one thing. The body of the Lord Jesus Christ, the worthy Lamb, still bears the marks of His suffering for us on the cross. The scars are not gone. Throughout eternity, each time we see Jesus we will see the reminders that He died for us. When John saw the Lord in his vision of Heaven he wrote, "And I beheld, and, lo, in the midst of the throne and of the four beasts, and in the midst of the elders, stood a Lamb as it had been slain, having seven horns and seven eyes, which are the seven Spirits of God sent forth into all the earth" (Revelation 5:6).

The sacrifice of Jesus for our salvation provides a salvation for us that is free through His grace, but it was purchased at great cost. And the evidence of that payment is still visible today. Those of us who have been saved for many years face the danger of losing the sense of how much our sins cost Jesus.

We speak of Jesus dying for the sins of the world, and He did. First John 2:2 says, "And he is the propitiation for our sins: and not for ours only, but also for the sins of the whole world." Remember, however, that His sacrifice was not general but very specific. It was *my* sin for which He paid: "But he was wounded for our transgressions, he was bruised for our iniquities: the chastisement of our peace was upon him; and with his stripes we are healed" (Isaiah 53:5). The joy of remembering that Jesus' sacrifice was for my sin in particular is that it was also for my salvation.

Today's Discipleship Principle: Rejoice today in the love of Jesus that kept Him on the cross as a sacrifice for your sins.

The Importance of the Physical Resurrection

And they gave him a piece of a broiled fish, and of an honeycomb. And he took it, and did eat before them.—LUKE 24:42-43

Even after Jesus showed the disciples the scars in His hands and feet from the crucifixion, they were not fully convinced that He was in fact alive. Many of the Jewish people of that day believed in ghosts that could appear in human form. To convince them that He was truly alive, Jesus sat and ate with them. His ability to eat food was a clear proof that He had been physically resurrected by the power of God.

The resurrection to which we look forward—whether the instant transformation of those who are alive at the Rapture or the rising from dead of those who sleep in Jesus—is only possible because Jesus first was physically resurrected from the dead. If He had not been physically resurrected, there would be no hope for us. All of our hopes hinge on the reality of the resurrection, and without a living Saviour there can be no salvation. Paul wrote, "But now is Christ risen from the dead, and become the firstfruits of them that slept" (1 Corinthians 15.20).

Because Jesus was raised with a physical, glorified body, we have the same future hope. The importance of the physical resurrection is not a new idea. We find this longing and hope expressed in the Old Testament book of Job: "And though after my skin worms destroy this body, yet in my flesh shall I see God" (Job 19:26).

The reality of death has been part of our world ever since the Fall of man, but the death, burial, and resurrection of Jesus changed everything—past, present, and future. Now we no longer fear the grave for its power has been broken.

Today's Discipleship Principle: Jesus is eternally alive, and His resurrection guarantees our eternal life.

All Bible Roads Lead to Jesus

And he said unto them, These are the words which I spake unto you, while I was yet with you, that all things must be fulfilled, which were written in the law of Moses, and in the prophets, and in the psalms, concerning me.—LUKE 24:44

I read of a veteran Welsh preacher who gave some advice to a new minister regarding the importance of preaching about Jesus. The old minister said, "Young man, from every town and every village, and every little hamlet in England, wherever it may be, there is a road to London. And so from every text in Scripture, there is a road to the metropolis of the Scriptures, that is Christ. And my dear brother, your business is when you go to a text, to say, 'Now what is the road to Christ?' and then preach a sermon, running along the road to the great metropolis—Christ. And I have never yet found a text that has not got a road to Christ in it."

The Jewish people divided what we now call the Old Testament into three sections—the law, prophets, and psalms. In Jesus' first appearance to the disciples following His resurrection, He declared to them that all of the sections of Scripture told of His coming—and that He had fulfilled the prophecies exactly as God had given them to the inspired prophets of old. They had spoken of His birth, life, ministry, death, and resurrection; and He had lived just as they said.

In addition to being a powerful statement about the complete reliability of Scripture, this is a pattern for us to follow in our lives and ministry. Jesus is to be at the center of everything in our study of Scripture and Christian life. Paul said, "For I determined not to know any thing among you, save Jesus Christ, and him crucified" (1 Corinthians 2:2). He should also be the center of every aspect of the local church: "And he is the head of the body, the church...that in all things he might have the preeminence" (Colossians 1:18).

Today's Discipleship Principle: The focus of our efforts should not be anything other than our blessed and wonderful Saviour.

Opened Understanding

*Then opened he their understanding, that they might understand the scriptures,—*LUKE 24:45

Solomon was presented with an opportunity that was truly unique. When he assumed the throne of Israel after the death of his father David, God appeared to him and presented Solomon with a blank check—he could ask for anything he wanted, and God would do it. Solomon had his priorities in the right place (although later in his life he would turn away from following God), and instead of asking for riches, power, or fame, Solomon asked for wisdom. "Give therefore thy servant an understanding heart to judge thy people, that I may discern between good and bad: for who is able to judge this thy so great a people?" (1 Kings 3:9).

All of us have need of God's guidance and direction for our daily lives. We understand that God does not speak to us in dreams or visions, but through His Word, and thus if we want His wisdom, we need to be careful students of the Bible. The wonderful news is that every believer has the Holy Spirit as a guide to help us live according to God's Word. Jesus said, "Howbeit when he, the Spirit of truth, is come, he will guide you into all truth: for he shall not speak of himself; but whatsoever he shall hear, that shall he speak: and he will shew you things to come" (John 16:13).

Rather than seeking guidance in signs and feelings, we need to read the Bible and find our direction and wisdom in the pages of Scripture. We have the same Holy Spirit who inspired the writers of Scripture to help us understand His meaning in the words. This is not something to be taken lightly. The greatest resource available to God's children is often overlooked because we fail to listen to the guidance and direction of the Holy Spirit as we make decisions and choices.

Today's Discipleship Principle: We have the promise of the Holy Spirit to help us understand and apply God's wisdom to our lives.

The Necessity of Christ's Death and Resurrection

And said unto them, Thus it is written, and thus it behoved Christ to suffer, and to rise from the dead the third day:—LUKE 24:46

There are many times when we can substitute one thing for the original without much changing the result. For example, if you are baking something and are short one egg, you may be able to use a little applesauce and baking powder and the results will be about the same. If you break a taillight, you can cover the hole with red tape and the light will still shine through when you step on the brakes.

But there are other areas in which no substitute will work. When it comes to our redemption, the death, burial, and resurrection of Jesus Christ were absolutely essential. These are the very foundation of our faith. Paul wrote, "For I delivered unto you first of all that which I also received, how that Christ died for our sins according to the scriptures; And that he was buried, and that he rose again the third day according to the scriptures" (1 Corinthians 15:3–4). The reason Paul started his preaching with this truth is that it is the core of all doctrine.

There were no alternatives to provide a way for our sins to be atoned and for us to be reconciled to God. No angel could die in the place of man. No man could live according to God's law. No one can pay the debt for another because we each owe our own debt. The only hope of salvation was the substitutionary death of the sinless Son of God. If there had been another way, surely God would have chosen it. But there was not, and so Jesus died in our place. The thing we need the most—salvation—is only possible through the sacrifice of Jesus Christ.

Today's Discipleship Principle: The cross is the true measure of God's love for us, and it should fill our hearts with gratitude and joy for our salvation.

A Vital Command

And that repentance and remission of sins should be preached in his name among all nations, beginning at Jerusalem. And ye are witnesses of these things.—LUKE 24:47–48

All four Gospels end with an expression of what we commonly call the Great Commission—the command of Christ to take the gospel to the world—and the book of Acts begins with the same command. There is little doubt about what Jesus considered to be important in leaving His last words for His followers. Even when Jesus first called the disciples, He called them to win lost souls: "And he saith unto them, Follow me, and I will make you fishers of men" (Matthew 4:19). And it was the same at the conclusion of His ministry just before He returned to Heaven.

Evangelist J. Wilbur Chapman said, "If today is the day of salvation, if tomorrow may never come and if life is equally uncertain, how can we eat, drink and be merry when those who live with us, work with us, walk with us and love us are unprepared for eternity because they are unprepared for time? If I am to stand at the judgment seat of Christ to render an account for the deeds done in the body, what shall I say to him if my children are missing, if my friends are not saved, or if my employer or employee should miss the way because I have been faithless?"

What was true nearly two thousand years ago is still true today: God's plan is for His children to take the gospel to the world. The population of the world continues to increase, but the number of Christians obeying this vital command is not rising proportionately. We decry the social and moral decay of our society, and it is a tragedy. But the only solution to human problems is found in the gospel, not in moral reform or political renewal. Only new life in Christ changes things. There is no substitute for obedience to the command of Christ to be a witness for Him.

Today's Discipleship Principle: Those of us who know Christ must make His last command our first priority.

Holy Spirit Power

And, behold, I send the promise of my Father upon you: but tarry ye in the city of Jerusalem, until ye be endued with power from on high.
—LUKE 24:49

D r. A. J. Gordon enjoyed telling the story of a Welsh preacher who was staying with a family prior to preaching in their church that evening. He asked the homeowner if he could spend some time alone before the service to prepare. As the time for the service grew near and the preacher had not come out, the man sent the maid to see if he was all right and let him know that it was almost time to leave. As she approached the door she heard him asking for God's power. "I will not go unless You go with me," he prayed. Without knocking on the door she returned to the homeowner. "He will be here soon," she said. "And the Other One is coming with him!"

How we need the power of God's Holy Spirit for every part of our lives. We cannot do it alone. One of the most effective strategies of the enemy is to get us to rely on our own strength and abilities as we work for God. But we lack the resources to accomplish meaningful and lasting results. It is only as our resources are empowered by the Holy Spirit that we are able to be effective in our ministry. Human ingenuity and devices are no substitute for God's power.

It was not until the Holy Spirit had come on them in power, as recorded in Acts 2:1–4 that the disciples were ready to begin their ministry. We are just as much in need of His filling and power. This is why Ephesians 5:18 instructs us, "And be not drunk with wine, wherein is excess; but be filled with the Spirit." This command is not for a one-time event, but an ongoing process of continual yielding to the Holy Spirit so we may be empowered by Him.

Today's Discipleship Principle: We cannot do the work of God apart from the power of the Holy Spirit of God working in our lives.

The Blessings of the Lord

And he led them out as far as to Bethany, and he lifted up his hands, and blessed them. And it came to pass, while he blessed them, he was parted from them, and carried up into heaven.—LUKE 24:50–51

As Christians we have received the greatest blessing possible in salvation through Jesus Christ. But God's love is so amazing that He offers us far more. David, who experienced great blessings throughout his life wrote, "Blessed be the Lord, who daily loadeth us with benefits, even the God of our salvation. Selah. He that is our God is the God of salvation, and unto God the Lord belong the issues from death" (Psalm 68:19–20).

We do not receive scanty blessings from the abundant resources of God. He constantly fills our lives with good things—good things which we do not deserve. A Christian who cannot find much for which to be thankful is simply not paying attention. We are surrounded by blessings every day.

The fact that we often are not grateful is not a testimony to God's lack of provision and blessing, but our lack of appreciation. Where would we be if God charged us for air, or there was a fee each time our hearts beat? How would we function if we had to create all the resources we need rather than using what God already created?

Charles Spurgeon said, "God's goodness to us is not merely *bene volens*, in which He wishes us well, but it is beneficence of good doing. His gifts and benefits are deeds of goodness, acts of goodness. He doeth to us that which is good. He doth not only wish us well, and speak to us well, and direct us well, but He doeth well unto us." Though God is gracious and patient, it must break His heart when we take His blessings for granted, or even worse when we complain because we don't have more.

Today's Discipleship Principle: Let us never fail to be grateful for the daily benefits we receive because of God's grace.

The Strength of Joy

And they worshipped him, and returned to Jerusalem with great joy:
And were continually in the temple, praising and blessing God. Amen.
—LUKE 24:52–53

When the disciples made their way back to Jerusalem after watching Jesus ascend up to Heaven, they were rejoicing. It was not because they were unaware of the trouble they were about to face. The night before the crucifixion Jesus told them that they would face hatred and persecution for His sake: "If ye were of the world, the world would love his own: but because ye are not of the world, but I have chosen you out of the world, therefore the world hateth you" (John 15:19). Instead they rejoiced because of Jesus.

Robert Murray McCheyne said, "The purest joy in the world is joy in Christ Jesus. When the Spirit is poured down, His people get very near and clear views of the Lord Jesus. They taste that the Lord is gracious. His blood and righteousness appear infinitely perfect, full, and free to their souls. They sit under His shadow with great delight. They rest in the cleft of the rock. They lean on the Beloved. They find infinite strength in Him for the use of their soul—grace for grace—all they can need in any hour of trial and suffering to the very end."

A Christian's joy is not the result of circumstances but of the fruit of the Holy Spirit in our lives. And it is that joy that equips and strengthens us to resolve that we will carry on no matter what trials or hardships we may face. As the prophet Nehemiah told those post-exile Jews in Jerusalem, "...the joy of the LORD is your strength" (Nehemiah 8:10). Remember that when Jesus ascended to Heaven, He left the disciples with an enormous task—to preach the gospel in all the world. Yet, because they had a real relationship with Christ and believed His promises of His power for the task, they could go to their assignment with joy.

Today's Discipleship Principle: When we lose our joy, we lose our strength for the battle.

Only the Beginning

The former treatise have I made, O Theophilus, of all that Jesus began both to do and teach, Until the day in which he was taken up, after that he through the Holy Ghost had given commandments unto the apostles whom he had chosen: To whom also he shewed himself alive after his passion by many infallible proofs, being seen of them forty days, and speaking of the things pertaining to the kingdom of God:—ACTS 1:1–3

The Gospel of Luke is the longest book in the New Testament in terms of the number of words and verses, yet even so it only scratches the surface of the life and ministry of Jesus. In the early verses of Acts, which is a follow up to the book of Luke and penned by the same human author (Luke), we see the work that Jesus did during His time here on Earth is only the beginning of God's plan for us. The lessons that He taught His disciples that were recorded by Luke under the inspiration of the Holy Spirit are meant for us as well. The work that Jesus did is the same work we are to continue.

Jesus said, "Verily, verily, I say unto you, He that believeth on me, the works that I do shall he do also; and greater works than these shall he do; because I go unto my Father" (John 14:12). The early church had a powerful and dramatic impact on the world. They did not have the programs, tools, and buildings that we have, but they had the power of a group of people who were committed to continuing the mission Jesus started, and in the power of His Holy Spirit they shook the world.

Today we have facilities and resources and programs, but we don't always have fruit. What we need is a renewed focus on the Saviour and a renewed filling with His Spirit. Only then can we truly continue the work that Jesus began. Only then can we serve Him with the power and passion that His sacrifice for our salvation demands.

Today's Discipleship Principle: The stories of the life of Christ are not given to us for information but for inspiration and duplication.

december

The Reality of Our Faith

It seemed good to me also, having had perfect understanding of all things from the very first, to write unto thee in order, most excellent Theophilus, That thou mightest know the certainty of those things, wherein thou hast been instructed.—LUKE 1:3–4

The Gospel of Luke was written for a specific purpose—to lay out in detail the events of the life of Christ, from the announcement of His coming to the announcement of His return. Though it is ancient, probably written somewhere around 60 AD, Luke is completely reliable. That is because he was not writing merely what he had personally seen or what he had learned by interviewing others, but because Luke was writing under the inspiration of the Holy Spirit. As a result, Luke, like all of the Bible, is completely accurate and without error.

When we talk and think about Christmas, there are many traditions and legends that have grown up over the years. Many of the things that people think of in connection with Christmas are not actually part of the story given us in the Word of God. Yet for all of the things that have been added and talked about over the years, there is a real, certain, absolute truth at the heart of the Christmas story. What is recorded for us in pages of Scripture is trustworthy.

We do not have to live with doubt. Luke told Theophilus (the name means "lover of God") that he was writing to provide a solid foundation—certainty—for his faith in the things he had been taught. The early Christians only had the Old Testament and what they were taught by the disciples. We have the completed Word of God and the Holy Spirit living within to help us understand and apply it to our lives. While we will never fully understand all of the Bible until we get to Heaven, we can fully rely on it. Our faith is real and has a solid foundation.

Today's Discipleship Principle: Everything that the Bible says is true, and we can trust it with complete confidence.

"In the Days of Herod"

There was in the days of Herod, the king of Judaea, a certain priest named Zacharias, of the course of Abia: and his wife was of the daughters of Aaron, and her name was Elisabeth. And they were both righteous before God, walking in all the commandments and ordinances of the Lord blameless. And they had no child, because that Elisabeth was barren, and they both were now well stricken in years.—LUKE 1:5–7

While we think of Christmas as a happy time, the years around the birth of Christ were anything but happy for the people of Israel. They had known a brief period of freedom following the revolt of the Maccabees, but then the Romans moved in and placed the land under the rule of Herod the Great. The wicked and bloodthirsty king was no friend to the Jewish people. He ruled the land with an iron fist and had anyone who opposed him put to death.

At the same time, the true worship of God was under attack from within as well. The Pharisees were focused only on the outward elements of the law, missing the matters of the heart, while the Sadducees brought in Greek and Roman philosophy and downplayed what the Bible actually taught. This is the background of the beginning of the Christmas story.

Yet in that time of darkness, as the nation lay under foreign rule and many had turned away from following God, there were still people like Zacharias and Elisabeth who served and obeyed and followed God with their whole hearts.

It is an undeniable fact that our world is getting darker—more like the days of Herod—but that does not mean that we cannot still be faithful in serving the Lord. When God chose parents for John the Baptist, who would announce the coming Messiah, He found a couple who did not yield to what those around them were doing.

Today's Discipleship Principle: The culture around us cannot force us to go against God—we can do right no matter what.

God Always Keeps His Promises

For he shall be great in the sight of the Lord, and shall drink neither wine nor strong drink; and he shall be filled with the Holy Ghost, even from his mother's womb. And many of the children of Israel shall he turn to the Lord their God. And he shall go before him in the spirit and power of Elias, to turn the hearts of the fathers to the children, and the disobedient to the wisdom of the just; to make ready a people prepared for the Lord.
—LUKE 1:15–17

The prophet Malachi was the last man in the Old Testament to receive a word from God. And then, for the next four hundred years, there was silence. The people of Israel were conquered first by Alexander the Great and then later by the Romans. God did not give new revelation through prophets. Despite the hopes and prayers of the people, they were not delivered from their enemies. There surely must have been some doubt in their minds as to what was going on—whether or not God could be trusted. God had promised through Malachi that a prophet like Elijah would come, but, years passed, and nothing happened.

Yet in His perfect timing, when all of pieces were in place, God sent John the Baptist. From the moment of his birth, John was prepared for a truly unique ministry. He would be the one who would identify Jesus to the nation of Israel as the Messiah they had been seeking. Though his ministry was not lengthy and ended with his death at the hands of Herod, John did the most important thing anyone could do—he told people about Jesus: "And many resorted unto him, and said, John did no miracle: but all things that John spake of this man were true" (John 10:41).

The life and ministry of John the Baptist is a reminder to us that everything God says can be believed, and in His timing it will come to pass. When we do not see God's promises unfolding on our timetable, we can remember that God does always keep His promises.

Today's Discipleship Principle: We can always trust what God says, no matter what may be going on around us.

Faith and Doubt

And Zacharias said unto the angel, Whereby shall I know this? for I am an old man, and my wife well stricken in years. And the angel answering said unto him, I am Gabriel, that stand in the presence of God; and am sent to speak unto thee, and to shew thee these glad tidings. And, behold, thou shalt be dumb, and not able to speak, until the day that these things shall be performed, because thou believest not my words, which shall be fulfilled in their season.—LUKE 1:18–20

Sometimes we find it hard to believe the promises of the Bible. We think that if we only had a supernatural experience with God—like Moses at the burning bush or the three Hebrew children in the fiery furnace or Peter walking on the water—we would believe. But the truth is that our hearts are, as the song says, "Prone to wander." The issue is not a lack of God's faithfulness, but our lack of belief.

When Gabriel appeared to Zacharias in the temple and told him that in his old age he and Elisabeth would finally have the son they had prayed for all those years, Zacharias should have been thrilled. He should have rejoiced and given thanks that his prayers had been answered. But after such a long time waiting, he did not have confidence in the message he received, even though it was delivered in person by an angel of God. As a result of his unbelief, Zacharias was not able to speak again until John was born.

Even people in the Bible who had supernatural experiences with God—such as Zacharias—did not always have supernatural faith. We do not need more evidence that God is faithful or some new revelation—we need to act on what He has already told us. God does not work on our schedule, but that does not mean He is not working. In His timing, we will see the fullness of His promises fulfilled.

Today's Discipleship Principle: Though we will never have perfect faith, we should always follow the faith we have, rather than listening to our doubts and fears.

The Reward of Obedience

And it came to pass, that, as soon as the days of his ministration were accomplished, he departed to his own house. And after those days his wife Elisabeth conceived, and hid herself five months, saying, Thus hath the Lord dealt with me in the days wherein he looked on me, to take away my reproach among men. —LUKE 1:23–25

In our society where some people choose not to have children, it is hard to understand the pain of parents in Bible times who were childless. Those who did not have children were looked down upon, and many people viewed having no children as a sign of God's judgment or condemnation for some heinous sin in the lives of a married couple. Despite the pain that must have filled their hearts, the Bible tells us that Zacharias and Elisabeth still faithfully served God. They did not insist on getting what they wanted as a condition of their obedience.

There are many people today promoting a "vending machine" view of God—that He is somehow obligated to dispense whatever we ask for when we pray. Though God is gracious and does answer many prayers, we do not deserve and should not demand that He act as we think. The kind of prayer patterned for us by Jesus and taught to us in Scripture is prayer that is in submission to God's will.

There are few things in life sweeter than seeing God answer a long-time prayer. While I rejoice in immediate answers, there is something very special about seeing God work, perhaps in a way we did not expect, to answer a petition we have presented before Him many times. When the answer is delayed, it does not mean we should stop praying or stop following God, but that the time has not yet come. As we continue to pray, even when the answer is delayed, we will see God accomplish His purpose in His timing in our lives.

Today's Discipleship Principle: When we do what God says regardless of circumstances, He always rewards us for our obedience.

A Special Woman

And in the sixth month the angel Gabriel was sent from God unto a city of Galilee, named Nazareth, To a virgin espoused to a man whose name was Joseph, of the house of David; and the virgin's name was Mary. And the angel came in unto her, and said, Hail, thou that art highly favoured, the Lord is with thee: blessed art thou among women. And when she saw him, she was troubled at his saying, and cast in her mind what manner of salutation this should be. —LUKE 1:26–29

N othing about the birth of Jesus was accidental or a coincidence. Everything that happened was part of God's plan. The Bible says, "But when the fulness of the time was come, God sent forth his Son, made of a woman, made under the law" (Galatians 4:4). One of the most important parts of the plan was the selection of the woman who would be the mother of the Messiah. In Mary, God found a pure, godly, and loving young lady who would be able to carry the great responsibility of being Jesus' mother.

Some have painted a picture of Mary that is distorted from what the Bible teaches. Mary was not born without sin. She herself declared her need of salvation: "And Mary said, My soul doth magnify the Lord, And my spirit hath rejoiced in God my Saviour" (Luke 1:46–47). Mary was not a perpetual virgin. She had other children with Joseph after Jesus was born (Mark 6:3). And Mary is not the mediator to whom we should pray for access to God—Jesus is the only mediator (1 Timothy 2:5).

But the myths that have grown up around Mary should not keep us from acknowledging her amazing level of faith in God. The plan Gabriel revealed to her represented a life-shattering change that would bring enormous criticism and eventually great sorrow. But because it was God's plan, she gladly accepted it.

Today's Discipleship Principle: We should cultivate the same loving and obedient heart that Mary had toward the things of God.

The Son of the Highest

And the angel said unto her, Fear not, Mary: for thou hast found favour with God. And, behold, thou shalt conceive in thy womb, and bring forth a son, and shalt call his name JESUS. He shall be great, and shall be called the Son of the Highest: and the Lord God shall give unto him the throne of his father David: And he shall reign over the house of Jacob for ever; and of his kingdom there shall be no end.—LUKE 1:30–33

Though we tend to think of Jesus as a baby when we think of Christmas, He was always far more than that. From the moment of His birth, Jesus was not just the son of Mary, but also and always the Son of God. He came into the world to be the Saviour—that is what the very name Jesus means. But He is also the King. Isaiah prophesied, "Of the increase of his government and peace there shall be no end, upon the throne of David, and upon his kingdom, to order it, and to establish it with judgment and with justice from henceforth even for ever. The zeal of the LORD of hosts will perform this" (Isaiah 9:7).

Of course, Jesus did not establish a kingdom during His first visit to earth. He was here to be the sacrifice and payment for our sins. He laid aside His rights as a ruler in order to pay our penalty for sin and offer us the gift of eternal life. But He was no less a king for the lack of an earthly kingdom, throne, or temporal power.

And when Jesus returns, it will be nothing like the first time. The second time He will come as an undisputed ruler who will put all things under His feet. When we worship the newborn King, we should not forget that He is also the returning King who will rule the entire world.

And what a reign that will be! It is easy to look around us today and grow discouraged over the sin and suffering in our world. But when Christ returns as ruler of the world, we will experience life as God meant it to be.

Today's Discipleship Principle: We worship and follow Jesus—the King of all Heaven and Earth—and He deserves our wholehearted devotion.

Doing Whatever God Says

And the angel answered and said unto her, The Holy Ghost shall come upon thee, and the power of the Highest shall overshadow thee: therefore also that holy thing which shall be born of thee shall be called the Son of God. And, behold, thy cousin Elisabeth, she hath also conceived a son in her old age: and this is the sixth month with her, who was called barren. For with God nothing shall be impossible. And Mary said, Behold the handmaid of the Lord; be it unto me according to thy word. And the angel departed from her.—LUKE 1:35–38

The angel Gabriel made two life-changing announcements six months apart. In each case he told the people to whom he appeared that God was about to do something impossible in their lives. To the aged priest Zacharias, Gabriel announced the birth of a son to two people who should not have been able to have children. To the young girl Mary, Gabriel announced that she would bear the Son of God even though she was a virgin. The contrast in their responses is remarkable.

The priest, who had served God faithfully for years, did not believe the news he received. He asked for a sign and as a result was unable to speak until after John was born. On the other hand, as soon as Mary was told what God had in store for her, she accepted and believed it. She wanted whatever God said to be the course for her life.

So many times we are more like Zacharias than Mary. Rather than simply accepting what God says and wanting to be part of His plan, we insist on understanding all the details and doubt that God really can do what He said. We want to make sure things make sense to us before obeying what the Bible tells us. Instead we need to be yielded to the Lord, considering ourselves to be His servants, and do whatever He wants us to do.

Today's Discipleship Principle: How we react when God calls us to do difficult things reveals the strength of our faith.

The Blessing of Belief

And she spake out with a loud voice, and said, Blessed art thou among women, and blessed is the fruit of thy womb. And whence is this to me, that the mother of my Lord should come to me? For, lo, as soon as the voice of thy salutation sounded in mine ears, the babe leaped in my womb for joy. And blessed is she that believed: for there shall be a performance of those things which were told her from the Lord.—LUKE 1:42–45

There is no more crucial aspect of the Christian life than faith. Not only are we saved by grace through faith, but each day we must walk in faith if we are to be obedient to God. The Bible says, "But without faith it is impossible to please him: for he that cometh to God must believe that he is, and that he is a rewarder of them that diligently seek him" (Hebrews 11:6).

If we only pay lip service to believing the promises of God, we will not be men and women of prayer. After all, if we do not believe that God is real and that He will hear and answer when we cry out to Him, why bother praying?

The reality is that without faith—a willingness to not only accept that what God says in His Word is true but to act upon it—we will never do the things that God has commanded us to do. As you read through Hebrews 11, sometimes called "The Great Hall of Faith," you discover that each of the people God praised for their faith *acted* on their faith. They didn't simply say they believed; they did soemthing about it.

Mary was greatly challenged by the message Gabriel brought to her. She knew that she would be accused of being immoral once word got out that she was expecting a child. She did not know how Joseph would respond to the news. But because she believed God, she willingly submitted to His plan. As a result, she received the blessing that comes to those who believe.

Today's Discipleship Principle: True faith believes God even when it appears there is reason to be afraid, and this kind of faith will be blessed.

The Worship of Mary

*And Mary said, My soul doth magnify the Lord, And my spirit hath rejoiced in God my Saviour. For he hath regarded the low estate of his handmaiden: for, behold, from henceforth all generations shall call me blessed. For he that is mighty hath done to me great things; and holy is his name. And his mercy is on them that fear him from generation to generation.—*LUKE 1:46–50

Every person on earth was born to worship God. It is part of God's design for our lives. The Psalmist wrote, "Let every thing that hath breath praise the LORD. Praise ye the LORD" (Psalm 150:6). And in truth every person does worship—some worship God, and others worship something else. When we do not put God in His rightful place on the throne of our lives, we find something to take His place. Often a lack of worship of God is an indication of a worship of self instead.

Mary was a young woman, possibly still in her teens, when Gabriel announced that she would be the mother of Jesus. In response, her heart of worship poured out in a beautiful testimony of praise to God. One of the things I like about Mary's worship is that it was clearly directed to God. It wasn't about her need to worship; it was about God and His greatness.

Mary's worship came from a heart of gratitude. She realized that it was God's grace that was providing her salvation and the salvation of the world. She humbly accepted God's plan and rejoiced that she was part of it.

Kent Hughes said, "The height of devotion is reached when reverence and contemplation produce passionate worship, which in turn breaks forth in thanksgiving and praise in word and song." This kind of worship should be a daily reality in our lives.

Today's Discipleship Principle: If we think about all that God has done for us, we will not find it hard to worship Him with our whole hearts.

Doing Things God's Way

And it came to pass, that on the eighth day they came to circumcise the child; and they called him Zacharias, after the name of his father. And his mother answered and said, Not so; but he shall be called John. And they said unto her, There is none of thy kindred that is called by this name. And they made signs to his father, how he would have him called. And he asked for a writing table, and wrote, saying, His name is John. And they marvelled all.—LUKE 1:59–63

When Gabriel appeared to Zacharias in the Temple and announced that he and Elisabeth would have a son, he also gave the aged priest the name for the boy—John. Nothing about the life of the "man sent from God" (John 1:6) was left to chance, not even his name. God had a detailed plan for John's life—who his parents would be, how they would raise him, and what his ministry would be. But it was up to Zacharias and Elisabeth to follow that plan, and, as is often the case, they received opposition even from well-meaning friends.

When it came time to name the baby whose birth was a miracle, the friends of the couple objected to the name God had chosen, thinking that the baby should instead be named after his father. Yet John's parents were wise enough and obedient enough to take a stand, even if it meant breaking cultural norms and even in the face of pressure, and follow the plan of God that had been laid out for them.

Though it is helpful when we have friends who encourage us to do right, we must be willing to do what God says even if no one else understands or supports us in the effort. The ministry to which John was called was going to require him to have great courage and stand firm even in the face of persecution and eventually death, and he needed this example from his parents.

Today's Discipleship Principle: There are times when following God's plan means that we must stand alone, but the rewards of doing right are worth the effort.

A Mission Worthy of a Lifetime

And thou, child, shalt be called the prophet of the Highest: for thou shalt go before the face of the Lord to prepare his ways; To give knowledge of salvation unto his people by the remission of their sins, Through the tender mercy of our God; whereby the dayspring from on high hath visited us, To give light to them that sit in darkness and in the shadow of death, to guide our feet into the way of peace.—LUKE 1:76–79

When John the Baptist was born, his father Zacharias gave thanks to God for the miracle birth and then spoke a blessing over his son that contained the mission for his life. John's purpose was to point people to the Messiah—to bring them the message of hope and salvation that Jesus was coming as the Lamb of God who would take away the sins of the world. John was faithful to that task, preaching the truth without fear or favor, and pointing many to the Saviour.

The life mission of John the Baptist should be our purpose as well. There is no more important task, because everyone we meet has an eternal soul and a need of salvation. There were many religious figures in John's day who were proclaiming messages that were not true. John fearlessly pointed out the difference between right and wrong, despite the fact that many people wanted a message more accommodating to their lifestyle.

Jesus praised John the Baptist, in the highest terms, for his commitment to his calling. He said, "Verily I say unto you, Among them that are born of women there hath not risen a greater than John the Baptist: notwithstanding he that is least in the kingdom of heaven is greater than he" (Matthew 11:11). Neither John's life nor ministry were long, but they were effective because he faithfully made Jesus known. Every Christian can and should follow the example of John in pointing others to Jesus.

Today's Discipleship Principle: There is no more important mission we can undertake than pointing people to our Saviour.

Believing What We Cannot See

And it came to pass in those days, that there went out a decree from Caesar Augustus, that all the world should be taxed. (And this taxing was first made when Cyrenius was governor of Syria.) And all went to be taxed, every one into his own city. And Joseph also went up from Galilee, out of the city of Nazareth, into Judaea, unto the city of David, which is called Bethlehem; (because he was of the house and lineage of David:) To be taxed with Mary his espoused wife, being great with child.—LUKE 2:1–5

Doing what God tells us to do is no guarantee that everything will work out the way we think it should. In fact, many times it is the very effort of following God that leads us into difficult circumstances. It was that way for Joseph and Mary. I would guess that few people believed Joseph and Mary's story that Mary's pregnancy was the result of God's Spirit rather than immorality. They had no doubt endured scorn and criticism from many as they told their unbelievable story.

Then, another wave of difficulty came in the form of the government-imposed census of all of Rome's occupied territories, including Israel. Caesar Augustus, the adopted son of Julius Caesar, and the first emperor of the Roman Empire, did not care what impact his edict had on the lives of those who were subject to it. At the point of Roman swords, the order would be enforced against anyone foolish enough to defy it. So Joseph and Mary made a long trip at an inconvenient time.

But they went in faith, believing that God was still in control. And in truth, the difficult journey was necessary for the prophecy of Jesus' birthplace to be fulfilled. Hundreds of years earlier, Micah had prophesied that the Messiah would be born in Bethlehem (Micah 5:2). God was using the difficult circumstances in this couple's lives to bring about His purpose. You can be assured that He will do the same through the most difficult things you face today.

Today's Discipleship Principle: God always knows what He is doing, and we can always trust Him even when we cannot see His plan.

No Place for Jesus

And so it was, that, while they were there, the days were accomplished that she should be delivered. And she brought forth her firstborn son, and wrapped him in swaddling clothes, and laid him in a manger; because there was no room for them in the inn. —LUKE 2:6-7

Though Bethlehem was just a small village, a few miles away from Jerusalem, it had a large place in Israel's history because it was the boyhood home of the great King David. As a result, when the Roman order was given for people to return to their ancestral homes to register for the census, the town of Bethlehem quickly filled up. Those who had close relatives there undoubtedly stayed with them, and those who did not took every room in what was apparently the only inn in town where visitors could find lodging.

By the time Joseph and Mary arrived in Bethlehem, there were no rooms available, so despite the fact that Mary was about to give birth, they had to settle for staying with the animals in a nearby stable. That is why on His first night on Earth, the very King of Heaven, the Lord of Glory, the Son of God was carefully wrapped and placed into a feeding trough for animals.

This would not be the last time the world would have no place for Jesus. During His ministry, Jesus was often rejected. He warned one potential follower of what to expect if he were to follow Him: "The foxes have holes, and the birds of the air have nests; but the Son of man hath not where to lay his head" (Matthew 8:20). This lack of room for Jesus is easily seen in our day as well. In fact, even though we profess to follow Christ, we must be on guard to make certain He really is the center of our lives. Just as in first-century Bethlehem, it is so easy for our lives to fill up with pressing cares that have no eternal significance.

Today's Discipleship Principle: It is a tragedy when the world has no room for Jesus, but it is an even greater tragedy when Christians do not put Him first.

The Shepherds in the Field

And there were in the same country shepherds abiding in the field, keeping watch over their flock by night. And, lo, the angel of the Lord came upon them, and the glory of the Lord shone round about them: and they were sore afraid.—LUKE 2:8–9

For centuries, since at least the time of King David, Bethlehem had been a center for shepherds. The hilly terrain was ideal for shepherds to keep their flocks fed and safe, especially in the winter. And the proximity to Jerusalem made Bethlehem an ideal place to raise the sheep for Temple sacrifices. They were close enough to the Holy City to be convenient but far enough removed to avoid the mess and smell that accompanied raising animals. The shepherds themselves didn't escape the reproach and were often looked down on by much of society.

In many ways, the fact that shepherds were the first to receive the news of the birth of the King of the Jews seems strange. Yet viewed from God's perspective it makes perfect sense. Shepherds were not the kind of people with whom kings usually associated, but Jesus was not a typical king. The ancient prophet declared that the Messiah would come, not in glory and pomp, but in humility. "Rejoice greatly, O daughter of Zion; shout, O daughter of Jerusalem: behold, thy king cometh unto thee: he is just, and having salvation; lowly, and riding upon an ass, and upon a colt the foal of an ass" (Zechariah 9:9).

Beyond that, Jesus Himself used the metaphor of a shepherd repeatedly to describe His life and ministry. He said, "I am the good shepherd: the good shepherd giveth his life for the sheep" (John 10:11). Just like the lambs raised by the shepherds for sacrifices in the Temple, Jesus would one day lay down His life to purchase our salvation.

Today's Discipleship Principle: If you feel insignificant or unimportant, remember that the first group God chose to announce the birth of His Son was the outcasts of society.

The Message of the Angels

And the angel said unto them, Fear not: for, behold, I bring you good tidings of great joy, which shall be to all people. For unto you is born this day in the city of David a Saviour, which is Christ the Lord. And this shall be a sign unto you; Ye shall find the babe wrapped in swaddling clothes, lying in a manger. And suddenly there was with the angel a multitude of the heavenly host praising God, and saying, Glory to God in the highest, and on earth peace, good will toward men.—LUKE 2:10-14

Though the message that the Messiah had been born was delivered first to the shepherds, it was not meant just for them. The angel specifically told them that the news he was bringing was for "all people." The message of Christmas is not the birth of a baby, although that is the start of the story. The real message of Christmas is the birth of a Saviour. The love, grace, and mercy of God provided for mankind what we most needed—a way to be reconciled with God.

There are many facets of the Christmas story, but this is the heart of everything. In the middle of shepherds, wise men, mangers, stars, and angels, we must never lose sight of what Jesus came to do. He is so much more than a good example, wise teacher, and powerful healer. He is the Saviour. This is what lies behind everything He did—not just in His birth, but through His life, death, and resurrection.

Jesus declared His purpose to be the salvation of men: "For the Son of man is come to seek and to save that which was lost" (Luke 19:10). If we truly follow Him, that will be our purpose as well.

In fact, after Christ's crucifixion and resurrection, He specifically told us that sharing the message is our purpose: "And he said unto them, Go ye into all the world, and preach the gospel to every creature" (Mark 16:15).

Today's Discipleship Principle: The story of Christmas is that there is a Saviour, and this is the message we must share with the world.

Shepherds in a Hurry

And it came to pass, as the angels were gone away from them into heaven, the shepherds said one to another, Let us now go even unto Bethlehem, and see this thing which is come to pass, which the Lord hath made known unto us. And they came with haste, and found Mary, and Joseph, and the babe lying in a manger.—LUKE 2:15–16

I really love the response of the shepherds to the message they received from the angels that Jesus had been born. They didn't sit around and debate the proper response to an angelic visitation. They didn't appoint a committee to study the history of miraculous births. They got to their feet and took off for the city.

The Greek word that is translated *haste* not only means to hurry, but it also carries the idea of wanting something very much, so that you do whatever it takes to get to where it is. No doubt it took a little arranging to make sure their sheep would be safe while they were gone, but they wanted to get to where Jesus was, and they hurried to do so.

How our hearts should long for the things of Christ—and too often we allow other things to be our true desire instead of Him. Jesus described this problem in His parable of the sower and the different kinds of ground on which the seed falls. He said, "And these are they which are sown among thorns; such as hear the word, And the cares of this world, and the deceitfulness of riches, and the lusts of other things entering in, choke the word, and it becometh unfruitful" (Mark 4:18–19).

Although we haven't received an angelic invitation to see baby Jesus, we have received invitations throughout the pages of Scripture to seek the Lord through His Word and through prayer. Nothing is more important than Jesus, and we are instructed to love, follow, and obey Him with all of our hearts. There should be nothing reluctant in our worship and service of the Lord.

Today's Discipleship Principle: Make sure your heart is eager for the things of God rather than the things of the world.

What We Have Seen and Heard

*And when they had seen it, they made known abroad the saying which was told them concerning this child. And all they that heard it wondered at those things which were told them by the shepherds. But Mary kept all these things, and pondered them in her heart. And the shepherds returned, glorifying and praising God for all the things that they had heard and seen, as it was told unto them.—*LUKE 2:17–20

Every Christian is commanded to be a witness to the world. Jesus said, "Go ye therefore, and teach all nations, baptizing them in the name of the Father, and of the Son, and of the Holy Ghost: Teaching them to observe all things whatsoever I have commanded you: and, lo, I am with you alway, even unto the end of the world. Amen" (Matthew 28:19–20). This is not an optional task—it is essential to our obedience to the Lord.

After the shepherds had gone to the manger in person and seen that everything had happened just as the angel had told them, they did not just go back to their sheep and keep the news to themselves. Instead they went across the countryside telling everyone they met what had happened. There are no people who do not need to hear the gospel message that a Saviour has been born, and God has no other plan for them to hear than for us to tell them.

Notice that the angels did not go from door to door announcing the birth of Jesus. After their initial announcement and song of praise, they went back into the heavens. The good news is not carried around the world by angels, but by men and women who are willing to tell what they have seen and heard. This is what the apostles did after Christ's resurrection. When authorities tried to silence their witness, they responded, "For we cannot but speak the things which we have seen and heard" (Acts 4:20). There is nothing more life-changing than meeting Jesus, and we must take the message to others.

Today's Discipleship Principle: Like the shepherds, we must be faithful witnesses to the hope of salvation in Jesus Christ.

The Name of the Saviour

And when eight days were accomplished for the circumcising of the child, his name was called JESUS, which was so named of the angel before he was conceived in the womb.—LUKE 2:21

There are nearly two hundred references, names, and titles given to Jesus in the Word of God. They reveal the different aspects of His character and nature, as well as the work that He did and continues to do in our lives. Among these names are:

> The Alpha and Omega
> The Bright and Morning Star
> The Good Shepherd
> The Bread of Life
> The Way, the Truth, and the Life
> Emmanuel
> Messiah

The list goes on and on, but no other name so fully captures the life and purpose of the Saviour than the name that the angel gave to Him before He was born—Jesus. The very name means "one who saves or delivers," and that is why Jesus left the glory and honor of Heaven to come into the world to live among sinful men. That is why He was willing to go to the cross as an innocent sacrifice to pay for our sins. That is why He laid down His life so that we could be saved.

The name of Jesus is truly the sweetest name, because of all that it conveys. And God has decreed that all men will acknowledge Him either in this life or at the judgment: "Wherefore God also hath highly exalted him, and given him a name which is above every name: That at the name of Jesus every knee should bow, of things in heaven, and things in earth, and things under the earth; And that every tongue should confess that Jesus Christ is Lord, to the glory of God the Father" (Philippians 2:9–11).

Today's Discipleship Principle: Give thanks today to God for the amazing, indescribable gift of a Saviour in the person of Jesus Christ.

Obedience Even in Lack

And when the days of her purification according to the law of Moses were accomplished, they brought him to Jerusalem, to present him to the Lord; (As it is written in the law of the Lord, Every male that openeth the womb shall be called holy to the Lord;) And to offer a sacrifice according to that which is said in the law of the Lord, A pair of turtledoves, or two young pigeons.—LUKE 2:22-24

Joseph and Mary had endured a great deal of upheaval in their lives before Jesus was born. When He arrived (right on God's schedule) they were far from their home in Nazareth and removed from any kind of family help. Add to that the fact that because of the crowds of people staying in Bethlehem they were actually camped out with the animals, and the first bed Jesus had was a feeding trough they had repurposed for His use. It is safe to say that Joseph and Mary were not well off financially.

We see this confirmed in the offering that they took to the Temple for Jesus—it was the offering that was used by those who were too poor to be able to make the regular offering of a lamb for a firstborn son. God had made provision for this in Leviticus 12:8 which instructed, "And if she be not able to bring a lamb, then she shall bring two turtles, or two young pigeons; the one for the burnt offering, and the other for a sin offering: and the priest shall make an atonement for her, and she shall be clean."

There is a wonderful example for us in the obedience of Joseph and Mary. They had little in the way of financial resources, but they still did what God had commanded. Sometimes we are more prone to make excuses for why we cannot do as God has instructed us, rather than simply obeying. Our obedience is not conditioned on having everything we need or think we need, but on our willingness to do what God says no matter what.

Today's Discipleship Principle: If we do not obey God with what we have now, we would not obey Him if we had more.

Waiting for the Messiah

And, behold, there was a man in Jerusalem, whose name was Simeon; and the same man was just and devout, waiting for the consolation of Israel: and the Holy Ghost was upon him. And it was revealed unto him by the Holy Ghost, that he should not see death, before he had seen the Lord's Christ. —LUKE 2:25–26

Those of us who have children or grandchildren who are young know all about the countdown to Christmas. The excitement builds as the days tick off on the calendar and we get closer and closer to the big day. When it gets to the point where there are only one or two days left until Christmas and the presents are wrapped under the tree, the excitement can almost be felt.

Imagine what it was like for those who were awaiting the promised Messiah. The Jewish people were living under terrible conditions when the prophesied time approached. Not only had they been conquered by the Romans, but the puppet king Herod the Great was a bloodthirsty tyrant who ordered people murdered on a whim. In addition, the spiritual condition of Israel had greatly declined so that many no longer followed the God of their fathers.

But for those who still believed there was hope. The promise had not yet been fulfilled, but they believed that God would do what He said—and He did.

For us who look back to the birth of Jesus, we also have a promise to which we can look forward. He told us before He left that He would return. "And if I go and prepare a place for you, I will come again, and receive you unto myself; that where I am, there ye may be also" (John 14:3). The fact that He has not yet returned does not make His Second Coming any less likely, and we can wait for Him with confidence.

Today's Discipleship Principle: God always keeps His promises, and even if the fulfillment of them is delayed, we should keep believing.

Christmas Praise

And he came by the Spirit into the temple: and when the parents brought
in the child Jesus, to do for him after the custom of the law, Then took
he him up in his arms, and blessed God, and said, Lord, now lettest
thou thy servant depart in peace, according to thy word: For mine eyes
have seen thy salvation, Which thou hast prepared before the face of all
people; A light to lighten the Gentiles, and the glory of thy people Israel.
—LUKE 2:27–32

When the aged Simeon, who had been promised that he would see
the Messiah before he died, met Joseph and Mary in the Temple
with Jesus, he immediately recognized the infant as the Saviour of the
world. Imagine what it must have been like for him to gently cradle
the little baby for whom he had waited so long in his arms. Simeon
recognized the truth of the Christmas story—that Jesus came to offer
hope of forgiveness and salvation, and he issued a heartfelt prayer of
praise and worship.

While it is always right for us to be grateful and praise God, there
is certainly no more meaningful time of year for us to remember and
worship God than Christmas. This is the time when we remember most
of all the amazing and enormous sacrifice that Christmas represents. The
Bible reminds us, "For ye know the grace of our Lord Jesus Christ, that,
though he was rich, yet for your sakes he became poor, that ye through
his poverty might be rich" (2 Corinthians 8:9).

Though many of the Jewish people in Jesus' day rejected Him because
He was not offering them political deliverance from Roman oppression,
Simeon recognized that the point of Jesus coming was to bring salvation
into the world. And even as we celebrate Christmas, we should focus on
the real purpose for the birth of Christ.

Today's Discipleship Principle: When we understand the true meaning
of Christmas, our hearts will be filled with praise for God's love and
mercy toward us.

The Cost of Christmas

And Joseph and his mother marvelled at those things which were spoken of him. And Simeon blessed them, and said unto Mary his mother, Behold, this child is set for the fall and rising again of many in Israel; and for a sign which shall be spoken against; (Yea, a sword shall pierce through thy own soul also,) that the thoughts of many hearts may be revealed.
—LUKE 2:33–35

I love the Christmas season and the special joy that it brings to those of us who know the Lord. It is a time when we celebrate with family and friends, exchange presents, sing songs, and spend time together. Yet even as we enjoy this wonderful time of year, we should never forget that the greatest gift of Christmas—the Son of God sent into the world to be our Saviour—came at a very high cost.

Man turned against God, violating the one instruction issued in the Garden of Eden. Even in the only perfect setting the world has known, Adam was unwilling to obey. As a result, death entered the world and is the only future of which all can be certain. Yet in mercy and grace, even before the Fall, God had already ordained a plan for our salvation, despite the fact that it would require the death of His sinless Son as a sacrifice for our sins.

It is only the amazing love of God for us that can explain why the high cost of Christmas was paid. And it is that love that should motivate us to follow the example of the Lord.

In explaining his lifetime of devoted service to Jesus, Paul wrote, "For whether we be beside ourselves, it is to God: or whether we be sober, it is for your cause. For the love of Christ constraineth us; because we thus judge, that if one died for all, then were all dead" (2 Corinthians 5:13–14). When the love of Christ fills our hearts, we are willing to pay any cost to demonstrate our love to Him.

Today's Discipleship Principle: The cost of Christmas should drive us to a lifetime of devoted love and service to Jesus Christ.

Rejoicing in Redemption

And there was one Anna, a prophetess, the daughter of Phanuel, of the tribe of Aser: she was of a great age, and had lived with an husband seven years from her virginity; And she was a widow of about fourscore and four years, which departed not from the temple, but served God with fastings and prayers night and day. And she coming in that instant gave thanks likewise unto the Lord, and spake of him to all them that looked for redemption in Jerusalem.—LUKE 2:36–38

When the elderly lady named Anna, who had faithfully served God all of her, life held the baby Jesus in the temple when He was brought for His dedication, she immediately broke out into thanksgiving and rejoicing—because she knew that Jesus was the hope of all those who were looking and praying for redemption. The same is true today. He remains the only hope of a world in desperate need of salvation. And those of us who have received that salvation can be filled with rejoicing.

When Jesus was born, the angels of Heaven could not contain their joy. Multitudes of angels filled the sky near Bethlehem to glorify God and praise Him for providing the hope of peace to a world in need. And yet, salvation is not for the angels but for us! How much more then should we be singing and rejoicing over the goodness of God toward us! His praises should fill our mouths and our hearts without end, and even more at Christmas as we celebrate and remember all that He has done for us. The wonderful carol Silent Night puts it this way:

> Silent night, holy night,
> wondrous star, lend thy light;
> with the angels let us sing,
> Alleluia to our King;
> Christ the Saviour is born,
> Christ the Saviour is born!

Today's Discipleship Principle: Christmas gives us reason to rejoice because Christmas gives us the hope of redemption.

Only the Start of the Story

And when they had performed all things according to the law of the Lord, they returned into Galilee, to their own city Nazareth. And the child grew, and waxed strong in spirit, filled with wisdom: and the grace of God was upon him.—LUKE 2:39–40

Joseph and Mary were not casually selected by God to be the earthly parents for His Son. They were faithful and obedient to God's commands, even at great personal sacrifice and hardship. When all the things that we associate with Christmas—the long trip, the birth in a stable, the shepherds, the wise men, and the trip to Egypt—were finished, the real Christmas story began. The new family went back home to Nazareth, and simply continued to obey God just as they had done throughout the process.

Though Jesus was perfect God from His birth, He was also human and He still needed to grow up and mature, and He did so with a constant example of obedience from His parents as they daily followed the law of God.

God's plan for our lives is not mostly composed of large events and miracles, but of daily devotion and obedience to His Word. Ellen Sturgis Hooper wrote: "I slept, and dreamed that life was Beauty; I woke, and found that life was Duty." Events like Christmas only happen occasionally, but each day we have the opportunity to live as Jesus lived in submission to the will of His Father. Rather than wishing for wondrous experiences and angelic visitations, we need to be content to walk in the footsteps of Jesus and live as He lived. This is God's purpose for our lives: "For whom he did foreknow, he also did predestinate to be conformed to the image of his Son, that he might be the firstborn among many brethren" (Romans 8:29).

Today's Discipleship Principle: The true meaning of Christmas is not found in a single day, but in a lifetime of obedience and service to God.

Godly Patterns

Now his parents went to Jerusalem every year at the feast of the passover. And when he was twelve years old, they went up to Jerusalem after the custom of the feast.—LUKE 2:41–42

Joseph and Mary had the only perfect child in all of human history. Yet Jesus was not only God, but also man, and as such He laid aside the power and glory that were His right and subjected Himself to the physical limitations of human form. As part of that emptying of Himself, He became not just a man but a baby, who would need to grow and learn and develop. And in that growth, Jesus had wonderful parents to guide Him.

Despite the fact that many Jewish people in the time of Christ were only paying lip service to their faith, or had completely abandoned following the God of their fathers, Joseph and Mary continued to obey the law given to the Children of Israel through Moses. Part of their obedience was making the annual pilgrimage to Jerusalem for the major feast days on the Jewish calendar. The Bible tells us that they did this every year. I'm sure there were competing obligations and important tasks that they could have chosen, but instead they continued to obey God's command.

In doing so, they set a good example for Jesus to follow. In the same way, we need to be aware that all of us are role models for others. We usually think of this only in terms of people in positions of authority—pastors, teachers, or parents. But no matter our role, there are people who are watching our lives to see and copy our conduct. There is a great responsibility on our shoulders to make sure that we are leading people in the way that they should go. Paul wrote, "Be ye followers of me, even as I also am of Christ" (1 Corinthians 11:1).

Today's Discipleship Principle: We need to live each day in such a way as to set a good and godly example for all those who are watching.

Assuming God's Presence

And when they had fulfilled the days, as they returned, the child Jesus tarried behind in Jerusalem; and Joseph and his mother knew not of it. But they, supposing him to have been in the company, went a day's journey; and they sought him among their kinsfolk and acquaintance. And when they found him not, they turned back again to Jerusalem, seeking him.—LUKE 2:43-45

In the days when Joseph and Mary took Jesus to Jerusalem for the Passover, it was not safe to travel alone, so often a large group of people from one city or region would join together to make the trip to the temple for the feast days. This was the case when Jesus was twelve and His family joined with friends and relatives to go to Jerusalem. After the week-long observance of Passover and the Feast of Unleavened Bread, the group headed home, but Jesus stayed behind. It was not until a full day had passed that Joseph and Mary realized Jesus was not in the group.

Often we think that just because we are regularly in church and carry on the outward forms of Christianity, we have a close relationship with God. Yet tragically, many Christians go through much of their lives without evidence of His presence and power. They assume that He is there (and of course the Holy Spirit never leaves a true believer) without stopping to realize that something is missing.

We should be so reliant on God for our daily lives that we cannot miss Him even for a moment without noticing. The devil tempts us to replace God-dependance with self-reliance. He does not mind if we do good things in our own strength, but he knows that it is only God's power that can stand against him. As the old hymn "Brethren We Have Met To Worship" puts it, "All is vain unless the Spirit of the Holy One comes down."

Today's Discipleship Principle: We need to be constantly sensitive to and aware of the presence of God in our lives.

God Comes First

And it came to pass, that after three days they found him in the temple, sitting in the midst of the doctors, both hearing them, and asking them questions. And all that heard him were astonished at his understanding and answers. And when they saw him, they were amazed: and his mother said unto him, Son, why hast thou thus dealt with us? behold, thy father and I have sought thee sorrowing. And he said unto them, How is it that ye sought me? wist ye not that I must be about my Father's business?
—LUKE 2:46–49

When God gave Moses the Ten Commandments, the very first one was that nothing and no one else was to be allowed to take His place: "Thou shalt have no other gods before me" (Exodus 20:3).

God alone is worthy of our complete commitment and devotion, and He will not share our affections. The history of the human race, from the time of Adam and Eve until now, is filled with people who have allowed all manner of things to take His rightful place. Any time that God is not completely on the throne, we are living in rebellion, no matter how much our outward lives may appear to conform to the Christian life.

Even as a twelve-year-old boy, Jesus was committed to putting God first. He believed and demonstrated throughout His life that obeying His Father was the priority that mattered most. And if we are to be like Him, we must do the same.

Jesus made the cost of truly following Him clear: "He that loveth father or mother more than me is not worthy of me: and he that loveth son or daughter more than me is not worthy of me. And he that taketh not his cross, and followeth after me, is not worthy of me" (Matthew 10:37–38). We cannot allow anything to take the place of our love for God. He always and in all things must come first.

Today's Discipleship Principle: The first and most important commandment is to love God completely, and we must obey that above all others.

The Obedience of Christ

And he went down with them, and came to Nazareth, and was subject unto them: but his mother kept all these sayings in her heart. And Jesus increased in wisdom and stature, and in favour with God and man.
—LUKE 2:51–52

We could spend the rest of our lives describing the wonderful attributes of Jesus and never run out of things to say. But certainly one of the most striking traits of His—all the more because it is in an area that is so difficult for us to master—is the humble obedience that Jesus demonstrated. The Lord of Heaven and Earth became a little baby and grew up in the home of imperfect parents. He never sinned, but they did. Joseph and Mary both needed a Saviour. Yet despite their failings, Jesus lived in submission to their authority the entire time He was in their home.

Why did Jesus obey His earthly parents? Even more, why did He obey His Father's will knowing what it would mean? It is because despite His power and honor and glory, our Saviour is humble. In his great passage describing the process by which Jesus came to be the sacrifice for our sins, Paul points this out: "And being found in fashion as a man, he humbled himself, and became obedient unto death, even the death of the cross" (Philippians 2:8).

If we are to be like Jesus, we must be willing to humble ourselves rather than insisting on getting our own way and having our rights respected and honored. Perhaps you've heard the old saying, "You are either a stumbling block or a stepping stone." That statement is often true, but the problem is that in order to be a stepping stone to lift up others, you have to be willing to be walked on sometimes. Jesus did that in order to provide our salvation, and we must do the same to help point others to Him.

Today's Discipleship Principle: When we submit ourselves to God's commands, we are demonstrating the reality of our faith in Him.

The Key to a Powerful Message

Now in the fifteenth year of the reign of Tiberius Caesar, Pontius Pilate being governor of Judaea, and Herod being tetrarch of Galilee, and his brother Philip tetrarch of Ituraea and of the region of Trachonitis, and Lysanias the tetrarch of Abilene, Annas and Caiaphas being the high priests, the word of God came unto John the son of Zacharias in the wilderness. And he came into all the country about Jordan, preaching the baptism of repentance for the remission of sins;—LUKE 3:1-3

Few people in all of history have had a ministry with the impact of John the Baptist. In a time of great darkness, he preached a powerful message of the need for repentance and the coming of the Messiah. And many believed the preaching of John. He was a vital part of preparing the world for the beginning of the ministry of Jesus. He would eventually lose his life because of his powerful preaching against sin in high places. In describing His cousin's work, Jesus said of John the Baptist, "He was a burning and a shining light: and ye were willing for a season to rejoice in his light" (John 5:35).

Truly our world is desperately in need of powerful proclamations of the truth. We need people like John who will cry out against sin and for righteousness. We need to point people to Jesus.

But if our message is to have power as John's did, it must come from the same source. John had power in his preaching because he preached the Word of God. We do not hear words from God as John did because we have the completed Bible (which he did not have). If we proclaim our ideas and opinions, we will not make an impact. It is only when we, like the prophets of old, say, "Thus saith the Lord" that we can shake the world. This is what Christians in the early church did, and the result was that even unbelievers referred to them as "These that have turned the world upside down" (Acts 17:6).

Today's Discipleship Principle: If we want to make a true impact on the world, then we must preach and teach the Word of God.

Preparing People to See the King

As it is written in the book of the words of Esaias the prophet, saying, The voice of one crying in the wilderness, Prepare ye the way of the Lord, make his paths straight. Every valley shall be filled, and every mountain and hill shall be brought low; and the crooked shall be made straight, and the rough ways shall be made smooth; And all flesh shall see the salvation of God.—LUKE 3:4–6

John the Baptist was the fulfillment of Old Testament prophecy. Isaiah foretold the message that he would preach announcing the arrival of the Messiah, and Malachi declared that the messenger would be a powerful witness: "Behold, I will send you Elijah the prophet before the coming of the great and dreadful day of the LORD" (Malachi 4:4). The powerful ministry of John the Baptist had one central focus, and on the day Jesus went to him to be baptized, John announced to everyone that the Messiah had come: "The next day John seeth Jesus coming unto him, and saith, Behold the Lamb of God, which taketh away the sin of the world" (John 1:29).

In our day, we need the same work to be done—not to announce that the Messiah is coming, but that He has already come and offers salvation to those who believe. We need to share the gospel with power and conviction so that people will realize their need of a Saviour.

Oswald J. Smith said, "The world does not need sermons; it needs a message. You can go to seminary and learn how to preach sermons, but you will have to go to God to get messages." If like John we are focused on declaring the message God has given us, and are willing to be humble, we can have a great impact on the world. Remember that it was John who said, "He must increase, but I must decrease" (John 3:30).

Today's Discipleship Principle: The most important thing we can do with our lives is to point people to Jesus Christ.

indexes

Title Index

May

1 A Pattern for Prayer
2 Importunity
3 Asking, Seeking, and Knocking
4 Trusting God's Love for Us
5 Rejecting God
6 Unity in God's Family
7 The Strength to Overcome
8 The Necessity of Replacement
9 The Sign of Jonah
10 Let Your Light Shine
11 Clean from the Inside Out
12 Ignoring What Really Matters
13 Carrying the Load
14 The Testimony of Blood
15 Hidden Sins
16 The Fear of the Lord
17 Consider the Sparrows
18 The Great Shame of Being Ashamed of Jesus
19 The Work of the Holy Spirit
20 What Makes a Life
21 The Peril of Prosperity
22 Time to Give an Account
23 Don't Worry
24 Worry Doesn't Make You Taller
25 How Great God's Love for Us Really Is
26 Where Is Your Treasure?
27 Ready for His Return
28 Overpowering the Enemy
29 Faithful Where We Are
30 A Matter of Responsibility
31 A Cause of Division

June

1 Understanding the Times
2 Sooner Is Better than Later
3 Give Heed to the Warning
4 Not Just for Decoration
5 Rejoicing in Our Deliverance
6 The Glorious Kingdom of God
7 Does God Know You?
8 The Reality of Hell
9 God Is in Control
10 A Rejected Invitation
11 Don't Delay Doing Good
12 The Shame of Self Promotion
13 How to Really Get Ahead
14 God Helps Those Who Help Others
15 The Folly of Excuses
16 The Urgency of the Gospel
17 Loving God Most of All
18 Counting the Cost
19 Clinging to Belongings
20 Staying Salty
21 A Complaint about Reaching Sinners
22 God Looking for Sinners
23 Making Heaven Happy
24 Searching by Candlelight
25 Focus on the Father
26 When the Party Ends
27 Reaching the Bottom of the Barrel
28 The Insanity of Sinners
29 The Father Running to the Son
30 God's Acceptance of Sinners

Scripture Index

About the Author

Dr. Paul Chappell is the senior pastor of Lancaster Baptist Church and the president of West Coast Baptist College in Lancaster, California. He is a powerful communicator of God's Word and a passionate servant to God's people. He has been married to his wife, Terrie, for thirty-two years, and he has four married children who are all serving in Christian ministry. He enjoys spending time with his family, and he loves serving the Lord shoulder to shoulder with a wonderful church family.

Dr. Chappell's preaching is heard on *Daily in the Word*, a radio program that is broadcast across America. You can find a station listing at: dailyintheword.org.

You can also connect with Dr. Chappell here:

Blog: paulchappell.com
Twitter: twitter.com/paulchappell
Facebook: facebook.com/pastor.paul.chappell

Other Titles for Your Daily Walk

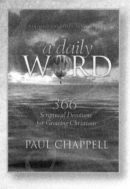

A Daily Word

Designed to compliment your daily walk with the Lord, this book from Dr. Paul Chappell features 366 daily devotional thoughts to strengthen and encourage your spiritual life. Each devotion features a one-year Bible reading selection. Also included are helpful reference resources as well as Scripture and title indexes. (424 pages, hardback)

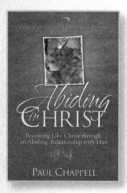

Abiding in Christ

In these pages, Dr. Paul Chappell will lead you on an exciting and encouraging journey to discover the authentic Christian life. You will learn how an intimate relationship with Christ produces a genuine heart and life change. You will find the source of true love, abundant joy, lasting fruit, spiritual maturity, emotional stability, and purpose in life. (168 pages, paperback)

Stewarding Life

God has given you one life and filled it with resources—time, health, finances, relationships, influence, and more. How you steward these resources will determine whether you successfully fulfill God's eternal purpose for your life. This book will challenge and equip you to strategically invest your most valuable resources for God's eternal purposes. (280 pages, hardcover)

strivingtogether.com

Visit us online

strivingtogether.com

wcbc.edu